Aberdeenshire Library and Information Service
www.aberdeenshire.gov.uk/libraries
Renewals Hotline 01224 661511

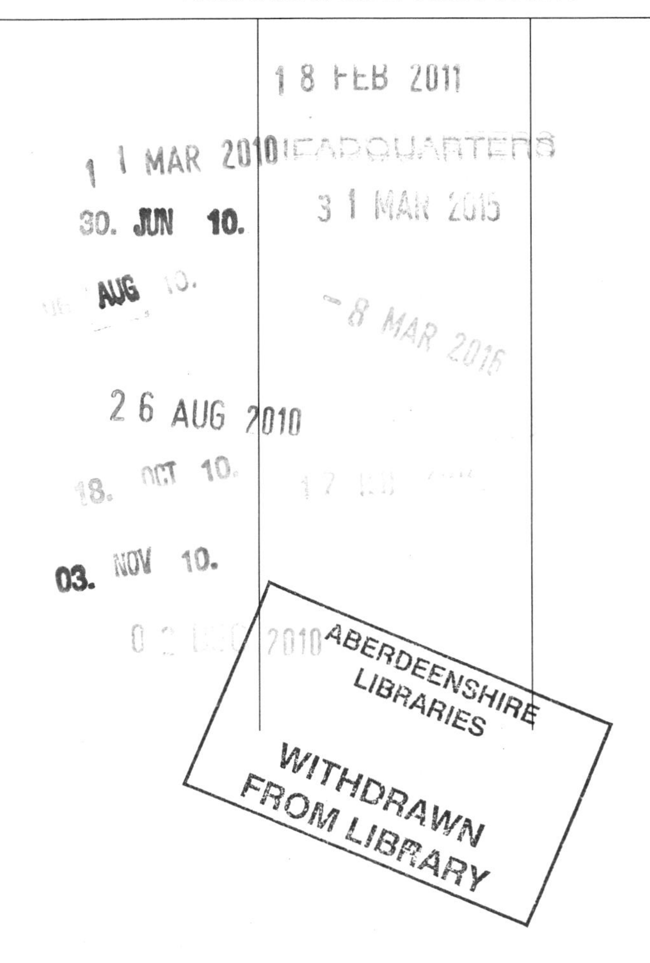

A COLOSSAL FAILURE OF COMMON SENSE

THE INCREDIBLE INSIDE STORY OF THE COLLAPSE OF **LEHMAN BROTHERS**

LARRY MCDONALD

WITH PATRICK ROBINSON

EBURY PRESS

1 3 5 7 9 10 8 6 4 2

Published in 2009 by Ebury Press, an imprint of Ebury Publishing
A Random House Group Company
First Published in the USA by Crown Business in 2009

Copyright © Lawrence G. McDonald and Patrick Robinson 2009

Lawrence G. McDonald and Patrick Robinson have asserted their right
to be identified as the authors of this Work in accordance with the
Copyright, Designs and Patents Act 1988

All rights reserved. No part of this publication may be reproduced, stored in
a retrieval system, or transmitted in any form or by any means, electronic,
mechanical, photocopying, recording or otherwise, without the
prior permission of the copyright owner

The Random House Group Limited Reg. No. 954009

Addresses for companies within the Random House Group can be found at
www.randomhouse.co.uk

A CIP catalogue record for this book is available from the British Library

The Random House Group Limited supports The Forest Stewardship Council
(FSC), the leading international forest certification organisation. All our titles
that are printed on Greenpeace approved FSC certified paper carry the
FSC logo. Our paper procurement policy can be found at
www.rbooks.co.uk/environment

Printed in the UK by CPI Cox & Wyman, Reading, RG1 8EX

ISBN 9780091936150

To buy books by your favourite authors and register for offers visit
www.rbooks.co.uk

332.
62

This book is respectfully dedicated to the many thousands of Lehman employees whose lives were thrown into turmoil when the firm collapsed, and among whom I was privileged to work for the four best years of my life.

Contents

Cast of Characters

Lehman Brothers (31st Floor) / Members of the Executive Committee

Richard S. Fuld Jr.: chairman of the board and chief executive officer

Joseph Gregory: president and chief operating officer

David Goldfarb: former chief financial officer; former global head of principal investing; chief strategy officer

Christopher O'Meara: chief financial officer, 2005–07; chief risk officer

Erin Callan: managing director and head of hedge fund investment banking; chief financial officer, 2007–08

George Walker IV: managing director and global head of investment management

Ian Lowitt: chief administrative officer; chief financial officer, 2008

Lehman Brothers (Traders, Investment Bankers, Risktakers, Salespeople)

Michael Gelband: managing director and global head of fixed income; head of capital markets; member of the executive committee

Alex Kirk: managing director and global head of high-yield and leveraged-loan businesses; chief operating officer of fixed income; global head of principal investing

Herbert "Bart" McDade: managing director and global head of fixed income; global head of equities; president, 2008; member of the executive committee

Eric Felder: managing director and head of global credit products group; global head of fixed income

Dr. Madelyn Antoncic: managing director and chief risk officer; government liaison

Thomas Humphrey: managing director and global head of fixed-income sales

Hugh "Skip" McGee: managing director and global head of investment banking

Richard Gatward: managing director and global head of convertible trading and sales

Lawrence E. McCarthy: managing director and global head of distressed-debt trading

Joseph Beggans: senior vice president, distressed-debt trading

Peter Schellbach: managing director, distressed-loan trading

Terence Tucker: senior vice president, convertible securities sales

David Gross: senior vice president, convertible securities sales

Jeremiah Stafford: senior vice president, high-yield credit products trading

Lawrence G. McDonald: vice president, distressed-debt and convertible securities trading

Mohammed "Mo" Grimeh: managing director and global head of emerging markets trading

Steven Berkenfeld: managing director and chairman, investment banking commitments committee

Lehman Brothers (Research and Analysis)

Christine Daley: managing director and head of distressed-debt research

Jane Castle: managing director, distressed-debt research

Peter Hammack: vice president, credit derivatives research

Ashish Shah: managing director and head of credit strategies, derivatives, and research

Karim Babay: associate, convertible securities research

Shrinivas Modukuri: managing director, mortgage-backed securities research

Lehman Brothers (Mortgage and Real Estate)

David N. Sherr: managing director and global head of securitized products

Mark Walsh: managing director and global head of commercial real estate group

Lehman Brothers Family and Former Lehman Brothers Partners

Robert "Bobbie" Lehman: chairman, 1925–69, and the last of the brothers to head the firm

Christopher Pettit: president and chief operating officer, 1994–96

John Cecil: chief administrative officer, chief financial officer, 1994–2000

Bradley Jack: president and chief operating officer, 2002–04

Peter G. Peterson: former chief executive officer; former U.S. secretary of commerce; founding partner of the Blackstone Group

Steve Schwarzman: former investment banker; founding partner of the Blackstone Group

Senior Government Officials and Banking/Investment Industry VIPs

Henry M. Paulson Jr.: former CEO of Goldman Sachs; former secretary of the U.S. Treasury

Ben Bernanke: chairman, U.S. Federal Reserve

Timothy F. Geithner: former president, Federal Reserve Bank of New York; secretary of the U.S. Treasury

Jamie Dimon: chief executive officer, JPMorganChase

David Einhorn: founder, Greenlight Capital

John Devaney: chairman and chief executive officer, United Capital Management

Corporate Financial Personnel

Anand Iyer: managing director and global head of convertible securities research, Morgan Stanley

Tony Bosco: managing director, convertible securities trading, Morgan Stanley, acquisitions

Gary Begnaud: Philadelphia branch manager, Merrill Lynch

Family and Friends

Lawrence G. McDonald Sr.: father, investor, golfer

Debbie Towle McDonald O'Brien: mother, fashion model

Ed O'Brien: stepfather and lawyer

Bob Cousy: family friend; point guard, Boston Celtics

Steve Seefeld: best friend at Falmouth High and Wharton; partner, ConvertBond.com

Kate Bohner: longtime friend and television financial journalist

Jack Corbett: longtime friend and successful retail stockbroker

Fallen Angels

Jeff Skilling: president and chief executive officer, Enron

Angelo R. Mozilo: chairman and chief executive officer, Countrywide Financial

Author's Note

It's been said that there are two distinct groups of people in America: "Wall Street" and "Main Street"—the former composed of people who keep the financial plumbing of the latter in good condition so that everyone will prosper. Wall Street has, however, become increasingly complex and opaque, and many on Main Street have only the most basic notion of what it does. In addition, Wall Street, particularly with the collapse and bankruptcy of Lehman Brothers in September 2008, was the epicenter of the worldwide financial crises that brought the global economy close to a complete collapse. My objective in writing *A Colossal Failure of Common Sense* was twofold. First, to provide Main Street with a close-up, inside view of how markets really work by someone who was on the trading floor in the years leading up to Lehman Brothers' calamitous end. And, second, to give my colleagues on Wall Street as crystal clear an explanation as possible about the real reasons why the legendary Lehman Brothers met with such a swift ending. The lessons therein are important for beginning to understand how we can prevent such disasters in the future and ultimately do a better job of serving Main Street.

—Lawrence G. McDonald, July 2009

A house divided against itself cannot stand.

Abraham Lincoln,
June 16, 1858

Prologue

I STILL LIVE just a few city blocks away from the old Lehman Brothers headquarters at 745 Seventh Avenue—six blocks, and about ten thousand years. I still walk past it two or three times a week, and each time I try to look forward, south toward Wall Street. And I always resolve to keep walking, glancing neither left nor right, locking out the memories. But I always stop.

And I see again the light blue livery of Barclays Capital, which represents—for me, at least—the flag of an impostor, a pale substitute for the swashbuckling banner that for 158 years was slashed above the entrance to the greatest merchant bank Wall Street ever knew: Lehman Brothers.

It was only the fourth largest. But its traditions were those of a banking warrior—the brilliant finance house that had backed, encouraged, and made possible the retail giants Gimbel Brothers, F. W. Woolworth, and Macy's, and the airlines American, National, TWA, and Pan American. They raised the capital for Campbell Soup Company, the Jewel Tea Company, B. F. Goodrich. And they backed the birth of television at RCA, plus the Hollywood studios RKO, Paramount, and 20th Century Fox. They found the money for the Trans-Canada oil pipeline.

I suppose, in a sense, I had seen only its demise, the four-year death rattle of twenty-first-century finance, which ended on September 15, 2008. Yet in my mind, I remember the great days. And as I come to a halt outside the building, I know too that in the next few moments I will be engulfed by sadness. But I always stop.

And I always stare up at the third floor, where once I worked as a trader on one of the toughest trading floors on earth. And then I find myself counting all the way up to thirty-one, the floor where it all went so catastrophically wrong, the floor that housed the royal court of King Richard. That's Richard S. Fuld, chairman and CEO.

Swamped by nostalgia, edged as we all are by a lingering anger, and still plagued by unanswerable questions, I stand and stare upward, sorrowful beyond reason, and trapped by the twin words of those possessed of flawless hindsight: *if only.*

Sometimes I lie awake at night trying to place all the if-onlys in some kind of order. Sometimes the order changes, and sometimes there is a new leader, one single aspect of the Lehman collapse that stands out above all others. But it's never clear. Except when I stand right here and look up at the great glass fortress which once housed Lehman, and focus on that thirty-first floor. Then it's clear. Boy, is it ever clear. And the phrase *if only* slams into my brain.

If only they had listened—Dick Fuld and his president, Joe Gregory. Three times they were hit with the irredeemable logic of three of the cleverest financial brains on Wall Street—those of Mike Gelband, our global head of fixed income, Alex Kirk, global head of distressed trading research and sales, and Larry McCarthy, head of distressed-bond trading.

Each and every one of them laid it out, from way back in 2005, that the real estate market was living on borrowed time and that Lehman Brothers was headed directly for the biggest subprime iceberg ever seen, and with the wrong men on the bridge. Dick and Joe turned their backs all three times. It was probably the worst triple since St. Peter denied Christ.

Beyond that, there were six more if-onlys, each one as cringe-makingly awful as the last.

If only Chairman Fuld had kept his ear close to the ground on the inner workings of his firm—both its triumphs and its mistakes. If he had listened to his generals, met people who formed the heart and soul of Lehman Brothers, the catastrophe might have been avoided. But instead of this, he secluded himself in his palatial offices up there on the thirty-first floor, remote from the action, dreaming only of accelerating growth, nursing ambitions far removed from reality.

If only the secret coup against Fuld and Gregory had taken place months before that clandestine meeting in June 2008. If the eleven managing directors who sat in ostensibly treasonous but ultimately loyal comradeship that night had acted sooner and removed the

Lehman leaders, they might have steadied the ship, changing its course.

If only the reign of terror that drove out the most brilliant of Lehman's traders and risk takers had been halted earlier, perhaps in the name of common sense. The top managers might have marshaled their forces immediately when they saw giants such as Mike Gelband being ignored.

If only Dick Fuld had kept his anger and resentment under control. Especially at that private dinner in the spring of 2008 with Hank Paulson, secretary of the United States Treasury. That was when Fuld's years of smoldering envy of Goldman Sachs came cascading to the surface. Could that perhaps have been the moment Hank decided he could not bring himself to bail out the bank controlled by Richard S. Fuld?

If only President George W. Bush had taken the final, desperate call from Fuld's office, a call made by his own cousin, George Walker IV, in the night hours before the bank filed for Chapter 11 bankruptcy. It might have made a difference.

If only . . . if only. Those two words haunt my dreams. I go back to the fall of Lehman, and what might have made things different. For most people, victims or not of this worldwide collapse of the financial markets, it will be, in time, just water over the dam. But it will never be that for me, and my long background as a trader and researcher has prompted me many times to burrow down further to the bedrock, the cause of the crash of 2008. I refer to the repeal of the Glass-Steagall Act in 1999.

If only President Clinton had never signed the bill repealing Glass-Steagall. Personally, I never thought he much wanted to sign it, but to understand the ramifications it is necessary to delve deeper, and before I begin my story, I will present you with some critical background information, without which your grasp might be incomplete. It's a ten-minute meadow of wisdom and hindsight, the sort of thing I tend to specialize in.

The story begins in the heady, formative years of the Clinton presidency on a rose-colored quest to change the world, to help the poor, and ended in the poisonous heartland of world financial disaster.

Roberta Achtenberg, the daughter of a Russian-born owner of a Los Angeles neighborhood grocery store, was plucked by President Clinton from relative obscurity in 1993 and elevated to the position of assistant secretary of the Department of Housing and Urban Development. Roberta and Bill were united in their desire to increase home ownership in poor and minority communities.

And despite a barrage of objections led by Senator Jesse Helms, who referred to Achtenberg as that "damn lesbian," the lady took up her appointment in the new administration, citing innate racism as one of the main reasons why banks were reluctant to lend to those without funds.

In the ensuing couple of years, Roberta Achtenberg harnessed all of the formidable energy on the massed ranks of United States bankers, sometimes threatening, sometimes berating, sometimes bullying—anything to persuade the banks to provide mortgages to people who might not have been up to the challenge of coping with up-front down payments and regular monthly payments.

Between 1993 and 1999, more than two million such clients became new homeowners. In her two-year tenure as assistant secretary, she set up a national grid of offices staffed by attorneys and investigators. Their principal aim was to enforce the laws against the banks, the laws that dealt with discrimination. Some of the fines leveled at banks ran into the millions, to drive home Achtenberg's avowed intent to utilize the law to change the ethos of providing mortgage money in the United States of America.

Banks were compelled to jump into line, and soon they were making thousands of loans without any cash-down deposits whatsoever, an unprecedented situation. Mortgage officers inside the banks were forced to bend or break internal rules in order to achieve a good Community Reinvestment Act rating, which would please the administration by demonstrating generosity to underprivileged borrowers even if they might default. Easy mortgages were the invention of Bill Clinton's Democrats.

However, there was, in the mid- to late 1990s, one enormous advantage: amid general prosperity, the housing market was strong and prices were rising steadily. At that point in time, mortgage defaults were relatively few in number and the securitization of mortgages, which had such disastrous consequences during the financial crisis that began in 2007, barely existed.

Nonetheless, there were many beady-eyed financiers who looked askance at this new morality and privately yearned for the days when bank policies were strictly conservative, when credit was flatly denied to anyone without the proven ability to repay.

And at the center of this seething disquiet, somewhere between the persuasive silken-tongued members of the banking lobby and the missionary zeal of Roberta Achtenberg, stood William J. Clinton, whose heart, not for the first time, may have been ruling his head.

He understood full well the goodwill he had engendered in the new home-owning black and Hispanic communities. But he could not fail to heed the very senior voices of warning that whispered, *There may be trouble ahead*.

President Clinton wanted to stay focused with the concerns of the bankers, many of whom were seriously upset by Achtenberg's pressure to provide shaky mortgages. And right before the president's eyes there was a related situation, one that had the deepest possible roots in the American financial community.

This was the fabled Glass-Steagall Act of 1933, the post–Wall Street crash legislation that prevented commercial banks from merging with investment banks, thus eliminating the opportunity for the high-rolling investment guys to get their hands on limitless supplies of depositors' money. Glass-Steagall was nothing short of a barrier, and it stayed in place for more than sixty years, but the major U.S. banks wanted it abolished. They'd tried but failed in 1988. It would take another four years for this Depression-era legislation to come once more under attack.

President Clinton understood the ramifications, and he was wary of the reform, wary of seeming to be allied with the power brokers of the biggest banks in the country. He understood the complexities of the Glass-Steagall Act, its origins, and its purposes—principally to prevent some diabolical investment house from plunging in big on a corporation like Enron and going down with a zillion dollars of small depositors' cash. No part of that did President Bill need.

On one hand was the belief of the main U.S. clearing banks that such mergers would strengthen the whole financial industry by increasing opportunities for hefty profits. But there were many people running small banks who were fearful that a repeal of Glass-Steagall would ultimately lead to large conglomerates crushing the life out of the minnows.

President Clinton always kept a weather eye on history, and he was aware the commercial banks, with their overenthusiastic investments in the stock market, had essentially taken the rap for the crash of 1929. They were accused of crossing a forbidden line, of buying stock in corporations for resale to the public. It had been too risky, and the pursuit of huge profits had clouded their judgment.

The man who had stood firmly in the path of the gathering storm of the 1930s was Virginia senator Carter Glass, a former treasury secretary and the founder of the U.S. Federal Reserve System. The somewhat stern Democratic newspaper proprietor was determined that the commercial banks and the investment banks should be kept forever apart.

He was supported by the chairman of the House Banking and Currency Committee, Alabama congressman Henry Bascom Steagall, and it was their rigid legal barricade that did much to solve Wall Street's greatest-ever crisis. The biggest banks were thenceforth prevented from speculating heavily in the stock markets. But even then, a lot of people thought it was a harsh and restrictive law.

With President Clinton in office for only three years, the major banks once more marshaled their forces to try for a third time to repeal Glass-Steagall, and once more it all came to nothing, with the nation's small banks fighting tooth and nail to hold back a system they thought might engulf them. But in 1996 they failed once more.

In the early spring of 1998, however, a Wall Street detonator exploded, sending a sharp signal that the market was willing to go it alone despite the politicians. On April 6 Citicorp announced a merger with Travelers Insurance, a large corporation that owned and controlled the investment bank Smith Barney. The merger would create a vast conglomerate involved with banking, insurance, and securities, plainly in defiance of Glass-Steagall.

The House scrambled to put a reform bill together, but the issue died in the Senate after it became clear that President Clinton had many concerns and was almost certain to veto it. The $70 billion merger between Citicorp and Travelers went right ahead regardless. The result was a banking giant, the largest financial conglomerate in the world, and it was empowered to sell securities, take deposits, make loans, underwrite stocks, sell insurance, and operate an enormous variety of financial activities, all under one name: Citigroup.

The deal was obviously illegal, but Citigroup had five years to get the law changed, and they had very deep pockets. Senators harrumphed, and the president, concerned for the nation's smaller banks, worried.

However, the most powerful banking lobbies in the country wanted Glass-Steagall repealed, and they bombarded politicians with millions of dollars' worth of contributions. They cajoled and pressured Congress to end this old-fashioned Depression-era law. Inevitably they won. In November 1999, the necessary bills were passed 54–44 in the Senate and 343–86 in the House of Representatives. In the ensuing days the final bipartisan bill sailed through the Senate, 90–8 with one abstention, and the House, 362–57 with fifteen abstentions. Those margins made it vetoproof. I remember the day well. All my life my dad had been telling me that history inevitably repeats itself. And here I was listening to a group of guys telling me it was all different now, that everything was so much more sophisticated, "doorstep of the twenty-first century" and all that, so much more advanced than 1933.

Oh, yeah? Well, I never bought it. It's never different. I knew that Glass-Steagall had been put in place very deliberately to protect customer bank deposits and prevent any crises from becoming interconnected and forming a house of cards or a row of dominoes. Carter Glass's bill had successfully kept the dominoes apart for more than half a century after his death.

And now that was all about to end. They were moving the pieces, pressing one against the other. I remember my concern as I watched the television news on November 12, 1999. The action on the screen was flying in the face of everything my dad had told me. I was watching President Clinton step up, possibly against his better judgment, and sign into law the brand-new Financial Services Modernization Act (also known as Gramm-Leach-Bliley), repealing Glass-Steagall. In less than a decade, this act would be directly responsible for bringing the entire world to the brink of financial ruin. Especially mine.

1

A Rocky Road to Wall Street

Right here, in a haze of tobacco smoke and cheap hamburger fumes, I was on the skid row of finance . . . places like this specialize in the walking dead of failing corporations.

At the age of ten, I resided in some kind of a marital no-man's-land, a beautiful but loveless gabled house in the leafy little township of Bolton, Massachusetts, some twenty miles west of downtown Boston. My father, Lawrence G. McDonald, had accepted the end of his marriage and had left my stunning fashion-model mother to bring up their five children all on her own. I was the oldest.

The general drift of the breakup was rooted in my dad's hard-driving business career. Owner and chief executive of a chemical engineering company, he might have stepped straight out of a suburban cocktail party staged on the set of *The Graduate:* "Plastics, son. That's the future."

And I guess in a way it was the future. At least it was his future, because plastics made him a stack of money, enough to start his own brokerage firm, and it only took him about twenty-nine hours a day, seven days a week, to do it. He was obsessed with business.

So far as my mom was concerned, that was the upside. The downside was his devotion to the game of golf, which took care of his entire quota of spare time. For all of my formative years he played to scratch or better. As the club champion of Woods Hole Golf Club, down on the shores of Nantucket Sound, he had a swing that was pure poetry, relaxed, precise, and elegant, the clubhead describing a perfect arc through the soft sea air as it approached the ball. Also, he could hit the son of a bitch a country mile.

Mom never really saw him, since she never landed a job as a greenskeeper. And he saw her principally in magazines and on giant billboards around Boston, where dozens of images showed her modeling various high-fashion accessories.

When I referred to the marital home being loveless, I was not quite accurate. There was a burgeoning love in that house, but it did not involve Dad. He'd moved out, and many months later, a new suitor for my mother appeared on the horizon. Years later they were married, but even at my young age I realized he must have been some kind of latter-day saint, taking on this very beautiful lady with the staggering encumbrance of five kids and a kind of rogue husband prowling around the outskirts of her life, keeping an iron grasp on every nickel of her finances.

The name of the new man, who would one day become my stepfather, was Ed O'Brien. He was an extremely eminent lawyer and a grandson of a former governor of New Hampshire. Ed was a very classy guy, and he adored Mom and helped her in every way. He was not so big and tough as Dad, who had a touch of John Wayne about him, a kind of western swagger and a suggestion of unmistakable attitude, which often goes with entirely self-made men.

Anyway, right now I want to get to the point. Remember, Dad did not live with us anymore, and Ed occasionally stayed the night. Well, on this particular morning I was standing in the living room staring out of the window at Ed's brand-new Mercedes-Benz convertible, a $100,000 car even way back then in the late seventies. Suddenly I saw a car pull up outside the front gates.

Into the expansive front yard strode Lawrence G. McDonald, wielding what looked to me like a seven-iron. He came striding up to Ed's automobile and took an easy backswing, left arm straight, and completely obliterated the windshield in a shower of splintered glass. The clubhead struck right above the wipers, a little low. I thought Dad might have raised his head just a tad on impact.

Never breaking stride, he walked resolutely to the front of the car, took aim, and smashed the right-side headlight. Moving left, he ripped the club back fast. I thought I detected a slightly tighter swing, hands a little farther down the club. Anyhow, he did precisely the same to the headlight on the left.

By this time there was glass all over the place, and still I just stood there, gaping, wide-eyed. I watched Dad stride around to the back of the car, and for a moment I thought he was planning to survey his handiwork. You know, like standing back after you've dropped a ten-footer.

I was wrong. Once more he took his stance, swung the club back, and fired it straight into the taillight on the left side, shooting red glass all over the lot. Then he moved two paces right and with precisely the same shot, slightly wristy with a lot of backspin, punched out the other one. If either taillight had been a golf ball, it would have flown high and dug in on landing, probably pin high. There was a lot of precision about Dad's play that morning.

I mention this because the incident is branded into my memory. It took me ten years to ask him about it, and he replied as only he, or perhaps John Wayne, could—real slow. "It wasn't a seven-iron, son. Didn't need any more than a pitching wedge."

It would be another thirty years before I would witness at very close quarters another such act of wanton, willful destruction. And that took place on the trading floor of a Wall Street investment bank.

I begin my story with that brief insight into the character of my father because he had, even after the divorce, a profound influence on me. By nature he was a bear. That's not a straightforward grizzly, seeing world disaster in every downward swing of the Dow. Dad was a permabear, seeing potential catastrophe every hour from the opening bell to the close of business.

For some investors the floor of the New York Stock Exchange is the last refuge of the Prince of Darkness, a place where demons of ill fortune lurked behind every flickering screen. Dad was not that bad, because he was an instinctively shrewd investor, often a wizard at stock selection, spotting the corporation that was about to tank. But his attitude almost caused him to miss the two greatest bull market rallies in history, because to Dad, cash was king, and he might need to prepare for the end of the world. He was the ultimate value investor. In outlook he was a cautious, somewhat skeptical pessimist. In personality he made Howard Hughes look like an extrovert.

In his own business Dad was extremely successful. He earned his bachelor of science degree in chemical engineering at Notre Dame, where he was number one on the golf team. Then he went to work as a salesman at General Electric's plastics division, the Google and Microsoft of its day. He ended up a multimillionaire, owning his own plastics manufacturing plant in Massachusetts.

When he told me to beware, that history, without fail, repeats itself, he was not thinking of the sunlit uplands of triumph and achievement. He had in mind events like the eruption of Krakatoa, World War II, the fall of the Roman Empire, the collapse of the Soviet Union, and above all the crash of 1929. Always the crash.

With a worldview like his, it was scarcely surprising that the peace and quiet of the golf course was his principal escape. And he was one hell of a player. He held the course record of 65 at Woods Hole for more than twenty years, and on one near-legendary occasion he nailed the three par-fives in birdie, eagle, and double eagle. He played the great golf courses in serious competition, once losing on the last green at Winged Foot Country Club to one of the best Massachusetts amateurs of all time, Joe Keller—and even Joe had to sink a forty-footer to beat him.

Dad had already set me on the road to becoming a scratch golfer when my world caved in. He and Mom split, leaving Mom with us kids in the big house without the means to support either it or us. Ed had a law practice in Worcester, and to that tough Massachusetts city we upped and transplanted ourselves, mostly because Mom needed a friend, just someone to be there, in the absence of Dad and his weighty bank balance.

Bolton, where we had always lived, was a little gem of a town, an upper-middle-class haven set in green rolling country with the families of well-to-do business guys in residence. From there, my mom, now in desperate financial straits, my three brothers and one sister, and I ended up in a housing project in the worst part of a distinctly suspect city—the absurdly named Lincoln Village Apartments, gateway to nowhere. I was too young to go into culture shock, but hell, even I realized that somehow the roof had fallen in on my life.

With five children to care for, my mom, the hugely admired Debbie Towle, could not possibly go back to work. She was still, by all accounts, spectacularly beautiful, and would once again have been in demand as a fashion model, but that was impossible. We were not so much hard-up as bereft.

The apartment was in a nightmarish neighborhood, run-down and dirty, with a slightly sinister atmosphere, as if at any moment some shocking crime might be committed. Mom was always in tears. I could tell she hated the place, hated living at the wrong end of this urban version of Death Valley.

As you can imagine, the people were an absolute treat, many of them shifty-eyed, leering, unkempt, and full of resentment: some really shaky kids, white trash, drug dealers. There were also gangs of trainee criminals staging shoplifting raids and nighttime burglaries all over the city. They kept trying to recruit me, but I knew enough to stay well out of it. I refused to join them, and one night their leader came to the door of our apartment, dragged me out onto the front steps, and punched me right in the face.

Mom nearly had a heart attack, and Ed O'Brien came to the rescue, trying to help with money. Dad? He pretty much disappeared. In my first eighteen months in Worcester I went to three different schools, each one a bigger disaster than the last. This was life as I had never imagined it. Academically I was slipping behind; mostly I was afraid to go outside the door because of the sheer danger of the place. It's hard to explain every vestige of the change in our lives. But the difference was total. There were no more trips to the Cape, no more golf, no more elegant dinners at our home. We were prisoners of the cells of Lincoln Village.

My dad did pull one masterstroke on my behalf. He arranged for me to report to tranquil, green Worcester Golf Club, where I spent time caddying. I was too young to understand I was hauling a huge bag around for one of the immortals—Bob Cousy, the six-foot-one point guard for the great Celtics teams of the fifties and sixties, and an excellent golfer. The sweet-swinging point guard called me "kid"; I called him "Mr. Bob."

But those trips around the course were only a tiny respite from my real world. I earned $100 caddying, all of which I gave to my mom. As a family, we were sinking into depression. I remember it all so well—no laughter, no joy, and the unmistakable feeling that we never should have been anywhere near Lincoln Village. Finally, the entire family got together, both Mom's people and Dad's, and decided, "We have to get those kids the hell out of there."

So one bright morning in the spring of 1979 we all moved to Cape Cod, where Dad had always had a home. We went back into the sunlight, back to life as we had once known it in Bolton, away from the glum recesses of Worcester.

When I began at my high school in Falmouth, I was at a huge

disadvantage, way behind in my work in all subjects. I fought an academic war to become a C student, struggling to catch up. During my junior and senior years, when it was time to make a decision about college, I most definitely was not regarded as a candidate for a top university. So you can imagine my surprise one day when Dad showed up and told me he was taking me out to his alma mater in South Bend, Indiana: Notre Dame, the hallowed campus of the Fighting Irish, which also houses one of the greatest libraries in North America under the watchful eye of the Touchdown Jesus, set in massive mosaic glory on the eastern wall of Memorial Library.

He took me to all the sacred places: the Grotto, the library, the Rockne Memorial, the Sacred Heart Church, the palatial South Dining Hall, and of course the stadium. I thought then, as I think now, it must be one of the most fabulous university campuses on earth.

Plaintively, I asked my dad, "But why now? Why bring me here so late? I obviously could never make it, not after the years in Worcester. If you wanted me to come here, I should have stayed at my school in Bolton."

He was a man of few words at the best of times, and he greeted my comments with even fewer words than usual. There was no explanation of his intentions. And we traveled home to the Cape with hardly any further discussion about my lack of academic future. I think Dad knew I was doing everything I could to regain lost ground at school, but there was no possibility whatsoever that I could ever aspire to a place like Notre Dame.

When we reached the house, Dad took me by the shoulders, turned me around to face him, and said in that rich baritone voice of his, "Son, remember this—it's not where you start, it's where you finish." Spoken, I have often thought, like a true hard-driving son of a mailman—and for that matter, a bit like John Wayne. A student's gotta do what a student's gotta do.

What I had to do was scramble my way into a university of some description. Any description. In the end I made it to the University of Massachusetts at Dartmouth, a small seaside town that sits in the southernmost corner of the state, where the Atlantic washes through the trailing headland of Cuttyhunk, the last of the Elizabeth Islands.

Before I reported to UMass for my economics courses, I spent a summer working in Falmouth pumping gas. I swiftly developed a deadly rivalry with the gas station next door, which was manned by one of my local buddies, Larry McCarthy.

He was a whip-smart kid, built like a jockey, 120 pounds wet through, and about five foot five. He got a pretty hard time at school partly because he was so small and partly because he was frequently seen reading the *Wall Street Journal* when he was in seventh grade. But he was a feisty little devil, and he fought like a tiger, ever ready to swing a roundhouse right at any perceived slight. Just how feisty he was would be demonstrated to me in Technicolor when we both had our backs to the wall at Lehman Brothers twenty years later.

His dad was a bank president, and he sent his son to the expensive Sacred Heart School. Right from the get-go Larry was being groomed for a Wall Street career. He sailed into Providence College to study economics and business administration.

Even as a teenager, I should have known he'd go far, because he was hell as a business rival. One week things were a little quiet, so I cut a cent off the gas price at my station, guessing the notoriously parsimonious New Englanders would go for that with enthusiasm. I was right, and for a couple of days I was doing real well. Then it all went south and I was back in the doldrums.

It did not take me long to find out why. Across the street Larry had slashed his price by more than two cents and mopped up almost all of the town's regular business at the pumps. The summer drew to a close leaving us still best friends, but with the business pecking order established.

As a freshman, I lived in Falmouth with my dad and made the hour journey to school each day. That had the advantage of being free except for gas, and the disadvantage of my being watched beadily by a very advanced financier as I toiled my way through the demanding curriculum. Dad was making a big effort, seeming to want to make amends for things in the past, and we got closer. I guess I started to like him more, as I have done ever since.

By the time I moved into junior year, I had become a top student, straight A's, while majoring in economics, with probably the best grades in my class. Dad regarded all this with a watchful gunslinger's gaze. Never said anything. Probably figured there wasn't any need. But I bet he secretly knew I could have made Notre Dame if I'd had a shot.

When we talked, it was usually about business. Sometimes about our other shared interest, golf, but mostly Dad let his short irons do the talking. Although I do remember he once told me he'd dropped a sixty-footer on the fifth green of the exclusive International Club out in Bolton. This was reputed to be the largest green in the game, a 120-yard-wide upside-down apple pie generally regarded as impossible from all angles. Dad, who was the best player in the entire membership, recounted that putt with a paucity of words. But he told it like it was, straight and true, the upholding of good over evil, like a scene from the back lot of *High Noon*.

Those were the terms in which he saw the world, and he looked at the financial markets with a mixture of suspicion and cynicism, watching, waiting for the chink in the armor of the mighty that would allow him to cash in. Like all bears, he was intuitively drawn to the art form of shorting stocks—acquiring shares in a corporation in anticipation of a downward spiral. In the broadest possible terms, if one thousand shares are acquired at $100 each and the price then falls to $50 per share, the bear tucks away a succulent $50,000 profit. It's a bit complicated, because the original $100 shares are not actually purchased by the bear. They're borrowed through a broker and immediately sold. All the old bruin needs to do is buy them back at the cheaper price and pocket the difference. And so, while all around him the stockholders are licking their wounds, losing their cars, selling their houses, and watching their portfolios blow up, men like my father bask in the sheer scale of the disaster, counting their cash and staring balefully around for the next potential casualty.

No doubt in my mind: Dad was a bear's bear.

And all the while he stressed to me that no matter how bad things were, they could always be that bad again, or worse. In his view, "it couldn't happen again" rates as just about the stupidest comment ever uttered. *Yes, it could, son. Yes, it could. History invariably repeats itself.* The mantras of my father. Forever in my mind.

By the time I graduated from college in 1989, I had learned enough about Wall Street to understand that was the place I wanted to be, right out there in New York with the big dogs, playing in the major leagues of finance. The trouble was, my chances of getting in were zilch. Those big finance firms recruit from the best colleges in the United States. They ransack the top business schools, scoop up the outstanding talent from Harvard, Princeton, Yale, and Penn. And they land them early, often bringing kids into the firms for work experience before they even graduate. UMass Dartmouth was not one of the regular stops on their recruitment drives. They wanted the best, and their recruiters headed straight for the institutions where they were most likely to find it.

I understood that big finance in the United States was probably the toughest of all careers. It was such a ferocious learning curve that young people were quite often burned out at forty, unable to take it anymore—the endless hours, the pressure, the fear of missing a chance. And yet I still knew that it was for me, even though it would be a long, hard road, mostly uphill. I didn't broach the subject with anyone. Instead I decided to tackle it alone, armed only with my economics degree from a relatively obscure university. Whichever way you cut it, I was at some disadvantage against a kid from Choate and Harvard with about seventeen relations in the boardrooms of the great finance houses. Still, as Dad had said, it's not where you start, it's where you finish.

So there I stood in search of my personal holy grail, metaphorically staring at the north face of the Eiger, wondering which way was up. I was long on ideas but destitute when it came to contacts and connections. I had no clue where to start. While a hell of a long way from Worcester, I was still light-years away from Wall Street. And I was braced for rejection on a mammoth scale, but I believed that every no brings you closer to a yes. See that? A psychologist, even at that young age!

In my secret thoughts I set myself a five-year target to make Wall Street—not some plush carpeted office, but right down there in the Colosseum of the trading floor, where the rubber meets the road, where the toughest characters in the game stand guard over the firm's capital. I was holding on to a dream that my dad had instilled in me, the lure of finance on the grandest scale, illuminated by another of his mantras: that someone somewhere is going to screw up big-time every trading month of the year . . . the anthem of the bears.

I can't say why, given that I had witnessed my dad stepping gingerly through those big bull markets, but I have always been sympathetic toward the bears, even though I understood that the real big hitters of the investment world traditionally have been men who seek stocks in corporations that are on the rise, the ones on the verge of a breakthrough with a new idea or discovery.

In any event, that summer of 1989 I set about establishing a career for myself. I would begin with a mass attack on the financial institutions of the Northeast, buoyed up by yet another of Dad's mantras: even a blind pig will occasionally find an acorn. I bombarded the industry with letters of application, probably a thousand of them, accompanied by a resume that was light on substance but long on ambition. I spent hours in the Falmouth library researching chief executives of New England brokerage houses, chief financial officers, marketing directors, human resource guys, and God knows who else.

When I hit them, I hit them big, dozens of letters at a time which I personally fired into the Falmouth Post Office, armloads. The rejection slips came back like a machine gun fusillade. But I never went down. I just kept mailing: Boston, Hyannis, Quincy, Plymouth, Buzzards Bay, and points west all the way down to Newport. Result: zero.

The fact was, I could not even gain entry for an interview, never mind receive a job offer. So if I wasn't invited, I thought, I'd get in some other way. Armed with my list of addresses, I went on a kind of brokerage house patrol. I just turned up with the name of the guy I wanted to see, trying to wheedle my way past the advance guard of receptionists and secretaries—all of whom, of course, tried to get rid of me, since I had no appointment.

As each one of these sieges was repelled, resulting only in ignominious defeat, I slowly came to understand I needed to be a great deal more cunning. So I evolved a new strategy. I would sneak in, barge in, lie my way in, or make my entry in disguise. From that point on I was a changed person, a new specialist in low cunning, deviousness, and subterfuge. Some of my tactics were so preposterous it was all I could do to prevent myself from falling over with laughter.

There was the out-of-breath, well-dressed young exec who was simply so late for an appointment there was no time to argue at the desk. At some of these brokerage houses I just charged straight in, as if I owned the place, and headed for the boss's door. (That was in the more innocent days of the early 1990s; today I'd probably be shot.) Other times I'd simply say I had an appointment, no ifs, ands, or buts, and I'd traveled two hundred miles to keep it. Other times I researched my target and turned up on his birthday or anniversary with chocolates or flowers that had to be delivered personally. I had to invest in a couple of blue tradesman's work coats for these forays into the enemy camp. Ed O'Brien, by now my stepfather, funded this operation right down to the flowers.

My most successful deception at the New England offices of Merrill Lynch, Lehman, Morgan Stanley, or Smith Barney was the role of pizza deliveryman. Ed stood me a long white coat that hid my business suit for that one and even offered to finance the pizzas. But since the boxes were always empty, I explained, that would not be necessary.

There's something magnificently ordinary about a pizza, something delightfully mundane. It's a word that can soften the stoniest heart. "Pizza for Mr. Matthews" was not the way. You needed the jargon of the pro: "Sausage, mushrooms, and extra cheese, Mr. Matthews, right away while it's hot." Or "Linguisa, peppers, and tomato, Rick Matthews, gotta be hot." Or "Rick Matthews wants it real hot—extra cheese and sausage. Let's go, let's go!" For that last one, I hit the reception desk with my best Italian accent and barged straight in, quivering with urgency, as if any delay would cost the receptionist her job, not to mention mine. Once I was past the receptionist I was able to ditch the white coat and the pizza boxes.

Of course, having stormed the first line of defense armed only with a pizza box, I was still one hell of a long way from my final objective, a job on the trading desk of one of the big Wall Street–based finance houses. But I was in the door, in the most literal sense, and I was seeing a few branch managers—mostly for about four and a half seconds before they had me escorted from the building.

A few, however, doubtless amused by my *chutzpah*, let me stay for a chat. Some of them were really good guys and seemed sympathetic that I wanted a job in the finance business so badly that I was ready to risk arrest for illegal entry. Strangely, I noted many of them saying the very same thing: aside from the fact that I needed to pass the Series 7 exam before I could earn employment as any kind of broker, every one of them told me I needed sales experience. It could be selling door-to-door or cold calling, but experience was absolutely vital. They all said they'd consider giving me a shot, but not until I had a genuine sales track record.

"Kid," one of them told me, "you're going to kick off as a retail broker, and before you get out there, selling stocks, bonds, and securities, you must know how to approach people, the buzzwords that will hold their interest, how to tempt them, how to warn them. I don't care what you sell for your first experience, but for Christ's sake get out there and sell 'em something, rather than wasting my time!"

I think he was the director of one of the Merrill Lynch branches, but he was really decent to me, and I remember he sent for a couple of cups of coffee while we were chatting. In the end he said we might as well get into one of the pizzas he thought I had. So I just made the excuse of another appointment and left his office under a cloak of dishonesty similar to the one I'd used when I entered. *Wow,* I thought, *this finance game will be the death of me.*

It was true the last guy had understood some of my desires. Deep within me there burned an ambition so powerful I sometimes thought it might burn me up with it. I was prepared to walk through fire to get where I was going. The words of one of my heroes, the author Napoleon Hill, were welded to my soul: *Winners never quit. Quitters never win.*

Almost immediately I switched tacks and went in search of a salesman's job, giving due thought to the advice I'd received. I went to about five interviews and settled for a sales rep's job with American Frozen Foods of Milford, Connecticut. My home office was in Sagamore, right on the Cape Cod Canal, hard by the high bridge that separates the Cape from the Massachusetts mainland.

My territory was the Cape and islands plus southeastern Massachusetts. The great wide canal that cleaves its way along the western coast of the narrow land defined my theater of operations. My specialty was pork chops, though I made significant headway with our pork roast. And I may as well reveal that the culture shock involved in going from dreams of becoming a billion-dollar Wall Street bond trader to the reality of being a novice pork chop salesman was much like the Bolton–Lincoln Village saga.

But I was determined to give it the old college try—UMass, that is, not Harvard. And I set about it in a scientific manner. I called about seven hundred million people, all along the banks of the Cape Cod Canal. I hit 'em by phone, I hit 'em by road, I even hit 'em by bus when my car was in for service.

My creed was that no pork, in all the colorful history of pig farming, had ever tasted even one-hundredth as good as this particular set of chops. I sold them to young ladies, young marrieds, and divorcées, to the rich, the lonely, and the dispossessed. I sold them to the up-and-coming, the has-beens, and the still-striving. The sharp young newlyweds were tough, unlike the pork, because of a reluctance to shift from their planned budgets.

But when I saw an old lady my heart sang. They weren't normally hungry, but many of them had a lot of grandchildren. My sudden appearance on their doorstep—a six-foot-three charmer, a bit of a Jack the lad, scratch golfer, future Master of the Universe, et cetera—saw me invited in for a cup of coffee so often I probably could have switched to being a coffee salesman, and the hell with the pork chops.

Anyway, given the amount of time I spent in deep conversation with these female senior citizens, I needed to sell hard, stressing the joy and convenience of having a fridge full of pork chops, a meal for all occasions. I studied recipe books, learning about fifty thousand ways to prepare the chops for the table. These formed my selling phrases—pork chops, perfect for every dinner.

I realized there was a heavy commitment involved in a delicious pork roast, since you need three or four people to eat one. So as soon as I detected that a lady was widowed or lived on her own, I instantly switched my pitch toward the chops, highlighting the ever-useful four-pack, perfect for the single-chop dinner.

There was one wealthy couple from Cohasset with whom I was so successful they must have purchased about 470 pork chops, creating so much storage pressure that I sold them a new freezer. In the end I was one of the top salesmen in the entire American Frozen Foods northeast region. And I was out in the lead midway through the second year when I called it quits: *The winner, and still the pork chop champion of the world, from Woods Hole, Massachusetts, Larry "Lean Man" McDonald!*

Meanwhile, my buddy Larry McCarthy had moved smoothly into finance. He made it to the majors while I was still trying to get into single-A. A Wall Street investment firm, Donaldson, Lufkin and Jenrette, gave him his chance, and his career immediately flourished, exploding upward. While I was selling the four-packs he was learning to specialize in bank debt and distressed bonds.

At that point our careers were so far apart it would have been laughable if it hadn't been semitragic. There was Larry marching around lower Manhattan like J. P. Morgan incarnate, while I was working the banks of the Cape Cod Canal with a vanload of pork.

At that time, I could not gain a foothold even close to where Larry worked, but still I hung on to my dream: that one day I would make it to the top table in the world's biggest business. Nothing could cloud my vision of the holy grail, and I vowed to keep chasing it, no matter how difficult that proved to be.

American Frozen Foods did their level best to keep me in their organization. After presenting me with the award for being best salesman—number one in pork—they asked me to move down to their corporate headquarters in Connecticut, where glittering prizes would await me: high-level management, head of marketing, czar of the sales force. And it darned nearly turned my head—but then I thought, *Whoa! This is not my objective. I don't plan to become the world's number one meat salesman.*

But the offer focused my mind. Suddenly I knew I had to get into finance somewhere, in some capacity. So with a single item added to my resume—"a top salesman with American Frozen Foods"—I blasted out my letters of application once more. Dozens of them. Response: zero.

I was rapidly losing hope when, from out of the wide blue yonder, there came a chance—not much of one, but a glimmer. A pal from Falmouth High, Steve Seefeld, who had been not only the smartest boy in the school but also the richest, called me one weekend and spoke to me as if he had read my mind. Commensurate with his status as the Einstein of Falmouth High, Steve possessed an elegant turn of phrase. "Listen, Larry," he said, "screw this pork chop bullshit. It's time you got the hell out of the fucking freezer."

Normally I might have dismissed this, but Steve was a very special character—special enough to have earned his sea captain's license before the age of sixteen, which made him a legend in the oceanside bars of Falmouth. Jesus, this kid thought he was qualified to drive a packed Martha's Vineyard car ferry when he was still in tenth grade—docking, navigation, tidal currents, the lot. Not only that, but Steve was now fluent in Java, C++, and Visual Basic, the most advanced new languages of computer programming. And that wasn't all. Steve had also gotten the highest possible score on the mathematics section of the SAT. He was studying at the world-renowned Wharton School of the University of Pennsylvania. He lived with a group of fellow business students close to the school, and suggested I break away from the Cape, get down there, and move in with him and his guys.

We agreed that I needed to get into finance right now. He said I should enroll at a nearby Philadelphia business school and start studying right away for the Series 7 exam, without which, he said, "a future bond trader would be like a butcher without a meat cleaver." Steve added that although he knew I had stacked away ten grand in what he called "porkbucks," I should still take a day job and maybe even find some bucket shop to sponsor me in the exam—not an uncommon maneuver.

And so I left American Frozen Foods. I think they were sorry to see me go, but my immediate boss, Dan Nectow, knew in his heart that my personal guiding light did not illuminate a path back into the freezer. I left with his good wishes, heading south to Philadelphia into uncharted territory. It was only 330 miles, but to me it was like a journey to Patagonia.

I gassed up my old Volkswagen Golf and stuffed into it my worldly possessions, which added up to a suitcase full of clothes, two or three coat hangers, some literature of doubtful merit, and about eighty prime pork chops, packed into a cooler as a gift for my new roommates. (Dan let me have them wholesale, prepacked.)

I enrolled in the Securities Training Corporation, a financial school that operated on the Wharton campus. From our house on Powelton Avenue, not far from Wharton, I began a new assault on brokerage houses, phoning and writing.

Philadelphia is a rougher, tougher business environment than the greater Boston area. I found out how just how tough on my fourth day in the city. I had secured an interview with the branch manager of a sleazy bucket shop in the downtown area, just off Chestnut Street. His offices bore about as much relationship to a Wall Street investment house as Soweto does to Beacon Hill.

About twelve guys, used-car-dealer types, were selling stocks, mostly penny stocks. All of them were fat, and half of them were eating hamburgers. All of them were smoking—every ashtray was brimming full. And every single one of the salesmen was shouting, some of them stamping on the floor. One guy was standing on his desk, yelling at some hapless customer, "You have to be long on this! People are stampeding for this . . . it's going . . . it's going!" The impression was of frenzied dealing, a veritable stock exchange uproar for these plainly fraudulent equities being offered on the pure pretense that the action was nothing short of huge.

Even I could see this was the wrong end of the business. I was never going in there. I'd starve before I set foot in their rathole. Through the thick smoke the guy standing on the desk was cajoling, urging, trying to persuade some poor old guy to pile his net worth into the stock—anything for the commission.

This was a classic sweatshop, a small outfit being paid by an obviously failing corporation to unload cheap stocks. These fat chain-smoking salesmen would say anything to their victims: "This stock is gonna double . . . it'll be two bucks by next Wednesday . . . you don't often get a chance like this . . . how many do I put you in for? What d'ya want? Gimme a number." It was right here, in a haze of tobacco smoke and cheap hamburger fumes. I was on the skid row of finance, the rock-bottom end of the business. Places like this specialize in the walking dead of failing corporations.

In their own way these bucket shops are specialists. They have no clients from whom to protect their reputation. They also have no reputation to defend. They just get out there and sell stocks and bonds they often know full well are worthless, and to hell with the consequences. They usually are paid a fee for hawking these fraudulent equities. That makes it a win-win. The sleazeball scavenges a living, and the doomed corporation gets one more bag of dough before filing for Chapter 7. That, by the way, is worse than bankruptcy. Chapter 7 is forced liquidation—goodnight Vienna.

Get me outta here was my only instinct. But the managing director, a total sleazeball in a shiny suit, led me back into his office and, with a colorful flourish, brandished a document in front of my eyes. "Check out the number, rookie—that's my paycheck for last month. Twenty thousand bucks."

All he wanted me to do was locate guys with cash and then sell 'em, jam them into worthless penny stocks with promises or anything else that worked. From my view across that hellhole of an office, just picking up the merest snatches of conversation, I could work out this was an underworld operation, selling stock in fake shells of corporations to raise cash, which was tantamount to ripping investors off, stealing them blind. My moral standards would not allow me to work for such an operation.

But the sleazeball manager was not finished with me, and he made me an offer to which I was forced to listen. "Hey, kid," he said, "you gotta pass your Series 7, right? Because if you don't, you ain't going no place. So here's what I'll do—you gotta have a sponsor, and I'm gonna be that sponsor, right? I'll fill in the papers, get 'em entered up in the right places. You pass the exam, you come and work for us, okay?"

I've never known whether he really believed I would work there, and he had no intention of paying for my exam, as most sponsors would. All he would do was file the papers as my official sponsor. I would have to pay for everything, including a $1,000 fee to the bucket shop.

We parted on good terms, and I made my way back to Powelton Avenue to face what I saw at the time as the daunting task of passing the Series 7—the only way you can get into the world of securities. Officially, I was trying to obtain "the general securities registered representative license administered by the Financial Industry Regulatory Authority (FINRA) that entitles the holder to sell all types of securities products with the exception of commodities and futures."

> *The bulk of the Series 7 exam focuses on investment risk, taxation, equity and debt instruments, packaged securities, options, retirement plans, and interaction with clients such as account management.*
>
> *In order to write the Series 7 exam, a candidate must be sponsored by a financial company that is a member of FINRA, or a self-regulatory organization (SRO).*
>
> *Successfully completing the Series 7 exam is a prerequisite for most of the FINRA principal examinations.**

That was my task, and I set off to work myself to death for five weeks, preparing for this six-hour bitch of an exam. It certainly was not as tough as the bar exam but was plenty tough enough for most of us. The official description scarcely did it justice. The entire paper was a demanding test of options, municipal securities laws, NASD rules and regulations, and that investors minefield, buying on margin. The main book I needed to study was about three feet thick, or at least that's how it looked to me.

Night after night, I pored through the book, memorized rules and procedures. Without knowing where I was going or where I would end up, I devoured that book, morning, noon, and evening, surrounded by

*FINRA, formerly the National Association of Securities Dealers, was established in 2007.

guys who were doing MBAs at Wharton and would soon head straight up the red carpet to the biggest firms on Wall Street.

But, in the fullness of time, each and every one of them would have to tread the same path and pass the exam. The main difference, of course, was that they would be sponsored by Merrill Lynch, Smith Barney, Lehman, J. P. Morgan, and Bear Stearns. Unlike me, who had nothing and was officially associated with one of the least attractive bucket shop gangs on the East Coast. Whether or not that Series 7 was a top priority or just a distant mountain to be climbed made no difference.

One by one my new Wharton buddies came and asked to see the study book, especially my pal and roommate Rick Schnall, a nephew of Carl Icahn, the most famous corporate raider on Wall Street, the Muhammad Ali of his trade. It was a big help being among guys like that, because when everyone is involved in the same subject, with similar insights and perceptions, the sheer velocity of the available information is ratcheted up a few notches. They were generous to me with their time and advice, and in turn I let them take a few peeps at the practice exams in the back of my book.

In the last couple of weeks my strategy was to take those practice exams over and over, and by the time I finally took the examination I'd completed a whole stack of them. Hell, I was darned nearly a veteran, and I crashed home to victory, scoring a 92 (the passing grade was 70). I was now licensed to walk in the steps of the mighty, and my elation was about 300 on the Richter scale.

Little did I know that the Series 7 exam was the very first step on my personal road to the greatest financial catastrophe in history, a global meltdown, the Armageddon of the world's stock markets—choose your metaphor. I was on the yellow brick road leading directly to the biggest bankruptcy of all time. Dead center, matter of fact.

But money was running out pretty fast, and my only prospect of gainful employment was back in the bucket shop with the sleazeball and the smokers, a group I regarded as the totally unacceptable face of capitalism. From where I stood, Danny and the porkers back in Sagamore looked like the boardroom of Salomon Brothers.

So once more I set off to storm the ramparts of the brokerage houses. But this time I was armed not only with my Pork Chop Man of the Century award from American Frozen Foods but also with my outstanding grade on the Series 7 exam.

Merrill Lynch was my first call. The Philadelphia branch was situated in a beautiful old bank building down near Independence Mall, pitching-wedge distance from the Liberty Bell, on Chestnut Street. I moved smoothly past the front line of the brokerage house's corporate defenses by unleashing a colossal whopper and telling the receptionist I had an appointment with the branch manager, Gary Begnaud. I think he must have been too busy to remember whether he had an appointment with me or not, but he summoned me into his mahogany-paneled office and listened to my story. He never did find out the true validity of my "appointment," but he liked the sales experience, and he loved the fact that I had achieved the Series 7 on my own.

He treated me seriously and tried to explain the requirements for a Merrill Lynch retail salesman. Tell you the truth, they were pretty damn basic—find as many rich people as you can and talk them into investing their money with the company. The bigger the amount, the better Gary was going to like it.

Would he give me leads?

"Nah."

Would I get lists of the right kind of people?

"Forget that. Get your own lists."

How about a desk in his office, where I could answer the phone and pick up a few leads that way?

"Larry, you get a desk and a phone in the bullpen. We'll teach you the new but noble art of cold-calling clients to sell money market funds, stocks, and bonds. Our analysts put together these financial packages, and you get out there and sell them."

He added that interrupting busy people with a sales pitch was no walk in the park. In fact, he suggested that if I was any good, I had a fighting chance of becoming, in a very short time, the least popular person in Pennsylvania. "But if you're good," he told me, "the money's good."

Would I get a salary?

"Oh, sure. Eighteen thousand a year. Plus commission on what you bring in."

He said "eighteen thousand" as if it was eighteen million, but I swiftly calculated I'd be lucky to get three hundred fifty bucks a week. Hell, I could earn that in a day with American Frozen Foods.

But this was my chosen road, the road to Wall Street, and Gary was Merrill Lynch's most trusted executive in what was then the fifth-largest city in the United States. I found out why when he imparted his final zinger to me: "Larry, you got a job here for six months. In that time I want you to bring in $6 million in assets and $100,000 in investment commissions. Fail and you're fired."

My mind raced, and I flashed from the sheer impossibility of the task to the joy of a paltry salary plus another $25,000 payout in commissions if I hit the minimum production threshold of one hundred grand. Would I give it a try? Damn straight I would, even though I suspected that Merrill Lynch in Philly operated on the same lines as the sleazeball and the smokers, except for the classy manners, the sophisticated product packages, and the towering reputation of this Wall Street powerhouse. That's all.

Let's face it—selling the stocks and bonds offered in the Merrill portfolio, offering a rock-solid 5 or 6 percent on clients' money, beat the hell out of selling fraudulent stock for some carpet maker in South Philly. And the uppermost thought in my mind was that I needed money, fast, and if I didn't take Gary's offer, then my only alternative was to report back to my sponsors, and I couldn't face that.

I shook hands with my new boss, took a swift tour of the office, produced my precious Series 7 diploma and my award from American Frozen Foods, and promised to report for duty the next morning at six. That night I made my transformation from earnest parka-wearing student to slick young hustler operating under the banner of Merrill Lynch. I went into Wanamaker's, the famous Philadelphia retail emporium, and bought myself a new suit and a pair of black shoes.

I felt good, though a bit uneasy, as I walked into the office early the next morning. It was, after all, the only time in living memory I'd entered a brokerage house without telling a grandiose white lie to one of the front office staff or hiding behind a couple of empty white pizza boxes—*sausage and extra cheese for Mr. Begnaud.*

In a briefcase I'd borrowed from Rick Schnall, one of my Wharton roommates, I had my new set of weapons, my salesman's attack blueprint: local maps, business directories, and lists of country clubs, golf clubs, and big-city men's clubs, anywhere I was likely to find people who fit Merrill Lynch's favorite marketing phrase, "persons of high net worth."

They were my targets, and by nine o'clock I was putting together a power list and trying to convert key phrases from the meat-selling business to fit the much more complex task of selling stocks and bonds. I was using every ounce of creativity I possessed.

For instance, one of the prime ways a reluctant potential client gets out of making a commitment to invest is to say, "I'm sorry, Mr. McDonald, I need to run this by my wife." Every salesman worth anything whatsoever is ready for that one. But because I didn't want to use any phrase the prospective client might have heard before, I racked my brains for a line I could be ready with. Finally I got it, and I used it for months. When the potential client said he needed to run it by his wife, I answered: "Sir, these equities do not come in different colors. Your wife probably hasn't picked a winner since she picked you." A couple of people were mildly shocked at this flagrant chauvinism, but if anyone laughed, I knew I was turning for home, whippin' and drivin' down the stretch to the finish line.

The problem was, my new suit and shoes had just about wiped out my cash, and after six weeks of sixteen- to eighteen-hour days I was not making it financially. I couldn't give up, but I couldn't go on, because my success rate was hovering somewhere near the red zone. I'd hardly clinched a deal in that time, and I was broke. Which caused me to make a thoroughly desperate move.

I located a loan shark to borrow $500. The terms were harsh: pay $600 back in two weeks. I presumed that failure would result in my lifeless body being dredged up from the Schuylkill River, probably wearing cement boots instead of my new black shoes. But I had no alternative. I was now on my own and didn't want to borrow from family and friends.

Somehow I had to sell these equities, and all I had was my brain and a killer work ethic. I cold-called until the phone was red hot, hundreds of calls every day, looking for the break, for the client with money to invest. I worked my way door-to-door all the way from the office near Eighth Street right down to Society Hill on the western bank of the Delaware River.

In the evenings I hit the suburbs, particularly the great mansions of Philadelphia high society along the Main Line. The name refers to the old Main Line of the Pennsylvania Railroad, which transported the rich home from Philadelphia to their castles, great and small. It's a megabucks sprawl where even small is great, palatial residences set back in wondrous manicured gardens all the way from Bala Cynwyd through Merion, Ardmore, Bryn Mawr, Devon, Wayne, and Paoli. Today the Main Line is not so much a rail line as a state of mind, and its residents are apt to regard all other suburbs as if they housed the boat people of Vietnam. Philadelphia believes it has its own aristocracy. They even speak differently, with a kind of rigid set to the jaw, especially when uttering the words *Main Line*—it's a kind of "Maayne Loyyyne" effect. I'm a pretty reasonable mimic, but I never quite mastered that pronunciation. I'm told you have to be born to it.

Anyway, the old Maayne Loyyyne became my new territory. Not as a resident, you understand, since I could barely afford the train fare, and the Volkswagen looked as if it belonged to one of their assistant pastry chefs. But it was a battleground where I would raise (a) the money to avoid being assassinated by the loan sharks and (b) the millions of dollars in assets that would put me on the fast track to Merrill Lynch's head office at 250 Vesey Street, a thirty-four-story building at the north edge of the World Trade Center site in lower Manhattan.

I realized that in most cases I might not get past the front gates, and certainly not beyond the housekeeper's telephone, but these guys had to put their cash somewhere, and I had a real good package to sell them. In my own mind wild horses would not stop me; I would use every trick and technique in the book, anything to get in front of the man with the dough.

The trouble was, I needed a human slingshot to get me in—a way to get noticed, some kind of an inside track—and I tackled the problem the way Eisenhower planned the Normandy landings. I attacked the alumni associations of every Ivy League university in the United States. Then I hit Duke, North Carolina, and UVA before taking a shot at Stanford, UCLA, and USC. All I wanted was a copy of the alumni yearbooks for, say, the classes of 1966 or 1967, because in there were hundreds of graduates. Those books gave birthdates and places, the names of their wives, and where they started their business careers. You'd be amazed at how many of the ones who'd started out in Philadelphia were still working in that city, and how many of them turned out to be in residence on the Main Line. I guess when a city has been a critical part of American industry and white-collar business since the Revolution it will always have a serious collection of blue-blooded tycoons in residence. And Philadelphia was for years, after New York, the second-largest trading port in the country.

The only trouble, as I saw it, was that much of the money was old. And people with old money are innately suspicious that someone is going to take it away. They've spent generations protecting themselves and their fortunes, and mostly they consider any Johnny-come-lately of the modern financial world to be radioactive. And boy, was I ever a Johnny-come-lately.

With that in mind I plotted and planned with immense precision. In addition to the alumni yearbook assault, I invented the country club offensive, compiling a list of every expensive golf and country club in the area, especially those along the Main Line—and in particular the revered Merion Golf Club in Ardmore, with its 6,846-yard championship East Course and lockjawed Maayne Loyyyne membership. My objective was simple: to acquire the private members' handbook with its complete list of members' addresses and phone numbers.

Now, smart golf clubs were places in which I was entirely at home, despite being secretly in hock to the local brigade of loan sharks. Places like Merion can be extremely intimidating, with their rigid traditions, exemplary manners, and the inbred etiquette of the game, which seems to pervade every room, every lounge, every bar, and even the locker room. But they were not intimidating to me. My dad had taken me to private golf clubs, and while at the time I was not practicing sufficiently to play to scratch, I was still a single-figure handicap player, and that gave me a natural clubhouse confidence.

I knew all about this place before I arrived. I knew that Bobby Jones had completed the legend of his 1930 Grand Slam here when he won the U.S. Amateur before an eighteen-thousand-strong crowd. I knew that Ben Hogan had won the U.S. Open here. I knew all about the fabled "white faces," as Merion's bunkers are known. My dad had played and won here.

I knew the dress code, and I knew the language of the golfers. I had studied the layout and noted the difficult holes. I was expert with the throwaway lines of the membership—*four-putted the eighth, again; hooked into the woods at the twelfth; couldn't get out of the bunker on the fifteenth to save my life.* By any standards I was ready.

I walked into the clubhouse locker room dressed like Jack Nicklaus and holding a putter. It was a Sunday morning, and the membership was out on the course. I did not even see an attendant, and there, lying on a bench, was a membership book.

I slipped it into my pocket and walked calmly out of the building and back across the parking lot. It was probably worth less than a dollar, that little white book with its club emblem, featuring the little wicker basket that sits, uniquely, on the top of every Merion flagstick.

But to me it was priceless, and I headed back downtown with the joy of the conqueror in my heart.

In the ensuing few weeks I learned one thing about club membership books: they can always be found lying around, but nine times out of ten you find them in the locker room or by the bar. The interesting thing is, no one takes a bit of notice if you pick one up. Somehow if you're in, you're in, a member of the brotherhood.

Every day I cold-called club members and a selection of the names I had picked up in the area from the college alumni books. And with my excellent Merrill Lynch financial products I made some progress. It was never easy, but every now and then I ran down a prospect and piqued his interest. Sometimes I sent official Merrill Lynch flowers or chocolates to their wives before I called. And somehow I persuaded my Philadelphia clients to invest $1.5 million. My own commission was of course only about $15,000, but at that time it seemed like one hell of a lot of money.

And then, after several weeks of work, I got my first big break, and it came from the most unlikely quarter: the police. I had been on a charm offensive with a guy who was a finance official in the Philadelphia fraternal order of police, and who, to my amazement, invested a huge amount of his colleagues' funds in the market. I made him offer after offer. I attended all kinds of police events. They even made me dress up like a cop for a Halloween party. Anyhow, I explained to him that the interest rate he was getting was not good enough, and I could do better.

In the end I was victorious. My new pal the cop invested $15 million with me. I was one of the top rookies for acquiring investment assets for Merrill Lynch in Philadelphia. The country clubs came through in the end, the alumni books proved to be a triumph of client location, and even the door-to-door offensive paid off. As it had been with the frozen meat, so it was with the stocks and bonds. I ended up one of the top first-year salesmen. Gary Begnaud was thrilled with my performance.

By now it was 1992. I was twenty-six years old, and I was not happy. I had money. I was comfortably placed, with a decent car and a lot of new friends. But I never liked Philadelphia, and every month that went by I was digging ever-deeper roots for myself. The Main Line was okay, and I had a few very good pals out there. But I missed New England, I missed Boston, I missed the Cape, and nothing in this historic but somewhat grim metropolis could ever feed my soul the way the beaches and the oceanside dunes of Cape Cod always did.

It was a real test for me to leave the world I had created for myself. But the feeling inside me was like that of a homing pigeon. And one day I walked into Gary's office and broke the news. I was going home.

He nearly had a fit at the potential loss of one of his top salesmen, the kid he had plucked out of nowhere who might or might not have had an appointment. But he could see I was determined to go, and I presented him with all my accounts, requesting only that he grant me an official transfer with a senior sales position to Merrill Lynch's office in Hyannis, which in financial terms is a kind of suburb of Boston. I could see he hated to do it. But for the second time in a couple of years Gary came through for me, in somewhat unusual circumstances.

On a bright autumn morning I gassed up my new car and headed north, out of Pennsylvania, up to New York, and on toward the Cape. Toward an old familiar world. Toward home. But with me I took a lesson issued to me over and over by my buddy Steve Seefeld, who for months had sworn to God that the only way forward in the world of finance was bonds, convertible bonds, which he personally had been trading since he was, ridiculously, about nineteen years old.

2

Scaring Morgan Stanley to Death

He yelled down the line, threatening bloody murder. "I'll sue your ass . . . I'll have you in court by Monday morning . . . I'll have five partners on your case from the biggest law firm in New York. I'll bankrupt you with legal fees."

I LEARNED ABOUT the rich in Philadelphia, especially that they can stand just about anything except some smart-ass trying to run away with their bread. The only issue for them is retaining their assets. They can live with low returns and low rates of interest, but their unbreakable rule is, *Don't lose my capital.*

As my months pitching and selling to the high rollers of Philadelphia had turned into a year and then another, I began to stick more and more to the creed of my roommate Steve Seefeld: *Sell 'em bonds, Larry, it's the only thing they're comfortable with. It's the least risky way you can ever invest.*

Steve, of course, spoke from a position of strength. The early death of his landowner father had seen him inherit a great fortune. He actually drove around in a Mercedes when he was still in high school. Happily, he had no inclinations to run off with my father's ex-wife, so his windshield and headlights remained intact.

The night before I left Philly, Steve and I had dinner. Our final conversation remained with me for the rest of my career. "Never lose sight of the critical difference," he reminded me, "between the holder of a corporate bond and the holder of corporate stock. The bondholder has massive protection. Even though it looks like he's bought something, he's really only lent money to the corporation. The owner of equity is powerless because he's just placed a bet on the company's cash flow. If the stock crashes, he's dead in the water, and there's nothing he can do about it."

Thus I drove back to Cape Cod a newly converted disciple of the new fashion for convertible bonds, an often misunderstood concept even today. There are always people, some of them quite shrewd equity investors, who remain confused about the literal meaning of the word *bond.* I can help right there. It means debt, pure and simple. It's an IOU between a borrower and a lender.

Corporate bonds, Treasury bonds, and municipal bonds all represent nothing more than a loan—or, if you wish, debt—for which the lender will be paid an interest rate, known as coupon yield. And this is why U.S. Treasuries are considered the least risky bond of all: you are lending money to Uncle Sam, and he's got the best credit score in the universe. That's why, generally speaking, Uncle Sam is very big out on the Main Line.

People often use the phrase *stocks and bonds,* but in truth there is a vast gap between them. Anyone can buy stock or equities in large or small amounts. Bonds are for the rich. When issued they come in at $1,000 each, but you typically have to buy a thousand of them, which means you need a million bucks minimum to get in the game. (This is a typical minimum investment for any institutional investor. Retail investors, in some cases, can invest smaller initial amounts.)

But all you have done is loan either the government or a major corporation $1 million. When you buy your bond, you are given two key facts—the amount of interest you will receive annually and the date your bond will mature. On that maturity date you will be given your money back. All of it, no bullshit. And throughout the time you hold that bond, receiving, say, a 5 percent rate of interest on that $1 million investment ($50,000 a year, free of state tax if it's a government bond), you have powers denied to the regular stockholder. In the great scheme of things, bondholders matter, with many carefully written covenants to protect them. Stockholders are cannon fodder. If the shares go up, they win. If the shares go down, no one cares.

But bonds . . . ah, those golden-edged bonds. They are just the ticket, because the large corporation that took your money is duty bound to give it back. Bondholders can have people hired and fired. If a few of them get together, they can throw out the board, unload the top executives. They can demand that the assets of the corporation be sold, and they rate real high on the pecking order for repayment if a corporation goes bankrupt.

And it's important to understand that a large corporation going bankrupt is not the same as a person throwing up his hands in the face of a couple of low-flying creditors and declaring personal bankruptcy. Because when a company goes very badly bust, especially a small company, it's usually because they have run out of cash and credit. They can't pay the staff or their benefits or their pensions. So they have to fire them, shut the gates, and call it a day—for the moment. But behind the shut gates are assets. Not liquid assets, perhaps, but temporarily frozen assets. Freed of their monthly obligation to hundreds, maybe thousands of workers, the corporation is rarely flat broke. Rather, most corporate bankruptcies happen because a company needs a breather and to reorganize, because their debt load is too big relative to their cash flow.

Bankruptcy by no means signals all is lost for the bondholders. Stepping over the bodies of the shareholders, who have lost everything, they have the key to the company's gates—behind which often stand acres and acres of concrete, massive plant buildings, downtown office blocks worth millions of dollars, and state-of-the-art machinery. There may be materials, electronics, steel, tires, aluminum. And product may still be sold, maybe at knockdown prices, but there is a cash flow.

First on the list of creditors is always the bank, and they can wipe out a lot of money. But next in line come the bondholders (senior secured, then unsecured), who now get their share of the spoils. Even if the corporation is in Chapter 11 bankruptcy,* those $1,000 bonds are still owed and must be repaid from the remaining assets. The bondholder even has a seat at the bankruptcy table along with the bankers and corporate execs.

Still, on the upside, if a corporation is either plainly going south or suspiciously heading that way, a bondholder is free to sell on the open market. He may only receive 80 cents on the dollar, but if he's been collecting the annual interest for three or four years, he's not going to come to much harm. Unlike the shareholder.

*Chapter 7 of the Bankruptcy Code provides for "liquidation" (i.e., the sale of a debtor's nonexempt property and the distribution of the proceeds to creditors).

The person who buys the bonds on the market through a broker for, say, $800,000 is still owed the full $1 million by the corporation at the end of the ten-year tenure, the maturity date. And if it's one of those traditional big, nearly impregnable U.S. corporations, it's probably a decent buy. The iron-clad rule is that the bonds were issued at $1,000 and, barring bankruptcy, will always mature at $1,000. However, they do not always trade at $1,000. They can trade at a lot less than $1,000.

The buyer in the open market looks at one critical figure, known as the yield to maturity. This is the figure that matters. And it's arrived at by a simple process. The bonds, with perhaps five years to run, issued by, say, the biggest chemical corporation in the world, are going to cost probably $800,000. They're paying a 6 percent coupon annually on that initial $1 million investment for another five years, which is a total of $300,000. When the bonds mature, the buyer gets the original $1 million back, not just the $800,000 he paid. Which represents a straight $200,000 profit. That's a $500,000 total return on the original investment of $800,000—a yield to maturity of 11.50 percent. Beautiful.

In the end, the bond was only a method by which the corporation was raising money, and it's reflected on their balance sheet as debt. Because that's what a bond is. The corporation was not trying to raise money to stay alive; it was raising money for a substantial expansion, maybe a new plant, a new retail branch, a new skyscraper, an acquisition, or, in the case of an airline, a dozen Boeings. Municipal bonds usually are for new roads, new bridges, or construction. U.S. Treasuries are for pretty well anything the federal government damn pleases, but they've never defaulted on one nickel.

Let me run through the bond creation process. A national chain of supermarkets wants to build a new superstore in a new development outside a prosperous U.S. city. It's going to cost $100 million. The CFO goes to a major Wall Street investment bank and produces the business plan, which demonstrates its potential profitability, the location, the lack of competition, and the prospect of building around it an entire community of retail outlets. If the investment bank likes the sound of it, they will lend the supermarket the money to proceed with the construction, at an agreed-upon coupon yield for a specified time. Typical would be 6 percent annually for ten years, like a gigantic mortgage.

The investment bank will then securitize the loan, which is a snazzy way of turning a debt into a bond, dividing the $100 million into one hundred thousand $1,000 bonds, and then putting together a prospectus to sell them. This was a primitive form of securitization, one that would become much more dangerous down the road. For now, they put them out to their bond salesmen, located on their own trading floor, and offer them immediately to a few well-heeled clients, the big hedge funds, mutual funds, and investing institutions.

You can imagine the sales pitch: *Just released this morning, a great new bond from Superfoods. Fantastic new retail facility right on the town line of Greenwich, Connecticut. According to their research, this can't miss. They've been trying for planning review board permission for three years, and so have three other smaller outfits, but Superfoods landed the project. You want this bond, trust me. They got a great balance sheet, double-A rated. You can have a thousand for a mill. Or ten thousand for ten mill, but this offer will last about twenty minutes.*

The successful selling of the bonds releases the investment bank from holding the $100 million debt on their books. It's the corporation that continues to hold the obligation—but now it's to the bondholders, and not due for ten years. With a stroke of the financier's magic wand, a $100 million debt has been turned into an investment with an annual yield of 6 percent.

For years, this was the core business for investment banks—Lehman, Morgan Stanley, Goldman Sachs, and Bear Stearns. It was mostly the institutional side of the business—the big leagues, the place I'd been trying to reach ever since I left college.

When I arrived back on the Cape, my plan was to ensure that the packages I would offer clients would be heavy with bonds, because they represent the supreme method to ensure the preservation of capital. It's been ever thus in the world of investment for both people and institutions with large amounts of principal. Investing now or anytime requires a continual search for ways to control risk and protect assets while still achieving above-average returns.

Bonds have been around for a very long time. In fact, America was built on bonds. Back in the second half of the nineteenth century, bonds were issued by the new industrial giants to finance the building of the railroads, which would open up the vast lands and wealth of the United States, still reeling from the devastation of the Civil War. They were issued on the same lines I have outlined. In the 1880s there was one far-reaching development: the emergence of the convertible bond, which had the added feature of allowing the holder to convert it into a fixed number of shares of common stock—equity shares—in an era when the market for railroads and anything connected with them were making fortunes.

The new iron horses, the enormous steam locomotives, took investors out of their covered wagons and onto the gravy train. Each bond was issued with a conversion value that permitted investors, if they sold before the maturity date, to partake of the profits engendered by a rising stock price. Equally, if the stock plummeted down, holders of convertible bonds were given a parachute that usually worked—that is, it would not let their price go below 70 or 80 cents on the dollar.

Also, same as now, the bond was still a bond, and whatever else, the corporation still owed that $1,000 when the maturity date finally arrived. You may ask why these corporations put the sweetener in there, and the answer is very simple: they needed to persuade people to invest, and the revolutionary idea of investing in a railroad, which somehow started near home and then kind of vanished over the hills and far away, ending up God knows where, unnerved some investors. The sweetener of the convertible bond often made the difference.

It also found great favor with the railroad companies whose bonds were not required to pay an 8 percent coupon.* They had to pay only 5 percent, because of the staggering rise in their stock price in that era. The beauty of issuing convertible bonds by a corporation is the ability to borrow money and pay a lower coupon. Investors are willing to accept the lower coupon because of the sweetness of the equity upside potential. That incentive still exists today with the modern convertible bond. And unless you make some lunatic selection of a doomed corporation, it's going to taste as sweet as ever. Especially out there on the Main Line, where the parties that often started way back in the nineteenth century continue.

I was only half aware, because the signs were not yet cast in stone, but when I arrived back on the Cape to begin work in the Merrill Lynch office in Hyannis, the world was on the verge of a revolution. Technology companies were about to become the growth sector of the stock market. Motorola, Ericsson, Oracle, Texas Instruments, 3Com, Cisco Systems, and EMC Corporation led the charge to a high-tech-dominated business environment. They were the railroads of the

*Companies loved issuing convertibles not just because the coupon was lower, but because in a rising stock market, investors actually converted their bonds to stock, saving the companies precious cash.

1990s. And many of them were about to make serious use of convertible bonds, the rock-steady way to raise money for expansion, with the coupon and equity kicker to encourage investors.

A corporation such as Motorola could borrow at 8 percent from Lehman because they could afford it. They wanted the major injection of capital, and they were happy to reward bondholders with a high annual coupon payment, because they were positive the new tech business would be highly profitable in the coming years. The task of the investment bank was to examine, investigate, and arrive at a yes or no that would not mislead their clients. I'd seen those beady-eyed analyst guys operate at close quarters, and I had enormous faith in them.

With my courage high, I straightened up to sell these convertible bonds that had been given the green light from Merrill Lynch. I'd already noticed this type of bond was beginning to outperform on a risk-adjusted basis every other kind of asset class, even residential property and gold. I also sensed the coming high-tech revolution, and I had visions of being carried directly into Wall Street on a wave of flying electronic sparks, flickering screens, and cyberspace mysticism. I was not that far wrong, either.

But first I needed to establish a business within the confines of Merrill Lynch in Hyannis. The work was not that difficult, and I cruised through the first few months, building a client list, selling the bonds, selling what equities I considered appropriate, and rekindling old friendships.

I realized, though, that there was a big difference between working in Philly and working on Cape Cod. Although Philadelphia wasn't New York, it possessed that big-city edge of toughness, and it demanded competitiveness and hard-edged selling techniques. Cape Cod had little of that, and almost surreptitiously the danger of losing my own edge began to creep up on me.

The fact was I could now conduct a retail stock and bond operation with consummate ease. I always started early in the morning, but not like Philly, where I used to report to the office in the middle of the goddamned night, consumed by a desperation to win that I believe is nurtured only in a big city.

Cape Cod was not about strange desperations. It was about cooling it, enjoying the slow relaxed pace of the place, light traffic, no charging around looking for cabs, people being at their desks having coffee, and business lunches. Everything was more, well . . . civilized.

There was the sheer vista of the land and seascapes. The long lonely ocean beaches up around the village of Dennis, the majesty of the surf at Nauset on the Atlantic side, the great sweep of the Monomoy headland jutting out toward Nantucket. There were Wellfleet and Truro up there on the bayside, then elegant and prosperous Chatham with its historic fishing fleet, snooty Osterville, rarefied Oyster Harbors, and the spectacular coastline around the working seaports of Falmouth and Woods Hole.

My territory stretched right up to the great sandy eastern hook of the Cape at Provincetown and then more than a hundred miles back to the two gateway bridges that lead to mainland Massachusetts and the townships near the canal.

Wherever you look there are tempting distractions, including many golf courses, and especially Woods Hole. And for a twenty-six-year-old single guy with a bit of money, there were other distractions, such as girls, bars, restaurants, boats, and parties. The lifestyle was intoxicating. The Cape was luring me in, and so was a girlfriend I had at the time. For more than three years Cape Cod had been a lot of laughs, and I was going comfortably soft, losing my edge, finding no urgency to fight.

I changed my job, switching to the excellent competitive retail brokerage house of Smith Barney, and it didn't change a thing. I was still cruising, making fewer phone calls to my old buddies in the industry, coming up with fewer new plans, kind of allowing the world to slip past. Jesus, looking back, it was great. It was also probably the most dangerous time of my entire career.

There's a word for Cape Codders who rarely cross the bridge to go, as they phrase it, "off-Cape." The place is like a drug. There are people who have never been off-Cape, never felt the need. These are the clamheads. But I could not become a clamhead. I needed to rev up my ambitions and start driving again toward Wall Street. I pondered my next move, because I now knew I had to get out, and soon. Otherwise I would have been there forever.

Around that time I also sensed there were big moves afoot in the market. For example, e-trades were beginning to catch on, and this process was lowering margins. For a few days I worried. And then I ran into an acquaintance in a bar. He worked for IBM and was about to start up one of the Cape's first Internet service providers (ISPs), a revolutionary gateway to the Internet. It would allow both businesses and private citizens to plug into the World Wide Web, the new information highway, the dot-coms. I only half understood what he was talking about, because the Internet did not figure prominently in my job. But the guy in the bar told me that the whole business world was going to end up operating online, that the whole of the New York Stock Exchange would end up on that screen. In the next two or three years, people would buy and sell stocks and bonds online; brokerage houses would be closing down by the thousand. This was the start of the high-tech revolution.

"Don't wait," he added darkly. "Get online with the rest of the world's business leaders. Because anyone who doesn't is dead." In his view, every scrap of information I would ever need in my entire career was going to find its way onto the screens. "Miss this opportunity to join the real world," he said, "and you'll be like a fucking dinosaur in a space station."

Holy shit, I said to myself, *the brokerage business is going to be destroyed.* The guy had scared the living daylights out of me. And the vision of the Internet as this encroaching monster from cyberspace stood stark before my eyes, snaking out its electronic tentacles into my cozy world, tempting my clients away, showing them how to buy and sell, helping them create their portfolios without me. Three years from now I'd be standing in a financial wasteland. Wall Street would look like Dresden in 1945, and my bank account would look like the Empty Quarter.

I walked out of that bar with my mind reeling. I was going through a very obvious epiphany. I had located a way into Wall Street: the creation of a corporation every financial business in the world *needed.* For the first time the future was not merely the holy grail shimmering somewhere out there in the mists of broken dreams. My future was a laser beam leading to a place that I could identify, a shining city not on a hill but in lower Manhattan. I had tried so darned hard for so long, but for the first time I could see my way forward with a clarity that would never again desert me.

This called for decisive action. So I called my trusted old buddy, Steve Seefeld, and he listened in silence while I explained how the IBM exec was switching on the whole of Cape Cod to the Internet, and that the world as we knew it was about to end. We talked for two hours about the unlimited potential of the Internet.

"Tell you what," said Steve eventually, ever the pragmatist, ever the poet. "The fucker's right." He confirmed that the high-tech revolution was upon us and that he was working on a way forward. Steve's game was cyberspace and the Internet. Like him, I was very interested in convertible bonds. And over the next three hours on the line between Greenwich, Connecticut, and the Cape, we hatched a plot for a new and revolutionary concept: a Web site that would educate institutional investors about the bond market and then provide an opportunity to trade online.

When we had finished the call, neither of us was clear how to proceed, but I think we both knew that we would proceed somehow. The following morning I called Steve in Greenwich again and told him that in my opinion we should kick our plan into gear right away. He was very positive about a new online corporation, for us to be partners. And so I packed up my stuff once again, gave up my job and my condo, said a few good-byes, loaded up the car, and drove away. So far as I was concerned, I was headed not off-Cape but off-planet. I was driving into unknown territory and I had no idea what awaited me, except that Steve and I believed we were onto something big, and we had the bit between our teeth. I was thirty years old.

When I arrived at his house, he was full of optimism. We outlined the project and then set about opening our new office, a world headquarters, from which we expected to hit 'em low, hit 'em hard, and hit 'em fast. No more bullshit. The new corporation was to be named ConvertBond.com. We needed to get up to speed both on the Internet and on the computers that channeled the World Wide Web into the places it was required. My new partner understood more about computer programming than anyone else in the country except Bill Gates.

We found a decent-sized office above a strip mall on Railroad Avenue in Greenwich. Chinese food to the left, printers to the right, pharmaceuticals dead ahead, dry cleaner down below—who could ask for more? We had our computers installed, hired a couple of programmers, and set about starting up a corporation that in time would knock people's socks off.

The idea was brilliant but simple, like most trailblazing plans. Steve's devotion to bonds was unflagging, but he had noticed over the years that when you wanted to know something about a new bond issue, it was a royal pain in the ass to find out. You had to call the corporation, explain who you were and what you wanted, and then request a prospectus. Bear in mind that some investors, especially big institutions, might want to know about perhaps twenty bonds. They wanted to study and understand them, and it might take weeks to gather the relevant material, which was all contained in these big, glossy, often overwritten prospectuses that often were full of bullshit.

In simple terms, we planned to collect these prospectuses from companies all over the country. We wanted to use them to build a huge back-end database that would contain details about every bond, either for sale or about to be issued, in the entire nation: coast to coast, north to south.

It was a mammoth task. Sometimes our goal seemed too far away. And sometimes we thought we were going too slowly. But we kept going, phoning, writing, e-mailing, visiting. Steadily our priceless database came into being. We talked to every mutual fund, hedge fund, and pension fund in the world, any fund that had any kind of record of buying or selling convertible bonds. We discovered their needs, and we tailored our information highway to all of their requirements.

"One day," said Steve, "the whole world is going to need this. In time, anyone buying a convertible bond would not dream of doing so without going online and checking out the bond issuer with ConvertBond.com. We're on the verge of something enormous. This, Larry, old buddy, can't miss."

The trouble was, it was so difficult to get any kind of income. All we did was spend. We had nothing to offer until the database was complete. We certainly had nothing to offer the big investment houses yet, and we were both terrified some national outfit would copy our idea and run with it a whole lot faster than we could.

We spent between $300,000 and $400,000 financing the operation. We worked night and day, sometimes even sleeping under our desks—anything to save time. We ripped open the prospectuses as they arrived in the mail, and then we set about transferring each and every one of them onto the computer, deriving a standard formula for them that in the not-too-distant future would allow investors anywhere in the world to go to ConvertBond.com and find out anything and everything significant to the bond in which they had an investment interest. Just at the touch of a few buttons.

As you can imagine, the sight of our office was amazing. We were trying to sort out more data than the U.S. Army's recruiting department did. We had floor-to-ceiling, wall-to-wall, out-in-the-hallway prospectuses. Once we had this mountain of information under control, we planned to slip into Steve's pet project. Each morning we wanted to highlight one single knock-'em-dead bond, deemed our Convert of the Day—chosen with the full and fearless approval of this new two-man operation, analyzed and researched right up here over the dry cleaner, next to the Chinese takeout. Stand back, America.

Of course, our own presentation was designed to make us look as substantial as IBM. It was the tried and tested American way, and we were following in the footsteps of the great U.S. entrepreneurs. There's never been anything like the Internet to provide instant status to minor-league outfits like ours. To tell the truth, our Web site made us look like the Pentagon. Our creed was printed boldly at the head of the home page: "Founded in 1997 [which it still was], the site offers terms, analysis, news and pricing relating to the 890 convertible securities that currently can be found in the U.S. market." The number 890 may not sound like much, but you should see what 890 looks like in stacks all over the floor, forming a kind of office minefield.

Our Convert of the Day was typically a bond issued by a corporation like Hewlett-Packard. That bond might offer a strike price of $63.15, which means, broadly, that a bondholder who had paid par for his convertible—that's $1,000—could, if he wished, convert that into regular Hewlett-Packard stock at any time at the fixed price of $63.15 per share. That meant he could *always* exchange the bond for 15.83 HP shares. The moment that share price began to rise, the price of the bond rose with it. So if the stock went from $55 to $90, you multiply that figure by 15.83, and your bond is worth at least $1,424—which is sweet for the investor, especially since the coupon yielded 5 percent. In the raging dot-com market of the next twenty-four months, if the HP stock eventually surged to $100 a share, the investor's bond went up again and was now worth at least $1,583. That's more than a 25 percent annual return. It was especially good if you happened to have a thousand of them, because, including your 5 percent coupon, that added up to a $683,000 profit. Because Hewlett-Packard had a credit score nearly as good as the U.S. government's, that bond was never going to be worth much less than $880—not with HP guaranteeing your 5 percent *and* the return of the original $1,000 in twenty-four months. The bondholder thus enjoyed the upside potential of the stock and downside protection from the mighty Hewlett-Packard. That's why we made it Convert of the Day.

Getting all this data loaded and providing breaking news updates was hellishly complex and absolutely impossible to put into action for anyone except a computer genius. I could help with the design, but the actual mechanics of installing this huge site on the World Wide Web was a project for Steve and his programmers. It was 1997, and I felt like some kind of techno-peasant. In the late nineties there were only a limited number of people in the entire country who could undertake such a mind-blowing operation, and Steve Seefeld was one of them because he could speak the language of cyberspace. I was learning as we moved along. But Steve was fluent, probably had been since birth.

While my new business partner toiled away in the literal engine-room of ConvertBond.com, my group continued to hammer the phones, order the prospectuses, and gut them for the key points, the parts that were essential for the bond buyer. My work was then moved over to Steve for uploading. It was without question the busiest time of both our lives. We had no time for real meals. We kept going mostly on chop suey, chicken chow mein, and fried rice from the restaurant downstairs. We were always driven by the fear of a new, bigger, and richer player entering the game and stealing our idea, because beyond the walls of our frenzied office the whole world was on the move in a kind of panzer-division march to the Internet. There were guys leaving Procter and Gamble, IBM, Johnson and Johnson, Kellogg's, and other massive international corporations just to join Internet companies. Outfits such as Ask Jeeves, America Online (AOL), dating services, and God knows what else were on the rise. Yahoo went public.

Like them, Steve and I could see the future. In a very short span of time we would inaugurate a convertible bond Web site that had to prove itself priceless, and the only thing we needed was data. We already understood that much of this information was on the very expensive Bloomberg system, and we needed to get hold of more of it.

When we launched, we immediately charged institutional investors $1,000 a month to access our Web site at will. We had other sliding-scale charges for investors of all sizes, depending on how much data they wanted. And right from the outset we attracted traffic, paying customers. Our debt was growing to maybe $100,000, times were quite tough, and we were putting in eighteen-hour days. But our vision of the future remained undimmed: the indispensable convertible bond research Web site.

Once we were up and running in late 1997, we had the system

operating virtually on automatic. My new project involved publicizing ConvertBond.com. Once more I hit the phones, bombarding the media with calls, this time targeting the financial journalists who knew a bit, but nothing like as much as Steve and I did.

I would get through to the reporter, oftentimes a woman, and my pitch was dead-on, to say the least. Remember, I knew a thing or two about pitching, principally to tell 'em what they most wanted to hear. *Oh, hi, Deborah, my name is Larry McDonald and I'm a co-founder of ConvertBond.com. I have some information that might interest you.* Key words: *dot-com* and *information,* both irresistible to a financial journalist in this climate.

I then proceeded to tell the journalist about the new project, but never too long, and never too complicated; I just kept feeding them the words they salivated over—*revolutionary, World Wide Web, the next stock craze, state-of-the-art system, groundbreaking method.*

Deborah, I am one of the frontline operators in this brand-new game. I can help you make sense of this. Take this new Amazon.com bond. It's got a 4 percent coupon with one hell of a valuation. I will help you with every sliver of intelligence on this bond. Show you the ropes when you access ConvertBond.com. Because there's nothing more important you're going to tackle this week, and I've read you, there's no one better than you. Trust me . . .

Jesus, McDonald, you silver-tongued charmer, you.

Steve and I left no publication untouched. We called reporters at the *Wall Street Journal, Barron's, Investor's Business Daily.* We hit newspaper financial editors in New York City, on Long Island, and in Connecticut. We hit magazines, columnists, broadcasters. And for a very short while not much happened. Then it did.

Greg Zuckerman of the *Journal* suddenly called me and wanted to know all about this new Amazon.com bond due to be released in a matter of hours. Next morning I opened up the *Journal,* turned to C1, the front page of the hugely read Money and Investing section, and saw a major article: "Amazon, Bookstore of the World." It centered around their new convertible bond, one of the biggest ever issued, involving institutions only and either marketed to or sold to firms such as Fidelity Putnam and Vanguard.

Shivers ran up my spine. There we were, ConvertBond.com, mentioned not once but twice, and given colossal credence: "According to ConvertBond.com . . ." We had arrived. Our Web site already had been clocking 1,000 hits a day, but now we exploded like Mount St. Helens—before close of business that day we had received 150,000 hits.

For months now the publications had been heralding some kind of a dot-com gold rush. Anyone who did not accept that such a surge was in progress was in danger of being mown down in the stampede. And here we were, one of the nation's newest dot-com outfits being swamped with hits on our Web site. Looking back, we were right in the midst of the boom: we were becoming the guiding light for the biggest institutional investors in convertible securities on Wall Street.

It was a crazy time. The whole ethos of U.S. business was changing. In this new, vibrant atmosphere we were seeing big high-tech corporations where people no longer bothered with pin-striped suits and ties but rather turned up for work wearing sneakers, jeans, T-shirts, and denim jackets. The geeks were taking over the world as corporations settled into business models that were entirely based on buying and selling in cyberspace.

The sudden low price of reaching millions worldwide and the possibility of either selling to or hearing from those people promised to overturn established business dogma in advertising, mail-order sales, and customer relationships. The Web was, in the jargon, a killer app—a computer program so useful that people were rushing out to buy computers just to get hold of it.

The big scorers in this new atmosphere were Hewlett-Packard, Dell, IBM, and all the components companies that supplied them, such as Intel, Sun Microsystems, Sony, and Cisco Systems. Also making fortunes were Yahoo, AOL, Netscape, E*Trade, and Microsoft. So far as we were now concerned, at the top of the entire pile was Convert Bond.com, right over the dry cleaner, the new 150,000-hits-a-day gangbuster operation blazing a trail through the pages of the *Wall Street Journal*. That was a self-view, of course, probably not universal. Yet.

Thus our business began its early march toward becoming a cash cow, generating dollars every hour of the day and through the night. But it was still very tough going, because every day we received several new prospectuses, and they still had to be gutted and uploaded. And between us, Steve and I still had to select the Convert of the Day. Hell, we had thousands of unseen investors out there relying on us, our judgments, our research and analyses.

And still we were aware of the value of publicity. We needed to keep our name out there in the front lines of the bond investment world. The one exposure we lacked was the business channels on television, Bloomberg and CNBC. A slot there would surely send us straight through the roof. But how to pull that off?

My favorite CNBC program centered around a very beautiful reporter called Kate Bohner, who produced a daily ten-minute essay on some quite difficult financial subjects. Difficult for the average reporter, that is. But I had always thought Kate was different. She showed a very astute grasp of complicated matters. To me she always seemed more like an executive in a finance corporation, a big commercial bank, or an investment house. There was just something more thoughtful about her, a quality that went beyond merely telling a topical story.

There was no question of telephoning her, because there was no chance of getting through. There was probably a network screening operation designed to snag perverts, to protect women as good-looking as Kate, and I did not think it was in the interest of ConvertBond.com for me to find my way onto that particular list.

So I pondered the problem, and decided, when the time was right, to launch my message through the Internet. By now I was certain Kate Bohner would have her own e-mail address, which, of course, was a secret that I had no way of finding out. But I worked in a hotshot Internet company with access to a lot of know-how, and I resolved to try to crack the Kate Bohner code.

I started with the e-mail address KBohner@CNBC.com and compiled a list of about thirty different permutations, waiting for the right moment to write a good friendly message. Days went by, and then one day I turned on the television, switched to Kate's channel, and saw to my delight that she had a brand-new hairdo. Very slick, a bit shorter, and it made her look fitter than ever.

I pulled up those thirty different e-mail addresses on the computer, composed my short message—"Really nice new hairdo today"—and signed it "Larry McDonald, co-founder, ConvertBond.com." I then fired them all out, a scattershot approach, fully expecting all of them to bounce back with "address unknown." And twenty-nine of them did. But fifteen minutes later, I got a reply from Kate: "Larry, so glad you noticed. Thank you."

I now had her e-mail address, and all I needed was a reason to send her another message. And that was real easy. I just waited until she broadcasted another good essay on a subject I knew a lot about, and then fired off a signal: "Kate: I really liked your piece about bonds today. Very insightful. I might be able to give you a hand with that type of stuff. Maybe even give you a few creative ideas. Yours, Larry. P.S.: Don't change your hairdo."

I made no attempt to suggest a meeting or even a phone call, just kept it easy and complimentary toward her. By this time I had made some provisional inquiries about this goddess of the airwaves. And the answers, given her astute grasp of finance, were predictable. She'd done business and international studies at Wharton and graduated from Columbia University School of Journalism. Her dad was a professor of English literature, and she'd spent several years in Europe. Just about what you'd expect from someone that good at her job. Would I hear from her again? Would she make contact?

Back came another response: "I'd appreciate that, Larry. By the way, what do you do?"

I waited a day and then sent her an e-mail explaining about our new Web site, told her I was sure it was sufficiently revolutionary to make a very good piece, and noted that we were riding the dot-com wave in a very big way. The *Wall Street Journal* had already mentioned us. So had *Barron's*.

Again she responded, and suggested that we meet, perhaps for drinks one evening after work. Of course I immediately agreed, and she suggested the bar at the Gotham Lounge in lower Manhattan.

On the appointed day, beside myself with excitement, I finished work early, drove out of Greenwich, and headed into the city. The traffic was heavy, and I almost crawled over the Triborough Bridge and onto the FDR Drive, heading south. At last I was going against the afternoon rush-hour flow, and I remember racing along the highway beside the East River toward Wall Street at a real good clip. The good news was that I was right on time. The bad news was that Kate never turned up. I waited for ages, sipping fizzy water and becoming steadily more disconsolate. I did not have a phone number for her, and to be honest, I was completely baffled by her absence. In the end, after forty-five minutes, I left the Gotham and drove back to Greenwich. I decided not to contact her; I thought that was her prerogative.

Next day she sent me an e-mail apologizing. And her reason was not anything simple, like working late or a car that wouldn't start. Kate had been in a car crash, a full-blooded wreck, and this time we swapped phone numbers in case she was in another one. Our new date was for the next week, Wednesday at six.

Once again I drove into the city, and this time the traffic was worse. I was two minutes late and double-parked outside the Gotham before running in. I spotted her immediately. She was sitting way down at the far end of the long bar with a girlfriend.

I introduced myself, and she introduced me to Candace Bushnell, the New York–based author of *Sex and the City.* I remember Kate ordered me a glass of wine while I dashed out through the bar to get the car legally parked. As I did so, I glanced into the mirror and could see Candace smiling and giving Kate a thumbs-up. I saw her mouth the words, "He's cute."

With my confidence high, I parked the car and went back in. Right away we all got along, and had a great evening together. The three of us went out for dinner, and ended up at Kate's place for a nightcap. Candace went home first, leaving Kate and me alone, an opportunity to show her I was a proper gentleman, not some smart-talking lounge lizard on the make. We concluded the evening with a chaste kiss on the cheek from Kate to me, and we parted, having established a friendship that has lasted to this day. I still think she's one of the best financial reporters in the business. But I knew right from the start that I could not really compete. I mean, Jesus, she'd been married to Michael Lewis, who wrote *Liar's Poker.* She'd been at the soccer World Cup in Paris.

But Kate came through for me in spades. We talked quite often, and under my tutelage she wanted to do two programs on convertible bonds. One would plainly be on Amazon, bookstore to the world. This was a bond I was a real expert on. And she wanted to do a second program, on a global corporation with a recently issued convertible bond. I knew just the outfit for her: Diamond Offshore, the Louisiana-based deepwater drilling kings whose services are in demand worldwide. This has always been a very exciting, brilliantly run operation, and I really believed in their new bond and credit quality. I regaled Kate with Diamond's history and their success searching for oil in the depths of the Gulf of Mexico. So far as I could tell, they had always made a stack of money in oil fields throughout the entire planet, especially off the coasts of Texas, South America, and western Australia and in the North Sea.

What I always loved about Kate was the ease with which her

imagination was fired. You could be talking about a bond, just a name, but you start painting pictures of a big sea off the coast of windswept Scotland, of men braving the storms, drilling into the ocean floor in freezing, dangerous conditions, pumping the crude oil, hundreds of miles from home, out there on a giant offshore rig. Right then you had a real audience, not just some impatient journalist looking for a sound bite. When Kate went on the air with her essays—CNBC coast to coast and worldwide, an international audience—talking about the bonds, the background, the price, and the potential profits, she was the best. And did she ever do us proud. She mentioned ConvertBond.com several times. She mentioned me constantly and prominently: *According to senior partner Larry McDonald . . . I have just spoken to ConvertBond.com partner Larry McDonald, and there's no doubt in his mind . . .*

Overnight Steve Seefeld and I became world oracles on the convertible bond. And we deserved it, because we both understood the subject as well as anyone and a lot better than most. Kate Bohner made us famous, and in turn we helped to make Kate look her peerless best. What a team.

I should perhaps mention here that at this stage in the proceedings ConvertBond.com's site went berserk. Those 150,000 hits we'd received off the *Wall Street Journal* story now looked like a real slow day. We had hits from all over the world, hundreds of thousands of them, inquiring about convertible bonds, extolling the virtues of convertible bonds, explaining about new issues. People were ransacking our site for information, sending messages, requesting interviews, hammering in their credit card details.

Steve and I, exhausted at the best of times, forgot our tiredness and looked to the future. Every week we fed our best ideas to Kate and kept her posted on all the new developments. She often told me it was like getting dispatches from the front lines of a war zone.

Four times more she did programs on convertible bonds, all of which featured us and our Web site. And right now she had the attention of the entire bond-investing world. The major publications, *Barron's, Fortune,* and the *Journal,* were forever writing about the convertibles, and we were getting hits from some of the biggest investors in the world, including Warren Buffett's Berkshire Hathaway and several other big value investors. Everyone was looking for information on ConvertBond.com. Everyone was talking about us. We were getting bigger and bigger, and shortly we would be named by *Forbes* as the Best of the Web.

Kate for one brief moment seemed to think this was getting bigger than all of us, but I steadied her, told her that with her Wharton expertise and her natural flair, she could do anything. And I would do my bit to help make her an authority on convertible bonds in the media world.

"Kate," I said, "you can handle this."

She looked at me and said, "Larry, you're damn right I can."

Finally, Steve arrived at the conclusion we both knew was inevitable: it was merely a matter of time before we launched our own corporation, aligned with our Web site, to trade convertible bonds online, to get into the sharp end of the game, buying and investing for clients, selling and advising. The slight drawback was that we would need a building the size of Fort Knox, with similar resources, to put such an operation together. Our present space above the Chinese restaurant could not house such an organization.

Without getting too deeply into the nitty-gritty of setting up a trading operation intended to rival Lehman Brothers, Salomon, Goldman Sachs, and Morgan Stanley, we concentrated on the intellectual requirements for such a scheme and the computer resources required. In fairness, we were too busy to delve deeply into even that. But, true to form, one of us let it slip to one of the many journalists currently in touch with us that those were our plans, to open our own convertible bond trading floor on the Internet, the first one in the world.

I have never really known what kind of a reaction that caused among Wall Street's big hitters except for one of them, Tony Bosco, Morgan Stanley's managing director of convertible securities trading, who elected to contact us. Somehow he located our phone number, and I answered the call. I'll never forget what he said, very quietly: "McDonald? My name is Tony Bosco, and I'm calling from Morgan Stanley."

There was a silence, just for a moment, while I gathered my thoughts. And then a deafening roar came from the other end of the line: "*Who the hell are you guys? And what the hell is going on?*"

I damned nearly dropped the phone, but I knew better than to hang around and get into a slanging match with this character. So I told him I was too busy right now and to call back later. Can you imagine, me telling the might of Morgan Stanley to call back? One of the great keepers of my lifelong holy grail, getting blown off by a guy who worked above a dry cleaner in suburban Connecticut?

Later that day he did call back and ranted and raved at us. It turned out his main gripe was about our rating system on the Web site, where we and thousands of our users around the world were apt to criticize new bonds that came out with, say, only a 3 percent coupon, the same as the bank. We would not have hesitated to dump on such a bond, and with our current 250,000-hit-a-day Web site having such influence over the global market, Tony apparently thought we had gone several steps too far.

One of the bonds Morgan Stanley was marketing had been clobbered by the ConvertBond.com analysts (Steve and me) on the grounds of "crummy credit and not enough coupon." Bosco was not having that. Even without our threat to become a bond-trading operation, we had already ruined his day.

He yelled down the line, threatening bloody murder. "I'll sue your ass . . . I'll have you in court by Monday morning . . . I'll have five partners on your case from the biggest law firm in New York. I'll bankrupt you with legal fees."

"Come on, Tony, that company's got shitty credit and a stupid coupon. Our own online poll of global users wouldn't give five bucks for 'em." Before I hung up on him, I added, "And you know it. So you can stop bullshitting me." We both sensed we had Morgan Stanley on the wrong foot.

At this time, there were Internet mergers and acquisitions all over the marketplace, like AOL Time Warner. And pretty soon there was a rumor that Union Bank of Switzerland was trying to buy us. The story broke in a couple of publications, and when it did, we thought that would really unnerve Morgan Stanley, who probably foresaw it would be difficult to market any convertible bond without our stamp of approval.

For a while Bosco was quiet, presumably assessing just how big a nuisance we really were. But one fact was obvious: if we gave a poor rating to any convertible bond, it would be more difficult to market, especially new issues, because people followed our advice, respected our assessments, and relied on our analysis and research.

I can just imagine Bosco's baleful stare as he glared at the screen, noting we had assessed one of Morgan's new bonds by saying, "This corporation has really shaky credit, too much debt, and the coupon's rubbish. Is this bond a buy? You must be crazy."

He called from time to time, mostly to remonstrate. I could just tell our presence was intermittently scaring Morgan Stanley to death. And in a very short time they made one of those decisions common to the bully boys of Wall Street. In the autumn of 1999 they made up their minds to buy us, just to get us out of the way, to get control of our loose-cannon Web site, the one that half the bond buyers in the country counted on for pragmatic assessments and information.

Tony personally opened the proceedings. Christ, he must have hated that—from loathing us to loving us in such a short time. He asked us gruffly what we considered ConvertBond.com was worth, and we told him that just then, with the dot-coms on the crest of a wave, the figure was possibly too much for him. He did not tune in to the joke.

Steve and I could feel him seething down the line from New York. But he kept his cool and requested a number. I told him I could not really put a price on it, but I'd definitely know it when I heard it. Former pork chop salesmen can be pretty tough that way.

Finally he fired out a number. "How does that sound?" he asked.

"Pretty modest," said Steve. "Let's not waste our time. Larry and I have sweated blood to make this business into a cash cow. We do not need to give it away."

Tony Bosco was noncommittal, but then he upped his bid. There was a sadness about the discussion, because I think Steve and I both knew there was a chance Morgan Stanley only wanted ConvertBond.com to shelve it, to get it out of their lives. Anyway, we turned him down. We both thought Bosco's interest represented imperfect timing. We gave him what we thought a fair price was at the time, but warned that in three or four months, if dot-com stocks continued going to the moon, we might be worth a great deal more.

We were growing fast, but we had to deal with now. Morgan Stanley was champing at the bit to get us out of the way. And Tony Bosco was ready to up his offer. The downside for us was the huge gap the loss of our corporation would make in our lives. Nothing would ever be the same again, and we'd miss the fun, the sense of flying by the seat of our pants trying to make it work.

The following day, Tony came back and made another offer for ConvertBond.com. It wasn't even close to high enough, but we thought it over and figured we might be near the top of the market, and we took it. We shook hands over the phone and agreed to the contracts being drawn up. Morgan Stanley wanted us both to join them and the deal did not take long to put together. Our Web site would be controlled by the investment bank, and now they would operate it with our assistance.

And so I said good-bye to my first entrepreneurial success. I was going to a place one step nearer to Wall Street. And, in a sense, I was closer to my dream of a place among the elite than I had ever been. At the time, I was a thirty-three-year-old millionaire, and I thought I knew what was going on.

But little did I suspect that looming right up ahead was an enormous stock market crash that I would experience at close quarters—when the dot-coms went south in some kind of an atomic cloud.

3

Only the Bears Smiled

What was wrong with the world that autumn after the catastrophe? Had it sent people off the rails? But after Enron collapsed, a spate of bankruptcies rocked our system. And they all involved convertible bonds.

NEITHER STEVE SEEFELD nor I had any idea about corporate structure. No clues about how things worked in a vast operation. We'd both been freewheeling too long, making our own decisions, paddling our own canoes. Together we'd founded a national business worth millions of dollars without ever having a meeting, writing a memorandum, organizing a conference call, or taking anyone out to lunch. To us, formality was just a pain-in-the-ass waste of time. If you've got something to say, say it. If there's something to do, do it. If you've screwed something up, admit it.

Big corporations do not function in that way. First of all, they've got too many people on the staff who don't know their ass from their elbow—legions of workers who could no more achieve what Steve and I had done with ConvertBond.com than fly to the moon.

The whole ethos of a major company is different. There's people forever trying to cover their own asses, people who have somehow carved an entire career out of making small but telling criticisms of other people's work. That's because in a big corporation the guy who spots a screwup is somehow cleverer and more valuable than the guy who wrote the forty-page marketing plan in the first place.

Fear is the key. Fear of being the one person in this whole morass of execs who got it wrong. Fear of being the scapegoat, fear of looking ridiculous, fear of being fired. Thus there develops a whole art form of corporate ducking and diving, staying out of the firing line, writing memorandums that somehow shift the responsibility, not being seen with your head above the parapet, subtly seeking the glory but always dodging the blame, carefully filing the memo that will ultimately exonerate.

Ideologically, Steve was not ready for Morgan Stanley, nor was Morgan Stanley ready for him. And there was probably a hint of things to come in the first few days. Our new bosses had taken a thorough look at our Web site, but they decided it needed changing. They actually said "refining," because that immediately made them look about twenty times cleverer than us.

But we didn't care. They could essentially do what they liked, and after three endless meetings with consultants and God knows who else, they finally figured out what they wanted.

"Okay," said Steve, who understood more about the system and its possible changes than all of them put together. "We'll get that done in a couple of days."

What? It was as if he had suggested we abandon Christianity to become Hindus. No, no, no, no. A full team of experts from the head offices of IBM would be called in, all of them doubtless earning at the highest possible rate. They'd move into Connecticut as soon as possible and begin work right away.

I can't remember how long they took, but they came to our new offices in Stamford, and the process went on for months. Steve and I were amazed, mostly because we had not tuned in to the corporate mantra that it doesn't matter how long it takes or what it costs, just so long as there isn't a screwup, with the attached blame and recriminations. Just so long as no one gets caught with their pants down.

I can't even remember what difference it all made in the Web site, but I should have noticed the difference it made in Steve. He became less interested. It ought not to be forgotten that he was a person utterly unused to talking to anyone cleverer or richer than himself. Such people need extra consideration, but that's not how corporations work. They are places where the pecking order is everything, where an unimaginative grunt may find himself in a superior position to someone like Steve. They might think that's okay. But it never is, because people like Steve cannot kowtow to anyone.

For a couple of months we soldiered on in our new quarters at One Landmark Square, Stamford. I think they originally only kept ConvertBond.com going as insurance, just in case the bond market did go online, as we had suggested. But Morgan Stanley clients loved it, and it was a perfect place to showcase the investment bank's immaculate research, masterminded by the peerless Anand Iyer. So we continued, spending some of our time in sales, some running the old database, and the rest in research. We also spent all our time writing memorandums and going to meetings. I should have guessed this could not last.

One morning we were informed there was a big meeting taking place that afternoon. Then we were told there would be a meeting in the late morning to prepare for the meeting in the afternoon. That wrapped it up for Steve. Uttering the Shakespearean phrase "I can't put up with this fucking bullshit for another minute," he quit, gathered up his stuff, and left, walking out of Landmark Square like Hamlet after realizing there was something rotten in the state of Denmark.

Before he left, we arranged to meet for dinner that night in a good local restaurant called Sixty-Four, right on Greenwich Avenue. And there, over a halfway decent bottle of wine and a couple of New York strip steaks, we celebrated our long partnership.

It's hard to recount my sadness. After all we'd gone through together, it was finally over. Outside the restaurant, we shook hands. Steve told me I was still the best friend he ever had. "Remember, we built it together," he said, "And I want to thank you for everything. I just can't put up with this corporate bullshit."

It was raining that night, and I remember I just stood there, getting soaked, stunned at the loss of my wingman, somehow losing a friend I had worked with every day for three years. Deep inside I was devastated; I had never felt so lonely. As I watched Steve drive away, it was almost impossible for me to accept that I would not see him at the office in the morning. I was all alone. Just me and the holy grail that lurked in some corner of Morgan Stanley—not in the Stamford office, but in the midtown office in New York. I pulled myself together and ran back to my car, resolving to find that holy grail the very next day and kick it right in the ass, for old times' sake.

As for Steve, he went off and bought himself a small twin-engine prop plane and spent his time flying to and from the Bahamas. We're still in touch, but it can't ever be the same.

With the original office now closed, my life began to center on Morgan Stanley, and that was not all bad. I had a decent salary plus bonuses, and one day a month I went into the main office in New York to learn the ropes among the heavies. I never did trade bonds, and then my main man, Tony Bosco, suddenly quit to run a hedge fund in South Carolina. For me, these events were not so much depressing as sad. I missed both Steve and Tony, and had obvious adjustments to make in my own career. You always do when your buddies suddenly vanish from your life.

But, in near silence and with relentless efficiency, another great force was gathering in Washington, one that would have an effect on my life approximately ten thousand times more drastic than anything appertaining to the absence of Steve and Tony. It was the embryo Commodity Futures Modernization Act of 2000, edging its way forward throughout the spring, summer, and fall of that year.

My new boss was Anand Iyer, an ex–Wharton man, managing director and global head of convertible securities research at Morgan Stanley. Anand was in his early forties, born in India and the best-dressed man in the bank if not the state of Connecticut; he lived in Old Greenwich. Now he assumed responsibility for the corporation Tony Bosco had purchased.

There are many different types of operators at the top of any big investment bank, but Anand could never escape the fact that he was a natural-born intellect, a thoughtful, scholarly guy who needed to unravel even the most complex of problems before he made a move. I guess one of the biggest faults you find all over Wall Street is guys making decisions about subjects they do not even remotely understand.

And so, as Wall Street lobbyists and politicians staged the great struggle for the Commodity Futures Modernization Act (CFMA) in faraway Washington, there was one pair of dark, penetrating eyes watching their progress. Anand did not, of course, know the future ramifications of the act. But he knew it mattered terribly, and he was aware that deregulation in this instance might or might not be in our best interest. As a matter of fact, he was not all that crazy about the repeal of Glass-Steagall either.

Let me just recap the significance of the CFMA, which would not be passed until the end of the year. A major purpose was to deregulate the entire business of trading a credit default swap (CDS). This is nothing more than a bet—for instance, that a mortgage company will go broke and its bond value will sink to, say, 4 cents on the dollar. We're talking about a bet that would allow a big bondholder to go to an investment bank and say, "I hold $1 billion worth of bonds in Countrywide. The coupon is 5 percent, which is 1 percent more than a similar Treasury bond. I'll give you 90 percent of that 1 percent if you'll insure me for the present value of the bond all the way to zero, in case the corporation goes broke and my bond becomes valueless."

So far as the bank was concerned, that was pretty good business. For absolutely nothing, they would be paid a fee of $9 million a year. That was great for the balance sheet—unless, of course, the corporation went down, in which case the bank would hold a $1 billion liability. More often, the bank would sell the CDS to a hedge fund, which was more willing to take the risk. The bank would pick up a fast $200,000 fee and be rid of the hassle.*

However, the unseen aspect of the CFMA, the one that would turn it into a weapon of mass destruction, was the section that made an ancient illegality into a legal transaction. That was the part that allowed *anyone*—bondholder or no—to take out that insurance, to have a bet against Countrywide staying alive, without even holding one single bond. In times to come, hedge funds and investors, even banks, would start betting against these big mortgage corporations' survival, against corporations with big debts, and against corporations that were just plain inefficient. The merchant banks would have many opportunities to pick up juicy multimillion-dollar annual fees while crazily racking up literally billions of dollars' worth of liability.

Just take our first example—the bank that, for $9 million a year, was risking a billion on the survival of a major mortgage house. Let's assume they accepted bets from a hundred such sources, and in the end the mortgage house went down. That's a liability of $100 billion. Not many banks have the cash reserves to pay out that much. What seemed so appealing in theory may not, in the future, look so hot in the grim reality of the market.

Anand and I spoke of the coming CFMA from time to time. And while neither of us actually nailed the true problem, we sure as hell wondered what might happen in the unthinkable event of the real estate market ever going south or if a large CDS financial counterparty was not there to make good on the transaction.

I had remained in touch with my old gas station rival Larry Mc-

*We assumed that the yield on a similar risk-free Treasury bond is 4 percent. At this time, Countrywide bonds paid only 1 percent more than the Treasury bond as compensation for risk that the bond could default.

Carthy, who was continuing to fly high in his own career and was now managing director of high-yield bond trading at Wasserstein, Perella.

We spoke on the phone most days, much of the time talking about my own career, and my next step up the ladder, one that I hoped would take me to Wall Street. Larry was always one hell of a good friend, and in some ways he was closer to me than Steve.

In those early days at the great investment bank Morgan Stanley, I was still riding the dot-com tidal wave when suddenly there came warnings from a highly predictable quarter. The old perma-bear, the one with the pitching wedge and the John Wayne swagger, was growling in his Cape Cod lair. While the entire investment world was making fortunes off this high-tech Internet bonanza, the word coming from that particular cave was full of foreboding, as was only to be expected. "Larry, this isn't natural," my father told me. "Therefore it has to be a bubble." He cared nothing that some of the great modern fortunes were being made in this new industry, which represented the ability to communicate and swap information with thousands of people at the touch of a keyboard. "It's crap."

"Sorry, Dad, didn't quite get that."

"Crap," he confirmed. "Nothing ever changes. History *always* repeats itself. This world has seen more bubbles than Moby Dick. Everything from silk to spices, from whale oil to tulips. They're all crazes, and in the end they all crash. And you can mark my words, this dot-com boom will end in tears."

That was not all that was vexing him. In early November it had become apparent that President Clinton was going to sign into law the bill repealing the Glass-Steagall Act, the 1933 law that had the express purpose of keeping a wall between commercial banks and investment houses. So far as I can tell, looking back, my dad was the first person I ever heard blow the whistle on that repeal. And he blew it real hard.

Nothing could persuade him that any good could possibly come from taking down the wall. "It wasn't put there just to pass the time of day," he told me. "It was put there because of the crash of 1929 when the banks went down with people's honest-to-goodness savings, ruined 'em. And Senator Glass knew why. That act of his was purposely designed to keep people's deposits out of the hands of the goddamned investment banking lunatics who gamble other people's money."

Somehow I always knew, like some kind of a sixth sense, that he was correct. But nonetheless I enjoyed playing the devil's advocate and reminding him of the new enlightenment, the current perceived wisdom on Wall Street.

"But, Dad, all the analysts on the Street say that things are different now," I would remind him. "Anyone will tell you that. The world is swinging toward global free trade, and most people think it makes no sense to constrain our investment banks any longer. Otherwise ambitious foreign banks, like Iceland's and the Brits, will run riot all over us."

"Crap," repeated Dad. "Wall Street investment houses darn near took this country down once in 1929, and given a chance they'll probably do it again. Clinton signs that bill, he does so at great risk."

I asked him if he thought Citicorp merging with Travelers and Chase Manhattan merging with J. P. Morgan were fascinating prospects for increasing the United States' financial clout on the open market.

"I do not," he said. "I see both as potential disasters."

Of course, he was just as bearish about the prospects of what he called the dot-com bubble. "The price of those stocks is just too damned high," he said. "Most of 'em have never earned a nickel, their P/E ratios are insane, and I am just waiting for the crash. You got a lick of sense, you'll start shorting them."

I always used to protest about this. Always argued how different things were today and what a revolutionary time this was. "This is the new economy," I told him.

"Not so," he once replied. "It's just the same as the old one. And the same rules apply. And right now we seem to have about seven thousand dot-coms when the world probably needs about two hundred."

He'd been reading some report that claimed shopping malls were darn near obsolete. That within two years everyone would do their shopping online. According to the analysts, there would be hardly any shops.

"Crap," said Dad. "The retail world will hit back."

"How the hell will a chain of bookstores hit back," I asked, "when an outfit like Amazon will deliver any book in the world to anyone within forty-eight hours?"

"I guess people like picking up books and holding 'em," he said, "checking 'em out. There'll still be bookstores. They've been there for hundreds of years, and they'll still be there in the next century."

I pointed out that the next century was only about eight weeks away, and he retorted that he didn't care if it was fifty years away, there'd still be bookstores. In his considered opinion, the market would darn soon find out that these dot-com no-profit operations with their crazy stock prices were just a bubble. And like all bubbles, this one would surely burst.

I shook my head at the sheer uncomprehending mind-set of the old-fashioned investor. And I didn't even hear my dad's parting shot about getting myself a crash helmet.

Anyway, President Clinton signed the act repealing Glass-Steagall into law on the afternoon of November 12, 1999, with or without my dad's approval. And some truly momentous events began to rumble into place.

Citigroup had been formed by a merger that was illegal at the time it took place, as it violated Glass-Steagall, but now it was legal. The old Citicorp merging with Travelers gave them ownership of Primerica, which represented the fulfillment of my dad's dread: a huge commercial bank owning an investment house. As he put it, it was like "giving the gambler access to other people's savings."

And that was not all. Chase Manhattan, which had long nurtured ambitions to get into the stock market and start making some serious investments, almost immediately began moves to merge with J. P. Morgan, another investment house. Once more we were on the road to a situation where the smaller high-roller could be given unlimited backing by its masters—my dad's recipe for disaster.

These machinations by the Wall Street giants were conducted in the lowest-profile manner possible. Certainly they were not the issues everyone was discussing on a daily basis. That topic was very definitely the dot-com boom, and in the Stanford office of Morgan Stanley I represented the future. Steve and I had been that dot-com boom, a couple of characters who had walked off with a pile of dough in the midst of the riotous climb of the high-tech stocks.

That Christmas, I spent a little time with my dad, and once more we talked about the boom that had made me reasonably well off. Still the old man didn't buy it. When I returned to the office in the New Year his words were often on my mind. And I kept seeing statistics that I knew would cause the bear to start growling all over again. One of them was the financial report I was studying on the hugely fashionable California-based multinational Cisco Systems. I was poring over its numbers, trying to get a handle on them, when I had a sudden intuitive leap of understanding.

Cisco Systems basks in the sunlight of San Jose, a few miles southeast of San Francisco near the Santa Clara Mountains. The only thing I really knew about the area was it contained the giant telescope of the Lick Observatory, through which one could perhaps see infinity. But right here in Morgan Stanley, Landmark Square, Stamford, I was staring at a number that surely must have come from outer space. Cisco Systems, which designs and sells networking and communications technology, claimed a market cap of $555 *billion.* That made it, so far as I could tell, the highest in the world, bigger than ExxonMobil, bigger than everyone else.

At first I thought it might be a misprint. *Better check out the price/earnings multiple.* At that point I thought fifty times earnings was exorbitant. My eyes almost popped out of my head when I saw Cisco's—they were valued at *160 times earnings.* One way of looking at that is to remember that if anyone bought the corporation at that price, at current trading levels, it would take 160 years to get the purchase price back. The same applied to buying its equity. This, I concluded, was nuts. But since I had only been at Morgan Stanley a short while, I didn't want to start raising hell. Still, that night I went into the market—not recklessly, just a modest investment—and shorted Cisco, just the way Dad had advised. I knew that if I told my dad about Cisco's numbers, he'd just laugh. You can't fool a bear, right?

In the ensuing weeks we started to see the dot-com bubble go south. Which was probably a major shock for those thousands of investors who had dived into new public offerings by the tech companies without even checking to see when, if ever, they might make a profit. Blinded by phrases like *networking, new paradigm, consumer-driven navigation,* or *tailored Web experience,* people had lavished money into this section of the market.

By March I was having serious doubts, as the son of any true bear would. The whole thing was a phenomenon, and pretty soon the dot-com corporations started reporting huge losses. Then they started to collapse. In the coming months Cisco Systems would eventually lose $400 billion of its market cap.

As the fall approached, the wreckage of the dot-com dream was scattered across the marketplace. And it did not escape me that if Steve and I had tried to sell ConvertBond.com nine months after we did, they'd have handed us a bucket of oats.

There were enormous losses, especially from the 117 dot-coms whose stock had doubled on the first day of issue in 1999. Altogether that year there were 457 dot-com initial public offerings (IPOs). In 2001 there were only 76, and there is no record of the stock price of any one of them doubling on the first day of issue.

No industry in the entire history of stock markets has ever evaporated that quickly. At that time there were 280 stocks on the Bloomberg U.S. Internet Index, and their value fell by a combined total of *$1.755 trillion in seven months.* Seventy-nine of them crashed 90 percent from their fifty-two-week high. Seventy-two more were down more than 80 percent.

Looking back, I can obviously see that it was one of the greatest fiascos of all time. It was a moment when investors were prepared to forgive anything: heavy losses, no profits, lousy management, half-crazed geeks trying to be businessmen, not enough advertising on the Web pages, and a grotesquely unrealistic estimate of future success. If it had anything to do with the Internet, no matter how remote or unlikely, there was a stampede to get involved. Steve and I had ridden high on that wave, of course. But from my perspective now, it was like walking out of a nuthouse with what seemed like a king's ransom.

I happen to be a world expert on hindsight, having been blessed with it myself. But as I reflect on that summer of high carnage in the first year of the new millennium, it seems fairly obvious that the world market needed only around four disk-drive makers. Venture capitalists, however, financed fifty of them.

I am thus drawn back to the views of my own father. He said it was a bubble. He said it could not possibly be either real or sustained. And he forecast an almighty crash, an industry that both went up and came down with a roar heard around the world—the dot-com crash of 2000, when only the bears smiled.

The events of that long summer had a profound effect on me. Every day I listened to those who had gambled, won, and then lost. But for me there was only one voice that was consistently right. And that voice lived in a somewhat luxurious cave on Cape Cod. Suddenly I realized something: in spirit, I was very much like my father. By inclination I was not a true perma-bear, but I was nonetheless a bear. Or perhaps I was a vulture; that's a slightly different breed, but much the same, one of God's creatures that can smell death when it's in the air.

Way back in the 1980s, during my final year in college and for the next two years, there were diabolical tremors in the financial markets. There was the stock market crash of 1987, when on Black Monday, October 19, computerized program selling caused the largest one-day percentage decline in stock market history. I remember my dad showing me the graph—it looked like the vertical drop from the high point of a Coney Island roller coaster.

And then there was the savings and loan crisis of 1988–90, which took years for the government to repair. That was a bank problem, when 747 of them failed. In a way, this was the forerunner of the trouble that loomed ahead when Glass-Steagall was repealed. Needless to say, throughout that entire time my dad was right about the market.

When the dot-com fiasco broke out, I felt I was living through the third market crisis of my adult life. My vivid recollection of that time is, naturally, how lucky Steve and I were to get out of it when we did. I was also very aware that I'd gotten a real bang out of shorting Cisco and being correct. I experienced a definite charge out of correctly forecasting gloom and doom.

I sensed this was my strong suit—the anticipation of upcoming disaster. It may have been in my blood, a God-given talent, or maybe my dad had just drummed it into me from a very young age. But ever since my front-row seat at the collapse of the dot-coms, I was wary, and ever on the lookout for trouble. I have never wanted to become a perma-bear, always hoping for a profitable short position. I just have an instinct that there is big money to be made when a great beast of a corporation is headed south. I was still devoted to the convertible bond, and that was my specialty, my principal area of expertise.

Allied to my instinct for sniffing trouble, I sensed my future may be as a bond trader in the rough end of the market. In our profession such people are known as distressed-debt traders. And as I sat there surveying the carnage of the dot-coms, my confidence increased that this was my path to the holy grail.

The distressed-bond folks work in an area of immense responsibility, assessing, valuing, and estimating the worth of companies with big problems. They truly are the vultures of the game, always watchful, circling over corporations that may or may not become a corpse. Such people observe workers being fired, gates being closed, pension funds going down. And yet there is an optimism about them, because their real task is to assess what remains and when to strike. When can that bond be bought for only 18 cents on the dollar and there is still heavy value in the bankrupt company's assets and real estate, making it worth perhaps 50 cents on the dollar or maybe even a little more?

It's only a rumor that the distressed-bond guys work in a crypt and wear high-collared black cloaks to work. Closer to the truth is their famous sense of reality. They are often the corporate brakes on the high rollers, the ones who don't quite believe the perceived wisdom. They are always watching the optimists charging ahead, swerving around on the winds of chance, occasionally flying into the teeth of a gale. I call them the high kites.

Warnings from the vultures have saved many an overeager trader from doing something catastrophic, mostly because the market's angels of death have the best handle on *value*. Warren Buffett's a vulture. You won't catch him plunging forward and buying a shaky concept. He avoided the entire dot-com disaster because he could see no intrinsic worth in the corporations. He also could not see enough advertising revenue.

And so I secretly consigned myself to the parking lots of life, where I would conduct a permanent patrol. I intended to be the one wandering around out back, where the vultures fly, with maybe a few stray bears for company. You see a lot of high kites (people who were always bullish no matter what the realities of the marketplace) in the parking lot looking for the big turbo-charged machine that will scream to the top of the hill, banners flying. I'm with the guys looking for companies driving 110 miles an hour with no brakes—the best stocks to short.

Somehow or another, everyone weathered the destruction of the dot-coms, and the year 2001 started more or less calmly until Pacific Gas and Electric filed for Chapter 11 bankruptcy in April with debts of $36 billion. This earned the attention of our West Coast offices, since it was the biggest bankruptcy in history to date.

But a few months later came 9/11—a landmark for so many people, and the start of a succession of financial disasters that would affect me for the rest of my career (including a slightly chilling dislike of working in a high tower near the window on an outside wall).

Within weeks of the fall of the Twin Towers the economy was on its knees. Travel and all of its attendant profit centers, such as airlines and hotels, was down by 50 percent. And that was when a very large fire alarm came echoing out of Larry McCarthy's midtown office. He told me he had just taken a substantial short position on the stock of the seventh-largest corporation in the United States and the dominant energy trader in the world.

Its name was Enron, and it made a living behind an enormous operation involving the buying and selling of petrochemicals, plastics, power, pulp and paper, oil, liquid natural gas transportation, other shipping, freight, and broadband. It was also involved in a vast network of futures trading in sugar, coffee, grains, and hogs. Its operations were conducted on a scale that was incomprehensible to most accountants. They were a global Gulliver based in Houston, Texas.

Also the analysts at the rating agencies, Standard & Poor's and Moody's, persisted in giving it blue-chip ratings, so the position of Enron seemed virtually impregnable. Larry McCarthy did not buy it. He said the accountants could not understand the company's balance sheets. Specifically, he said those balance sheets were constructed specifically to confuse the friggin' life out of anyone who studied them. "Larry," he told me, "you have to trust me on this. These balance sheets are designed to bamboozle people. The whole company is structured to bamboozle people. So far as I am concerned, there's something real shaky going on here."

He also knew, as I did, there was an Enron convertible bond being issued, and I had customers to whom all this mattered. I began to examine Enron's financials with renewed vigor. As an analyst in a major finance house, I was able to plug into the Enron conference call, in which shareholders and bondholders could speak to the corporation's financial officers and ask questions about the way things were running.

All kinds of financial institutions were on those phone lines, including guys from Goldman Sachs, Smith Barney, and Merrill Lynch, all paying attention to the opinions of Andy Fastow, the chief financial officer, and the president and CEO, Jeff Skilling. I was on the line when a nervous stockholder fired a hostile question at Skilling about off-balance-sheet debt. Skilling, in front of everyone, called him an asshole, which I thought was a slightly unorthodox name to give a part owner of your corporation. It's funny how little things like that can make a huge impression, but I remember thinking right then, *Whoa! I'm not too sure about this crowd.*

I delved into their financials, studying them night and day, until I could see that many of Enron's debts and losses simply did not appear on the balance sheet. I helped clients to bail out of the Enron bonds.

It seemed that within days the company started to come unraveled, and the fraud, the false accounting designed to inflate their revenue, came glaringly into the spotlight. That did it—the stock, which had been trading that fall at $85, crashed to 30 cents once it became obvious what had been happening. The scandal took down the hitherto respected accounting firm of Arthur Andersen, the fifth largest in the world. The colossal deception was so convoluted that it managed to provide the illusion of billion-dollar profits when the company was actually losing money. If a deal looked bad or went wrong, they just left it off the balance sheet, which was of course effective, if blatantly dishonest.

There was one astonishing issue that resulted in several convictions. Like many of Enron's more nefarious operations, this one took place in a relatively remote part of the world—off the coast of Nigeria, where three energy-generating barges were anchored. Enron sold a stake in this business to Merrill Lynch for $7 million but promised to pay it back, thus making the cash a loan. The Enron accountants subsequently booked it as a $12 million profit.

Many insiders knew what was happening and began wholesale selling of stocks before the crash. Regular stockholders or bondholders were trapped in the disaster unless they were clients of Larry McCarthy, or to a lesser extent me.

Skilling and his cohorts, meanwhile, kept talking up the stock, swearing to God it was going to $130 or even $150. And they had issued bonds on such a scale that it was impossible for investment advisors to get everyone out. Kenneth Lay, the founder and chairman, was as guilty as Skilling, and, if anything, even worse in his demeanor, assuring shareholders who were losing money on a daily basis that all would be well if they just kept their nerve. Even his wife, Linda, was unloading the stock while he continued to exhort the supporters of the corporation to keep the faith.

Before his trial for fraud and conspiracy, Skilling had a nervous breakdown and turned into a gibbering wreck on a New York Street, afraid, as well he might have been, to face the majesty of the United States law courts. Enron, his mighty corporation, had already gone bankrupt on December 2, its $65 billion in unpayable debt a new high-water mark, almost double that of Pacific Gas and Electric. It was also a brand-new landmark for massive and unending accounting fraud, and for pure corporate villainy.

I have never understood what was wrong with the world that autumn, or whether the catastrophe in lower Manhattan had sent people off the rails. But in the seven months after the Enron collapse, a spate of bankruptcies would rock our once-conservative systems. And they all issued convertible bonds: Global Crossing, Qwest, NTL, Adelphia Communications, and WorldCom.

But these crashes made a major impression on me, as they were my first close-up lessons in corporate greed, dishonesty, and corruption on the grandest scale. Little did I know they had been mere dress rehearsals for something a hundred times worse in the not-too-distant future, when the double-edged sword of gigantic debt again would figure prominently.

Quite honestly, I could not believe how significant the convertible bond was in all these fiascoes. Every one of those doomed corporations, including Enron, had issued bonds just before they filed for bankruptcy, bonds to help them raise money, even though all was lost. I was rapidly arriving at the undeniable truth that many convertibles represent Wall Street's Last Chance Saloon—the only bar where you can still get a drink at 3:00 A.M., when it's starting to get real late. They're that magic wand, the one investment banks wave when they suddenly turn unadulterated debt into an investment opportunity. All those corporations are doing is borrowing money. Bond means debt, nothing else.

In the case of the aforementioned outfits, we're talking about the most dangerous bonds ever placed on the market by reputable finance houses, and all issued by corporations that must have already known the barbarians were at the gates. I guess they just wanted to keep the dream alive, at whatever cost. They issued several bonds in the months leading up to their demise, and you may see this happen again in the future. Should it do so, remember my words about the Last Chance Saloon, because these guys are headed for their last drink.

My job at this time was as a convertible bond securities analyst and researcher, and it fell upon me to study the bonds when they were issued and assess how reliable they were. After those months, I was becoming more careful than I had ever been—and I'd been pretty careful before. My clients were counting on me as much as on the long reputation for excellence of Morgan Stanley. But I noticed that these days their questions were ever more searching, always probing, testing me to ensure that I really understood what I was talking about. That kind of atmosphere concentrates the mind. Everywhere you looked there was something that seemed fishy, and no U.S. corporation was above suspicion; there were too many guys headed for the slammer. We had gone through a period that was like the Battle of the Somme with bank statements. And I ended up expecting to find dishonesty around every turn in the road. My cynicism, generally speaking, was without boundaries.

Don't let me sound as if I was some kind of one-man troubleshooter. Morgan Stanley had wall-to-wall experts on every subject, including plenty of high-yield credit analysts. I was talking to them constantly, because at that time—late 2002 and early 2003—anything with a high-yield coupon was something that needed to be investigated. I became particularly close to Anand, who understood the subject as well as anyone I ever met, and I think together we developed sharp instincts for spotting the suspect, the unlikely, and the downright dishonest. Anything Anand did not know about high-grade credit analysis was not worth knowing. Like me, he was keenly aware that those giant corporations had made one last-ditch bid to raise money with convertible bonds just before they crashed.

In the end, when a new bond issue was announced by any corporation in a troubled industry, my inner voice was shouting at me—*Watch it, Larry. These bastards are probably going down.* It might not have been healthy or optimistic, but it sure as hell eliminated mistakes. I still was not a true bear, but I was certainly learning the trade of the vulture, perfecting the fine art of locating impending death.

These months permitted me to lay the cornerstones of my future—the ability to assess value and to spot the deep flaws in proposals and the possible corporate weakness in new bond issues. For a while I was closer to becoming a detective than a trader. This was not all bad, given the enormous number of financial wizards who had been successfully lied to over the previous year. However, I was rapidly arriving at the conclusion that some of those so-called experts couldn't find an elephant in a chicken coop.

Larry McCarthy's view was very similar. He believed that very brilliant financiers who worked on the inside of major corporations and set out to baffle, bemuse, and generally bamboozle the outside forces that sought to regulate them were, as a rule, a whole lot cleverer than the regulators. Some of those guys had gone on for months, even years, pulling the wool over the eyes of accountants. Their only problem was the sheer volume of people who began to grow restless when things got shaky, when guys like Larry and to an extent me started to get beady-eyed, wondering what the hell's going on.

We start checking. And investigating. And telling people. Until someone screams bloody murder and everyone rushes for the exit. The choreography is consistent and, in the end, brutally predictable, because the villains always alienate too many people, and that's when things start to go south. In this business, they always get caught when the money runs out.

All of this did not escape the government. The controversial Sarbanes-Oxley Act was enacted back on July 30, 2002, nine days after the WorldCom collapse. Its purpose was to create a near-hostile environment for corporations planning to issue bonds. The CFO and the CEO were suddenly obliged to sign a statement declaring that everything was truthfully disclosed, personally guaranteeing the validity of both their financials and the company's assets. The requirements applied to any and all SEC filings, especially companies' 10Q and 10K statements, quarterly and annual. The penalty for failing to comply or withholding the truth was a jail sentence. The sheer anger of the government affected everyone. In turn, the big lenders and mutual funds felt so burned by all the fraud that had taken place in the past couple of years that they pulled in their horns and at the slightest hint of suspicion refused to lend anything to anyone.

By the end of 2002, Wall Street was predictably in trouble; not only was it reeling from the lingering effects of the dot-com bust and September 11, but its lucrative fee engines, the huge income generated from major bond issues, had ground to a halt. Balance sheets were beginning to look a bit ragged. And in the time-honored way of that particular world, the big hitters of investment banks began to rally their forces, searching for a way to slide under the SEC regulations. What they were after was a method of dodging the stiff penalties that now went with any type of dishonesty appertaining to bonds. They were seeking a new investment vehicle that did not come under such heavy scrutiny from the SEC. Just as crooked financial officers in now-bankrupt corporations had sought to bamboozle their accountants and investors, now the Wall Street elite, the lawyers and bankers, set out to bamboozle the SEC regulators. We suddenly had a commando squad of MIT- and Harvard-educated multimillionaires preparing to go into combat against $120,000-a-year civil service regulators. It never did seem like an even match to me.

What Wall Street's financial maestros came up with while the SEC guys were consumed with backdated options, insider trading, and naked short-selling was something brand-new—a fee-generating machine hereinafter referred to as the dreaded credit derivatives, also known as securitization. They invented a method of turning a thousand mortgages into a bond with an attractive coupon of 7 or 8 percent. This high-yield bond could be traded, and hence turned into a profit generator; it would enable the mortgage brokers, investment banks, and bondholders to reap a very nice annual reward—*just so long as the homeowners kept right on paying on time every month, and the U.S. housing market held up the way it always had.* One of the unintended consequences of Sarbanes-Oxley was the drying up of the corporate bond market. Securitization of credit derivatives helped fill the revenue gap.

Meanwhile, Larry McCarthy's firm had been taken over by Dresdner Bank of Germany, and there was a brand-new set of executives, none of whom would ever be suspected of moonlighting as nightclub comics. The fun seemed to drain out of Larry's life, and he's one of those characters who cannot survive without some lightheartedness. You often find that people with giant brains need the stimulus of humor. There was, for instance, no finer wit or humorist than Sir Winston Churchill. It's as if their minds leap so far ahead of the pack they have an unstoppable compulsion to satirize a tricky situation. Of course, there is always a danger that those lagging in their wake don't get either the problem, the solution, or the joke. Which is when McCarthy is apt to become a bit tetchy. He likes dialogue, interaction, repartee, and cross fire. He's always sharpening his wits, and usually comes out well in front. It would not be uncharitable to assess that his new German masters from Dresdner Bank failed to tune in to their very brilliant managing director of high-yield bond trading. Larry could be hugely amusing, but his boardroom jokes now fell upon stony ground, his consummate ability to find humor in the most parlous situation was unappreciated, and his capacity to make his new colleagues laugh was no longer possible. While almost all of his colleagues were running around kissing German asses, trying to ingratiate themselves with the new leaders, Larry McCarthy was not among those particular executives, and there was no possibility he was going to last there for more than three or four months, his great expertise notwithstanding.

It all came to a head one evening during a corporate dinner, at which, having failed utterly in his attempts to get one single laugh out of his audience, Larry reached the point of total exasperation, his repertoire exhausted. Glaring at the new German chiefs, he suddenly decided the hell with it, and snapped, "Fuck this. You've got the personality of a lampshade." Still no one laughed, and Larry quit that week, for several reasons, not just the lack of humor.

Two months later he was being sounded out by Lehman Brothers, and his hiring is another one of those Wall Street tales that might seem too good to be true, but it is. According to the story, Larry arranged to meet two of Lehman's top people in the bar at Ben Benson's steakhouse. This is home ground for Larry, so much so he has his personal plaque on the bar, a space reserved at all times for one of Wall Street's most revered figures. The Lehman guys arrived, Alex Kirk and Tom Humphrey, extremely powerful figures, and Larry McCarthy told them his best stories, and in the end stood them sufficient drinks to ensure they were absolutely shit-faced. When he was quite satisfied that Kirk and Humphrey had achieved this state of grace, he hit them with one of the most demanding sets of requirements ever presented to a Wall Street firm. One of them, according to Larry, was they laugh at his best jokes at all times. In fairness to Kirk and Tom, they both knew Larry well, but now they knew he had true chutzpah as well as recognized brilliance.

At this point Tom delved into his pocket and produced a short document that guaranteed Larry McCarthy a $2 million bonus for the year, win, lose, or draw. Larry stared at it, then ripped it into a dozen pieces. "Two million?" he exclaimed. "I haven't earned that little since I was in high school. If I only earn $2 million we're both in trouble. Pay me what I'm worth at the end of the year." And they hired him right there, on his terms. Larry joined Lehman as managing director and head of distressed trading, a position of enormous responsibility and one which he occupied with immense distinction.

Meanwhile, back at Morgan Stanley, along with all the other bond people, we were experiencing an upsurge in the market after mid-2003. Alan Greenspan, head of the Federal Reserve in Washington and probably the most powerful man in the country, was in the process of cutting interest rates to near-unprecedented lows. He began the process to prevent damage to the U.S. economy from the dot-com bubble, and he cut rates again to prevent a sharp recession after 9/11. He cut and cut, all the way from 6 percent in December 2000 down to 1 percent on June 30, 2003. Thus began one of the greatest consumer-borrowing bonanzas since the 1920s.

There was, of course, not the slightest use in putting savings in a bank. Yields were so low that the money might as well have been under the mattress. Better to put it on a couple of short-priced favorites at Belmont Park. Better yet, buy high-yield bonds. In those months around the summer and fall of 2003, high-yield started to become once again a mantra for American investors. Especially high-yield bonds, because those little darlings had the advantage of hewing to sound business practice and providing important protection for the investors. (This is inclined to be absent with beaten favorites at Belmont.)

Greenspan, in some quarters, was a national hero because his actions essentially provided people with free money, with hardly any interest to pay on funds borrowed at 1 percent. Mind, there were rumblings of discontent in very high places, and as ever, the bears thought the whole system could go south. But no one argued with Alan Greenspan.

Into the picture came the soft tread of the Chinese, with their dirt-cheap consumer products and an economy exploding with growth. China made it possible for Alan Greenspan to hold those interest rates down, avoid inflation, and keep the U.S. economy buzzing. China actually made it possible for the whole world to keep the lid on inflation, which surely would have gone mad without the armies of devoted workers slaving away in the Chinese industrial cauldron.

It's always amusing to hear European leaders, especially England's, blithely pointing to their own exemplary records in holding down inflation and talking about their own prudence and foresight, when in truth it had nothing to do with them. It had to do with China and their cheap products. Nothing else. From ports like Shanghai, freighters were steaming toward the United States, laden to the gunwales with consumer products priced at around half of what anyone else would have charged. The whole world was trying to buy inexpensive goods from China, and the Chinese were delivering, loading up on cheap American money. All this did keep the lid on world inflation, but as many as ten thousand American jobs a week were disappearing over the long horizon to the Far East—to India, Malaysia, and Taiwan as well as to China. The key to all this was, of course, the abundance of cheap labor available in the People's Republic, with its population of well over one billion souls.

Never in modern history has a labor force numbered so many and been prepared to work for so little. At least not since the Egyptians laid to rest the Fourth Dynasty Pharaoh Khafre, in his pyramid 2,500 years before Christ. In turn, the Chinese purchased billions of U.S. Treasury bonds at 3 percent, which in effect meant they owned a vast obligation from the U.S. government. In simple terms, China made one heck of a bet on the success of Uncle Sam, and it's a bet they could not afford to lose. America's ultimate success must be theirs as well. But let's face it, when you have a cash flow like Niagara Falls and that much money in the bank, there's not much left to buy except U.S. Treasuries.

There were American economists who were concerned about the Greenspan strategy and how long his free-money approach could continue, but he was a man of such influence it was impossible to utter any criticism except in the softest terms. Nonetheless, there were people who simply thought it was too good to be true—that this new nirvana, where anyone could borrow anything, with hardly any interest, would last forever.

The truth was, this was the starting point of America living in a false economy, because all this free money was in defiance of the natural laws of the universe. All bubbles, down the centuries, have started that way, leading to the inevitable time when people begin to think it's normal, that nirvana has finally arrived. It happened with a resounding clash of heavenly cymbals when the dot-coms went bananas, and people all over the planet began to believe this was a brand-new easy-money world. But of course it wasn't. It never is. You can ask my dad, who watched the start of the insane credit boom in late 2003 by observing, dryly, "Here we go again. Straight back to the edge of the cliff."

This was a time when the convertible bond analysts and researchers were still being ultra-careful and were still mindful of the spate of bankruptcies in 2002. Investors began to grow quite cavalier about their stocks and bonds. They had easy lines of credit but increased personal debt and decreased savings. They were part of a consumer-spending bonanza in a country that would ultimately lose several million jobs to China. The United States had a trade deficit with Beijing that amounted to billions of dollars of debt. There was a new category of money, "borrower dollars"—dollars that weren't quite real because they had been borrowed from banks and credit card companies by the consumers. And they were winging through cyberspace by the trillions, headed for China and India.

Back home, where it was impossible to make money in bank accounts with a 2 percent rate, high-yield bonds were plainly the answer, and they became as fashionable as stock in dot-com companies had once been. But Wall Street had outsmarted everyone, and instead of the old-fashioned regular reliable bonds, investors now stampeded for residential mortgage-backed securities (RMBS), commercial mortgage-backed securities (CMBS), collateralized debt obligations (CDOs), collateralized loan obligations (CLOs), and structured investment vehicles (SIVs), paying around 5 to 8 percent.

Securitization. What a stroke of pure genius. Turning those mortgage debts into tangible entities. Hardly anyone noticed the minor flaws that would, in time, bankrupt half the world.

The year 2003 turned into 2004, and still the flame of my ambitions burned as strongly as ever. I still wanted a seat at Wall Street's top table, right up there in the major leagues, and I thought I had what it took to make those final steps. And there I would prove my dad was wrong to be so gloomy, and so devoid of optimism. In short, I was still trying to become a trader.

Larry McCarthy, currently setting the world alight at Lehman, remained encouraging, and somehow even in the early part of the new year, I was aware that my future did not lie with Morgan Stanley, because there was seething unrest in the old firm. Guys began to leave, big important guys, such as Steve Newhouse and Vikram Pandit. Our head of investment banking, Guru Ramakrishnan, also headed for the exit in what became a massive exodus of talent. Even Anand quit, a devastating blow for me. It was a terrible time. The atmosphere was poisonous. Most people dreaded coming to work. Everywhere you looked there was disquiet, unhappiness, malice, and unrest. New people arrived who did not fit in, and established staff members could feel the difference so sharply that at one point it seemed everyone I knew was looking for a new job.

It's a strange truth, but when you have the right mix of people, and there's mutual respect for what other people do and how they operate, a corporation such as an investment bank runs really smoothly. But it never takes much to screw that up, and once that happens, suddenly the chemistry has gone. I suppose it's like that in sports teams too, probably in everything.

All I knew was I had to get out of there. I was still seeking the holy grail, and the son of a bitch had to be somewhere. But it was not in the hive of buzzing discontent that was my present office.

Larry McCarthy knew the situation. Even from his battle station in midtown Manhattan, he was amazed at what was happening to us. One day he called me and uttered the words that would change my life, "Don't worry about it, Larry. There's a place here at Lehman for you."

Thus began a series of interviews with the great investment house I had revered since I left college. I was totally focused on leaving Morgan Stanley and I trusted Larry, so six times I made the journey from Stamford to the city to speak with the top brass of the 154-year-old investment bank.

Lehman was one of the giants of Wall Street, and they acted like it. Everyone I met was a class act. And then on the morning of July 14, 2004, a letter dropped into the mailbox at my apartment on Forest Street in Stamford. It came from the office of a Lehman vice president I had met, Deborah Millstein. Its words swam before my eyes:

> *Dear Lawrence:*
>
> *We are pleased to extend to you our offer of employment to join Lehman Brothers Inc as a trader in the High Yield Department in the Fixed Income Division, reporting initially to Larry McCarthy and Richard Gatward. Your title of vice president will be submitted for official approval by the Executive Committee of our Board of Directors . . .*

How about that? Into the hierarchy, alongside some of Wall Street's smartest guys. Sixteen years had passed since I'd been rejected by more brokerage houses than any other applicant in history. And now one of the biggest had finally seen the light.

Better yet, I'd be working with my old and trusted pal from the rival gas station in Falmouth when we were sixteen, Larry McCarthy.

There's a French saying, *Plus ça change, plus c'est la même chose*—the more things change, the more they stay the same. I'd just made the move, as it were, from my gas station to his.

Larry had been the catalyst who propelled me into Wall Street. And I could never really express my gratitude to him, because there aren't enough words in the English language for me to do that. But hell, just give me the chance, I'd laugh at his jokes all night for what he did for me.

4

The Man in the Ivory Tower

There were mind-blowing tales of Dick Fuld's temper, secondhand accounts of his rages and threats. It was like hearing the life story of some caged lion.

I ENTERED THE marble halls of Lehman Brothers on Wednesday morning, July 21, 2004, at the usual start time, six o'clock. The sun was rising over the distant East River, yellow cabs were thundering through quiet streets at the highest speeds they would reach all day, and God was in his heaven, probably applauding me as I pushed open the doors below the towering glass ramparts of 745 Seventh Avenue.

The breathtaking history of this great finance house had not begun in here. That had happened back in 1868 down in lower Manhattan, where the ghosts of the long-dead Lehman brothers probably still resided. But nothing died when the corporation made its move here in 2002, and a thousand Wall Street legends, fables, and sagas down all the years somehow slipped silently into the carpeted hallways of this modern Tower of Babel. I could feel them, every step I took.

Lehman. The very name conjures up visions of a select men's club, a paneled haven from the world's vulgarities, especially formed for men of breeding and high intellect; a dining room in which was served only the finest Bordeaux, and a boardroom where stimulating conversations abounded and great fortunes were created.

Much of the wealth of the United States owed its beginnings to the dazzling brilliance of financiers, all named Lehman, who had plotted and schemed on behalf of the firm. The roots of the place stretched back to the 1840s, to the fields of Alabama and the town of Montgomery, which had four thousand white citizens and two thousand black slaves. When cotton was king. To that thriving heart of the Old South, Henry, Emanuel, and Mayer Lehman, cattle merchants from Bavaria, had journeyed, and they made it their home. Since every other immigrant of the time headed like homing pigeons to New York, gateway to the New World, it was probably not a fluke that these three future financial titans made straight for the center of the cotton industry, the place that really counted in the world's shipping and trading operations. In 1850 they established their own trading and dry goods business and called it Lehman Brothers.

The Civil War devastated the South and caused tempestuous highs and lows in the cotton industry. By 1868 the Lehmans had moved to lower Manhattan, where they not only founded the New York Cotton Exchange but joined in boldly in the postwar expansion of trading stocks and bonds. In particular, they sold bonds to raise money for their home state of Alabama, which was almost bankrupt and desperately trying to build textile mills and railroads. They also helped found the Coffee Exchange and the Petroleum Exchange.

The Lehmans made their breakthrough into cooperation with the old Wall Street families by helping to build a couple of major banks, Mercantile National and Manufacturers Trust. By the turn of the century they were in heavy cahoots with Goldman Sachs and they raised money to help launch Studebaker (with the first pneumatic tires) plus the General Cigar Company and Sears Roebuck.

I looked around the walls as I walked through the third floor to meet Larry McCarthy. Everywhere there was evidence of one of the most illustrious investment banking corporations in all of history: photographs, stern portraits of Lehmans past. This was the family that had spawned four generations to run their corporation, all the way from the cotton fields of Alabama in 1850 to the death of the immortal Bobbie Lehman in 1969. Almost 120 years of excellence.

During that time the firm had raised the capital, even invested their own wealth, in helping to start huge retail operations such as Gimbel Brothers, F. W. Woolworth, and Macy's. They nurtured the airlines American, National, TWA, and Pan-American. They raised the capital for Campbell Soup Company, Jewel Tea Company, and B. F. Goodrich.

Bobbie Lehman personally was the driving financial force behind a new outfit that believed it could transmit moving pictures—RCA, the birth of television. Lehman, under his guidance, also backed the Hollywood film studios RKO, Paramount, and 20th Century Fox, plus the TransCanada pipeline and Murphy Oil, along with a giant of the oil service business, Halliburton, and the exploration and production newcomer Kerr-McGee.

Like his father, Philip, and his grandfather Emanuel, Bobbie led a corporation that was long on integrity, trusted and admired. Though the family's Jewish origins evoked mild hostility from social giants such as the Astors and the Morgans, the pure decency and efficiency of the Lehmans overcame all. Down the years many other partners from outside the family joined the corporation, and they were all men of stature and achievement. For almost a hundred years Lehman represented a business aristocracy, an organization all other New York investment banks secretly aspired to emulate.

I had obviously been reading up on the Lehman history in the days leading to my arrival. And the magazine articles about Bobbie were fantastic. He owned a string of racehorses and a $100 million art collection. The firm's longtime New York headquarters at 1 William Street was hung with paintings by old masters such as Botticelli, Goya, Rembrandt, and El Greco. There were works by Renoir, Matisse, Picasso, and Cézanne, all part of his private collection. They were also part of an enormous gift of three thousand works he later made to the Metropolitan Museum of Art, a gift that the curators described as "one of the most extraordinary private collections ever assembled in the United States."

Bobbie was a close friend of some of the most powerful men in the country. He played on one of the great United States polo teams, with teammates such as Jock Whitney and Averell Harriman. He made the banker and car rental king John Hertz a senior partner in Lehman, and the two of them often went to the races together. Like Whitney, Hertz was a major owner-breeder of thoroughbreds, and owned the 1928 Kentucky Derby winner Reigh Count, sire of Hertz's 1943 Triple Crown winner, Count Fleet. Bobbie Lehman was a member of New York City's aristocracy. His cousin Herbert Lehman was governor of the state, and later became a U.S. senator.

Bobbie focused the firm on venture capital. And he had an inspired touch at spotting new businesses, leading his family firm into an undeniable golden age. There should have been a crystal ball on his desk. Over and over he listened to people, helped them develop their ideas, and then backed them either with the firm's money or by raising it for them. "I bet," he once said, "on people."

And now I walked the hallowed floors of this bank, and it's still difficult for me to explain what it meant on that first morning. I knew the place had made a twenty-first-century move from its famous old headquarters in the financial district, but so far as I was concerned it was like moving a cathedral. The real estate was different, but the holiness remained.

God knows what Bobbie Lehman would have thought if he'd known the real reason why Lehman had paid $700 million for this 1,000,000-square-foot office building. Because the real reason was the terrorism of 9/11, when Lehman had occupied three floors of One World Trade Center, with another 6,500 employees in Three World Financial Center, amidst the carnage and the debris.

Bobbie died two years before the Twin Towers were completed. He never saw them rise to their heights, and he'd been gone 32 years when the gleaming Boeing 767, owned by the airline he had helped to create, smashed into the 84th floor of the North Tower.

Larry McCarthy took me down to the trading floor, which looked a lot like that at Morgan Stanley. There were well over a hundred people already there, all standing up in front of banks of computer screens—and, it seemed to me, all shouting. The temperature was around sixty degrees, which felt freezing even on this hot July morning. Larry told me it was kept that way even in the winter: cool, with oxygen being pumped in to give everyone as much energy as possible. I knew a lot of casinos in Las Vegas and even the Mohegan Sun complexes followed that policy, just to keep the gamblers energetically hurling their cash at a system geared to stop them from winning. That was not the objective at Lehman Brothers.

My opening day was spent meeting and spending time with two top female operators with whom I would be in constant touch every day. The first was Christine Daley, who was in her thirties at the time and head of distressed-debt research. Christine was a vulture's vulture. They say she could tell you to the penny what General Motors was worth at any given moment in the week, even in the auto giant's darkest days—*particularly* in the auto giant's darkest days.

Christine was a beautiful, slim, immaculately dressed Italian-American. I heard she earned over $2 million a year. She was watchful, and very skillfully set out to find out precisely what I knew. And she was no pushover, not the kind of person to whom I could easily have sold a couple hundred pork chops. And she had a towering reputation as a researcher who could slice and dice any big corporation, and swiftly come up with an eye-wateringly correct valuation. Unsurprisingly, she had graduated magna cum laude from the College of New Rochelle with departmental honors in all semesters. At New York University's Stern School of Business she graduated number one in her class, which was doubtless no shock to anyone.

Her second-in-command was a corporate brainiac, Jane Castle, thirtyish, a petite woman whom Larry described with undiluted admiration as "one hundred pounds of hell." She was married to another big-hitter at Lehman, Joe Castle. Their double-barreled income had provided them with an apartment in the city and a summer house at the Jersey shore. Jane was reputed to be Christine's equal at assessing the value of a corporation down to the minutest detail. Larry had told me, "Jane can tell you what Delta Air Lines is serving for lunch in first class on their morning flight from JFK to Berlin, and what it cost them. There's nothing she doesn't know about that company."

Jane came from Queens, a borough of New York City. She should have been from Missouri, because she accepted nothing at face value. No statement by any executive of any corporation, large or small, was good enough for her, because it might have been inaccurate or careless. She had to *know* the truth. I knew I would have to earn her trust in the weeks to come. It wasn't just there for the asking, even though I was one of Larry McCarthy's oldest friends.

I knew from the first moments I spent with Christine and Jane that this was the major leagues. I was in the presence of greatness with these two. I might be shorting major corporations in the near future, with millions of Lehman dollars on the line. But I had access to these two steel-trap minds. And right from the start my confidence was high.

The only thing that was not high about my situation was the floor I worked on—the third. But I quickly learned this was not a permanent state of affairs. Lehman moved their departments up and down in the building all the time, trying to ensure no one became too comfortable in their environment. They already made sure no one became warm either, with that chilly air they kept pumping through. The day I arrived the elevator order was: second floor, equities; third floor, fixed income (high grade and high yield); fourth floor, mortgages; fifth floor, capital markets investment banking; sixth floor, CDO and CLO structuring; seventh floor, municipals and investment management. Within weeks that would change.

Right off the bat, I was placed next to Larry, the best place to learn the ropes fast. On my other wing was a twenty-eight-year-old big-league bond trader named Joe Beggans, whom I already knew from trips on Larry's fifty-two-foot Viking powerboat. Joe was a gutsy operator, still recovering from the battering he'd taken during the dot-com uproar and from trading Enron and Adelphia bonds. That was like standing under a falling chain saw. And that was how Big Joe had learned his trade.

He stood about six foot six and had been the number three quarterback on the University of Pennsylvania football team. We all knew that meant not a whole lot of playing time, but only Larry took it to its humorous limit. With Joe in full cry about some bond issue, Larry would solemnly get down on one knee and stretch both arms out in front of him, palms facing each other, ready for the snap in the dying moments of the game. After a few seconds, without a smile, he would return to his screen having made a charade of what he claimed was Joe's entire quarterback career: about two minutes. Of course, everyone fell over laughing, which was why Larry performed the ritual in the first place. But Joe really liked Larry and took it in good humor, chuckling at the hysterical sight of his diminutive boss down on one knee ready for the snap in the middle of Lehman's bond-trading floor.

Another member of our team was Peter Schellbach, whom we called Schell. A calculating and somewhat skeptical bear, he was our senior bank-debt man, specializing in power plants, making sure of our first claims when anything went wrong. Schell bought distressed power-plant bank debt at 40 cents on the dollar, but he always worked on the innate value of a power plant, and often correctly assessed it would go back to 70 or even 90 cents once the corporation cleaned house and got rid of the excesses. He told me he was hugely helped in these ventures by Christine and Jane. They made a hell of a team, the ladies' academic caution allied to his aggressive trader mentality. One year they made profits for Lehman of well over $100 million.

Schell was a very good golfer and owned a house in the Hamptons. He was married with two sons, and played in a rock band that gigged at the Red Lion in New York once a month. He played the electric guitar, stuff from the Grateful Dead and the Who—classic rock. He was a fantastic musician, and a whole group of us used to go and watch him.

Alex Kirk was probably one of the most respected men at Lehman, and he was only about six years older than I was, still in his mid-forties. Wall Street legend has it that he was one of the biggest distressed-debt traders on the dot-coms and telecoms, and made about $250 million for the firm when they all crashed. That put him on the map—hell, it would have put anyone on the map. He'd gone to Trinity, the private liberal arts college in Hartford, Connecticut. His job title was global head of high-yield and leveraged loan businesses. He wasn't a real bear's bear. He was just a calculated skeptic. He and Larry were big pals.

My new desk among the traders faced the salespeople. I spent the first month learning, watching, doing the research, particularly in subjects I knew a lot about—convertible bonds, airlines, energy, technology. But I was blown away by my new colleagues' depth of knowledge and the intricate types of modern debt instruments they worked with.

There were times when I did not know how the hell I'd gotten in here, especially since Lehman was famous for recruiting battalions of the best young minds in the country, highly educated Ivy League types, magna cum genius, born and bred for Wall Street from the time they were infants, and then sent to private schools such as Choate, St. Paul's, Exeter, Tabor, Andover, and St. John's. Almost everyone I met at Lehman had attended Harvard or Harvard Business School, MIT or the Sloan School, Yale, Princeton, Penn or Wharton, Northwestern, Stanford, North Carolina, or Duke. It should have been downright intimidating, but I'd been through the mill by now. I'd founded a million-dollar corporation, I'd worked at Merrill Lynch, Smith Barney, and Morgan Stanley. My resume would stand up to anyone's.

My own mantra was close to that of Mike Douglas in *Wall Street: Most of these Harvard MBA types, they don't add up to dog shit—give me guys that are poor, smart, hungry, and no feelings. You win a few, you lose a few, but you keep on fighting.* Didn't impress Lehman, though. Every year they sent out their best and brightest to talk to and lecture these kids, take them out to dinner, take them to events, have them as interns in the summer, even at Christmas. They paid them well as interns, nurtured them. I could not believe the coddling, the opportunities they were given. Perfect lives, blessed at birth.

I guess by this time, at the age of thirty-eight, I had caught up to them. But the main thing was, I wanted to make Larry proud of me. I mapped out my work regime: up at 4:00 A.M. and into the gym, a full planning program evolving in my head while I worked out. On my second day, armed with the card that would get me through the vast marble entrance hall, I moved swiftly to my third-floor desk, touching down at 5:55 A.M. I had always outworked every one of my colleagues.

But to my amazement, there were a lot of people already at work on the trading floor. It was not yet at full blast noisewise. But there was heavy action, since it was 11:00 A.M. in London and noon in Paris and Germany, and they were still trading on Hong Kong's Hang Seng and the Nikkei in Tokyo. The cries of the traders split the morning air, which was blasting in cold. Everyone was in their shirtsleeves, unwilling to show the weakness of being bothered by the temperature. All around there are shouts—"Lift!" "Hit!" "Source!" "Five up!" "Five by five!" "Work five on the follow!" "Work it!" It was about three ticks from pandemonium, and more and more people were arriving, apparently oblivious to the whole new language I was hearing. Later I realized that I was pretty well in tune with everything being said, but some of the phraseology was unique to Lehman.

By seven o'clock the place was jumping. At 7:10 there was not one empty coat hanger in the five huge closets with their splendid mahogany doors. You needed to go about half a block to find somewhere to put your jacket, a closet in a less frenetic section where it did not appear the world was facing a cash meltdown every five seconds unless you stayed sharp.

No one, repeat no one, went out for lunch. You couldn't. You dared not. You might miss a $50,000 trade, which at Lehman was tantamount to running up a white flag of surrender and looking for a different career. There were two in-house kitchens on each floor, one for the workers, traders and vice presidents on down, and one for the managing directors. Our kitchen specialized in outstanding egg sandwiches, and there was a Danish and muffin mountain the size of Mont Blanc. You could get Coke and candy, glazed doughnuts and cream-filled doughnuts, and other minor cholesterol bombs rich in energy-sapping sugar. In the afternoon you could get hot dogs, burgers, and ice cream. If you decided to make that Lehman kitchen your sole restaurant, you had a fighting chance of being dead before you reached forty-five. The managing director's kitchen was distinctly upmarket. They could get filet mignon, shrimp, and God knows what else.

Our section, however, was more or less immune to all this, because Larry was our self-appointed gourmetmeister. He rarely used the kitchen, and almost every day he sent the kids—newly hired analysts—out for pizzas or tacos for everyone. He ate with his men. And he refused flatly to collect one cent for anybody's lunch. He was, and is, probably the most stand-up, generous person I have ever met.

Lehman Brothers, like the great city beyond the massive glass windows, never slept. When the trading bell sounded on the New York Stock Exchange at four o'clock in the afternoon, a lot of equity guys packed up because there was nothing more for them to do. Bank debt and high-yield debt often went till seven o'clock or later. And there were always people waiting for late calls, often from the West Coast. Those guys were there for dinner, working until ten o'clock. But the key moment in the trading day came around 6:00 P.M., when all the traders had to present their profit/loss numbers to the pit bosses—in my case to Larry and Richard Gatward. Most days the traders had normal-looking balance sheets, not too drastic one way or the other. But losses were not loved at Lehman. And if you turned in a sheet with a drop of $500,000 on the day, that was trouble. The Lehman hotshots would be aware of that in a New York minute.

In a way, Lehman was run by a junta of platoon officers. They'd all learned the basics, but they'd also spent a lot of time in combat. I think of them as battle-hardened, iron-souled regulars, guys like Larry and Alex Kirk, Mike Gelband, Peter Schellbach, Richard Gatward, and Christine Daley. My new commanding general was missing, however. Not missing in action, you understand. Just plain old-fashioned missing, locked in some rarefied war room on the thirty-first floor, an unseen but apparently malevolent presence. His name was Richard S. Fuld Jr.

As one of his new troop commanders, I looked forward to meeting this famous CEO. When I mentioned this possibility to Larry McCarthy, I recall him laughing, a touch sardonically, which was not all that unusual for him.

"That probably is not going to happen, buddy," he said. "I've never met him myself."

Huh? A managing director, the head of distressed-debt trading, had never met the CEO? Beat the hell out of me. But slowly in the coming weeks I learned about several unorthodox aspects of Fuld's character. I spoke to a few people who met him a couple of times a year. But there were a few guys who had never even seen him.

When Lehman's CEO arrived by limousine in the morning at a VIP entrance at the back of the building, his driver had already called ahead alerting the front desk in the lobby of his majesty's imminent arrival. The front-desk attendant then hit a button programming one of the elevators in the rear bank to go directly to the thirty-first floor. A security guard would then hold the elevator until Fuld's arrival. This was Fuld's private transport to the heavens, the one that preserved his godlike existence. Into this rarefied capsule he slipped silently, and was, in a way, beamed up to his somber mahogany-paneled office, far from the madding crowd. He left the building the same way, which was not, I thought naively, much of a way to keep your finger on the pulse.

"I hear he's a very defensive guy," said Larry.

"You mean he's paranoid?"

"Paranoid? Hell, no. He just thinks everyone's out to get him." Which was, in case you hadn't noticed, vintage McCarthy.

There was, it seemed, no doubt that our spiritual leader and battlefield commander was an extremely remote and watchful character, surrounded by a close coterie of cronies, with almost no contact with anyone else. And I suppose that was fine so long as the place was chugging along without civil war or mutiny breaking out, and continuing to coin money, which is after all the prime objective of the merchant bank.

But I sensed there was something deeply disquieting about this oddball demigod who ruled everyone's lives. Quite simply, people were afraid of him, even though they couldn't see him. And this was a fear based upon reputation, because through the years Fuld had fired many, many people, for a thousand different reasons. Popular local intelligence, however, suggested that the most prevalent way of incurring his rank displeasure was to threaten his power base.

He worked within a tight palace guard, protected from the lower ranks, communicating only through his handpicked lieutenants. And as the years went by, Dick Fuld had tightened his circle, shutting out more and more key people from the downstairs floors where the daily action seethed, where the trading battles ebbed and flowed, where more critical information flew around than anywhere else in the city. That was the place from which he had, to all intents and purposes, removed himself. In the process, he had become separated from the most modern technology and the ultramodern trading of credit derivatives—CDO (collateralized debt obligations), RMBS (residential mortgage-backed securities), CLO (collateralized loan obligations), CDS (credit default swaps), and CMBS (commercial mortgage-backed securities).

Stories about long-departed commanders were legion. There were secondhand accounts of his rages and threats. It was like hearing the life story of some caged lion. Tell the truth, I ended up feeling pretty darn glad I wasn't meeting him. There was something of the night about this guy, and it all dated back to the early part of the 1980s, when he and his chief cohort had not quite covered themselves in glory. In fact, he had been instrumental in one of the biggest screwups in Lehman's long history, and not surprisingly, there was a touch of Prince Machiavelli about the whole episode.

Richard S. Fuld, New York born and bred, graduated from the University of Colorado and earned his MBA at NYU's Stern School of Business. He joined Lehman in 1969, which was, with terrifying irony, the year Bobbie Lehman, the last of the family partners, died. Some say the grand old Wall Street firm died with him.

In any event, Fuld, who began his career fresh out of college as a commercial paper trader, moved steadily up the organization. By the high summer of 1983 he was a well-established bond trader, and in a ferocious bull market, Lehman was under the rule of joint chief executive officers, who were just about as similar as JFK and Nikita Khrushchev. On one hand, there was the urbane former secretary of commerce in the Nixon administration, Washington heavyweight Peter G. Peterson, and on the other there was Lewis Glucksman, the short, overweight, hotheaded man who occupied the position of Lehman's chief of trading. It was Peterson who as CEO had elevated Glucksman to share the position of co-CEO in June 1983. As a general expression of his undying gratitude, Glucksman had Peterson paid off and thrown out of the corporation within eight weeks of his own elevation to one of the two big chairs.

It was a shocking error in judgment by Glucksman, rooted in some perceived slight by the establishment investment banker Peterson toward the rambunctious, hard-driving trader. And it ended an unlikely ten-year partnership that had taken Lehman into a realm of profit never before seen. In 1982 Glucksman's traders had made an astounding $122 million, twice as much as the more staid but rock-solid investment bankers who were being forced to take a backseat.

When Glucksman struck, he struck hard, if a tad gracelessly. He told his old boss, Peterson, he wanted him gone by September 30. He was, it seemed, tired of Peterson's image, wining and dining media types and other CEOs and appearing in the society pages, while he, shirtsleeves rolled up, never even went out for a quick lunch because he was so busy trading, making money, and getting the results that counted. In truth, it was Peterson's priceless contacts that had allowed this old-style merchant banker to make Lehman the fourth-largest investment house on Wall Street. But the sloppy, disheveled Glucksman did not see it that way. He saw only this beautifully mannered, highly educated former member of the Nixon administration moving effortlessly around town in a way he could never hope to achieve.

When Peterson took his money and left, Glucksman elevated his thirty-five-year-old protégé, Richard Fuld, to become a member of the board, and appointed him global head of equity and bond trading. With Lehman turning profits of more than $15 million a month, Glucksman could do more or less as he wished, and it swiftly became obvious that the venerable bank had moved into a new era—the Glucksman/Fuld era, when these swashbuckling, rough-edged traders took over from the traditional sure-footed bankers.

With Glucksman rampaging around the premises doing his level best to establish a reputation comparable to that of Attila the Hun, a curious power struggle was developing between the traders and the bankers, who still dominated the ranks of the firm's seventy-six partners. In the end, though, there could only be one winner. Glucksman's traders were moved onto the board, and some partners, most of whom lived in fear of the tyrant from the wrong side of the tracks, began to depart. Lew assumed complete control in October 1983, and almost from that moment things changed.

It should be remembered that my sources were mostly old-timers at the bank, probably with a few axes to grind. Nonetheless, there are several indisputable facts that should be conveyed, especially as Fuld's career is so significant. From the moment Glucksman took control, Wall Street was in a raging bull market, and that year profits soared from $122 million to $148 million. The traders were on a ferocious roll, with America's baby boomers, now hitting their forties and getting richer, piling their cash into new mutual funds and Wall Street private money management accounts. It was a trading paradise. And Glucksman's plain desire to be respected and feared, not liked, saw him swiftly attain all-powerful status.

He expanded the board, installing his cronies, not so much with the other directors' approval but because none of them wanted to rock the boat when the bank was coining money at a breathtaking rate. Glucksman turned into a steamroller, driving through his wishes and whims, uninterrupted, unencumbered. It was a serious and destructive misuse of power. Dick Fuld looked on with admiration for his rampant mentor, certainly not disapprovingly.

Glucksman had the board and all of his department heads in his back pocket. And almost immediately he began to take on more risk, such as the venerable investment house had never dared in all their history. There was a growing suspicion that this hustling trader was in over his head, but that did not prevent Glucksman from approving an annual salary and bonus of $1.6 million for his protégé. The Lehman traders were now responsible for $4 of profit for every $3 made by the corporate bankers.

Glucksman seized control of the executive committee and forced several of the investment bankers to sell shares back to the corporation at book value, for immediate distribution to the traders. Fuld did well. Thanks to Glucksman's largesse, his own share count went from 1,700 to 2,750, valued around $1,000 apiece. As your average bonus grab goes, this one went high and tight.

Divisiveness and tension were rife at Lehman during this time, and by early 1984, predictably, the talent started to walk. Six prominent bankers, led by Eric Gleacher, left that spring. And, as partners, they took the firm's capital with them, at book value—17 percent of it, straight out the door. Lew Glucksman adopted an increasingly embattled stance, detested by many of his own banking partners.

At around this time, there were large financial supermarkets popping up all over Wall Street. Created by mergers and acquisitions, there were suddenly new and powerful entities in the game, outfits with balance sheets that were already big and burgeoning by the hour. There was Prudential Bache, Shearson American Express, Dean Witter Sears, and Salomon Phibro. Suddenly there was fear and insecurity among the smaller "boutique" investment houses, and nowhere was this more pronounced than at Lehman Brothers, where the remaining partners were braced for another walkout, since talent had become so transferable. There was a suspicion that Lehman Brothers was too small, too dependent on winning all of their trading skirmishes while the big guns of Wall Street exploded with capital and threatened to crush the life out of even the most powerful old-school investment banks, like Bear Stearns and Goldman Sachs.

Some bankers on the Lehman board believed the only way forward was to merge with a much bigger partner and proceed from there. They accepted this would mean a total loss of identity, and that the oldest continuing trading partnership on Wall Street would be gone forever. But no one was having much fun under the Glucksman/Fuld axis and several of the partners were happy to cash out and leave.

At the back end of 1983, in response to persistent rumors that the Lehman board might be open to offers for the firm, the agricultural commodity giant ConAgra made a $600 million bid. Lew Glucksman did not report it to the board, which was a truly heinous act of treachery in an old established partnership, especially since the offer erred on the reckless side of generosity.

However, both Lew Glucksman and Dick Fuld, for different reasons, did not want to sell. They wanted to hold their positions of power and command in the vanguard of this famous old Wall Street warrior. They wanted that power and influence as dearly as they wanted life itself. It was an all-consuming hunger both shared.

It was true that both Fuld and Glucksman loved money, personal money, stuff-it-in-your-pockets money—more, more, more, millions and millions of dollars. And there was an attraction in the fast buck for the quick sale. But Lehman's boardroom gave them status, and they each liked that at least as much as cash.

In the early 1980s, there were still many gentlemanly traits left in the traditional old finance houses in New York. And one of them is extremely difficult to understand unless you were born with it, which neither Glucksman nor Fuld was. In the broadest terms, it is the difference between natural greed—quiet, well-concealed avarice, understated self-interest—and the kind of obvious greed that men like Glucksman and Fuld wear like a misplaced badge of courage. They wear it not because they mean to offend but because that's the way they are. They know of no other way. And it betrays them every time;

they are unable to act as the cool, enthusiastic amateur rather than the self-seeking capitalist. The tragedy is that men like Glucksman and Fuld are unable to see what it is about them that can turn others against them. But deep inside, they are aware there's something. And this is precisely what leads them to those beleaguered positions, almost barricaded inside their ivory towers, snarling and growling at bad news, taking every scrap of credit for good news, learning to enjoy the fear and dislike of others, pretending that respect is all they really want.

In the end there is always mutiny. Even one of the greatest seagoing autocrats of all time, Captain Bligh, found that out on the quarterdeck of the *Bounty.* Lew Glucksman and Dick Fuld found it out at Lehman Brothers in 1984. A mutiny was building right before their eyes, in the form of a splinter group around three of the most influential Wall Street financiers of all time—Peter Solomon, Steve Schwarzman, and later Shel Gordon, all Lehman partners, all of them certain a sale was the best answer.

The year 1984 did what it had been threatening to do: it turned bad for the markets. Fuld's trading desk was headed south, and he compounded his own problems by staying close to deals he had made that were unlikely to come up trumps. On the Street, it's called marrying a bad trade. Since the ConAgra bid, the Lehman balance sheet was declining, and even if it had been possible to revive it, an offer would never look anything like the $600 million Glucksman had played so close to his chest.

By midsummer, Lehman Brothers was on the run. At least Glucksman and Fuld were on the run. The board of directors had veered against them, and there seemed to be nothing they could do. Both men made attempts to trade their way back into the game, but it was too late. Power was slipping away from them. Glucksman made one last roll of the dice, persuading the board to sell Lemco, Lehman's asset management business. But this was simply burning the furniture in order to stay warm. For several days, they just sat there in a kind of trance, racking their brains to solve the ever-present identity crisis that was paralyzing the firm. Did the bank want to remain the classic boutique investment house on which the firm was built? Or did they want to be all things to all people, like Merrill Lynch?

Their other problem was that Glucksman and Fuld had saved

nothing from the prosperous years of 1982 and '83. They'd spent the money on capital investment, and increased operating expenses and technology expansion. Not to mention those heavy bonuses for themselves.

And right then, the bombshell dropped. A cover story in *Fortune* not only pointed out the current losses but elected to air the Lehman dirty laundry, highlighting the boardroom clash of philosophies and personalities. Temporarily, this story killed all interest in anyone paying $600 million for Lehman. It was a relatively punchy example of financial journalism, and it painted a grim picture of an old investment house dominated by a couple of bullying leaders, with schisms of unrest lurking throughout the company.

Fuld did not come out of it very well, which was not really all his fault. By far the greater problem was the explosion on the Lehman balance sheet, which showed that Dick Fuld's trading operation had lost a staggering $30 million in the six-month period from October 1, 1983, to March 31, 1984. It would not be the last time a Lehman committee sat in dumbfounded amazement at the marks Fuld made on Lehman's trading positions. An added worry was the possibility that Lehman may have been hiding assets that would have materially affected the merger with Shearson.

Some people questioned why the five-year European certificates of deposit on the Lehman books were not marked to market but held at face value, or par, 100 cents on the dollar. But nothing altered the big numbers, which were going from bad to worse. Lehman's profits were in free fall, its overall value plummeting at one stage to $325 million. The issue of what is known as "performance smoothing" is one that would raise its head in 2008.

The sharks were still circling, and thanks to *Fortune* they sensed a bargain, that Lehman could be grabbed for a lot less than the $600 million ConAgra had mentioned. Shearson American Express's Peter Cohen and James Robinson were now in active talks with the Lehman executive committee. But they were shocked by the discovery of more hidden assets on the Lehman books, used to offset trading losses.

In the final reckoning, the firm's book value had fallen 33 percent. Lehman's banking partners were afraid that even more discrepancies would be found, but Shearson wanted to buy the firm, and in the end they went to $360 million for Lehman, a $175 million premium over stated book value.

Thus 132 years of Lehman history was quietly dissolved. Once the envy of Wall Street, the revered private partnership had been swallowed whole by a financial supermarket. They'd survived the Civil War and two world wars but could not survive Glucksman and Fuld. Without the counterbalance of the canny sophisticate Pete Peterson, Lew and Dick had taken exactly seven months to wreck the Lehman legend. The thirty-eight-year-old Fuld pocketed a net of $7.6 million for his 2,750 shares.

Shearson Lehman muddled through for almost ten years under the Amex umbrella. Lehman traditionalists were unhappy being a part of a financial supermarket during this time. Glucksman and Fuld, much to their credit, helped keep the Lehman spirit and camaraderie alive. Their salvation came in 1994 when Lehman was spun off as a separate entity. Fuld grabbed the vacant helm. And from that moment, stories about him abounded, as they would continue to do throughout my own tenure at the firm.

I had read the two most prominent histories of the firm, one old, the other older, and I could not help being struck by the sharp similarities between the Fuld of the eighties and the Fuld of the present. It seemed to me he was still in some kind of ivory tower. At least that's what everyone was saying. Down on the trading floor no one ever saw him, and that represented one hell of a lot of important people, many of whom knew almost nothing about their leader.

Greed and Glory on Wall Street, one of the books on Lehman's history, pointed out that in his previous incarnation twenty years earlier, Dick Fuld was extremely sympathetic to the concept of golden handcuffs—paying people generously with stock in the corporation, albeit stock they could not cash in for years. It held them in some kind of highly paid bondage, with their own money consistently out of reach. From what my new colleagues told me, that was still the system: big rewards and huge bonuses, but too often beyond the horizon.

Looking back down the years, Dick Fuld had seen what had happened to Pete Peterson, stabbed ruthlessly by Glucksman. Whatever affection he may have had for his old mentor, nothing could obfuscate the sheer nastiness of Lew's move against Peterson. Fuld had plainly made a vow that nothing like that would ever happen to him personally, which was probably why he had never worked with a really strong number two. Throughout all the years of his long reign at Lehman Brothers, Dick Fuld had never had a powerful deputy. That *modus operandi* continued in May of 2004 when fifty-four-year-old Joe Gregory was appointed president and chief operating officer. A key factor in the appointment was that his ambitions did not apparently include becoming CEO. His great concern was with what he called the "culture" of Lehman Brothers.

Down where I worked, on the gundeck of the ship, where financial cannons roared and real people found themselves in the thick of the battle, I never once heard the name Joe Gregory as a possible commanding officer if Fuld ever decided to retire. Joe was a man who stayed well clear of the action, heard the explosions only from afar, never smelled the cordite. Never saw the blood of heavy losses.

Joe was mostly closeted with Fuld up there on the thirty-first floor. In the coming years, I would constantly hear of their scheming to keep Lehman's stock prices high, quietly obscuring bad news, loudly announcing good news, gathering vast mountains of shares for themselves.

I had no idea whether either Fuld or Gregory possessed the kind of giant brain that was necessary on twenty-first-century Wall Street, though there were certainly grave doubts cast on this score. But there was one shining truth in Lehman Brothers that could never be conquered: down here on the trading floor, there were four people who possessed, without question, the cleverest, shrewdest, most decisive minds I had ever encountered in my business career. I watched Alex Kirk, Michael Gelband, Richard Gatward, and Larry McCarthy at close quarters. I saw them snatch victory from apparent defeat. I saw them probe weakness, scent triumph, switch strategy, and lay siege to the unwary.

Whatever the hell else happened in this great financial man-o'-war, where no one could see the hand that held the tiller, I was among the safest possible company. I thought back to my dad's old alma mater, Notre Dame, and the legend of the most famous college folklore in the world. I even made my own rewrite: *Outlined against sunny New York autumn skies, the Four Horsemen rode again. In financial lore, their names were Debt, Bankruptcy, Short Selling, and Fraud. Their real names were Kirk, Gelband, Gatward, and McCarthy.*

The backup battalions, which surrounded them every step of the way, were no less accomplished. Especially Christine Daley, for it was she who administered my first serious test of character and knowledge in the first week of my employment at Lehman.

The subject was one of the largest energy producers in the United States, the wholesale electricity giant Calpine, out of San Jose, California. At their peak, they owned almost a hundred gas turbines and power plants in twenty-one states, with natural gas fields and pipelines in the Sacramento Valley and 22,000 megawatts of capacity. Calpine ranked among the world's top ten electricity producers, with assets worth billions and billions.

They did, however, have one serious problem. Christine Daley, our iron-souled Lehman researcher, thought they would almost certainly go bust, and she was recommending we take a massive short position in this company. That took a lot of guts, because Calpine's creed of clean energy—the cleanest possible energy, turbines off which you could eat your lunch, emissions from which spring flowers would sprout, electricity so pure and spotless it would safely caress a newborn child—made it beloved among investors.

"Bullshit," said Christine inelegantly. "They're going down. That CFO of theirs could dance through raindrops without getting wet."

Anyhow, to return to my first major meeting, I stood before Christine, and in the first five seconds I understood why I was there. She knew all about my background in convertible bonds. She knew about ConvertBond.com, and she plainly knew that at Morgan Stanley I had never sold any of the many, many bonds issued by Calpine.

Instantly I was aware of her skepticism toward this darling of the investment world. "What do you know about them?" she asked. "And what do you think about Bob Kelly, the CFO?"

I told her I knew two major facts. They had one hell of a debt load, a lot of it convertible. I'd never been entirely convinced about Calpine, and in turn she questioned me about who would get paid, and when, upon the bonds' maturity. She wanted to know if Calpine could settle their convertible preferred shares for cash, or whether they could just box their way out and issue more shares.

I mentioned the convertible preferred stockholders—the guys who stand one tier higher than equity in the corporate capital structure. I utilized the finest Wall Street jargon, stressing that each one of the convertible preferreds had a different delta and a different gamma.

I will not easily forget the speed with which she cut me off in midsentence. "Never mind that ConvertBond.com mumbo jumbo," she snapped. "I am concerned with what the company can do to defer paying the dividends and defer their obligations to repay these preferred shareholders, because I can see a big fight developing right here."

"What kind of fight?" I asked, a bit lamely.

"The kind that starts when the preferred shareholders are senior to about $19 billion worth of debt, some secured, some unsecured," she replied. "That kind."

"Because the convertible preferred stock matures well before the debt, right? Kind of seniority by maturity," I said.

"Exactly," she agreed. "But I think the bank debtors will organize, hire some hotshot lawyer, and stage a battle in a courtroom, try to force Bob Kelly's hand, force him to cram down the preferred stockholders, while the bankers grab what there is of Calpine's assets."

"That would be a dividend roadblock, stopping all payments to the preferreds that mature in the next two years."

"Correct. They'd all lose out to the banks."

Christine Daley was as sure of her ground as anyone I'd ever met. She was convinced the cash flow of Calpine was nothing like good enough to support the gigantic debt the corporation carried. She knew there were bonds all over the place, many of them in different parts of the capital structure. There was first-lien and second-lien bank debt, senior secured notes, and a ton of unsecured straight debts. The last in line for repayment were three different convertible preferred debts.

In Christine Daley's opinion, Calpine was constantly robbing Peter to pay Paul, and constantly pushing the legal envelope, ducking and diving around the covenants that governed the financial structure of their debt. The entire corporation was structured to confuse the life out of the analysts as the company moved money from place to place, trying to stay solvent.

Christine did not buy it. And I could see she cared passionately. The look in her eyes was one of pure defiance, and it was backed by a laser beam of logic from which she could not be deviated. She was determined to persuade Lehman Brothers to take a huge short position. I thought of the massed ranks of lawyers and smart-ass execs who must be lined up against her, this one voice of profound certainty that stood alone against them.

"Calpine cannot last a year," she said as I was leaving. "And we are going to make millions of dollars watching them go bankrupt. It's just a hall of mirrors. Trust me, they're already broke."

"I'm with you all the way," I told her. "I always thought they were suspect. Which is why I never traded their bonds." But she needed no encouragement. I never heard anyone express a corporation's forthcoming woes better than Christine. You don't often meet a soothsayer with an AK-47.

As I walked away from her desk, back to my own little space on the computer line, I pondered that Calpine scenario. It was, of course, the oldest trick in the corporate playbook, building a vast network of separate components, corporations with different identities, and moving cash between them. One plant needs a few million, so you get it from another, pay it out, then pay it back from somewhere else. It's a process that can go on for years, removing the money and making big transfers all over the place, until no one knows where the money is, where it came from, where it went, or even whether it's real. All the while firms like Calpine would keep coming to Wall Street and issuing more debt.

Christine knew real when she saw it. And among all of that vast sea of numbers that made up Calpine's introverted/extroverted, hot/cold, now-you-see-it-now-you-don't balance sheet, only two mattered to her: her own year-end prediction of $650 million of Calpine EBITDA (earnings before interest, taxes, depreciation, and amortization) versus a truly daunting debt load of $18.5 billion.

"They have only one real chance," she had told me. "They'll have to trip at least one of those bond covenants. They don't have any choice."

It should be remembered that the end of 2004 was a very rosy time for the fixed-income markets. And for Christine Daley to come out and predict a major bankruptcy in a healthy market and economy was, I thought, an act of supreme daring and high confidence. Also, she was vocal in her views. Her faith and resolve knew no bounds.

She knew, of course, that Calpine was continually coming to the convertible market with bond after bond, 6 percent converts—the Last Chance Saloon for an outfit trying to get their hands on heavy capital. They were always trying to convince one of their largest bondholders, the gutsy Ed Perks of Franklin Mutual Funds, to lend them even more money through those convertible bonds. That's probably the soundest way out when you have mounting operating costs, a debt mountain with rising interest expenses, and falling earnings.

Meanwhile, out on the Street there was no letup in the lovefest for Calpine stocks and bonds. For cynics like Christine and me, it seemed nothing short of a cult following, with wide-eyed investors eager to play their part in the world's cleanest industrial energy program. We could see them rushing to the colors of the green flag with missionary, idealistic zeal. Oh, to be a part of the least-polluting, newest fleet of gas turbine plants in the world. Oh, to repair that shuddering hole in the ozone layer, re-ice the Arctic, stem the warming tides, save the stranded polar bears, replant the rainforest . . . *Mayday! Mayday! Save our planet!*

Of course, Christine Daley and I knew it should have been *save our ship,* not *save our planet,* because the green ship Calpine was holed below the waterline. For *mayday,* read *payday*—for the Calpine directors, that is. Not for the preferred stockholders, who were about to get crunched by the banks. As were the holders of Calpine equities.

The only interested party likely to come out of this laughing was Lehman Brothers, because they had Christine Daley and they were listening to her. *Go short, baby, go short, in the biggest possible way.*

Of course, back in Calpine's headquarters in San Jose the name Christine Daley was not universally loved. Wall Street has one of the most sensitive radar systems in the world. The network is a 24/7 communications sprawl in to which every single member of the finance industry is, on some level, tuned. Christine, conducting her traditional scorched-earth policy while researching critical information, spoke to many, many important people. I am sure they asked her advice, I am equally sure people asked her about any new bond that had just been issued by Calpine. And these people were often clients of Lehman Brothers. Christine was honor-bound to provide them with an honest assessment. I am sure that for many months she turned people off Calpine, shared with them her fears that this giant archipelago of power plants carried too much debt to be considered a buy, either shares or bonds.

In sunlit San Jose, I have no doubt she was regarded as the Princess of Darkness. They did not, I hasten to add, believe she was treating them unfairly, because they knew the score as well as she did. Christine was the Wall Street sleuth who had them nailed.

After that first meeting with her, I wondered just how many

people around there knew as much as she did. And it did not take me long to find out. Lehman Brothers had a meeting every Tuesday morning at seven for the high-yield/distressed-debt traders' teams, always with a guest speaker and thirty-five to forty traders and researchers in the room. Lehman believed in keeping the best information and analysis in front of its traders at all times, rotating different levels of expertise—the CDO maestros, the head of U.S. Treasury trading, the head of credit strategy. I could not help thinking how utterly disadvantaged the investing public was against this giant arsenal of research and talent at the immediate disposal of Wall Street's frontline traders. The standards I would be working to, once I settled in as an active trader, were the highest possible. The quality of the people was exemplary. At least it was down here on the third floor.

Aside from Larry McCarthy, I had to answer to the English-born managing director and global head of sales and convertible trading, Richard Gatward. He was a Lehman veteran of many years' standing, around thirty-six years old, a hard-nosed, stocky character who could see right through you if he suspected for one split second that you did not know precisely what you were talking about. If he'd been a Navy SEAL, he'd have been a combat instructor, drilling his team, driving them forward, testing them, letting them decide for themselves. But he was ever-present, ready for the screwup, listening for the bullshit, poised to pounce, probing to discover your inner reserves and whether you could take umbrage and learn from it. Because if you couldn't, he had no use for you. You might as well quit right now.

Gatward wanted respect, not personal popularity. He operated on some kind of radar that informed him precisely when things might be going awry. He knew when any one of us was losing money on a trade, knew it and disliked it intensely. He treated the firm's money as if it were his own. He was loyal to a fault, and he'd have gone to the barricades for Lehman Brothers.

In my first couple of weeks as an operational trader I found out all about him. One day I had the flu. I was on time and at my post, but I was trying to fight a headache, I felt colder than usual, and I simply was not on top of my game. As usual, the pressure was mounting. The traders were yelling, instructions were being called. I had a client on the line trying to sell $5 million of Calpines, unwinding a hedged position in a convertible bond. I was on my feet, calling a swap trade. I knew full well the bond had a 60 percent delta, which meant that if the stock dropped 10 percent, the bond would lose only 6 percent of its value. For a fraction of a second my concentration slipped, and I did the trade on a 30 percent delta. That left me exposed to Calpine's mountain of debt, which we were about to short massively, and I was suddenly and inadvertently long.

The trading floor is an arena of instant decisions: all traders are called to make markets all the time, to price the stock, price the bonds, buy, sell, or hold. And I'd just made a mistake. A big one. There was nowhere to turn. No one could help. My word was my bond. There was no going back.

Which was precisely when Rich Gatward appeared on my left shoulder, like the angel of death.

"That Calpine trade . . . what delta did you do it on?"

The equity trading floor around me suddenly seemed like the petrified forest. It always does when Gatward comes over. Everyone stops, watching for the scene to unfold. I knew only one thing: I'd shorted only half the stock I should have.

"Ah . . . er . . . Rich, I did it on a 30, but I probably should have done it on a 60."

"What's this word *probably*—what do you mean by that?"

"Er . . . I mean we should have done the trade on a 60 delta . . ."

"How many shares of stock do you need to sell right now to be hedged?"

I grappled for the bond calculator on the screen and hit the buttons as my entire career flashed before my eyes, the way it does, I believe, when you face instant death.

"Forty-five thousand two hundred, Rich."

"Well, don't look at me. Sell the fucking stock," he snapped. I could feel every eye on the floor trained on me, and he was not finished yet. "If you're gonna work on my desk, you don't fly blind. You'd better know your deltas to the fucking penny."

"You're right. I screwed up, and I'm sorry. It won't happen again."

"You're goddamned right it won't, because if it does we're going to have a big fucking problem. Do you understand that?"

"Yes, I do. It was a mistake. It won't happen again. I'm sorry."

"You'd better be fucking sorry. Right here we're dealing with the firm's capital. You're on my watch, and I have an eye on every fucking penny of risk on this desk—and if you have a problem with that, you can get the fuck out."

And with that he stormed off, back to his desk. It was as if the entire place could breathe again. People went back to work and the whole shouting, yelling, tempestuous atmosphere of the trading floor swiftly resumed business as usual.

Reeling from the humiliation, embarrassed beyond belief, I moved back into action. I'd always heard there were guys like Gatward on the big Wall Street trading floors, overseers whose creed was to keep everyone on their toes. I'd never been in any doubt that I wanted to be in the thick of the action, up there at the sharpest end of the business, where the bullets fly and you can get hit during your personal charge to glory.

But this Gatward was something else. He could have landed a job on a Viking ship. He'd just threatened to make me walk the plank, and I'd only just gotten there. But the venom he had unleashed on a staff member who had mistakenly endangered the firm's capital was something to behold. I never spoke about it, but the essence of his words was branded on my mind. These were words he never uttered, not literally, but the message had been hammered home: *McDonald, we only hire the very best people here. And the best don't fuck it up. You want to be one of us, don't fuck it up again. Ever. Hear me?*

It worked too. I never did. Bottom line: I knew he was right. He just wanted to get the very best out of all of his traders. And in case that public roasting ever preyed upon my mind, I kept in my desk a small framed copy of a very famous quotation from America's twenty-sixth president, Teddy Roosevelt: "Credit to the man who is actually in the arena, whose face is marred by dust and sweat . . . who strives valiantly . . . his place shall never be with those timid souls who knew neither victory nor defeat." Just to remind me that I had strived to be right there. It was demanding, it was all hell about six times a day, and it was hard. Real hard. And it was the hard that made it great.

5

A Miracle on the Waterway

It pioneered the early development of the NINJA mortgage—that's no income, no job, no assets. It was a paradise on earth for the sun-bronzed mortgage salesmen who worked hand in glove with the home builders.

I USED TO think occasionally that our colleagues on the fourth floor, the mortgage and property guys, arrived at certain meetings a few minutes after everyone else in order to make a grand entrance. You know the style, like long-ago film stars trying to maximize the applause: the flurried grandeur of Fontaine and Crawford, the sassy tardiness of Monroe and Liz Taylor.

Later, having given the matter due reflection, I adjusted this opinion, and put the lateness of the mortgage guys down to their suspected love of long walks on the lake in Central Park.

In that bright fall of 2004, we were in the presence of gods, the new Masters of the Universe, a breed of financial daredevils who conjured Lehman's billion-dollar profits out of one of the most complex markets ever to show its head above Wall Street's ramparts.

This was the Age of the Derivative—the Wall Street neutron that provided atomic power to one of the most reckless housing booms in all of history. Derivative number one was the fabled CDO, the collateralized debt obligation. This new "technology" was created and perfected in Wall Street's investment banks, including Lehman but especially at Merrill Lynch.*

* Lehman's biggest derivative positions were in RMBS (residential mortgage-backed securities). While technically not a CDO, we will, for the sake of simplicity, refer to them as CDOs throughout the remainder of this book. (A CDO can contain many different types of financial assets, including mortgage-backed securities, corporate bonds, and credit card receivables.)

Like most sensational ideas, this one was simple, and in a sense solidly based. The process began in the offices of large U.S. mortgage brokers, particularly in California, Florida, and Nevada, where the prospect of a fast buck has never antagonized the natives. This was the start of a lending twilight zone, the advance of the shadow banks, places with no depositors, no customers filing in and handing over their paychecks to carefully run commercial banking organizations. The shadow banks would lend, finance, and provide capital for house purchases, but they had to borrow the money in the first place from proper banks, mainly because they didn't have the money themselves. Presto! We have a lender who's not really a lender, a lender who has to *borrow* the money in order to make the loan. Huh?

They began to spring up all over the place, operating under the most creative banners in the history of marketing, naming themselves with comfort titles, ever friendly, ever ready to help—Right-Away Mortgage, No Red Tape Mortgage, LowerMyPayment.com, Deep-Green Financial, LoanCity, OwnIt Mortgage, Sea Breeze Financial Services, Mortgage Warehouse. All shadow banks, just like the giants New Century, Aurora, BNC, and Countrywide.

It quickly occurred to these mortgage houses that if they could provide financing in the very short term, they could then sell the mortgage to one of the Wall Street banks. What they did was package together a thousand mortgages—that's one thousand homeowners who had borrowed around $300,000 each to purchase property. The money had been loaned to these borrowers at an initial annual rate of around 1 or 2 percent, which would be adjusted upward within one to three years. It's called an adjustable rate mortgage, known in the trade as an option ARM. The mortgage house then telephoned Lehman and explained that this package of one thousand mortgages represented a debt of $300 million. It was fully collateralized by the property deeds, and in this boom housing market, when everyone paid up monthly on the wave of soaring prices, it carried zero risk. On a $300,000 mortgage at 2 percent, no down payment, the monthly payment would be $500 a month. Multiply that by 1,000 and you get $500,000. Every month. No bullshit. All Lehman had to do was buy the loans for the $300 million and create a bond by securitizing the debt, just like one of the normal bonds I mentioned earlier. It could then be sold to investors, who could sit back and collect a share of the massive monthly repayments from the homeowners.

In order to buy the loans, Lehman would borrow the $300 million in the short-term commercial paper market. Because the debt was secured by the mortgages, it could be turned into a mortgage-backed security (MBS). Now it was essentially a $300 million CDO bond, which the Lehman traders would slice up into, say, three hundred bonds at $1 million each and take to market as an investment vehicle that would pay as much as a 7 or 8 percent coupon, straight out of the gate. These would be sold in various numbers to major hedge funds, banks all around the world, and major investors, all jumping in for a cut of that interest payment, which might rise to 9 or even 10 percent in two years. (We're simplifying here. Lehman and other investment banks used a technique called assets swaps to, in effect, provide immediate returns to investors, even though some of the mortgages started paying just the teaser rate of 2 percent for the first couple of years).

Now, it did not take long for the original mortgage salesmen to realize that to earn their commission, all they needed was a signature. The head office did not care one way or another whether the loans were sound or not, because the mortgage house would sell them on to Lehman or Merrill Lynch within a month. Lehman didn't much care either, because once the bonds were sold the problem was no longer theirs, and in the rampant housing market that was an extremely fast process, with the bonds being distributed all over the world to banks such as HSBC, Iceland's Kaupthing Bank, or Japan's Mitsubishi.

The final holder of the bond, the distant bank or fund, also held the deeds to the original houses. Which meant that a homeowner in sunlit California could be sitting in a house that was owned by a couple of Eskimos out on the ice floes chasing polar bears, six thousand miles away. *Has the world gone stark raving mad?* I asked myself—or, more correctly, *should* have asked myself. But of course I didn't in 2004. I accepted the words of Lehman's fourth-floor gods that everything was, as the British say, tickety-boo.

One of the great glories of the process was the vast distance it placed between the ultimate lender—say, some hedge fund in Hong Kong—and the person who had taken out the mortgage in the first place, because this had the effect of diluting any complaints there might be. In essence, no one needed to worry whether it all ran smoothly or not. Hence the new gods of Lehman, the mortgage men, were able to take their daily walks on the lake in Central Park, unapproachable by mere mortals like ourselves. They were a study in fine-tuned hubris.

As if their arrogance was not sufficient, Lehman had recruited another battalion to provide the mortgage division with credence beyond even their dreams: all three leading credit-rating companies, Fitch Ratings, Moody's, and Standard & Poor's. These three did much more than just rate the CDOs for risk; they played an integral role in putting the CDOs together. The agencies offered guidance and expertise to the biggest investment banks on Wall Street. For Lehman they investigated the quality of each mortgage and then supervised the packaging of the bond. The agencies instructed the CDO assemblers how to squeeze the most profit from the mortgage-backed securities. Each CDO contained a fair share of good-quality homeowners who were expected to pay on time every month. There were also swaths of borrowers who might be a bit suspect financially, and these mortgages were spread evenly among the CDOs, which lessened the risk of selling any really poor product. Thus I firmly believe that Fitch, Moody's, and S&P were complicit in the entire program, not merely because of their skill in advising on both good and vulnerable mortgages but also because they gave the banks credence, allowing them to issue CDOs with triple-A ratings, signed and certified by the three biggest names in the business.

By the time I reached Lehman Brothers, those CDOs were the bedrock of a new Wall Street bonanza. Corporations such as Lehman Brothers were making fortunes in fees. And so, of course, were the ratings agencies.

All three of them had been handed overwhelming responsibilities by the financial regulators, who had in effect outsourced the monitoring of CDOs. Never had the agencies been on the right end of such an enormous cash cow. CDOs were exploding as thousands of people were given mortgages, and the agencies quickly decided to charge three times as much as normal to rate them. Even early on, there were those who wondered if the three agencies' principal motive for providing the investment houses with favorable CDO ratings might have been money. A couple of years later Moody's reported annual profits of $1.52 billion—almost half of it from the structured financing boom. S&P was not far behind, charging as much as $600,000 to rate a $500 million CDO.

In any event, it was one heck of a plus for Lehman's salesmen to go out with a bond which they could prove was investment-grade rated, because investors needed little encouragement to go for AAA-rated CDOs* that offered the same yield as investment-grade corporate bonds. At least they would, within twenty-four months, when the interest rate on the adjustable-rate mortgages ripped upward to 9 or 10 percent. The bond was solid, guaranteed by the burgeoning housing market, in which prices were rising 10 percent per annum. That's the way it worked—the U.S. housing market had never dropped more than 5 percent in any year since the Great Depression. Plus the bonds were highly rated by either Fitch, Moody's, or S&P, all of which most people believed were some kind of quasi-governmental organizations, and which had spent decades rating stodgy, traditional stocks and bonds.

All of this was being pulled by the ferocious undercurrent of rock-bottom interest rates. Bank rates were hovering near zero, bank interest wasn't worth having, and government bonds were paying so little that most people would have been just as happy burying their cash in their backyards. The ten-year Treasury yield in 2004 was only 4.05 percent. This was the beginning of a vicious cycle known on Wall Street as the "positive feedback loop." So long as China kept churning out underpriced goods and purchasing U.S. Treasury bonds by the shipload, nothing much seemed likely to change. Investors flooded into those mortgage-backed securities to get a higher yield on their money.

The CDOs seemed safe, well recommended, highly rated in the hottest market around—a market with a fantastically low default rate. The real granite-hard backup for these securities was, of course, the house, which cost $300,000 and would swiftly go to $330,000, like every house in the country, up 10 percent per annum. That's the way it worked. The U.S. housing market had never dropped more than five percent in any year since the Great Depression.

And it was making fortunes for my new employers. Which was why the Lehman mortgage guys wore those smug expressions as they walked through the hallways, supremely confident of their judgment, sure of their market, thrilled by the lion's share of Lehman profits they alone engendered.

*Amazingly, AAA-rated CDOs yielded only 10 to 15 basis points more than U.S. Treasuries in July 2006. AA-rated CDOs yielded 20 to 25 basis points more. One hundred basis points is equal to 1 percent.

Unsurprisingly, they became the blue-eyed boys of the thirty-first floor, demigods who rubbed shoulders with the mighty, who saw, and sometimes even spoke to, Fuld and Gregory. There could surely be no higher honor than that. Not at Lehman. Their words were not so much heard as acclaimed; their budgets were enormous, their bonuses magnificent, their freedoms enviable. And the risks they took were nothing short of awesome. In truth, they made the rest of us feel slightly second-class as we toiled away, pitting our wits against the market, making good steady traditional profits, millions of dollars each week, every one of which paled by comparison with the zillions being coined on the fourth floor by the mortgage guys. From our standpoint it seemed everyone was admiring them and helping them. Whatever they needed—extra budget, permission for more risk, permission to invest colossal hunks of the firm's capital in their market—they got.

Their most important helpers, however, were unseen, unsung, hardworking toilers in the market, a bit like ourselves in many ways. I refer to the mortgage salesmen out in the golden West, that Shangri-la where the locals shiver, gripe, and moan when the temperature drops below 72 degrees in January. The place where sales reps look like bodybuilders, toned and bronzed, teeth like piano keyboards, surfboards in the back of their cars. California, where the living is easy, and mortgages are even easier. Somewhere out there, a vast army of these salesmen was writing mortgage deals for people who wanted, in many cases, a first home.

Of course, in times past, buying a home required sufficient personal capital to make a sizable down payment, usually 20 percent, sometimes a little more. It also required the person to sit right down in front of the banker or mortgage executive and prove beyond a shadow of reasonable doubt annual income, job, and prospects of remaining employed. In many cases people were asked what they proposed to do about the mortgage if for any reason they became unemployed. And honesty was a watchword, because the local banker was an integral part of the community, a familiar figure, who shared schools, sports, and friendships with many of his clients. These were the standards of American banking, and they had stood the test of time, the pivotal issue being in every case the reliability of the customer and his ability to repay the money his home had cost.

But as the year 2004 drew to a close, there was a brand-new culture in real estate. The mortgage broker was no longer the lender, because he was about to unload the whole package, one thousand mortgages at a time, to Lehman Brothers or Merrill Lynch for the now-well-established parceling-out process, masterminded by the ratings agencies, Fitch, Moody's, and S&P. So the brokerage house did not care what happened after that, because they no longer had their own capital on the line. And those bodybuilder salesmen, those affable Californians, were free to run amok among lower-middle-income earners and sell them anything they darned pleased. There were no standards, no consequences, no responsibilities, and no recriminations. Because, and I stress this once more, nobody cared. There was no need. The brokerage firms could sell any and every mortgage they wrote, sell it on to Lehman Brothers or Merrill Lynch, or any other major U.S. bank, on faraway Wall Street.

No team of salesmen ever had a more liberal, freewheeling brief. Just sign up the prospect, write his mortgage, and collect your commission. Needless to say, this heaven-sent career path attracted literally thousands of a certain type of salesman. One of the biggest of the California brokerage houses, New Century, a corporation with many, many direct lines to our mortgage-backed securities trading floor, staffed 222 branch offices coast to coast and used a network of 47,000 mortgage brokers, many of whom worked in their "satellite offices"—that is, their apartments or cars. Those salesmen were applying deceptive, high-pressure tactics to people who never even realized they needed a mortgage, never mind a refinance, or a reverse mortgage, or a no-documentation mortgage, or an adjustable-rate mortgage, or a balloon mortgage, or a cash-back mortgage, or an easy-money mortgage, as advertised by the more ruthless of the breed on local gospel radio stations. There was a whole new language evolving, creating selling strategies that had never been heard of before. What the hell's a balloon mortgage? What do you mean, an easy-money mortgage? Don't ask, for Christ's sake—they'll try to sell you one.

For the record, an easy-money mortgage is a mortgage for $330,000 on a house that costs only $300,000. The salesman just hands over the change to the homeowner. *Sir, I'm not just offering you a brand-new home; I'm about to write you a check for $30,000 for yourself. What could you possibly be doing with your wife and children in this little apartment when I'm right here to change your life? Just sign here. And don't worry about the repayments. We start off at 2 percent, go to* *maybe 10 percent, but not for another couple of years. By then your property will have increased in value. Don't worry about it.*

Every day, there were around half a million mortgage salesmen working California alone, out there pitching, signing up more and more prospects, and to hell with the consequences. More than 40 percent of all U.S. subprime mortgage lenders originated in California. It was easier to finance a new house than it was to finance a new car. In fact, it was cheaper to buy a house than rent an apartment. No wonder those mortgage brokers made more money than any salesmen ever made since records began. And all roads led, ultimately, to Wall Street, especially to Lehman Brothers, fourth floor, where the mortgages were being flipped into CDOs, sliced, diced, packaged, and shipped on to Reykjavík, London, Dublin, Frankfurt, Hong Kong, and Tokyo.

We were watching an almost unprecedented bonanza. And from where I stood on the Lehman trading floor, it was a bonanza that had to be respected. The fourth-floor guys were making this banking corporation enormous profits, and no one could deny that. Their status was beyond question, and no one had come to any harm yet. Their performance was not far short of miraculous. I didn't think we'd need to buy wine for the Christmas party, since the mortgage guys could probably produce chateau-bottled vintages from tap water, a technique hitherto regarded as a dying art.

There's one thing I definitely know about miracles: they hardly ever happen. But I was watching one, the mystical transformation of debt, some of it highly shaky, into one of the biggest profit booms seen on Wall Street for years. Thousands and thousands of people, from faraway places, all contributing to our balance sheet on the anvil of the fourth-floor number crunchers. Everything I had ever been taught, everything I had ever learned, suggested that such seemingly miraculous events rarely last, and occasionally end in catastrophe.

And yet, and yet . . . There seemed to be no end to the irresistible force of the United States housing market as it rolled straight ahead, crushing all objections, problems, and hesitations. That market lumbered its way forward, muttering its omnipotent creed: *The U.S. housing market has never dropped more than 5 percent in any year since the Great Depression.*

My personal instincts were plainly out of sync with the Lehman philosophy. Hell, we were the leaders in this property rampage; we'd helped invent the CDOs, and no one could sell these gold-edged derivatives better than us. I didn't dare mention even a semblance of doubt, not to anyone. That would have been tantamount to high treason, as if the president of the United States had invited Osama bin Laden to Camp David for the weekend.

Still, without one iota of reason, evidence, or fact, I wondered. Deep in the night I wondered. Sometimes I went to sleep trying to make sense of the billion-dollar mortgage debts against our breathtaking profits. And then, four days before Christmas something happened. Something that was a puzzle more than a truth, and it did not occur to anyone else. At least I don't think it did. No one ever said anything. It occurred perhaps only to a guy like myself, a natural worrier, who had been lying awake at night, wondering.

Four days before Christmas, December 21, 2004, the news flashed onto my screen. Franklin Delano Raines—named for the thirty-second president of the United States—had suddenly quit his exalted post as chairman and chief executive officer of the colossus of the Federal National Mortgage Association, Fannie Mae to the rest of us. The first black man in history to head a Fortune 500 company was now history himself. He accepted what was being called an early retirement, but in truth, he was trying to duck out from under shocking allegations of accounting irregularities—cooking the books to increase his multimillion-dollar bonus.

Franklin Raines, a graduate of Harvard Law School and a Rhodes scholar at Magdalen College, Oxford, served in both the Carter and Clinton administrations. His departure from Fannie Mae was not a surprise because of the serious investigations being conducted by the Office of Federal Housing Enterprise Oversight (OFHEO), the body that regulates the largest American financer and guarantor of home mortgages.

But what did surprise me was another related item that suddenly zipped onto my in-house screen within hours of Raines's controversial departure. Fannie Mae was issuing, through Lehman Brothers, a massive $5 billion deal—$2.5 billion convertible preferred and $2.5 billion straight preferred stock. It totaled one of the biggest convertible deals I'd ever seen. And they wanted it done fast. Real fast. By December 30.

I sat at my desk for a few minutes and mentally digested that. And then I thought, *Here we are in the biggest, can't-get-beat housing explosion for half a century, and the government-backed mortgage house, the biggest in the country, suddenly needs urgent cash, emergency cash, in a big hurry, right out of the Last Chance Saloon, in the middle of the friggin' Christmas vacation. Now* that *I don't understand.* Was there a connection between that and the removal of Franklin Raines from power? Could this sweet-talking son of a Seattle janitor have taken so much of Fannie Mae's money for himself he'd wiped them out? Plainly not. Not to the tune of $5 billion. But he'd obviously done something pretty spectacular, since he'd managed to pay himself $90 million in bonuses, and OFHEO wanted it back.

Raines had been behind a strongly promoted policy at Fannie Mae to issue bank loans to people with low to moderate incomes and to ease their credit requirements. By the time of his "early retirement," Fannie Mae was already buying up subprime loans and loading up on mortgages from all kinds of shadow banks.

Now, in the space of a few hours, Raines was out, and Fannie Mae was acting as if they were on the breadline, being asked by a government agency to restate its earnings, marking them down from $9 billion to $6.3 billion.

Something's wrong here, I thought. But I had to get back to the task at hand: the $5 billion in preferred stock had to be sold overnight, and my group was in charge of the operation. It was a sensational piece of business, selling what was virtually a government bond for a 2.5 percent commission, adding up to a $125 million fee for Lehman. Rich Gatward and our convertible securities sales team stayed up all night to complete the deal, because the bond market never closes. When it's 8:00 P.M. in New York, it's 10:00 A.M. in Tokyo, 9:00 A.M. in Beijing, Shanghai, and Hong Kong. At 11:00 P.M. in New York they're trading in Bombay. At 3:00 A.M. in New York they're open in Munich and Rome. At 5:00 A.M. on Wall Street they're trading Brent crude oil in London.

As daylight broke over Manhattan and the team wearily put the finishing touches to the gigantic deal, everyone was pretty tired, and I was still wondering just why the biggest U.S. mortgage operators, backed by the federal government, in the most reliable property market for years, should suddenly require a huge and instant injection of capital, when they should have been opening their Christmas presents or decorating the tree.

Maybe some politician was sick of them asking for money. Maybe the antics of this Raines character had seriously pissed someone off, and they'd temporarily slammed the door on Fannie's credit with the government. But something did not add up, and around here things were supposed to add up.

Despite that long night's work on the preferreds, the plight of Fannie Mae remained. All through that morning we were hearing the occasional bursts of good news from the fourth floor, and for me, this made the contrast even more pronounced. By lunchtime, however, I'd cast my disquiet aside. *Face the facts, Larry: those guys upstairs are in the driver's seat, Fannie Mae or not.*

Business was so sensationally good they'd decided to cut out some of the several middlemen involved in the process of creating the CDOs. Lehman had been permitted to purchase a couple of real bucket shops, mortgage outfits with thousands of salesmen out there pressuring old ladies into loans they didn't need and might not be able to pay back. We owned those teams of salesmen, and they gave us one hell of a start on the opposition. But if anything ever did go wrong, Lehman Brothers would surely take their share of the blame. For the moment, though, there was no blame, just glory, profits, and other miracles.

The bucket shops I referred to were both out west. One was called BNC and was located in Irvine, California, a town southeast of Los Angeles and about five miles inland from Newport Beach. The second was Aurora Loan Services, out of Littleton, Colorado, a suburb of Denver, due south of the mile-high city. The temptation of the housing explosion in California had proved too much for Aurora, which had opened a large office in Lake Forest, ten miles down the coast from Irvine, in the shadow of the Santa Ana Mountains. I don't know what it was about that area, but New Century—a broker we did not own—was in Irvine too, headquartered in a huge black-glass palace, writing the mortgages and selling them right on to Wall Street, mostly to us.

Lehman had owned a stake in Aurora since 1997, which was well before most investment banks even dreamed of owning a mortgage broker. They had bought a piece of BNC in 2000. But by now, Christmas 2004, Lehman owned them both outright, which was a situation made in heaven for fleet-footed bankers, traders, and salesmen, because the mortgage brokers were not regulated by any government agency, unlike retail stockbrokers or real estate agents. The mortgage brokers could do anything they pleased.

And Lehman was an outstanding owner. They transformed Aurora from a small loan servicer into a nationwide lending powerhouse in the Alt-A market—that's one level above the subprime candidates, people with less risky credit scores who were able to swing at least a small down payment. However, the Alt-A loans required little or no proof of income—no formal documentation. These were known in the business as no-doc loans.

Aurora also had offices in Sunrise, Florida, and Florham Park, New Jersey, and Scottsbluff, Nebraska. They had twenty-five hundred employees, with sales reps earning six-figure incomes and working eighty-hour weeks to meet the cascading demand for mortgages to buy homes that instantly increased in value.

BNC worked out of a rented 73,000-square-foot space on several floors of an eight-story building out near John Wayne Airport. The rent cost them almost $200,000 a month, but business was sensational and they were writing billions of dollars' worth of mortgages and, like Aurora, feeding them back to Lehman. Thus there were armies of salesmen out there, with no greater complication in their lives than to get a prospect to agree to a mortgage and sign on the dotted line.

Much of the time the mortgage was out and on its way to Lehman before the ink was dry on the contract. Aurora and BNC could not get rid of them quickly enough. The Lehman mortgage group could not wait to get their hands on them, feeding them into the system, getting them packaged, rated by the agencies, and moved out into the world market as securities—CDOs, the best profit earners on earth. In 2004, BNC and Aurora originated $40 billion in subprime and Alt-A mortgages.

It seemed to me that everyone and his brother was trying to jump onto this bandwagon. Even General Motors, at the time the world's largest automaker, was in on the action. They owned General Motors Acceptance Corporation (GMAC), which operated ResCap, a wholly owned subsidiary that allowed the auto giant to get into the vast home mortgage market. Indeed, in the third quarter of 2004, GMAC, riding the explosion of the shadow banks, made a $656 million profit, perhaps a blessing in disguise, because it masked a $130 million loss by GM on its North American automotive operation.

I could not help thinking what a privilege it was to be working at the trading desk in Lehman Brothers. Because there were times when it seemed like this throbbing merchant bank was the hub of the entire business world. Take the General Motors situation. Because our mortgage guys were right on the front line, buying from the biggest brokerages, which owned mortgages by the thousands, they knew, and consequently we knew, the sheer scale of GM's ResCap operation, and its lifeblood importance to the guys who made Buicks, Chevrolets, Pontiacs, and Cadillacs.

And yet, down here on our floor, there was Jane Castle, poring over her charts, studying the financials of the corporations that made the parts that went into those automobiles. She could see with total clarity what was happening—sales were slowing, and the enormous U.S. factories were slowing with them. You want to know why? Ask Jane. The problem was a world commodity uprising, and she was already expert on the subject.

A couple of months previously she and I had sat in her office and gone over the charts for Tower Automotive. Tower was a global designer and producer of structural automotive components, used by virtually every major car factory—Ford, Chrysler, General Motors, Honda, Toyota, BMW, Fiat, and Renault. They had more than eight thousand employees in thirty-nine factories in thirteen different countries spread over North America, South America, Europe, and Asia. Their specialty was the frame of the car, the steel chassis and suspension systems. In Detroit, Tower was regarded as the endless heartbeat of the industry. But Jane thought they were going bust.

She was looking at the price of steel, which was going through the roof, currently standing at around $800 a ton, having more than doubled in the past several months from $380 a ton. The problem, it seemed, was China, struggling to complete its Olympic stadiums and buying steel from anywhere they could locate it. Their appetite was ravenous, and from where we stood, it appeared half the world's steel production was heading for Shanghai on any given day. In addition, China kept announcing plans to industrialize the entire country. At one point the People's Republic threatened to build twenty cities the size of Chicago, complete with towering steel-girdered skyscrapers, which would have swallowed up just about every hunk of metal on earth, leaving the rest of us to live in friggin' wigwams.

Jane was really negative about the makers of the car chassis. Especially the bonds. She had it in her mind that the high cost of steel was causing the auto companies to cut back, and in her view that must have an impact on Tower Automotive, which she envisioned sitting in the shadow of a mountain of spare steel chassis the size of Tiger Stadium.

It was the new Tower convertible bond that concerned her. It was a senior unsecured convertible bond, which meant that in the event of a total collapse of the company, it ranked number two in terms of priority for repayment. However, the language of the covenants was imperfect. That's my term; Jane had already read the indentures from end to end and considered the language as somewhere between weak and downright diabolical. Should the corporation collapse, Jane thought, both the banks and the straight bondholders would move in, wiping out every single asset, every last steel bar. I was trading the Tower convertible bonds and realized that such a chain of events would put our clients in considerable danger.

Jane felt the situation was so bad that she had already consulted our lawyers, and her view was simple: we should short the Tower bonds and the stock, big-time. In her view, their bank debt of $1 billion was too great; with a slowdown in cash flow, they would go bankrupt, and soon. I agreed with her entirely, and I went up to see Richard Gatward to make our case.

He was very cool about it. I mean that in the modern relaxed sense. "Okay, buddy," he said, "you want to short five million? Let's make it ten." Since the bonds were trading at 78 cents on the dollar, that meant to go in for ten times $780,000, borrow the bonds, get them sold, and wait for their value to decline.

So we went ahead, and waited. November went by, and in December, Tower Automotive bonds crashed by 15 percent, from 78 cents to 67 cents. In the coming weeks they fell much further, from 67 cents to 40 cents. That Jane. That brave, brave little bear had called it. And hardly had the smile faded from her face when Tower crashed again, all the way down to 10 cents on the dollar. They filed for Chapter 11 bankruptcy protection on February 2, 2005.

We unloaded half of our position at 40 cents all the way down to 10 cents, which gave me a trading profit for our department of $5 million. Joe Beggans was trading the straight debt and made $5 million, and Peter Schellbach was trading the bank debt and made $5 million.

The next day, Jane said the bonds had fallen too far and there was still a mountain of steel hanging around somewhere. Yes, it probably was the size of Tiger Stadium.

She told me, "We should get back in at 10 cents, Larry. They could go to 30. But we need to get a few clients together with us and buy all of them, get into a strong position, controlling the entire issue. That way the banks will almost certainly pay a high price to get rid of us, on the grounds of nuisance value. Get Lehman out of the picture, they can form the creditors' committee, sort out Tower, and reclaim their money without a lot of grief from us."

So we went back in, and Gatward and I bought just about every available Tower bond, mopping up the market at 10 cents on the dollar. We nearly traded the bond's initial size that day. That gave us a strong controlling group, and we went into the first meeting armed with lawyers. In fact, Jane went in person, accompanied by our legal counsel, Dan Kamensky. Jane and Dan demanded that the bank respect the legal position of the convertible bondholders, and threatened to paralyze the bank's entire strategy for months if it did not.

The bankers hemmed and hawed, hedging their bets, uncertain whether to plunge in and buy us out. But the market found out, and the rumors drove up the price, with everyone waiting on the banks. When the bonds lifted above 25 cents on the dollar, we went in and sold, all the way to 32 cents, leaving the bankers standing there. Again.

It all made another $4 million profit for the firm, and constituted a very reasonable day's work. Not with the flash and flourish of the mortgage boys, but still, a nice profit, cleverly earned, at relatively low risk, given our seat at the bankruptcy committee, and bondholding in a corporation that owned a pile of steel the size of Tiger Stadium.

The U.S. housing market had essentially gone berserk, and all through the winter of 2005 we heard nothing but roars of triumph from the fourth floor as prices for homes, new and old, continued to climb. And the CDOs with their glorious high yields were selling faster than the properties.

The boom stretched into every part of the country, even the staid northeastern urban strip up the Atlantic coast from Philadelphia to Boston. They were not quite in the same league as the burgeoning markets in the Sun Belt—Florida, Arizona, California, and Nevada—but they were strong and profitable nevertheless, especially in millionaires' enclaves such as the Hamptons on Long Island and Newport, Rhode Island.

House prices were actually creating millionaires out of the most unlikely people. It seemed that every time someone put a residence on the market, it was worth more than it had been six months before. I said *worth,* although I probably meant *cost.* They are not, of course, the same. The phenomenon reached the point where it was a media event, and in newspapers and publications everywhere, there were constant stories and features about the boom, some of them incredulous, but all of them taking it seriously.

It was not until the early spring that we began to hear the first jokes about the housing market. Wall Street is *always* the first place you hear jokes about any national event, political, financial, sexual, or even catastrophic. And the jokes, tentative though they were, involved all those different kinds of mortgages, offered to buyers who didn't need to provide proof of income—you know, the $400,000-a-year bus driver and the $10,000-a-month janitor. Wall Street, which as a rule understands more, or at least should understand more, *always* finds the funny side. Well . . . mostly. Because it didn't matter, did it? Even if the homeowner found it difficult or even impossible to make the payments, that $300,000 house would go up by $30,000 in a year, so everyone kept right on winning.

One name in particular kept popping up on the joke menu: a place called Stockton, the seat of San Joaquin County, east of San Francisco, and one of the largest agricultural areas in the United States, the asparagus capital of the world. Stockton sits on the south side of the wondrous California Delta, that sprawling complex of inland waterways where the mighty Sacramento River flows out of the north and meets the picturesque San Joaquin River washing up from the south. The result is a geographic marvel, a lush and fertile area perhaps fifty miles long by forty miles wide, with spectacular lakes, islands, tributaries, creeks, backwaters, and wetlands, all set some 60 miles east of San Francisco, deep inland, in the California Central Valley, with a wide waterway navigable all the way to the Golden Gate Bridge.

Stockton was one of the locales that pioneered the early development of the NINJA mortgage—that's no income, no job, no assets. It was a paradise on earth for the bodybuilders, the sun-bronzed mortgage salesmen who worked hand in glove with the home builders. Together they were shipping in potential clients by the busload, hundreds of people fleeing east, away from the incredible house prices in the San Francisco Bay Area, and finding hope and shelter in Stockton, where a brand-new four-bedroom single-family home cost only $230,000.

And these slick-talking brokers actually paid you to buy. That NINJA loan was nothing short of a miracle for so many financially strapped families, because it was quite often 10 percent bigger than the amount required to buy the house. You just signed documents that specified a 100 percent mortgage, put the change in your pocket, and moved in. The population of Stockton increased by five thousand every year between 2000 and 2005.

An added advantage for the salesman was that Stockton had the highest rate of illiteracy in the United States. Half their clients could not even read the mortgage contract, never mind comprehend it. One suspects that might apply particularly to the section of the contract pointing out that the artificially low 1 or 2 percent interest rate offered initially would probably increase fivefold or even tenfold in the not-too-distant future, rendering the mortgage unpayable. The body-builders, somewhat playfully, referred to this part as the "teaser," a phrase that was increasingly finding its way into the Wall Street joke lexicon that spring.

I should point out that the Stockton jokes were always surreptitious and never—repeat, never—uttered during any meetings in the Lehman building when the mortgage guys swaggered in with their balance-sheet-busting results for the month. Because they had access to the perfect retort: *We're making this much money because we know precisely what we're doing and because the U.S. housing market always goes up. That's* always, *not sometimes, not usually. So get on with your own very modest activities and leave the big corporate profits to us.*

The trouble was, no one really knew much about Stockton except that it had a population climbing toward 290,000 and consisted of rows and rows of brand-new houses. They were digging up the asparagus fields to build more, and according to one feature I read in one of the financial journals, there were several tons of glossy brochures crammed into mailboxes every day, scams offering people who might not be able to pay their mortgages the opportunity to take out a new mortgage, or a refinance, or a credit card with a million-dollar limit. According to the *Wall Street Journal,* when they called to activate the card, they were sold another loan to pay off the loans they already couldn't pay. The current joke on Wall Street was that Stockton was the only town in America where you had to send in an application in order *not* to get a loan. This was subprime nirvana, attracting the kind of clientele that caused *Forbes* to note that there were 6,750 crimes per 100,000 Stockton residents that year.

I remember reading the article and wondering how many of those particular felons had mortgages that had gone through Lehman and ended up on the books of a Japanese or Icelandic bank. There was not one shred of evidence that the mortgage bonanza would ever go wrong or that house prices would fall, but by golly, if they ever did, Stockton would surely be ground zero for financial crisis. I imagine there were other people sharing my own doubts and skepticism about all this, but it would have been grotesquely unfashionable to state them. Not to mention politically incorrect.

Anyway, my thoughts didn't matter, because the housing market simply would not slow down. For the twelve months through May 1, 2005, U.S. housing prices nationally had already beaten the previous year's record 11.2 percent increase. Right now the increase stood at a whopping 12.5 percent and rising. But the Sunbelt was checking in at around 30 percent. In Florida prices were up 33 percent, in Nevada 31.2 percent, and in California 27 percent—everywhere except Stockton, where the rise was 50 percent. The same $230,000 four-bedroom residence I mentioned earlier was now worth $325,000. And even with some of the interest-rate resets kicking in daily, it was still worthwhile to buy, albeit just, because the market was *still* rising.

When you work on one of Wall Street's major trading desks, there are a million graphs you need to check out, even study, on a daily basis, just so you don't get caught on the wrong side of a trend. One of the main market indicators is the credit spread. This is a measurement between the yield of U.S. Treasury bonds, which carry the smallest possible risk, and the yield of a publicly traded corporate bond. In a smooth market, the Treasury bond will probably yield a rock-solid 5 percent, and a corporate bond rated investment grade (AAA or AA) might yield half a percent more. The language for that on Wall Street is "50 basis points," or "50 bips." Thus when we talk about a credit spread—say, between Treasuries and AAA corporate bonds—we are discussing the difference between those two yields. Typically, we might say, "This bond is trading 50 bips wide of Treasuries." In the case of a junk bond, rated CCC and obviously loaded with risk, you'd expect a very high yield, anywhere from 500 up to 900 basis points, to compensate the bondholder for the fact that he might lose all his dough. Risk and reward: the oldest rule in finance. That's basically what the credit spread is measuring.

In the early spring of 2005 the spreads on junk bonds were becoming ever tighter. In the seven days leading up to May 21, they came down another 100 bips, to 400 basis points. A CCC junk bond was now paying a coupon of just under 9.00 percent, against ten-year Treasuries that were paying 4.30 percent, and a few months before in March, the yield on the Lehman Brothers High Yield Index was as low as 6.80 percent, a credit spread of just 250! By any standards that was a tight squeeze, but nobody cared. Everyone had become cavalier about risks in this raging bull credit market. Everyone was taking them, because of the near-insatiable desire to earn something on their money. With the banks paying only 2 or 3 percent and a truly staggeringly low default rate in the housing market, with billions of free dollars circulating in the fabulous credit boom, it seemed to make sense.

But in my deepest, never-tell-a-soul, cross-my-heart-and-hope-to-die, most secretive thoughts, I thought they were taking risks up on the fourth floor in the mortgage department. Sometimes I thought my facial expression might betray my unspoken fears about this property market. But I've always been a pretty good poker player, and I don't think it ever did. And while sometimes I looked around at the top brass in this corporation, at least the ones with whom I came into regular contact, and searched for a flicker of cynicism or annoyance on their faces, I never saw a flash of mild exasperation or even irritation at the men who plainly believed the unstoppable security of the property market was cast into American folklore as firmly as that other set of rules that came down on stone tablets from Mount Sinai.

There was, however, one exception to that, an exception about which I'm colossally uncertain, fearful that it might have been my imagination. But I twice thought I saw my ultimate boss, Alex Kirk, Lehman's global head of high-yield and leveraged-loan businesses, and a huge power in the land, look just a tad hard-faced at some of the more optimistic assumptions coming from the guys who walked on water. On anyone else I might not have noticed, but Alex was a terrific guy, of very even temperament, displaying nerves of steel in all of our trading sorties. He was six feet tall, had an extremely commanding presence, and was never prone to unnecessary displays of emotion.

My observation took place at one of our 7:00 A.M. meetings. The discussion was about the U.S. real estate market, and I thought I noticed something. It wasn't a lapse in concentration, because he was listening intently, no doubt about that. But for just a split second I thought he might say something, and I sensed it might be an unfavorable comment. But whatever it was, he reined himself in and said nothing.

Just before we broke up, to return to the trading floor, I thought I noticed it again. And once more the subject was property. But once more our leader refrained from making a comment, and I never gave it another thought. At least not until we were outside the room. That was when Alex pulled Larry McCarthy and me aside and looked at us with a deadly serious expression.

"This housing market," he snapped, "it's all 'roided up." I quote him with pinpoint accuracy because it was the very first time in hundreds of hours of discussions, both formal and informal, in Lehman's headquarters that I ever heard anyone utter a single detrimental phrase against the mortgage and property guys.

I quote the precise words because he used sports jargon for athletes who have been taking steroids, building themselves up with an illegal drug, mostly for events that require explosive power, such as baseball hitting, track and field sprinting, bike racing, and the like. That's how they describe an opponent: all 'roided up. And Alex Kirk used the phrase to describe the state of the real estate market in various sections of the United States, the ones upon which a large chunk of our balance sheet was poised, and upon which we had truly awe-inspiring risk and exposure.

I actually could not quite believe he had said it, and I could see Larry McCarthy standing there, wide-eyed with amazement. If he'd used the phrase himself, no one would have batted an eye because such inflammatory remarks are expected from him. But Alex? Cool, calculating, select-your-words-with-care Alex? Wow, this was big. "The whole thing is fucking ridiculous," he confirmed, obviously not wanting to sugarcoat the issue completely. And then he added, just for good measure, "This market is on fucking steroids."

The three of us just stood there. And for once Larry was lost for words. He looked straight at Alex, nodded curtly, and held out his right hand. I watched them shake. I witnessed an unspoken bond forged between them. And it was not convertible. We might as well, all three of us, have cut our thumbs with a bowie knife and allowed our blood to mingle, because right there outside that conference room we three had locked our minds into a potential mutiny. And it was one I think we all sensed might one day save this organization, which to a man we believed could be heading for very serious trouble.

Larry finally found his voice. "Alex," he said, "I could not agree with you more. This property market has to be on borrowed time. And we have to get the hell out. Couldn't you just smell the hubris in there, that mindless fucking smugness?"

Alex Kirk nodded. I had rarely seen him look this concerned. And it should be understood that he was a huge presence in the corporation. He was a fifteen-year Lehman veteran, dedicated to the cause. Deservedly, he was an extremely wealthy man. He lived in the most beautiful oak-paneled apartment, with a unique Asian theme, on the Upper West Side of Manhattan, overlooking Central Park. He had an outstanding fine art collection. He was the precise opposite of Richard Fuld, because Alex really liked all of his people, and liked to take them out to dinner, to talk and scheme. (Funny, but even over the sirloins you automatically stayed on your toes in the company of our leader.) He loved to mingle and share thoughts and plans. The 7:00 A.M. meetings were his idea. Communication was one of his many strong suits, and I was always thrilled to be taken into his confidence. Just standing there with the great man, sharing a sacred trust, wondering if perhaps we three alone stood square against the forces of evil, was an honor I still remember and treasure to this day.

But I cannot explain how deadly serious this was. Alex Kirk was thinking on his feet as fast as he knew how. He was developing a strategy, and he wanted it put into play right away. "Okay, guys," he told us, "get straight down to the analysts. Let's locate the major home builders with the highest debt leverage, plus the ones with the most exposure to first-time buyers. We need to get some huge short positions, because if this fucking thing blows, it could take everyone down with it. We have to get hedged out there."

We retreated downstairs, heading for the researchers. Jane Castle was completely preoccupied with two airlines, Northwest and Delta, both of which she believed might go bankrupt before the end of the year. And Christine Daley was up to her ears with General Motors, which she thought could not survive and might take down half of Detroit with it. So Larry and I grabbed Rich Gatward and we put analysts Karim Babay and Pete Hammack on the case, telling them to research the biggest home builders, particularly the ones that were active in California's Central Valley and carried hefty bank debt. In the next few hours Pete pulled them up onto his screen, scanning the building projects in the nation's property hot spots—Marin County, north of San Francisco; the vast developments in the desert outside Scottsdale, Arizona; Florida's Broward County, which sprawls to the west of Fort Lauderdale, in the southern part of the state.

I took a look at Broward County on the map and noticed it included a huge area of the Everglades. I asked Pete whether he thought the goddamned alligators might default on their mortgages, but he treated the remark with the contempt it obviously deserved. He said he had no direct information on that, but there were a lot of stats proving that seventy thousand people a day were going to live in Florida, and so far as he could tell, none of them were alligators.

The housing boom was so widespread it was difficult to know where to start. But we kept coming back to California, and that invariably led to the central part of the state, especially along Route 99, the original old two-lane highway that starts just south of Bakersfield and runs to Sacramento, 350 miles to the north. Along the way, Route 99 snakes through the more populated eastern portion of the Central Valley, towns such as Visalia, Fresno, Merced, Modesto, and Stockton.

One name kept popping out at us: the publicly traded Beazer Homes USA, an Atlanta-based builder currently responsible for literally thousands of new houses. Beazer was operational in twenty states, with the modern specialty of selling dwellings right from the plans, complete with one of the smorgasbord of exotic mortgages, especially the no-doc. But what set this builder apart was that they had purchased a mortgage company, which slotted it into the most dangerous territory, that of vendor financing—they were both building the homes and lending people the money to buy them. Every analyst on Wall Street understood that this was a highly risky procedure. "If this goes wrong," said Pete, "they'll go down in flames." He pointed out their balance sheet, which was currently showing long-term debt of $1.275 billion.

In addition, Beazer was about to issue a brand-new $300 million senior unsecured bond, with a 6.875 percent coupon. This was a classic example of a corporate bond, not secured by assets, being pushed out there to investors, just 300 bips wide of Treasuries—hardly any reward for the risk of such a bond from a corporation already in the hole for more than $1 billion, and trying to lay hands on $300 million more. Just to give you a snapshot of the amount of money involved, $1 million stacked up in $100 bills is a couple of feet high. A billion is more than three times as high as the Washington Monument.

And this was not an AAA-rated bond. Fitch Ratings had stated in the past few days that the Beazer Bond was BB+, hardly a riskless investment. And this suggested we were not the only ones wondering whether Beazer could actually handle this new $300 million debt, which was about to land like a cement mixer on their balance sheet.

But the strongest feeling I had about this construction giant involved the bodybuilders. Most home construction companies worked with the big brokerage houses and had a fairly tenuous connection with the fast-talkers out there selling mortgages. But Beazer actually owned them: it hired them, paid them, nurtured them, prepared their mortgage sales packages. And since neither I nor Larry, and certainly not Alex, trusted those sun-bronzed cowboys one inch, I was assailed by a feeling that I didn't trust their bosses much either. In my view, Beazer was surviving only because of the housing market, and if that market shifted, these guys could easily get caught with their girders around their ankles. My own view was that we should short Beazer, because it did not require a massive stretch of the imagination to envision a sudden housing slowdown, as perhaps supply might overrun demand. At which point there might also be a hefty number of first-time buyers starting to default when the mortgage resets began to kick in. This could leave an outfit like Beazer hanging out to dry with several thousand unsellable homes in a falling market. For a company with $1.3 billion in debt, that would almost certainly prove fatal.

Larry called a meeting for the following morning, to be attended by Rich Gatward and Karim Babay. Alex, if he was in the building, would very definitely sit in. The discussion would center around one of Karim's charts, which showed the Beazer sales graph climbing straight up the side of the mountain the way Yahoo's stock price had in 1999.

We checked all the data, and from where we sat it looked like Beazer was planning to pave over the entire California Delta. They were building everywhere, hundreds of people were already in their new homes, and presumably some of them were starting to pay for them. Karim understood our intentions but was uncertain whether a huge trading short on the corporation was justified. We, however, whose entire expertise was in the distressed-debt market, could see the signs, and Larry McCarthy was all set to throw a barrel at them, because Beazer was the one company that fitted all of our criteria. We decided to deploy 100,000 shares at $75 each and wait for the property market to cave in, which we thought it surely must. The only problem was, when?

Larry McCarthy took out $500 million worth of protection in the form of a five-year credit default swap. That meant he agreed to pay a 1.8 percent* carry on the $500 million, which was $9 million annually. However, if Beazer filed for bankruptcy, Lehman would be paid the $500 million,† provided the counterparty on the other side of the trade had the ability to pay. In addition, we all bought equity options—another bet that Beazer would crash, but in this case in the form of puts, which came into play if the stock went down.

That meant we'd unleashed all our artillery at this Atlanta builder: the shorts, the swaps, and the puts. And all because each and every one of us had an instinct that the real estate bonanza would probably not continue, and we suspected those mortgage resets could bring the whole market to its knees in the not-too-distant future. In a strange way, the guys upstairs making all the money while the going was good were our Public Enemy No. 1, because their risks were gigantic, and they appeared not to sense the potential danger.

When a high-rolling market goes wrong, history tells us it happens with lightning speed, as everyone stampedes for the door at the same time. Just imagine if Lehman was caught with a half dozen of those billion-dollar mortgage securitizations, the CDOs. Imagine if suddenly the guys who walk on water were no longer able to sell those CDOs, if the market just dried up because the defaults were too great in number. Holy shit! That really could be goodnight Vienna. Trouble is, when things have gone so right for so long, some traders tend to go soft, often failing to keep their guard up, failing to dodge the bullet that would kill them.

*Lehman would be paid the $500 million, less the recovery rate on the bonds.

†Beazer Homes' five-year CDS spread in 2005 was on average 180 basis points over the London Interbank Offered Rate (LIBOR). When an investor buys $500 million of CDS on a corporation like Beazer Homes, unlike buying a bond, the CDS investor (our counterpartyon the other side of the e-trade) does not have to put up $500 million in cash. We, as buyers of the CDS protection, are simply responsible for paying a premium (or cash flows above LIBOR to the counterparty) and can get paid as much as the face value if the corporation defaults. So in the Beazer example above, we were responsible for paying the 1.8 percent per year of $500 million at the time of this trade.

I'd never heard one sentence from any of the mortgage guys that would suggest they were ready to take cover in the event of a market correction. In fact, we were once more hearing rumors that Lehman was giving serious consideration to the possibility of buying New Century, the California mortgage brokerage.

I remember walking home after our meeting and reading a report Jane had given me. It actually caused me to stop dead on that summer evening and give thought to the possibility that the entire world had lost its marbles. It was an account of some Miami high-rise that had not yet been built, and there were reports of real estate speculators actually buying off the plans, holding the "apartments" until the foundation was laid, and then selling at a profit. Buying property and then turning around and selling it for a quick profit is known in the trade as flipping. But in the past, most people used to ensure there was some real estate to flip. What was going on in Miami wasn't flipping real estate. It was flipping fresh air. There was no real estate, just a 3,000-square-foot pocket of warm air twenty-three stories above the ground where one day an apartment was planned to be.

But what really caught my eye was the fact that this was apparently being done online. The deals were being conducted in cyberspace. The buyers had never even seen the building site, probably never even been to Miami. And they were making money from some computerized selling network hundreds of miles away. This was not a raging bull market where great fortunes were being made by the shrewdest operators. This was nut country, a simple demonstration that the whole property world appeared to have gone mad. I stood there on Seventh Avenue wondering whether that empty space up in the sky somewhere over South Beach had increased in value in the few minutes I'd been goofing off on a Manhattan sidewalk.

6

The Day Delta Air Lines Went Bust

I called the same price, 16 cents, and then we got hit again. Another five million, and then again. Instantly I dropped the price—"Fifteen, seventeen!" And our client took it. "You're done!" I yelled.

ON MONDAY, June 6, 2005, at 2:03 in the afternoon, I received one of those e-mails that *really* mattered. It came directly from Alex Kirk, and it announced the special nature of the next day's 7:00 A.M. meeting of the traders. There would be a guest speaker: Mike Gelband, a newly promoted Lehman managing director and global head of fixed income, a man most of us hardly knew. I'd seen him only two or three times before, spoken to him once, But Mike's immense reputation had preceded him.

He was a twenty-year Lehman veteran, mid-forties, with a closely shaved head and gold-rimmed glasses. Six feet tall, broad and athletic, Mike reminded me of Steve Seefeld—you did not instantly know how clever he was, but you sure as hell knew he was a lot cleverer than you. He was one of the best and bravest traders in Treasuries and mortgages Lehman had ever had, a corporate icon. It did not matter which department you worked in, you knew precisely who Mike Gelband was. And when he spoke, people stopped what they were doing and listened.

Mike had earned his MBA in 1983 at the University of Michigan, home of the Wolverines. He graduated from the celebrated Ross School of Business, long ranked among the top five business schools nationally and considered by the *Wall Street Journal* to be "very probably No. 1."

Mike lived out in fox-hunting country in Short Hills, New Jersey, with his wife and four children. On our floor, he occupied the northwest corner office, and was reputed to be one of the hardest, most meticulous workers in the entire building. He was an "inside man" and not naturally inclined to spend time with people socially. He played a lot of poker, which I think suited his temperament, because Mike was a studious character, somewhat like Bill Gates—not quite a financial geek, but close. To this day, I've never met anyone who could grab and comprehend a difficult new idea faster than Mike Gelband.

Anyway, he was to be our special guest speaker, and there was something about the way that e-mail was written that suggested Alex Kirk understood this was not likely to be a routine Tuesday morning gathering. Alex actually showed up at my desk in person about twenty minutes later to make sure Larry McCarthy and I understood this was a very important meeting and to make certain we would be there. Some of the guys occasionally skipped the Tuesday morning get-together because of domestic stuff like taking the kids to school. June 7 would not be one of those Tuesdays.

During the day, I was surprised how few people expressed curiosity about the Gelband meeting, believing it was just to introduce him on the heels of his new promotion. That was not quite how I read it.

It quickly became apparent that all the high-yield, distressed-debt, and high-grade traders were under orders to attend. Christine and Jane both told me they would be there, and so would almost every other research analyst on the floor. Alex Kirk's e-mail had stated there would be a half-hour presentation from Mike and then a fifteen-minute question-and-answer period.

And so, on that warm, clear June morning, shortly after 6:45 A.M., we gathered in the third-floor conference room. There must have been forty-five of us in there, all the traders and researchers, and anyone who could not tell this was an important briefing simply did not possess antennae. The atmosphere was charged. Alex Kirk was already seated when Larry McCarthy and I arrived. Mike Gelband was right next to him, and the two of them were in close conversation. Before them was a pile of presentations, which were immediately distributed among us. They were about thirty pages thick.

When the last person arrived and the clock clicked over to 7:00 A.M. precisely, the door was closed. It was as close to a special forces military briefing as anything I'd ever attended. I was rather surprised our cell phones were not confiscated, thus severing all connection with the outside world.

With the presentations now before us, virtually unread but intended to be a permanent record of the proceedings, Mike formally, and unnecessarily, introduced himself as Lehman's new global head of fixed income. There was not a soul in that room who did not understand exactly who he was.

As a hotly illuminated example of failing to beat about the friggin' bush, this one was right up there. Mike said flatly that in his opinion the U.S. real estate market was pumped up like an athlete on steroids, rippling with a set of muscles that did not naturally belong there. Those muscles gave a false impression of strength and in the end would not be sustained. He pointed accusingly to a massive amount of leverage in the system: money that was not real money, home prices that were not real prices, mortgages that were not grounded in any definition of reality with which he was acquainted.

He cited the shadow banks, the vast complex network of mortgage brokers that were not really banks at all but managed somehow to insert themselves into the lending process, making an enormous number of mortgages possible while having to borrow the money themselves to do so. He cited outfits such as Countrywide, New Century and NovaStar, among others, and he accused them of creating well over $1 trillion worth of economic activity that was comprehensively false money and would *never* be converted into genuine economic power.

You could see by the faces around the table that many members of the gathering found this somewhat bewildering. But Mike continued relentlessly. "Many U.S. economists are completely out of touch," he said. "They do not understand derivatives in the property business and how those derivatives provide a huge and totally unacceptable stimulus to the economy. Unacceptable because they are demonstrably false. But in effect they are more powerful than a Reagan-Laffer tax cut because they make everyone feel richer; they make people believe they are richer."

He had something like twenty analysts led by the highly respected Shrinivas Modukuri working on this study of the causes and effects of the real estate boom and how it was being conducted out there in the market. Gelband knew all about the bodybuilders and their methods. He knew all about the exotic mortgages and the way they were being sold to the lesser intellects of the American population. He cited the interest-only loans, the no-down-payments, the no-docs, the negative amortization loans (that's the one where the loan gets bigger as you pay), and the optional ARMs, which gave you a good cheap run for a couple of years and then knocked you clean out of the box with huge rate rises on the reset. His study concluded that by the end of the current year—2005—one-third of all mortgages issued in the United States would be of the highly dicey, buy-now-pay-later variety. His assessment suggested that the number of buyers obtaining mortgages but putting down no money would almost double compared to 2003. In his view this was a nuclear-fueled catastrophe waiting to happen.

He assured us that the bodybuilders were earning double commissions on these mortgage sales and were thus operating with incentives beyond all known reason. They just needed to sell, collect their double commission, and press onward to the next victim. The consequences were relevant neither to them nor to their employers, who were merely selling the mortgage packages to Wall Street. That was us, in case anyone hadn't noticed. Not a one of them, neither the commission guys nor the mortgage brokerage houses, shared one iota of the responsibility should the homeowner, for any reason whatsoever, find himself unable to make the repayments. In Mike's opinion, this process posed the greatest threat to the U.S. economy, and it would hit home in 2007 and 2008. "You cannot," he said, "model human behavior with mathematics. There's no computer model that will ever tell you whether someone will pay their mortgage. And there never will be. The risk will always be there. You cannot calculate it. Risk and reward are beyond the intellectual limits of a computer."

In the meantime, so far as he could tell, there was already a rapid increase in the number of homeowners who were starting to draw equity out of their properties in this sensational rising market. A new phrase was creeping in: HELOC, home equity line of credit. It referred to the process of turning your home into an ATM machine, drawing out cash against its rise in value. That's the extra money not required to collateralize the mortgage. Might as well cash in, right? Mike's guys were estimating this ATM extraction against homes in 2005 would hit $200 billion, and the next year $260 billion.

His report also demonstrated an enormous amount of discretionary income going into homes over the next three years. "It's a figure that will skyrocket," he said. "And it's all leverage, essentially false money from false housing prices and false mortgages that may never be paid." Mike was plainly appalled by the research showing that massive mortgage resets would be occurring soon: a total of probably $325 billion resetting to higher rates in the next twelve months, and $490 billion over the next thirty-six months. He wanted to know what the hell good it was to reset a guy's mortgage rate from a repayment of, say, $400 a month, the teaser rate, to $2,000 a month if the rate shot up to 8 percent or $2,500 if it went to 10 percent. What the hell was that all about? A goddamned baboon could tell you the poor bastard couldn't pay it. I have to say, the room was stone silent, transfixed by the sound of Mike's voice.

Next he turned his firepower on the feckless government mortgage giants Fannie Mae and Freddie Mac, which had issued their own estimates of that ATM number over the next couple of years. In a gigantic discrepancy, they were billions of dollars on the light side, and Mike plainly regarded those estimates with the same unbridled contempt we all had for Fannie's recent balance sheet, which had misstated its profits by a mere $2.7 billion—nothing serious, obviously. Mike blew their ATM estimates out of the water and declared the new financial mortgage products were masking the actual leverage debt in the U.S. economy. He pointed out that steep resets signaled some kind of death march for mortgage holders, because if they didn't meet the new minimum payment, the principal would go onto the back end of the mortgage and it would never be paid.

There was no one in the entire building who did not understand that a monumental fortune was being made from the CDOs and that Lehman Brothers was buying up $300,000 mortgages ten thousand at a time, parceling them out into collateralized bonds, getting them highly rated by the agencies, and moving them into the market—$1,000 bonds, sold in tranches. A 1 percent commission on a $3 billion bundle of collateralized debt like that adds up to $30 million on the Lehman revenue line while that $3 billion bundle stays on the Lehman balance sheet until they are sold. Mike Gelband's pitch was that these huge CDO numbers masked an enormous problem. That thousands of these mortgages had been issued to people who ought never to have been living in a $300,000 home anyway, and those mortgages were about to tank.

How about the market caves in and we get caught with around twenty of those big $3 billion securitizations and can't sell them? That was Mike's unspoken question. And there was, of course, another, also unspoken: *What happens then? When we're hanging out to dry for $60 billion and the CDOs cannot be sold because every other son of a bitch in America is trying to sell at the same time? How about that?* At this time the firm was leveraged to twenty-two times its net worth, and we were playing with money we didn't really have, betting on an outcome that could go wrong.

Everyone could see there was not one member of Lehman's mortgage department sitting in on the meeting. This was a special briefing, and it was clear that Alex Kirk and Mike Gelband had already conferred about this perceived danger to the corporation. But this was the first time we had heard it actually put into numbers, the language we all understood. And everyone could see Mike really meant it, that it had been on his mind. We could also see that Larry McCarthy and Peter Schellbach agreed with every word he was saying. And it should be understood that this kind of brutal talk was being conducted in a place where the exploding real estate market was making us fortunes in profits, that our mortgage guys were riding the wave, investing and winning, risking huge amounts and coming out in front on the gamble by selling the mortgage packages to banks, funds, and investors worldwide.

The question that now stood starkly before us was, were they locked into a bubble, and was it likely to burst anytime soon? No one knew the answer to that, any more than we could know that the raging U.S. property market would make its first downturn in decades less than six weeks from now, and that this summit meeting was being conducted at the very pinnacle of the market—at a time when the mortgage guys were still able, with consummate ease, to stroll on the lake in Central Park.

No one was in any way ready for Gelband's bombshell. No one had ever heard anyone else in the entire organization even attempt to break down the data on the housing market, far less arrive at what appeared to be an irrefutable conclusion that it could not possibly go on like this. There were many young bulls in the room who were doing a little shrugging and rolling their eyes heavenward, kids without fear in the teeth of the gale that now blew through us. They were, nonetheless, kids. Kids who had never seen a bear market, whose antennae had not properly developed. They were kids who did not comprehend one simple truth about Wall Street: that if you cannot hone your instincts to react to big trouble when it comes stalking across the horizon, you will ultimately be ripped to shreds by the monstrous anger of the market.

The only people in this room whose expressions betrayed profound concern at the words of Mike Gelband were the proven best brains on the trading floor. I noticed Alex Kirk, Larry McCarthy, Peter Schellbach, Joe Beggans, Pete Hammack, Jane Castle, and Christine Daley all frowning, unmistakably concerned by the words of one of Lehman's master traders and risk takers.

And because he delivered his conclusions without interruption, Mike inevitably sounded isolated, as if he was somehow moving forward but carrying a huge burden all alone. Except, that in a sense, we all went with him—Alex, Larry, me, and the rest. Looking back, it's clear that Mike's performance was a chilling one, with him standing up there against the surge of popular opinion, in near-defiance of both the president and CEO of the corporation and their cohorts. It took a lot of courage, in my opinion, but I guess that's what you expect when you have a Wolverine standing guard at the gates.

When the meeting ended, Alex Kirk stood up and advised us to think carefully about Mike's conclusions, because they were very important. He advised discretion when the subject was raised, but informed us that Mike intended to hold a less candid meeting with Dick Fuld and possibly Joe Gregory later that afternoon.

I left the meeting with Larry, who looked about as grim-faced as I had ever seen him. "Funny," I said, "but there were so many people in there who plainly didn't agree with Mike."

"Funny?" he growled. "More like fucking tragic. Last time we had a bear market, those kids were in diapers." Larry had a way of taking a salient point and kicking it straight between the posts. I guess it was the gambler's instant acceptance of the way the cards were falling, the lightning grasp of danger. But I think in that moment we were both determined to assist Mike in any way we could. Inwardly, I vowed to keep my eyes open for any and all indications that the real estate market might be heading south sometime in the foreseeable future.

I actually promised myself more than that. I would spend some time each day searching the databases for clues that things were moving the wrong way. I understood that there would be only slender indications, and that they would be concealing mammoth consequences. But in my view, it was the duty of everyone who occupied a position of trust to act as Lehman's sentries in what we believed might be a fragile situation.

And, of course, all of us had disquieting thoughts about the reception Mike Gelband could expect when he dropped his personal hand grenade onto the floor of the mortgage and property department. The question was, would even those guys dare to cross swords with him, seeing as many people thought he would one day aspire to the highest office in the building?

The answer was not long in coming. Without even a formal e-mail or any other form of official communication, we all heard on the Lehman bush telegraph that those guys *had* dared to challenge Mike. In their opinion he was too conservative. One of them had replied to his studies, "Yeah, right, Mike. Have you missed the fact that this bull market's exploding? Right now, we're carrying Lehman's balance sheet, and this kind of talk will have a bad effect on people." Someone else pointed out that real estate schools up and down the East Coast and all over California were packed, no vacancies, and working guys were stampeding out of other professions and heading for real estate offices. There were real estate guys on the television being interviewed, guys who talked about friggin' countertops and views from the goddamned master bedroom, claiming to make a million bucks a year.

I heard one guy that summer on television discussing his three cars: a Mercedes, a Range Rover, and a Bentley. I don't know if he'd paid for them, but the pinnacle of his craft was telling some crazy lady how to work the garbage disposal. Only in real nut country could a guy like that be driving a Bentley and earning as much money as a top Wall Street trader with full honors from Harvard Business School and unbelievable responsibility involving billions of dollars every day.

Right then I seriously began to accept that the real estate market was probably a gigantic bubble. Alex and Larry were sure it would burst, but the general drift upstairs at that meeting was that Mike Gelband had developed some kind of an attitude problem, and it needed to be changed, real fast. That was not, however, the way his views were perceived down here in this corner of the more hard-nosed bond-trading floor.

You probably had it in the back of your mind, but never really brought it forward, that the location of the "World Capital of Creativity" is in Hollywood. But with all due respect to the Burbank crowd, they just may pale when compared to the armies of investment banking teams on Wall Street.

Lehman Brothers had a Chinese Wall separating traders from investment bankers. Beyond that wall was the exclusive little garrison of Lehman's investment bankers, shadowy but self-satisfied folks who could come up with schemes to outwit the Holy Spirit itself. So revered was this group that they were permitted to invent, along with other Wall Street firms, a moneymaking scheme that by the middle of 2005 took off like a whirling dervish and made billions and billions of dollars before finally disappearing up its own backside, helping bankrupt half the planet.

The engine behind this mind-blowing escapade was Ros Stephenson, Lehman's global director of the financial sponsors group. She was a veteran managing director and led the LBO investment banking team. Because of the enormous size of LBO deals coming in at the time and the relatively small size of Lehman compared to big commercial banks, she and the Lehman team should have had a brain-numbingly conservative, careful philosophy, and been, by nature and declaration, highly conscious about risk. And for a long time we imagined she was the safest of managers, until she was handed the sword of the CLO (collateralized loan obligation), which was a new derivative based on the same principles of securitization that had led a hitherto unsuspecting world into the mighty CDO. Except instead of vast legions of new homeowners who might or might not be capable of paying their mortgages, the CLO represented a conglomerate of chancy takeover debts, or leveraged loans, created by people who were busily trying to buy overweight U.S. corporations. The CLO created a new powerful demand for leveraged loans globally. Ros was a beneficiary of this innovation.

CLOs can be explained by starting with the leveraged buyout companies that made it happen: private equity outfits such as Kohlberg Kravis Roberts, Bain Capital, Blackstone Group, Texas Pacific Group, Providence Equity, and Carlyle Group. All of these companies, and many others like them, share certain idiosyncrasies. None of them manufactures any product, none of them sells anything. They exist to make money for their investors. By every known standard, they are predators, but they also represent a stratum of creative genius in U.S. business that had not been matched for many years. Their business is the leveraged buyout (LBO), in which a corporation goes to Wall Street with a glittering prospectus that explains why the company needs $10 billion to buy out, say, a hotel chain. Mostly the investment banks like what they hear and often are willing to make such an enormous loan because it is secured against the thriving business the LBO guys are trying to buy.

You may be among the people who find it a little odd that someone wants to buy a corporation they cannot afford when that corporation is perfectly healthy and profitable and has no need to sell itself to anyone. Which is why LBOs are often hostile takeovers, in which the buyers, armed with borrowed cash from a firm such as Lehman or Morgan Stanley, start buying up the stock in enormous quantities until they gain control of the shares. They then take the company private, start selling off the assets, and repay both the interest and the loan from the profits of the original corporation, which did not need to change ownership in the first place. Another party trick they sometimes use instead is to saddle their new acquisition with an enormous bank loan that is used both to pay back the original loan and then hand over a fat dividend to the new owners. The buyout guys ultimately pay little or nothing for the company, and then feed off its assets and reputation. As an example, in late 2004 there had been a truly spectacular example of three private-equity corporations putting together a leveraged buyout of Mervyn's department stores for $1.2 billion. But no one knew at the time they had foisted an $800 million debt on the company as soon as it was purchased, and paid $400 million of that to themselves as a dividend. (You will doubtless note I did not use the word *predators* lightly.)

In fairness, these private equity funds were filled with some of the most brilliant financiers on Wall Street. They targeted corporations that they believed were either fat, inefficient, failing to maximize profits, or being milked by bad management. They always moved in fast and began stripping assets to pay off their own debts. And then, quietly and privately, they prepared the company to go public once again, almost certainly at a better price than the original shares.

Meanwhile, Lehman, which had financed dozens of these deals, was also parceling the loans into carefully constructed CLOs. S&P, Fitch Ratings, and Moody's were in there handing out AAA ratings like candy bars, collecting huge fees and helping to organize the bonds to be sold worldwide. The difference between these CLOs and the mortgage CDOs was the difference between a raft of corporations and a raft of homeowners. Same system, different players. Same massive fees and profits. Same level of risk—high.

The risk for an investment house such as Lehman was similar in both cases. It involved getting caught with these billions and billions of dollars' worth of bonds and being unable to sell them fast enough. The investment bankers on the other side of the Chinese Wall were honing their product into a viable market entity, and none of them was giving the slightest thought as to how to get out—and certainly not if everyone found themselves heading for the exit at the same time.

The other similarity between the CDOs and the CLOs was the ease with which they would both continue to be sold—confirming, once again, investors' rabid desire for some decent yield on their money at a time when short-term Treasuries were still offering around 3 percent or less. Four to six percent on one of those bonds, collateralized by a public corporation, looked very, very good from where most people were standing.

In a land as innately avaricious as Wall Street, the kind of cold-blooded corporate raiding involved in LBOs is simply too big a temptation for the kind of grotesque personal greed that has slithered through Wall Street for more than a century. And in the middle of 2005, determined to compete with big boys such as JPMorganChase and Citigroup, the powers that guided Lehman's destiny decided to climb in up to their eyebrows in this seamy, high-risk profit engine, which would make such a fortune but, in the end, cost the company something infinitely more precious.

However, in summer 2005, Lehman was getting more than just its feet wet in this fine new adventure. LBOs had exploded on a scale beyond anyone's imagination, and the third quarter of the year produced the best results ever for investment banks. Across the industry, stock sales and mergers and takeovers amounted to $117 billion, which allowed JPMorganChase, Citigroup, Goldman Sachs, Morgan Stanley, Lehman Brothers, and others to share $3 billion in revenue fees. The value of takeovers over three months in mid-2005 was up 41 percent on the previous year. The leveraged-buyout specialists estimated $50 billion worth of takeovers in the same three months, with a year-end figure likely to be around $180 billion.

Lehman's bankers were in a central position during the second-largest LBO in history, when the Hertz Corporation was bought out from Ford Motor Company for a total of $15 billion. There was perhaps a poetic edge to Lehman's participation in this particular deal, since Bobbie Lehman had been such a close friend of his fellow racehorse owner John Hertz, who was also a partner in Lehman. But the two great financiers doubtless would have been astounded at the sheer sophistication of the deal as the Wall Street guys rustled up the cash for the world's biggest car-rental corporation to essentially buy itself for the corporate raiders from New York: Clayton Dubilier & Rice, the Carlyle Group, and Merrill Lynch. This one set the standard, as they put the debt from buying the corporation onto the balance sheet of the Hertz Corporation, repaying it with the company's own cash flow. John D. Hertz was once described by that bard of the casting couch, Louis B. Mayer, as "the toughest man who ever wore shoes." But even Hertz might have flinched from an act of such astonishing opportunism against the business that still bears his name.

But it's unlikely that anything would have made much difference in these days of reborn corporate pirates. Not since Kohlberg Kravis Roberts grabbed RJR Nabisco for $31 billion sixteen years previously had a deal of quite such audaciousness been conducted. And this was only the start. Hundreds more would follow, and Lehman would be among the leading players in the rush for leverage and the subsequent selling of the buyout CLOs on a worldwide scale.

Lehman was often not sufficiently big to join in this jamboree of the giants. But its investment bankers were ambitious, and jealous of their place in the pecking order. Thus when Morgan Stanley and Goldman Sachs started blazing trails and raising money for the buyout boys, the Lehman guys felt they had to join in, at any and all cost. And since they were world leaders in the noble art of selling corporate bonds, it did not take them long to join the top table. One of their first moves was to swoop in and hire Richard Atterbury, the London-based head of Morgan Stanley's leveraged-buyout financial team. Atterbury became co–global head of Lehman's financial sponsors, the group that advised buyout firms. Lehman was the fourth-largest U.S. securities firm, but it ranked only thirteenth among the group of advisors to buyout firms worldwide. Morgan Stanley was number two in this group, and the Atterbury move was a clear indication of Lehman's ambitions.

At that time there was nothing but optimism in the market, but as the hot New York summer continued, my own studies of the financial markets began to reveal one or two very minor but significant pointers. And then one day, during the dog days of August, I spotted two of them, presented in an interconnected mode. According to the National Association of Realtors, sales of existing homes had fallen by 2.6 percent in July, which meant, to a reasonable person like myself, that hundreds of houses had gone on the U.S. market and failed to find a buyer, many, many more than usual. However, sales of *new* homes had risen by 6.5 percent compared to June of that year and by 28 percent from July 2004, hitting an all-time high. Could this, I wondered, be where all those dicey-looking mortgages in the subprime sector were ultimately leading—to homes built by the mortgage provider? I was pretty sure something was going on. And this was confirmed by yet another number: despite the rise in sales, prices for new homes fell by more than 7 percent in July—which was not spectacularly good news for Beazer Homes in any of their endeavors.

For me it posed one almost sinister question: had the housing market reached its peak, or would it come storming back again? The jury was still out, but on August 24, the *New York Times* business section came out with an article headlined "July Slowing of Home Sales Stirs Talk of Market Peak." It did not go unnoticed, but neither did it bring down the ceiling, which it probably should have. The reason was that at this time the trading floor was flooded with optimism because of the new LBOs, which surely pointed the way to the future, and Ros Stephenson seemed to grow in stature with every passing day.

Whatever one may have thought about the moral issue of these buyouts, the buyout team really knew what they were doing, and seemed to be able to turn huge profits on everything they touched. They also seemed extremely reliable, and every month there was a stampede for the new bonds. In 2003 only $17 billion worth of CLOs were issued. By the end of 2005, that number had blasted off to $50 billion. This provided the rocket fuel for the leveraged buyouts. Concern that the housing market might be propelled by legions of people who might not be able to pay their mortgages was not a factor in the world of LBOs, where major corporations were standing behind the bonds. This provided confidence to hungry investors, and even those of us who thought real estate might crash were optimistic about the leveraged buyouts.

Indeed, when the investment banking department posted its profits for the third quarter of 2005, there was a round of applause. They'd made $815 million for the quarter, up 55 percent from the previous year, and up 41 percent from the second quarter. These profits were driven by an all-time record performance in debt underwriting in the buyout game, which accounted for $336 million, an increase of 39 percent over the same period the year before.

The LBOs were a bonanza, but they were someone else's. On our section of the trading floor there were three enormous situations in progress. The first was Delta Air Lines, for which we were the main bond trader and market-maker, and which might be on the verge of total collapse. The second was the massive short position Christine Daley had led us into with Calpine, the squeaky-clean electricity giant with the smoke-screen balance sheet. The third was Beazer Homes, where we held gigantic short positions in a stock showing not the slightest interest in falling further, and Larry McCarthy became daily more likely to wring the neck of the researcher who had led him into it.

Delta was Jane Castle's bailiwick, and her plan was to play a waiting game. Generally speaking, she thought Delta would be driven into Chapter 11 bankruptcy and that the bonds would crash, at which point we should buy, buy, buy, because she, tenacious little Jane, swore to God they were worth more than 50 cents on the dollar. At the moment they stood at 36–38.

Beazer was driving Larry McCarthy nuts. I'd like to say driving him quietly nuts, but that would be a lie on too grand a scale. Beazer was driving McCarthy very noisily nuts. Everything about it was getting to him, especially their profits in the boom markets of the California Delta. Karim Babay had been extremely influential in arriving at our Beazer conclusions, and he above everyone else was tuned in to the foibles of the stock market's home-building sector. On days when Beazer's shares slipped back a little, Babay would without fail come strolling by for a chat about the market, especially the Atlanta builder, which he'd say was about to go into free fall. Thus far he had not been correct, and on the much more frequent days when Beazer shares climbed higher, from our price of $75 up toward $80, Karim seemed to go missing. He doubtless understood the bath you can take chasing a short that won't go down. His absence totally infuriated Larry—*Where is he? Where the hell is he? That's all I want to know. He has to be somewhere, right?* He would set off in pursuit of the elusive researcher, prowling the corridors, checking out the likely retreats for a guy who was afraid to face his accuser. Once, in a fury, Larry searched the god-damned john, checking out the shoes under the doors in the stalls, trying to find Karim and bawl him out over the rising Beazer shares.

With Delta kind of static for the moment and Beazer going up, the only ray of light was coming from Calpine, which suddenly reported a mediocre second quarter with growing concerns about their cash levels, the same levels Christine Daley had flagged a whole year previously. There were announcements that Calpine was mulling over the possibility of selling more assets, trying to reduce that crippling burden of debt. Privately I thought things were looking bleak for the electricity empire, because there was a ferocious battle brewing about claims on their remaining cash, even though they had not yet filed for bankruptcy. Indeed, the New York law firm Strook hosted a conference call after Calpine's first-lien debt holders tried to stop a coupon payment on the second-liens. There were lawyers everywhere, getting ready to fight over Calpine's use of their cash. And I noticed that whenever the subject came up at Lehman, there was a soft tiger-smile on the face of Christine Daley.

Calpine admitted their second-quarter net loss of $300 million was ten times worse than for the equivalent period the prior year. The reasons were reduced electricity generation as well as heavy costs related to canceled service contracts and suspended construction work on several plants. Calpine's shares had dropped a further 56 cents to $3.32, down 16 percent for the year to date. And the situation had obviously unnerved the directors, who were facing the fact that Calpine had posted losses in eight of the last eleven quarters. They'd slashed their wildly ambitious expansion program and sold off assets, but they were still sitting on a corporation with debts of $17.5 billion. That's a pile of $100 bills the height of fifty Washington Monuments—about five miles straight up. The image is useful, because one of the most irritating aspects of modern finance is that the numbers tend to be so enormous that they can't really be grasped.

Christine Daley was still smiling, for she had long ago sensed that the head honchos at Calpine operated their business along the guidelines laid down by *Field of Dreams:* if you build it, they will come. And while those guidelines might have been rock solid when it came to ghostly ballplayers in a cornfield, they did not apply to electricity consumption in the twenty-first century. Calpine was building it, but they weren't coming.

As summer drew to a close the Lehman trading floors remained inordinately busy. The late afternoon of September 14 was typical. People were packing up and heading home. The Yankees were fighting the dying embers of a disappointing season, and the media was in a collective fit of utter depression over the continuing conflict in Iraq. Forecasts of doom, gloom, and endless strife were everywhere, and you'd have thought George W. Bush, the beleaguered president who had rid the world of Saddam Hussein, was the devil incarnate. Gasoline was still flowing freely, but it was costing the West $50 a barrel. Prices at the pump were scaling ever upward, and since President Bush was considered directly and solely responsible for both the Iraq war and the catastrophe that had followed Hurricane Katrina, he was resolutely blamed for the rise.

Perhaps the biggest problem around that September was the price of jet fuel, because that was hitting the airlines hard—and none harder than Delta, which was already reeling from financial blows that would have darn near leveled any airline that ever flew. The great Atlanta-based southern carrier was assailed by an $18 billion debt. In addition, it had $180 million in pension obligations, and every time jet fuel went up by one penny, it cost Delta $25 million annually. Under siege from cut-price airlines, which had slashed hundreds of dollars from basic ticket prices, Delta was consistently flying around with half-empty aircraft. Delta had its back to the wall. It had wrung a $1 billion wage and benefit concession from its pilots, and it had a plan to shed seven thousand jobs by closing down its Dallas operation, but none of it was enough.

Jane had been telling us for several months that Delta was a candidate for bankruptcy, and at eleven minutes after five o'clock on the afternoon of September 14, 2005, she was proved right. It flashed onto my screen—"Delta Air Lines Files for Bankruptcy Protection." And I swear to God, the collective heart of Lehman Brothers skipped about six beats. Larry McCarthy was not in, and as the principal Delta convertible bond trader, I had markets to make.

I was on my feet in an instant. Big Joe Beggans was right there next to me, armed and ready to trade Delta's straight nonconvertible bonds. Alex Kirk was walking directly toward us, fast. I opened up a line to Larry, and I could see Jane making a beeline for my desk, just when I needed her. That's what I loved about her. During any time of crisis she was always right there. Because for the next hour there was going to be pandemonium, as millions of Delta bonds, crashing through the floor, were going to be launched onto the market by people trying to get the hell out of them. Many of those bondholders were our best clients, so we were duty-bound to purchase them, and the hits would be flying like cannonballs. Millions and millions of dollars' worth of Delta Air Lines bonds that no one wanted any longer. Holy shit! My blood was pumping.

Just for a few moments the floor was very quiet, and Alex Kirk, standing right at my shoulder, said quietly, "Steady, Larry. We're ready for this."

I looked at Jane, who was unsmiling. "Stay focused," she reminded me. "They're worth fifty-two cents each, no matter how many come up for sale." What Larry had once said about her flashed through my mind: *Jane can tell you what Delta Air Lines is serving for lunch in first class on their morning flight from JFK to Berlin, and what it cost them. There's nothing she doesn't know about that company.*

I understood the position of most of the bondholders. They'd do darn near anything to get out. But I had to make the market in what would be an avalanche of selling. Millions of dollars depended on my decision, which was I guess why every eye on the entire floor was trained on us, everyone waiting for my first call on the price I'd buy at and the price I'd sell at (though to whom, God alone knew).

Vividly I remember the phones around me ringing. And then, in the middle of this opening salvo, friggin' Northwest Airlines also declared bankruptcy. There was one of those audible gasps around the floor, the noise you hear in a big ballpark when a fastball rips past the batter on a full count in the ninth. Jesus Christ, I thought the roof was going to fall in, because we could also get hit by Northwest bondholders bailing out. But it was too late for strategy. My heart was pounding.

The boss of high-yield sales, Mike Pedone, hurled his right arm into the air and snapped, "Larry, I have AIG on the wire and what do you know, they're a seller. Where are you on Delta? Gimme a bid on five million. I need a bid right now." For a split second I hesitated, and Mike yelled, "They got five million to go! Where are you?"

That's when I called it: "Sixteen, eighteen!" And the moment those words were out of my mouth, Lehman Brothers was committed to an $800,000 purchase, five million bonds at 16 cents on the dollar.

"You're done," I said, snapping out the trader's no-going-back phrase and confirming our first trade in Deltas was now cast in marble. I heard Mike fire out his own confirmation to the customer, "Okay, you're done."

Twenty seconds later, we got hit again—Terence Tucker on the line from converts. "Where are you on Delta? Five million up!" These people were desperate, trying to get rid of their holdings in the bankrupt airline. I called the same price, 16 cents, but the words were hardly out of my mouth when we got hit again for another five million, and then again. Instantly I dropped the price—"Fifteen, seventeen!"—and our client took it. "You're done!" I yelled. Maybe they'd settle at 15, I thought. But they never did.

Lisa Konrad, our distressed-bond sales diva, called out, "I got Silver Point on the line—where are you on Delta right now? Five up."

In the middle of all this, someone wanted to sell about a zillion Northwest bonds. Joe Beggans and I were trying to cope with these twin issues since we traded both Northwest and Delta. Larry was on the phone, and I was trying to talk to him. Amid the all-enveloping frenzy to sell, he bawled down the line, "If Delta goes to thirteen, buy 'em all!"

Three more sell orders came flashing in. Beside me, Joe was talking in all directions—"Hit! Buy! Lift! Ten million up! Where are you on the follow?" He was a trading machine and on that day he was at his best. Everyone was shouting now, the salesmen and the traders, and millions of dollars were changing hands, darn near all of them in the same direction: outward. There was nothing we could do except buy and hope that Jane knew what she was doing. You've heard of the trenches. I was in there. Right above me, the sellers were circling, trying to get in line for a landing, like big passenger jets in a stack somewhere above JFK.

I dropped Delta's price again, to 13, and still the sell orders came in. I guessed the ratio of sellers to buyers was about ten to one. I got hit immediately for another seven million. Larry on the phone bought around $5 million worth. Then Terence, the best salesman I had, bellowed at me, "I got a buyer at fifteen, five up. You want to let some fly right here?"

This was the only buy so far. It was the only lift I'd had all day. *Way to go, Terence.* I took it. Then I dropped the price once more, to 12. Two more huge sell orders came in, and we bought yet again.

Sitting right next to me, Jane said quietly, "We're stealing them, Larry, we're stealing them. Stay focused. They're worth fifty-two cents, trust me."

I trusted her because she knew the reality, not the far-removed fury of the investors and traders. She knew about the lines of gleaming aircraft, the value of the Delta fleet, their name, their reputation, the jet fuel problem that was strangling them, and the murderous debt. But above all she understood that bankruptcy would allow them to regroup, and she knew there was an intrinsic value to those bonds beyond the debt and into the future. Jane could probably have run the airline, and here she was right next to me, telling me to buy at the lowest possible price, telling me I was stealing them as I blasted away at the Lehman balance sheet in this outrageous spending spree.

When the dust finally cleared, Joe and Larry had bought $95 million face-value worth of Delta bonds, I'd bought $40 million, and Peter Schellbach had bought $60 million. When we added all the orders up, the tally when you include those bonds we already owned was about $350 million, buying all the way down to 12 cents, from outfits like Putnam and Fidelity.

There's an old traders' rule: never sell your holdings on a day of bad news. Stay away from the exit door while the mob is trying to get through. Because there's sure to be a bounceback, just as soon as the panic-stricken sellers have all run for their lives.

When the phones finally went quiet, Alex Kirk returned to his office. Jane said jauntily, "Don't worry about it. We're golden." And I sat down for the first time in an hour to assess the situation.

Four of the seven biggest air carriers in the United States were now operating in Chapter 11—that was half the passenger seats in the nation being operated by bankrupt airlines. They'd only recently recovered from the aftermath of 9/11. And now here was Lehman Brothers with a huge holding in Delta's bonds, and I couldn't help wondering how long it would take to climb back to the value Jane so confidently forecast. If she was right, we'd probably make the biggest one-day profit in the history of Lehman. If she was wrong . . . let's not even go there.

The one person in all of the corporation who believed implicitly that Jane was correct was Larry McCarthy. One of the most fearless traders ever to work on Wall Street, he would hear no word against her assessment of the Delta situation; indeed, working in concert with Joe

Beggans, he'd bought $95 million worth of the airline's bonds. He was keenly aware that it might be months before the price rose to the levels Jane predicted. But he was sure of our position. And like all true gamblers, he was sure that his luck was running strong. As a matter of fact, he kept buying all through the next month, whenever an opportunity came up.

The situation at Delta did not really improve. Unrest in the Middle East continued, and the pilots were threatening to strike, which would blow Delta's normal operations apart and cut off their cash flow, their lifeblood. But Larry was adamant. "It's what Jane says. Those bonds are worth a lot more than twelve cents on the dollar. They got fucking Boeings, hundreds of 'em, parked all over Georgia."

It's difficult to grasp the size of the gamble Larry was involved in, just as it's difficult to grasp the type of man Larry was—his astuteness, the speed of his calculations, and the depth of his nerve. You'll have to take my word for it: there was nothing ordinary about him. Larry McCarthy had stepped straight out of a scene from *The Cincinnati Kid*. He had a nose for victory and an instinct for trouble. And when he scented the former, there was no shaking him off.

I'll tell you just one story about McCarthy, and then you'll know precisely what manner of man held those Delta bonds. He and I used to go gambling together. I suppose it was in our blood; there are a lot of guys like that on Wall Street, cold and determined with the firm's cash but addicted to the chase, calculating the odds, the risk-to-reward ratio. I guess we're all junkies for the thrill of being right, of winning, always winning. Anyway, later in the fall of 2005 we decided to go up to the Mohegan Sun casino in Connecticut for a couple of days. After dinner at Michael Jordan's Steak House, we headed for the tables for some blackjack.

I settled into a modest corner where the stakes were around $50–$100. McCarthy went to $100–$500, a spot he had occupied many, many times before. But by any standards you'd have to say the cards were not running for him. He slogged it out, going head to head with the dealer, but nothing could change his luck. After two hours he'd blown a very large hole in $75,000. An hour later he'd lost $100,000. The dealer was pulling seven-card 21s and never busting.

Three times I saw Larry double down on a 10 and then pull a 10, only for the dealer to hit 21. The pressure was relentless, the bad luck apparently endless. But McCarthy never flickered, never stopped smiling, never stopped wisecracking his way through the evening. Never once did he lose his cool, laughing cheerfully with the pit bosses and the dealers, who knew, to a man, that the cards had turned against him before he even started.

After four hours he had blown out $165,000. Nothing had gone right, nothing had been even reasonable. But Larry stayed positive, once handing the cocktail waitress a $500 tip. Finally I took him aside and told him, "Come on, buddy, this is a disaster. I've calculated your losses. You're down a hundred and sixty-five thousand. Let's call it a night."

I'll never forget his reply. He stared at me hard and said, "This is all about staying positive, old pal. Most people quit in life when they're just three feet from the gold. But you got to be there with the big bucks, for the turn. Because it always turns. Remember that. Everyone has good luck. Everyone has bad luck. Just don't stampede for the fucking exit when there's a minor setback. Trust me, it's gonna turn, and that's when you want to be there." And then he told me to call the pit boss and get another $100,000. He was playing on, and his credit was good. I just shook my head at the sheer guts of the man.

Both on the trading floor and in the casinos, most guys run for the hills when things aren't going their way. Bad negative attitudes, whiners and complainers. But not Larry. On the trading floor and at the tables, he was always Captain Cool, waiting patiently, lying in wait for his moment.

He asked us to give him a little room. Then he collected his $100,000 and took over the whole table, all six slots. They roped off the area, except for him and me, and he started with $2,500 on each hand—that's $15,000 on each round against the dealer. That gave him a very slight advantage, because there was no one else playing, catching the good hand. I watched him win a few, then lose a few.

And then suddenly the dealer busted two hands in a row for the first time in close to five hours. Larry hauled back $15,000. Then he pulled nothing less than a mind-blower. He gestured to the pit boss and requested permission to up the table max from $5,000 a hand, $30,000 a table. "Let's get this baby up to ten thousand," he said. "Sixty thousand a table."

The pit boss nodded.

Larry proceeded to pile on his $1,000 chips, ten each on all six slots. The cards were not pretty. His best was a 16, but the dealer's cards were worse. There was a six, but when the second card turned, it was the dreaded five. This meant if she drew a face card she'd have 21, and Larry would be down another $60,000.

The dealer, still under 17, had to go again. Almost thirty people crammed together outside the ropes, watching this fight to the finish, holding their breath. The dealer turned the card. It was a three, which made 14. Larry never blinked. The dealer turned again, an ace, for 15. Larry stared straight ahead. The dealer turned once more and pulled yet another ace. That was still only 16.

This was sensational. But the dealer had to turn again. And it was as if the entire casino had come to a halt. The pit bosses had moved in and were standing watch with the crowd. Cocktail waitresses stopped serving, and a kind of telepathy swept around the gaming room. It was as if everyone was aware of the titanic struggle between the casino's ace dealer and Larry McCarthy from Wall Street, with $60,000 riding on the turn of a card.

I watched the dealer gulp and then reach for the shoe, selecting the card. For a split second, the hand that covered that card paused, and then flipped it over to reveal the queen of spades. Dealer's bust—26.

After five hours, Larry's luck had finally turned. He leapt to tackle me, taking both of us right off our stools, into the velvet ropes, and onto the floor in front of all the spectators, both of us laughing fit to die.

When we finally climbed back to our feet, Larry just said, "Okay, guys, let's play some cards." He swapped the $1,000 orange chips, the "pumpkins," for the $5,000 "gray ladies" and placed two of them on each spot—another $60,000 hand. And when the cards came up they were devastating for the dealer: four blackjacks and two 20s for Larry, against the dealer's pitiful 17.

In thirty-five minutes, Larry had come back from the dead to be $25,000 in front. "Remember this," he said. "You've seen for the past four hours the best part of this game, and the very best part of life. When things can't get any worse, they always do, and when they can't get any better, they always do."

What he said was true. I'd watched this man get beat over and over again, and then I watched him ride his luck all the way back. When we walked out of there two hours later, he was $475,000 in front. I saw it with my own eyes. I think for the first time, I finally understood why Larry McCarthy was a full-blooded legend of Wall Street and why his name would live for a long time.

On the way out, he told me one more truth, as applicable in the market as it was at the table. "Never blow your powder too early," he said. "Start nice and slow, nice and low. Get the feel of the market, get centered, make sure you got a ton of ammunition, and don't quit too early. Never do that. When they're running against you, keep going, because they're gonna turn. And the split second they make that turn, hit it, buddy, hit it real hard. Because that's when you're gonna fucking *win*."

Which was all very well, until we returned to the office the next day only to see that Beazer, the home builder we'd shorted so ferociously, was chugging upward yet again. With all of its thousands and thousands of suspect mortgage holders and all of its debt, the market didn't care. Beazer rode up to $82 against our short position of $75. The sons of bitches were killing us. That morning we dropped another $2 million, which made $4 million altogether. Christ, we were losing $600,000 a point.

"Where's Babay? Where the fucking hell's Babay?" Never had I seen Captain Cool so angry. He'd searched the entire floor, raging from one section to another. Most people were too scared to laugh. Larry decided to take it on the chin and take the short off, just to stop the hemorrhaging. Never before had I seen him go against his own instincts that severely. Jesus, if he'd done that at Mohegan it would have cost him $600,000 personally.

And still Karim Babay never showed. Once more Larry searched the floor, and when he came back he was even more angry—angry with himself for losing his nerve, furious at Karim, who was not there to offer words of encouragement and advice, and incandescent at Beazer Homes, which had the temerity to defy every form of known logic.

Words failed him. Any vestige of humor he had left had flown the coop. And with an outrageous display of brute strength he reached up, ripped the computer screen from its mounting, and hurled it to the floor, obliterating it in a shower of glass and electronic sparks. The noise was amazing, and of course it was too much for a lot of the younger traders, who started to crack up at the temporary disintegration of Captain Cool.

But Larry was not sorry. He leaned down, picked up the shattered monitor, raised it above his head, and once more hurled it downward, blasting the frame asunder, with sparks and glass once more flying every which way. Then he turned to face the crowd, and suddenly the anger seemed to drain right out of him. At last he chuckled, raised his fist into the air, and shouted to the cheering traders, "Fuck 'em, right?" The roar of applause almost took the roof off the building.

Right then Beazer jogged up another 50 cents. "Screw 'em," said Larry. "We'll get 'em back on the way down."

That 'ole dog, he could still hunt.

But not everything was going wrong. In fact, hardly anything was. And several weeks later we stood back and watched Calpine go down in flames. The clean-as-air energy corporation vindicated every last word Christine Daley had ever uttered about them. They crashed under the overwhelming burden of their own debt and made a few headlines on November 29 when their stock price lost 57 percent of its value after they fired their CEO and founder, Peter Cartwright, and their CFO, Bob Kelly, who Christine had said could dance through raindrops without getting wet.

The stock drop was not in fact that serious, since it had already plummeted from its high of $58 to $1.25, but now it had lost another 71 cents, which more or less wrapped it up. I've never been exactly certain of the amount of money we made from that classic short, which we'd leveled at the corporation based on the words of one of the great Wall Street researchers. But it was, by all accounts, close to $100 million.

On Tuesday morning, December 20, Calpine filed for Chapter 11 in the U.S. Bankruptcy Court in New York. It was the eighth largest in history. They'd gone down under that massive debt, now $22.5 billion. The news flashed on all of our Bloomberg terminals, and I traded over $100 million in Calpine bonds that day, having been short $50 million face. It gave me my first-ever $5 million profit day. Larry and Joe Beggans were short $175 million.

I talked to Christine later that day, the day of her great triumph. And like a true researcher, she was slightly preoccupied with a historical fact. How could it be, she wondered, just a few years after the Enron catastrophe, that a crazily overleveraged U.S. corporation, in complete denial of its untenable position, could keep right on pulling off questionable accounting moves, one after the other? And from her perspective the fact that she had spotted it while no one else seemed to care made it worse. You rarely find such a realist who is also ultimately such a purist. But Christine Daley was that person. She had watched from afar and her assessment was that Calpine executives were attempting to pull the wool over investors' eyes, and she'd contemptuously dismissed all that as a smoke screen. It was the pure darned wrongness of the evasions, the half-truths, the exaggerations, the unfairness to investors. That's what had gotten to her. That's why she was so unforgiving in her assessment of that corporation. Just the goddamned lack of truth in their dealings with stockholders.

I felt I'd been with Christine from the start, since Calpine had been the topic of our very first conversation on my first day at Lehman. And I will always remember her astute determination. Just as I will always consider it a privilege to have known her.

7

The Tragedy of General Motors

"I am ninety-nine percent certain," said Christine, "that General Motors is going bankrupt. It's not even a car company; it's a health care provider with an auto manufacturer on the side."

THE NEW YEAR came howling out of the northwest in 2006, and we struggled to work every morning, the sun not yet up. Huddled into our top coats and fur hats, chins tucked down into our scarves, feet encased in galoshes, we made our way along the icy sidewalks, jumping slush puddles. Manhattan, winter-bleak, shouldering its way into the new day.

Yet once we'd fought our way into the warmth of our building, there were smiles on the faces of the traders in our little corner on the floor. There was even a smile on the face of the elusive Scarlet Pimpernel of the research department, Karim Babay—*they seek him here, they seek him there . . .*

In faraway California, slumbering on the warm banks of the Delta, Beazer Homes had just copped it. Their stock peaked in the first couple of days of the year at around $82.50, then began a relentless dive to where it belonged, losing $20 initially, then heading for $40 and then ultimately almost to zero, complete with its gigantic debt, and all of its dicey mortgage holders.

That January, the determined Larry McCarthy steamed back in and initiated a new short position on Beazer and was quickly on his way to a super $10 million profit as the stock finally plummeted. For one split second, I thought he was going to hug Karim for joy. And I never once noticed even one computer terminal in any danger whatsoever.

We were, at that time, in what some people regarded as a Goldilocks economy—a relaxed and calm state of affairs when everything moved gently and, like Goldilocks, we were keeping the three bears at bay. The first sign that Mama Bear was about to spill the porridge came in late January 2006 when David Rosenberg, chief economist for Merrill Lynch, suddenly came out and announced that existing home sales had started to collapse in October, three months previously, when they were down 36 percent compared to October 2004. That was the steepest decline in ten years, he noted.

Collapse. Down. Decline. Those words should have been time bombs in our fourth-floor mortgage sector, as if someone had yelled "Satan!" in the Sistine Chapel. But they were not. They were ignored.

And Rosenberg wasn't finished yet, not by a long shot. He reminded everyone that the U.S. housing boom had been built on cheap credit, mostly financed by the shadow banks. In 2005, 43 percent of all first-time home buyers had put zero money down. This figure had risen from 27 percent in 2003. Whatever was happening was looking kind of popular, the way free houses often are.

Rosenberg, echoing Mike Gelband six months before, added that 35 percent of all 2005 mortgages had been of that highly dicey, buy-now-pay-later variety—the ARMs, negative amortizations, and interest-only loans, not to mention the truly shaky no-docs issued to the $400,000-a-year bus drivers. For the first time in years, unsold inventories of U.S. homes were ratcheting higher. And he pointed out that the more than three hundred shadow banks in the United States amounted to little more than a steroid distribution center, funded by Wall Street's creation, the collateralized debt obligation. (Today CDOs sound uncannily like the product of a snake-oil salesman: *cure your ills, cure your depression, cure every damn thing.*)

I, along with every other member of our group, could not shake off the feeling of disquiet that a price drop in the real estate market, which sparked off any form of negative home equity, would not be a pretty sight. It was a source of near-wonderment to me that hardly anyone else could see that the U.S. economy and the stock market were being pumped up by a credit bubble the size of the planet Saturn—that's nearly ten times bigger than the Earth, 235,000 miles in circumference, not including the moons and rings.

Even *Time* magazine, that bastion of reality, was swept along by the bulls. In that very same January, they mentioned that the "big-spending

U.S. consumers" being fed low-priced products from China had spurred worldwide growth of over 4 percent for the second year running, the strongest two-year growth period in three decades. "And there's more good news to come," said *Time*. "The world economy is on track to enjoy another bumper year in 2006 as this twin American-Chinese engine continues to power ahead." Those forecasts emerged from a discussion among economists that *Time* brought together at the World Economic Forum in Davos, Switzerland, that month.

And many of the world's financial big-hitters went with the flow. "The outlook is basically for another Goldilocks kind of year," stated Laura D. Tyson, at the time dean of the London Business School and a former chairman of the President's Council of Economic Advisers.

I can state categorically that in our group there was not one person—not Alex Kirk, Michael Gelband, Richard Gatward, Larry McCarthy, Joe Beggans, Pete Hammack, Jane Castle, nor Christine Daley—who agreed with one word of that, *Time* magazine or not. We all thought this Goldilocks bullshit was running on borrowed time, and that Lehman should be shorting its backside off, to compensate for the wrath to come. Especially when it smacked into the fourth floor. Not to mention the thirty-first.

Just consider the dark warnings issued by these prophets in our group: Kirk called the "steroid problem" in the property market before anyone; Gelband laid it on the line to the mortgage guys before anyone else at Lehman understood the figures; McCarthy jumped on and acted upon every one of the warnings, believing them to be accurate; Castle could see the airlines collapsing at least a year in advance; Daley called the demise of the energy titan Calpine more than a year in advance; Hammack called the demise of one of the biggest publicly quoted home builders and mortgage giants in the country, and Babay supported him, almost ending up wearing a computer terminal as a New Year's party hat. We weren't on anyone's bandwagon; in fact, we put the wheels on the friggin' thing. And none of us bought Goldilocks. We didn't even buy the porridge.

And while *Time* was printing its issue and Tyson was forecasting, there were yet more ominous signs in the housing market. Perhaps the only person outside our team worth listening to was Warren Buffett, who remarked on the growth cycle, not just of real estate, but of anything: "You always have three I's. First, the innovator, then the imitator, then the idiot." Right on, Buffy. Here came the idiots, going for construction, piling into the hideously swollen gargoyle of the Florida real estate market. More than 27,000 condominiums were recently completed in Miami, with permits pending for 50,000 more. In the ten years prior to that, only 9,000 condos were built in the whole of greater Miami. And of course there was the automatic response there always is at the top of an out-of-control bull market—in this case, *There are between 75,000 and 100,000 retirees a day flooding into Florida.* Yeah, right, trying to keep up with the death rate.

In company with Peter Schellbach, I stared down at the figures for the southern construction boom. "There's always reasons at the top why we're going higher," he said. "And there's always reasons at the bottom why we're going lower. But this has got to be a top."

Aiding and abetting in this dizzying rampage around the top of the mountain were Lehman Brothers' two in-house write-'em-up, knock-'em-out mortgage brokerages, BNC and Aurora. Neither of them showed any signs of applying the brakes. These were outfits that fed on the optimism, nurtured the expansive ambitions of our mortgage team, and joined in the universal celebration of the boom times which would never end. They never even spoke to us, never even knew us, as we never really knew them.

In the first quarter of 2006, BNC was lending more than $1 billion a month. Aurora, the Alt-A market specialist, was right up there in the top three in this market for no-down-payment mortgages, which was in the process of growing from $190 billion to $400 billion in under three years. And of course this meant they had to keep growing, faster, faster, faster.

We all knew this meant their standards must be dropping. When there is heavy pressure to grow, those standards always drop. Mortgages that didn't meet the proper company requirements were surely being approved. They'd already dispensed with borrowers having to prove anything, either income or assets.

It had to be risky, and we were the corporate experts on trouble, identifying it whenever and wherever it lurked. Anyone wanted our opinion, we'd give it: we'd research the shaky area, and come up with a reason to either go short or forget it. Distress was our game. We'd have blown the whistle on BNC and Aurora a long time before anyone else did. That was our business, even in this bust-the-rules, make-the-sale Wild West real estate market of 2006.

The truth, unhappily, was that for Lehman's mortgage guys it wasn't about the loan. It was about getting the parts (mortgages) for their securitizations. Even if money was lost on a mortgage, no one cared. They made the money up ten-fold on the securitization process. And, with the help of the ratings agencies, they thought they had the risk all figured out, as they packaged and sold the CDOs. If there was a high risk attached to any given security, a higher interest rate was paid.

The least risky securities carried that AAA seal of approval by the credit-rating agencies. The problem emerging, in the opinion of our group, was that all of the loans carried about ten times more risk than the agencies thought. Some of the ratings, we suspected, had been issued on the south side of ridiculous. And every time we looked at the consumer spending charts or the mortgage origination chart, there grew a sneaking suspicion that we were somehow on the verge of the greatest debt binge in the history of global finance. Worse yet, it was emanating from the United States of America.

Starting in 2001, when Alan Greenspan dropped interest rates to 1 percent, the chart that tracks U.S. consumer debt as a percentage of income suddenly broke out, upward. It showed an alarming rise from the acceptable average of between 95 percent in a recession and 85 percent in boom markets. But now, in early 2006, it was on a relentless ascent, driving through 135 percent and still rising.

But perhaps the most thoroughly alarming of all the charts we studied, week in and week out, was the one that tracked the amount of debt Wall Street had repackaged, rebranded, rerated, and remarketed. We now called them RMBSs, CDOs, CLOs, and God knows what else. But they really were only debt, U.S. consumer and U.S. corporate debt. The chart showed that in the year 2000, the number was $1 trillion. In 2005, the number was $2.7 trillion. That's in the new modern language you need to describe a pile of $100 bills 475 miles high. Which is, by the way, beyond the pull of gravity.

Alex Kirk, Peter Hammack, and Ashish Shah, our global managing director, the analysis king of structured credit derivatives for the entire firm, were in no doubt. Lehman's foreign sales of these securitizations, especially to Europe, were astronomical, up 600 percent in six years. Every month we sold them more. And our relationships with banks and funds in Asia were often stronger. We were selling them securitized debt like lottery tickets.

Globalization—we darn near invented it, and we were quick to praise it: *the global economy, the security of the banking brotherhood, the interdependence, the global safety in numbers.* Someone estimated that 23 percent of all Wall Street's revenue stream for the last three years flowed out of securitization sales.

I had a different perspective. Globalization was when a financially strapped subprime mortgage holder in Stockton suddenly defaults, dumps his house keys in the mailbox, and then vanishes—and the $300,000 default shows up on the balance sheet of a side-street bank in Shanghai, Singapore, Tokyo, or London. That's Globalization with a big *G*. God help everyone if the default number ever went high, into, say, the thousands.

This was plainly a beginning. Our group had identified beyond any reasonable doubt that this thing was about to turn bad. There were trouble spots throughout U.S. industry, and the world was exploding with derivatives—the intangible financial products that Warren Buffett first described as "weeds priced as flowers" and later branded "financial weapons of mass destruction."

Have you ever noticed how, both in life and in corporations, one small piece of economy with the truth often leads to full-blooded deceit and then a copper-bottomed southern-fried lie? And following right behind that lie, you usually find a real shady area, a kind of no-man's-land where no one goes, not even in discussion with each other. We had one of those at Lehman. A deep dark secret. Matter of fact, it was the deepest and darkest you could get. Its name was Grand Cayman.

For there, in that sun-drenched Caribbean paradise set 170 miles south of the western end of Castro's Cuba, Lehman, in company with several other investment banks, held a controlling hand over a succession of hidden trusts. And, being Wall Street, they were awarded a truly fancy title that no one could possibly understand: qualified special purpose entities, or QSPEs. (Throw in the word *international,* and you could have been talking about any subject, in any place, at any time on earth. Obfuscation, thy name is Wall Street.) And in those QSPEs they stored money, bonds, derivatives, and CDOs—all of which had the glorious advantage of never appearing on corporate balance sheets. They were "selling" the CDOs to the trust and reporting the sale as profit on the Lehman balance sheet. This could be regarded as somewhat eccentric, since they were effectively selling the damn things to themselves.

Altogether, the Grand Cayman connection provided three big advantages to a firm like Lehman Brothers, which was trying desperately to compete with the biggest banks on Wall Street. The first was entering questionable profits from the "sale" onto the balance sheet. The second was receiving all the coupon payments from the derivatives they still held in the trusts. The third was that the Financial Accounting Standards Board (FASB) required them only to put aside 3 percent of capital, a tiny amount, to cover any losses in an offshore trust.

This 3 percent requirement was the highly controversial Rule 140, written in 2000, and the one Enron broke most spectacularly on its way to universal disgrace. They could not come up with the 3 percent when asked by the government, despite claiming to have made huge profits. That 3 percent brought them down: they were forced to admit insolvency and file for bankruptcy. In 2003 FASB attempted to raise the threshold to 10 percent, but the banks reacted with fury, arguing about the major impact such a rule would have on them. The banking lobby had not been so up in arms since Bill Clinton first declined to sign the Glass-Steagall repeal into law nearly ten years previously. Citigroup had massive holdings offshore, and their comptroller almost had apoplexy. He publicly stated on behalf of the global giant that Citi would be "significantly impacted" if the rule was changed to require 10 percent. Citigroup estimated they would have to raise $20 billion in fresh cash, which was a measure of the extent of their offshore, off-the-record, off-the-hook, off-balance-sheet holdings on the Caribbean island of dreams—sorry, schemes. In late 2003, after intense political pressure, FASB backed down, thus proving that the Securities and Exchange Commission was definitely still asleep, allowing Wall Street to careen forward, unchecked, unregulated, and unaccountable. Wall Street, of course, knew the SEC was still asleep, and, generally speaking, hoped to hell it would stay asleep.

This lack of regulatory oversight allowed Lehman Brothers to continually visit the short-term commercial paper market and borrow more and more money—massive amounts, billions of dollars—always pledging their new toys as collateral. You'd have thought someone might have yelled "Stop!" or *"Basta!"* or *"Arrêt!"* or *"Achtung!"* or even "Holy shit!" because the toys were bought with borrowed money. And those toys were time bombs despite their fancy names: RMBS, CDO, CLO, CMBS. It was like an arms race of leverage on Wall Street, and it all started with the demise of Glass-Steagall, the firewall that had kept the mighty commercial banks separate from the ambitious, fleet-footed investment houses. But now they were legally together, with one bank outdoing the next, pushing the leverage envelope, borrowing on an unprecedented scale, getting rid of the evidence that said they couldn't afford it. And there was no way for anyone accurately to measure the risk.

But the battle to reform Rule 140, involving some members of the government and the Wall Street heavies—the guys who came up with the big political contributions—was developing into a knock-down-drag-out contest. And with a presidential election not so far away, the bankers were punching way above their weight.

The issue was truly simple: leverage. If a new rule came in that forced the banks to haul their billions down the Cayman beaches and back to Wall Street, all hell might break loose. Because they would no longer be dealing with 3 percent offshore. They'd be looking at a domestic 10 percent holdback, to cover U.S. losses, standard procedure in banks throughout the nation since the Revolutionary War. This would have the obvious effect of depleting the balance sheets. Not only was holding back capital unacceptable emotionally, but most of the banks simply did not have it—especially Lehman, which was now leveraged thirty to one. If that rule was changed, the U.S. government might have to face up to a rash of bankruptcies in the financial capital of the world. Alan Greenspan was plainly wary of damaging the banking system with regulations and controls while the game was still in progress. But the risks and the leverage kept right on piling up.

The regulators continued to delay, never imposing the stricter rules, which would bring the inevitable deleveraging—the only way to slow down a market like this. They had let the grass grow four feet high because they were afraid of damaging the lawn.

Once more utilizing my perfectly astounding grasp of events aided by hindsight, I have to say that none of this was obvious at the time; not even to the line of crystal balls that decorated the desks of my group at Lehman. But it was one giant SEC procrastination, fueled by an overriding sense of not wishing to face the harsh discordant music of deleverage, which means getting smaller fast.

At that time, however, Ashish Shah and I did speak about the situation and concluded that there was a clear danger the way everyone was dragging their feet about disclosure of off-balance-sheet assets. It plainly could not last. Somehow it would have to come to light.

Looking back, it's clear the revenues were always what really mattered in the secretive boardrooms of Manhattan. Because those revenues mean bigger bonus pools, and that meant more money for the partners, very flashy houses in the Hamptons, beautiful cars, and fine art collections. Wasn't life absolutely great?

For all of us, the bonus pool was of paramount importance because the bonus represented most of our income. That's how we were paid. We also were paid half of our compensation in our own corporate stock. And everyone knew the inevitabilities of life. We had to earn the money to keep the profits and the stock high. Otherwise we were all spinning our wheels financially. Many of us were naturally far less ruthless than others, and many of us had a clear moral code about what was right and what was clearly wrong, but we were all working at the very sharp end of Wall Street, and making money was our game.

We were all more or less on the same salary. It was the bonus that made the difference. For instance, I needed to make $20 million for the firm to earn $1 million in bonus for myself. And I strived to do so, writing up my order book with immense diligence every day, recording the wins, recording the losses. Right next to me, the vastly experienced Larry McCarthy had a huge pool of money to play with because of his track record and length of service. Therefore he would always earn more than I could until I could increase my own money pool by making winning trades and building my own track record. It was always about money, nothing else.

I had an excellent first year, and I read somewhere that the average Wall Street bonus was almost 250 percent bigger than the average salary for all nonfinancial jobs in the city. Since 2003, thanks to the derivatives, our total compensation had increased by 49 percent. Which, when you stop to think about it, is on the high side. But that's what it was all about—record leverage, record bonuses.

In a sense, when any of us took a position, we were putting not only the firm's money but also our own bonuses on the line, our own personal wealth and annual income. This, I assure you, is apt to concentrate the mind. None of us takes lightly any position in the market, long or short. And when we do, it takes real courage. The same applied to the researchers, those hard-eyed corporate detectives upon whose words the traders depended.

Thus, in that cold New York January of 2006, everyone sat bolt upright and paid attention when Christine Daley made an observation about General Motors, once the world's largest automaker, and still employer of around 266,000 people in thirty-five countries. "I am ninety-nine percent certain," said Christine, "that General Motors is going bankrupt. It's not even a car company; it's a health care provider with an auto manufacturer on the side."

Of course, GM's troubles had been around for many years, and forecasts of doom were not earth-shattering items of news. But Christine Daley's business was to identify major problems in major corporations, and when she spoke up professionally, it was to recommend that Lehman Brothers invest millions of dollars in a short position. And this time it was on the Detroit car giant.

In her opinion, General Motors could not live. She cited their huge retiree health care and pension program, which covered more than 1.1 million people and entailed a total obligation of $56 billion, which the corporation could not possibly go on supporting. GM, said Ms. Daley, was engulfed by its obligations. She spoke of those now notorious GM job banks, possibly five thousand strong, where GM workers who had been laid off sat around in vast cafeterias reading and still received $30 an hour. She spoke of continuing problems with union cooperation, of GM's 2005 loss of $8.6 billion. She argued that every move GM made was creating long-term devastation for bondholders. She actually considered that if GM did not get rid of GMAC, their car financing and mortgage corporation, they might be gone by Christmas. Her last and final warning involved the burgeoning commodities market, fueled by the fact that China, in the run-up to the Olympics, appeared to want all of the world's steel, iron, rubber, zinc, and God knows what else. Commodities, in Christine's view, were going through the roof, and GM needed those commodities but could not possibly pay the price. "That," she said, "will finish them." She was planning, she noted, to make a presentation in March to the entire fixed-income division, and expected to demonstrate that this was indeed the time for one of the most almighty short positions Lehman had ever taken.

The GM stock price was already down below $19, and as a group, we elected to take a gamble on Christine's logic. We made some initial short positions in GM stock, starting out at $20, assuming the market would immediately notice the problems that were slowly strangling the auto manufacturer. But the stock instantly jumped up $2 and we covered our position—that's trader-speak for "all bets are off." We waited for the rally to end and then went back in, shorting GM at $24, expecting a quick sell-off. It never happened. GM went to $27.

Then *Forbes* magazine came out with a sad and melancholic examination of the company, headlined "The Tragedy of General Motors." It was as if Christine Daley had stood at the elbow of the author. The conclusions were identical: how could the Detroit colossus possibly continue? Nothing could have spelled out the plight of GM with more damning and sorrowful evidence. This was no witch hunt. This was a shrewd and professional assessment of the situation, and it was delivered by a national magazine upon whose word great judgments were made, right down to who was the richest person in the country. Forbes had a voice, a big, booming voice that, when it issued a warning, would surely be heard.

We went back in and placed the trade for a third time, shorting the stock at $27, confident the high debt load would finally drive it down. GM went to $31. Again we covered our position and bailed out, and that evening we caucused with Christine Daley, who thought the world must have gone mad. She was apologetic, angry, and slightly embarrassed.

But we had all forgotten one thing—the stock market in 2006 was not a normal stock market. It had an element of death-defying bravado about it, a prolonged denial of the obvious. Under the weight of $32 billion worth of debt, deteriorating cash flow, and insurmountable obligations, General Motors stock soared to $32. We at Lehman could have caught a very nasty cold, several million dollars' worth, and the old bonus sheets would have taken a full-blooded hit from this runaway Humvee.

But we were accustomed to an iron form of discipline, always prepared to take the hit before it grew into something serious. In this case we had covered three times, getting out and suffering only minor damage, limiting our losses. Alex Kirk pulled Larry and me aside and said "the market can stay irrational a lot longer than your trading ledgers can stay solvent. Cover the GM now." That's the way of the professional. Only a damn fool takes a position for a specific reason and then marries it when it goes the wrong way. You have to get out the instant it goes wrong, and the road to hell is paved with those who did not do so.

I mention this as one of the great shining examples, way beyond the derivatives, of a market that did not want to hear bad news and could not understand potential danger of leverage in the system. It was a pure one-way transmission. Wall Street was listening for *calm seas, record profits, best-ever growth, joy, wealth, prosperity,* and *b-o-o-o-n-u-u-s.* Anything less was essentially out of the culture.

And there was nowhere, repeat nowhere, on the planet Manhattan where this hyperoptimism, this self-aggrandizing, preening success story, applied in greater measure than at Lehman Brothers, the sorcerers of securities. When we shorted GM and were proved temporarily a bit hasty, there were those in the firm who nodded wisely at the obvious folly of our little group of pseudo-pessimists who could not understand the reality of modern investing.

In one small sense they were right, because it was certainly beyond Christine's grasp that anyone in their right mind could possibly lend GM several billion dollars to go on losing it and almost certainly never pay it back, and we all agreed with her. *Wrong.* In this market there were banks that would continue to loan cash to Detroit's version of the *Titanic,* even as the icy waters of debt and failure came splashing over the bow.

GM could roll the debt in the short-term commercial paper market, meaning the carmaker could take out a thirty-day loan and pay it back by borrowing the money from someone else. There were still many banks that would lend to General Motors for thirty days, since death did not seem imminent. But the big picture, moving the loan from one bank to another, would in the end turn out to be a lunatic game of Russian roulette, because someone somewhere was likely not to get paid. In the current climate of hyperliquidity, though, all this was disregarded, and the show rolled on.

Rick Wagoner, CEO since 2000, the tall former Duke University basketball player, strived valiantly to hold the place together. He created an enormous layoff plan to get rid of workers the corporation did not need, paying them $100,000 to go, up to ten thousand people. It probably was not going to solve the gargantuan problem he had inherited from GM policies of long ago, but it sent precisely the right signal to Wall Street: that here was a CEO who would do whatever it took to pull the corporation into shape. That was one of the reasons the stock kept edging up despite everything.

Another was the instinct of most Americans that General Motors ought not to go bankrupt. That may be irrational, and it may be soft-hearted. But there is a place in American hearts for the corporation that was the global leader in auto sales for seventy-seven years. It was the largest company in the world for an extended time, and it stood for everything that made the United States great. It was an industrial giant glowering on the banks of the Detroit River beneath the Stars and Stripes, a symbol of world power, U.S. know-how, engineering, and excellence. It was the biggest, the towering Goliath of the auto industry. Most people would feel a tinge of sadness if GM went under, because it wasn't just a car company, it was a part of America's soul, a breath of times past, proud and significant times—times that, I hope, will come again.

A very large section of the American public did not want GM to go down. Perhaps that's where Christine and the rest of us misjudged it. Not everything has to do with money.

I am keenly aware of the pure pain-in-the-ass quality of Wall Street's acronyms. RMBS, CDO, CLO, SIV, LBO, MBS, SEC, NINJA, and on and on. But right now I must return to a subject we touched upon only briefly—the credit default swap, or CDS. In the merry month of May 2006, Wall Street took hold of this gambling concept and decided to transform itself into something between a Las Vegas casino and an off-track betting parlor. You'll recall, I hope, the fancy-free nature of the CDS, which was nothing more than a bet on the total demise of a company, financial institution, or people defaulting on their mortgages. It was disguised as insurance, which is of course just a euphemism for bookmaking. Insurance companies are bookmakers in pinstripes: *We'll offer you hundred-to-one odds your house won't burn down—a $3,000 premium against a $300,000 payout.* Like an insurer, a real bookmaker carefully balances the odds, taking in hundreds of bets, balancing his book to cope with the unhappy circumstance when the favorite wins, trying to ensure that the other bets amply cover his risk. Naturally, this occasionally fails, and a horse everyone has backed wins at tight odds. But this time-honored system, perfected down the centuries by the oddsmakers, does not fail often. Wall Street, however, which has zero experience at balancing such a book, did not take these rudimentary precautions.

And that brings us directly to May 2006, when a kind of gambling fever hit the hub of America's financial industry. The CDS became the flavor of the month. I'll just refresh your memory on how it works.

Say a major pension fund loans General Motors $1 billion at 13 percent. The pension fund contacts Lehman or one of the other big investment houses and says, "Will you insure my billion-dollar bond in return for 8 percent of the loan amount each year as a premium? That's $80 million a year for you, and all the risk." But what is the risk? Will GM go bust and default totally on that billion-dollar bond? Highly unlikely in May 2006, with GM stock up at over $30. So Lehman agrees to shoulder the risk and prepares to collect the $80 million a year. But it does not stop there. Lehman contacts Morgan Stanley to do what bookmakers call "laying off." Lehman offers to transfer 90 percent of the risk, $900 million, for a premium of $72 million per year. Morgan Stanley thinks the CDS is sound and accepts, leaving Lehman with an income of $8 million a year, and the risk of the remaining 10 percent of the billion, or $100 million.

You might describe this as like running in front of a 100-mph express train to pick up $50. Some may think this a harsh simile, but the fact remains that you make all this bullshit profit, and the very first day one of your counterparties goes down, you lose the whole lot, everything you thought you made. Still, at this point nothing had gone down, and despite our warnings, the CDS market, certainly inside Lehman, had become the coolest, most fashionable trading Wall Street had to offer. No one had been asked to pay out a massive loss. At least, not yet.

But Lehman's CDS group did not worry too much about the potential losses. They had enormous trading fees on the lucrative spreads in this less transparent over-the-counter market. But they also saw that millions of dollars a year, and thought if we could collect little more than hundred of those bets, we'd earn a billion dollars a year with no outlay, no need to purchase the bonds or anything else. We just collect that huge income stream. The downside, a payout of more than $10 billion if the market went south, did not appear to trouble anyone.

And there were seventeen other Wall Street banks that thought precisely the same, including Bear Stearns, Wachovia, Bank of America, Citigroup, Goldman Sachs, Morgan Stanley, Merrill Lynch, and Credit Suisse. In 2006 the total notional value of the CDS market hit $26 *trillion,* up from $800 million in 2001. That $26 trillion represented an eye-popping *eight times* the amount of the underlying bonds. Deep down I knew this was a truly lousy idea. Where does it all stop—$600 trillion, $900 trillion?

And therein rested the charm/terror of the CDS, depending on your point of view. There was no limit to the amount you could sell. It was nothing like regular bond trading, where the limit was the number of bonds issued by the parent corporation. The credit default swap, the wager on success or failure, was endless. You could sell as many as you liked, because the CDS was not attached to anything. It was just out there in the ether. And no one owned anything. The only real cash flying around emanated from the original loan, the coupon paid by the corporation. The rest was a kind of phantom.

"It's fucking voodoo," said Larry at one memorable meeting, referring to the gigantic risks. "There's young traders in this organization who never even saw a grizzly bear up close and personal. And they're just printing money against the risk of some kind of ephemeral catastrophe that may or may not happen. What do we do if it does?" So far as Larry could see, we were just trading CDSs, which are IOUs or bets between dozens of Wall Street counterparties. He was a classic old-school realist, a cash bond trader, accustomed to the sale of bonds in exchange for a cash payment. Like several of our group members, he could sense something really odd about a world that was being built on side bets about the viability of corporations, where no one owned anything, where the risk was vague but nonetheless real.

We all had an uneasy feeling. The same group of people who were so jumpy over the shaky mortgages were just as jumpy over the CDSs. Because we were all far more grounded in reality, we found it impossible to ignore the risks inherent in these modern forms of hypertrading, where rules were bent and tried-and-true methods went straight out the window.

So far as we were concerned, risk was an absolute. At some point in the argument, the *degree* of risk becomes irrelevant: either there's risk or there isn't. And in this case, however remote it may have seemed, there was risk. I agree it may have seemed a bit far out from where we all stood right then. But when you get slammed by a friggin' rogue comet from outer space, no one gives a rat's ass how far it traveled. And the risks to the financial system from the explosion of CDS contracts were a lot more likely to rear their ugly head than a comet hitting Earth.

There were risk meetings when Larry would ask disarmingly, "What's going to happen to all the profits built into your trading ledgers when your counterparty is not there on the other side of your trades?" There were, of course, no answers. The bigger problem was that no one wanted to search for answers. The CDS profits were great; what else could matter? So Lehman just went right ahead and kept selling the CDSs as if we were just printing more stock certificates. No one really paused to consider that if a regular stock trader had ever done that, without asking permission from the principal corporation, that trader would have been led away directly to the slammer. And the record keeping was close to impossible to keep up with. Some firms, Lehman included, were months behind. To make matters worse, Lehman had to buy boatloads of CDs to protect themselves when they sold too much, leaving us exposed to yet another counterparty.

The whole environment was innately illegal gambling, and the law had always made it clear you could not gamble on stocks or bonds unless you owned them. A rash of Wall Street betting parlors did spring up in the early years of the twentieth century, but they were closed down by the feds. In fact, this government precaution began at the end of the eighteenth century, when "insurance" betting parlors began to spring up in seaports like New Bedford, Nantucket, New York, and Boston. People were actually placing wagers on whether or not ships would return from their voyage. And with this there came rumors of diabolical dishonesty, of ships being sunk in order for friends of the crew to collect the "insurance." Plainly, this could not be tolerated, and for two centuries this kind of wagering by people who had no connection with the principal was outlawed. Not until 2000, with the Commodities Futures Modernization Act, did Congress, in its wisdom, legalize the process, with some kind of special dispensation for Wall Street to bet and take bets on the success or failure of a stock, a bond, or its components.

And now there was rocket fuel driving the market to stratospheric heights—the trillions of dollars in side bets on those mortgage securities and corporations, the CDSs. By 2006 well over half of CDS bets outstanding were pure speculation by people who did not even hold the underlying corporate bond. They were essentially private insurance contracts that paid off if the investment went sour. But now it was not necessary to own the investment to collect the insurance. These were the beginnings of casino capitalism. The irony was that it was no longer insurance. It had nothing to do with insurance. It was a bet. And not many proper bookmakers would have taken it.

Even bookmakers in Las Vegas are regulated. But this booming marketplace for CDSs was not regulated. The corporate bond market is regulated by the TRACE system, options are regulated by the Chicago Board Options Exchange, and stocks are regulated by the SEC. But the CDS boys could do anything they pleased. They traded over the counter, which was invisible. There was no central exchange, only private bets between parties, and these bets were dominating the most virulent part of Wall Street in the year 2006. There were no SEC limitations—possibly because the SEC really didn't understand the risks involved.

And, in a way, we on the third floor had to let them all get on with it, and look after our own very substantial corner of the Lehman operation, trading and earning, always searching for the weak link in the mortgage and home building market that would guide us to major short positions, and try to save Lehman from a real estate Armageddon we alone believed might be around the corner.

It was Larry and Mike's firm belief that the U.S. housing market could darn near take us down. Massive shorts the other way could provide a lot of help toward rescuing us on the other side. But it would have been a hell of a lot better if we somehow could have stopped these lunatics from betting the farm on poor people making their mortgage payments.

I look back at the hours and hours Peter Hammack and I spent poring over charts, trying to spot the flaws in the balance sheets of some of the biggest brokerage houses in the country. My number one target remained the LA-based New Century, with its 222 branch offices and 47,000 salesmen, the bodybuilders.

I sensed rather than saw the tiniest trend, so small that no one else, except Peter, would have given it a second thought. But then no one else was looking for the same things we were. The first inkling we had that all was not well came when Peter somehow gained access to a database and unearthed the thirty-day and sixty-day mortgage delinquency numbers. Both of them showed a slight uptick. *Hmmm.* Then we came across an ad from NovaStar Financial, the huge Kansas City–based specialists in "nonconforming residential loans" (that is, loans to guys who haven't got any bread). The ad was offering a program to help borrowers get a job.

"What d'you think about that?" I asked Pete.

"Fucking weird" was his reply.

We checked NovaStar's numbers, and during the process ran into a small announcement that a very key executive had recently quit. To me, that's always like a red flag to a bull. Even more important was the volume of mortgages—just a little off, not much, but sufficient to raise our antennae. They were still lending $20 billion a month nationally, but their earnings were slightly off too, and there was a small blip in the credit lines of the new homeowners.

And then there was the Lehman June 12, 2006, second-quarter conference call at which we invited anyone in the business to call in and question executives on certain aspects of our operation. Shareholders and analysts were also free to come on the line and ask about anything that was bothering them. On this particular day, during a mortgage-related discussion, we had a question from Guy Moszkowski, a Merrill Lynch analyst. His query was made in the soft, polite manner that analysts are inclined to adopt when they're going in hard. He asked, "Maybe you can give us a little more color on volumes and revenues on the mortgage origination side and how you are dealing with the slowdown that we've been seeing." He was making a request that even I had not heard before, and I worked there.

There was a brief silence before the chief administrative officer, David Goldfarb, stepped up to the plate on behalf of Lehman Brothers to reply to Guy's question. It was not what you might describe as a perfectly straightforward answer. Indeed, David's opening sentence was as close to unadulterated gibberish as anything I've ever heard: "You know, again, our mortgage platform in the U.S. as well as in Europe and Asia is predicated on a diversified set of products and a diversified set of regions, and with that diversification it has led to, you know, resiliency overall. As Chris [Chris O'Meara, the recently appointed CFO of Lehman] mentioned in his formal remarks, the overall securitization volume is slightly down; however, there was a slight mix shift this quarter, more going toward Europe; our small lending platform basically had a couple of large securitizations."

Note the words that mattered: "the overall securitization volume is slightly down." Because they really did admit that this enormous U.S. real estate market might already have peaked. Some way or another, the volume of people grabbing onto those tricky mortgages was down, despite all the efforts of the bodybuilders. The question was, was this just a slowdown or were we heading for a crash? What did that lower volume of mortgages really mean? And can you believe that there were people in this firm discussing the possibility of buying New Century when we already owned two large mortgage brokerage houses, Aurora and BNC?

I leave it to David Goldfarb, still valiantly going forward on the phone: "So, broadly," he said, "there are certain pockets that continue to have less volume. We have built very much of a variable cost base around the business, and certainly we basically have our infrastructure tied very much to a variable platform, and as we believe volume gets reduced so does our cost base."

On reflection, I'll take a shot at explaining it myself. For some reason a whole lot of people declined the tricky mortgages. It could be market saturation; with 47,000 salesmen, New Century alone must have banged on the door of every potential buyer in the free world. In addition, by this point there had to be hedge funds that were in CDOs up to their eyeballs, with billions invested on behalf of their clients. However, I believed the biggest danger to the market was the bush telegraph of the poor—families and friends passing along hair-raising tales of people's mortgage payments ripping upward as much as threefold as the interest rate resets kicked in.

They say that in the book business, the finest advertisement of all is word of mouth. My instinct was telling me that the resets had scared the life out of a lot of people who were stuck with payments they could never afford. That kind of really god-awful news, and especially when it involves repossessions and defaults, is apt to zip around the NINJA community real quick.

For all of us, these disparate facts, none of them of magnetic importance, added up to the very first suspicions of a trend—one that involved the possible crash of the mortgage market. We had taken a penetrating look at the risk factor that most people seemed happy just to ignore. And according to Larry, the real culprits in Lehman Brothers were the guys who would not recognize risk if it walked up and bit them in the ass. This was the risk management department, a group of quasi-analysts whose sole job was to assess where we were vulnerable in our trading and holdings.

I have to say, they drove McCarthy nuts for several reasons. But the main one was their assertion that our Delta position was somehow lethal and kept each and every one of them awake at night to the detriment of wives, families, and sundry pets. They were forever calling nervously, checking, worried we had overstepped the mark, with $180 million of the firm's cash exposed against Delta bonds worth up to $600 million in face value. Remember, we had bought most of them below 18 cents on the dollar, and Jane currently had a satellite picture of lines of gleaming Delta-owned Boeing passenger jets parked in the desert. Delta, of course, was still flying, and had a cash flow. Jane's opinion remained intact: we'd stolen those bonds.

This was not precisely how the risk management guys saw it. And they never stopped griping and moaning about the way Alex, Larry, Gatward, Schell, Beggans, and I had so recklessly committed the firm to the bankrupt southern airline named after the delta of the mighty Mississippi.

On the other hand, risk management seemed thrilled to bits about the $10+ billion subprime CDO securitization position held by the mortgage guys up on the fourth floor. The risk department viewed that as far less harrowing than our Delta bond position, despite the fact that those CDOs were entirely dependent on the financial capabilities of some of the least capable people in the West: Kmart checkout staff who'd claimed a comfortable income of $250,000 a year on their application for a no-doc mortgage to buy a house out there in the asparagus fields. One month, in fact, we logged five times the volume of worried phone calls from the risk managers than did the mortgage guys, with whom we did a comparison.

But who could blame them? The CDOs were considered the same as government bonds, AAA, by the most prestigious ratings agencies in the United States. In contrast, we were foolishly invested in some bankrupt air transportation company whose pilots were about to go on strike.

Risk managers in Lehman Brothers were guided, advised, regulated, trapped, imprisoned, and threatened on pain of torture and death by a tyrant who stood in their back office with a bullwhip and branding irons. His name was VaR. His strength was beyond that of a normal man; he could terrify legions and lay down the law in a manner that made empires shudder. VaR had a brain the size of a caraway seed and the imagination of a parsnip. The acronym that provides his name comes from *value at risk,* a technique used to estimate the probability of portfolio losses based on the statistical analysis of historical price trends and volatilities. It measures the worst expected loss under normal market conditions over a specific time interval at a given confidence level. Which means it measures both fear and optimism.

In this particular instance, VaR knew that the market had no problem with the confidence level of those who bought CDOs. There was as yet no volatility in this market. There had not been any volatility for years. It was a calm, tranquil place, like Nantucket Sound on a still and windless August morning, without even the wash of the passing Martha's Vineyard ferry.

The one great flaw with VaR was its insistence on putting heavy emphasis on recent volatility. This meant that if a security did not have a history of volatility, it would irrevocably be marked as riskless despite the fact that it currently gazed into the abyss. VaR was a prisoner of its own guidelines.

And like all systems that place too much faith in a philosophy, especially one as widely used on a global scale as VaR, it ends up with too much power and influence. It ended up ruling the department it was supposed to assist, because at Lehman no one wanted to be the renegade who stepped over the sacred VaR guidelines. Should there be a disaster, there could be only one scapegoat: the man who kicked over the traces and failed to obey the tried-and-true rules of VaR. Therefore, right or wrong, VaR was obeyed.

In our case its flawed reasoning was obvious. The CDOs were fine because they fell within the no-volatility rules, they were AAA-rated, and there had never been a default. But Delta was another story: much lower-rated because of the bankruptcy, a shaky history with the unions, operational problems because of the rise of jet fuels, undercutting by no-frills rivals, and a questionable future. When the risk management guys ran Delta through the computer program, the damn thing nearly blew up. Result: love CDOs, hate Delta. Verdict: VaR was a bonehead. It's just a goddamned machine. And it's only as good as the information it's given. You cannot implicitly rely on it. And our risk management guys never should have idly switched off their own brains and paid attention only to the friggin' robot.

Still, that stupid piece of equipment, with its blinking lights, colored screens, and softly lit keyboard, was not the only brain around Lehman that was ignoring all of us. Someone should have given the son of a bitch a kick in the butt and told it our Delta bonds were worth a thousand of those collateralized debt obligations on a risk-reward basis. My department had a total risk of $180 million on the Delta bonds, with an upside of up to $600 million in the bond's face value. The mortgage guys were sitting on more than $10 billion of subprime; their only upside was the income from the mortgages, with billions on the downside.

The deepest irony was that our group was more worried about the real estate market than the mortgage department was. One evening, Alex Kirk and I went for a drink after work, down to Nobu 57, New York's fabled celebrity Japanese sushi restaurant on West 57th Street between Fifth and Sixth Avenues. And right there I asked him if he could give me a little guidance about the size of Lehman's exposure to a possible subprime default. I knew it was privileged information, and I knew it might be very difficult for Alex to confide even in me, one of his right-hand men. But I needed to know. And he knew I needed to know.

He was about as cagey as I'd ever seen him. "You know I can't go there," he said. "But I understand why you're asking. You want to know how big to short on the other side, just in case we might need a rescue operation?"

"Correct," I said. But I could not pry the information out of him.

"I just wish I could get a handle on the size of the problem," I told him, and he nodded very seriously. He knew. If ever anyone knew, it was Alex. Hell, he and Mike Gelband were the first ones in the entire corporation to call the problem of the steroid-boosted property market.

But Lehman, like all investment banks, was a real black box, with its secrets and its untold revelations. Alex hinted to me that we had his total support in our endeavors to balance the property books.

"You mean you won't object to us shorting those big mortgage brokerages and mortgage insurers in a major way?"

"That, Larry," he said, "sounds like a very sensible idea."

I mention that incident only to illustrate the depth of our anxiety. The problem was constantly on our minds. Ashish Shah, Larry McCarthy, and I were always talking about it. And we finally evolved a plan in which David Gross ("Grossy"), one of the top convertible bond salesmen on our floor and a very good friend, would come with me on a trip to the West Coast. Its purpose would be twofold. First, visit with several important clients to discuss airline bonds, one of my principal areas of trading responsibility. The second—and perhaps more important—would be to do some high-quality professional spying. The name's Bond, Larry Bond.

We had to be extremely careful, because on no account did we want the mortgage department—or anyone else, for that matter—to find out what we were doing. We just wanted to make a discreet trip out west and try to take the pulse of places like New Century and the rest, out there in the world headquarters of the bodybuilders. Grossy and I were going behind enemy lines, and we could not afford to have the tough-minded head of our mortgage securitization business, Dave Sherr, made aware of our presence in the cradle of the CDOs in Orange County.

The fortyish Sherr was a property bull. It was he who had opened the attack on our group at a meeting when he declared we did not understand the workings of that market. It was he who was ready with the instant retort that the U.S. housing market had never gone down more than 5 percent in any year since the Great Depression. He was a well-educated graduate of Babson College, the business school out in leafy Wellesley, Massachusetts, due west of downtown Boston. The global head of every aspect of Lehman's mortgage securitization business had an ill-disguised dislike of our ideas about his bailiwick. His belief in the everlasting validity of the CDOs was inviolable. Secretly we planned our trip. We first flew to Chicago where we would entertain clients for a couple of days. Dave Gross would be a key man here, since he was a salesman and knew them all personally. We made a point of allowing this trip to the Midwest to be well known inside the building. But only Larry McCarthy, Pete Schellbach, and Pete Hammack knew where we were really going.

For the first two days of the trip we entertained our clients out there by Lake Michigan, advising every last one of them to get in and short New Century, NovaStar, and an outfit called Accredited Home Lenders. We both explained there were small but significant signs that this housing market might have peaked or, worse yet, might crash. I told them how some of the cleverest people at Lehman Brothers were extremely concerned that the roof might fall in on the biggest mortgage brokers.

I know that many of them took our advice, mostly because any Lehman trader commands great respect beyond Wall Street, but also because our trip was a very warm, sociable time. We took two clients out to Cog Hill Country Club, west of the city, and played a memorable round on Course Four, the tigerish Dubsdread, where great professional and amateur championships have been held.

Dubsdread is 6,940 yards long with tight tree-lined fairways. Tiger Woods had recently fought his way around there to win his third straight Western Open. I've mentioned that I'm a lifelong golfer and the son of a very fine amateur player. But it still gives me a huge thrill to follow in the footsteps of the immortals. I guess it's similar to standing on Wimbledon's Centre Court, in center field at Yankee Stadium, or down on the hardwood at Madison Square Garden. But there's nothing like standing in solitude on a world-class golf course and knowing that great champions also stood here, with the same thoughts running through their minds: *a slight fade into the green . . . stay left of the bunkers . . . is this club long enough?*

For every reasonably accomplished player, the ghosts of golf's legends are always present. And at places like Cog Hill you just knew they were all once here: Sam and Ben, Arnie and Jack, Gary and Tom, as well as the sweet-swinging Tiger himself. And I'll tell you one secret: when I hit the sloping green at the par-five six-hundred-yard ninth with a drive and a three-wood, hell, I thought I *was* Tiger. Darn near filed an entry for the 2007 U.S. Open Championship at Oakmont.

In the end I shot 75. But Grossy and I made some good friends, and the following evening we flew west to Los Angeles. No one met us, and we rented a car, then drove to the Beverly Wilshire Hotel, checked in, and had dinner with two very big clients, hedge fund managers who had bought a lot of product through Lehman. Again we gave the warning about the housing market, and again we advised on some serious short positions against New Century, NovaStar, and Accredited Home Lenders.

At seven o'clock the following morning we received a scary signal from a retail equity broker from the Cape, Jack Corbett, who called the hotel to let me know that Accredited had massively missed their second-quarter earnings target. Jack was a good old buddy from Falmouth High, and he knew I was interested in the subject. Interested? My annual bonus was locked up in a corporation that was up to its eyes in CDOs, so many we weren't even allowed to know the number.

However, Peter Schellbach and I had shorted Accredited in a major way, so we weren't unduly troubled when the stock crashed 15 percent that day. In fact, we each made over $2 million profit that day for the firm. It was our first subprime trade, and it felt good. This was the first tangible evidence that we were correct in our assessment of the mortgage market, and that Dave Sherr and his band of subprime securitization brothers might be on borrowed time.

I wondered if Dave Sherr was still so utterly certain we had no idea what we were talking about. There was no sense of triumph. We just wanted them to come to their senses, to listen to the biggest brains in the company: Alex, Mike, Larry, Ashish, and, I suppose, the rest of us.

The tumultuous events of that early morning immediately instilled a charge of urgency into our mission. What if all these brokerage guys started missing their earnings? What if we could not stop Lehman from buying New Century? What if we could not get big enough short positions to counteract the problem?

I called Larry, who'd already heard about Accredited, and he thought Grossy and I had better get right down to the sprawling headquarters of New Century and try to get some solid information from someone—God knows who, because we couldn't just walk in and demand facts. That much was obvious.

We saddled up our hired Buick and picked up Route 405, running southeast for almost 50 miles, following the coastline toward San Diego. It was still quite early in the morning when we arrived, and we decided to take a scenic side trip down to Lake Forest, ten miles beyond Irvine, and take a look at the West Coast HQ of the Lehman subsidiary Aurora. There was not much to see, but it sure looked like a prosperous operation. So we turned around and headed back to Irvine, first of all scouting around the headquarters of BNC, our other subsidiary—another campus that looked suspiciously like a billion dollars.

But we pressed on to our objective, the giant mortgage factory in this manicured section of outer Los Angeles. We knew this would not be a simple reconnaissance mission, taking a look and moving on. We needed to go undercover, find somewhere to make contact with the enemy, and then make some serious assessments, validate the dangers.

We drove down typical California upper-middle-class streets, following our map and keeping an eye on the GPS system. It was pretty easy to find. In fact, the world headquarters of New Century seemed to pervade the entire area, as if the expensive shops, bars, and restaurants were all somehow a part of this grinding coast-to-coast money machine with a sales force that seemed like the size of the U.S. Army.

Finally we located it and pulled up outside its impressive front entrance, with its perfectly clipped lawns. New Century stood back, a palace of black glass—at least I guess it looked like a palace to its employees. To us, Wall Street special agents with a jaundiced eye, it looked like the Lubyanka—that's the Moscow headquarters of the old KGB.

We eased forward, making a quick recon of the front parking

area. For a split second I couldn't work out whether this was a mortgage brokerage or a Ferrari dealership. But I definitely never before saw one single spot on God's green earth with that many top-of-the-line automobiles parked shoulder to shoulder. Alongside the Ferraris, we saw two low-slung 160-mph Lotus sports cars from England. We saw brand-new Jaguars and the most opulent BMWs. Mercedeses were two for a penny. We even saw a dark blue Bentley.

And walking with the merest suggestion of a swagger, across the immaculately paved driveway, were two unmistakable salesmen—flat-top haircuts, two-piece suits that fit slightly too tight, gold earrings, leather briefcases with gold fittings. They climbed into a metallic blue Jaguar that started with a throaty, confident growl.

Grossy burst out laughing. "Holy shit!" he said. "Did you just see those two lugheads? Are we in the wrong business?"

8

The Mortgage Bonanza Blows Out

These were people who, in the five thousand years of recorded human house construction, never would have been granted a mortgage to purchase even a dwelling of mud, reeds, or palm leaves. And they were very, very frightened.

WE DID NOT linger very long outside the New Century parking lot. We drove maybe half a mile back toward the freeway and parked on a side street. We then walked back to New Century and took a long look around the outside of the building.

There was plainly no point in even contemplating entering, since we had no appointment and in any event had no right to be snooping around asking questions. It would have taken someone mere moments to call the mortgage department back in New York and demand to know who the hell we were and what we wanted, at which time the game would be up and Dave Sherr would want some embarrassing answers.

"We'd never get in there," said Dave Gross. "Not under any guise."

"I wouldn't be absolutely sure about that," I replied. "Gimme a couple of big pizza boxes; I'll be through that door and in the president's office in about three minutes—'Brad Morrice insisted, real hot with extra cheese.' "

Grossy looked at me, plainly considering whether I'd completely lost it. I decided not to elaborate on my misspent youth, and instead outlined our strategy. We needed a restaurant close to the building, where we could locate a few bodybuilders on their break.

We found a place that was almost perfect—snazzy, pricey lunch, nice bar, expensive décor, glamorous waitresses—just a few hundred yards from the New Century building, and made it our HQ for a couple of hours. Sitting at a corner table, we assessed the events of the last few days.

First off, Merrill Lynch, according to a fast phone call from Ashish, now had $50 billion worth of CDOs filled with mortgages on their books—a whole mass of subprime, scads of them from California, some of them probably sold from this very restaurant. Grossy reminded me of Pete Hammack's very last words before we left: "If, in just one month, New Century cannot move those subprime mortgages out into the market, they're dead. Their balance sheet could not stand it." Pete meant not just New Century but all of us. No one can afford to hold on to the scalding hot potato of subprime mortgages that cannot be sold. "Larry," he'd told me, "this market right now is like a line of traffic, with everyone moving up to the head of the line and waiting for the green light—get the CDOs sold and keep going forward." In Pete's opinion, if that traffic light malfunctioned, and the first two vehicles were somehow stuck, everyone else would back up. There would be a whole line with nothing moving, all jammed up, and the carnage would be indescribable.

New Century was selling $5 billion worth of mortgages every month, and David Einhorn, the founder and president of the multibillion-dollar hedge fund Greenlight Capital, had just joined its board of directors. He's probably the smartest short-seller on Wall Street, maybe the world. So what was he doing on the board of this New Century outfit, with its billion-dollar headquarters and lugheads riding around in brand-new Jaguars? His presence on the board gave me pause. Could we all be wrong? Did they really have a golden business, upright and aboveboard? Could Alex, Mike, and Larry all be completely wrong in their assessments? This was, after all, the second-largest subprime lender in the nation.

The thoughts were racing through my mind. And I guess my expression betrayed my concerns, but Dave, one of our best bond salesmen, did not share them. "Listen," he said, "New Century had a real shake-up couple of months ago, new CEO, this guy Brad Morrice. And quite frankly, I don't care whether David Einhorn is on the board or not. I don't care who the hell's on the board.

"But I do know one thing—we both saw those documents Pete pulled on the New Century's mortgage portfolio, and they showed nothing less than a factory, thousands and thousands of those mortgages, subprime up a hundred percent in 2004, a hundred percent in 2005, and God knows how much in 2006. And now we got signs the housing market might be heading south. Finally."

Worse yet, the interest rate resets were about to kick in. We'd seen the documents. Hundreds of thousands of poor people were about to see their monthly payments rocket up from $800 to possibly $2,400 a month, maybe more. It had to be a house of cards, because these people could not afford that much. Suddenly my certitude was restored and I knew that Pete Hammack's traffic jam would ultimately start right here. Maybe not for a while, but the traffic lights that would stop turning green were just outside this restaurant door, on the grounds of New Century.

By now it was around twelve-thirty and the bodybuilders were coming in for lunch. You could not miss them, with their slick hair, toned muscles, and tight-fitting shirts. You could smell them as well, expensive cologne in the middle of the day, reeking of success, and so cocky. Our waitress told us she'd just been given a $100 tip for three plates of pasta.

You could tell everyone was doing great. They were confident, slightly too loud, with a brashness common among people who are paid huge amounts of money for tasks that require no real brilliance. These guys were pleased with themselves, pleased to be talking about sport, girls, or automobiles. The stock market could have fallen and not raised a flicker in this particular chophouse.

We finished our lunch and moved into the bar, where I could see two or three bodybuilders having a beer. We easily fell into conversation, and they were happy to chat to a couple of vacationing Wall Street guys. They told us that mortgage brokerage was the greatest business on earth. Bar none. They were all earning between $300,000 and $600,000.

We mentioned there were rumors back on the Street that this booming real estate market might be turning. There were small but clear signs, the market had flattened and would probably fall. But they dismissed the possibility out of hand: *That's no problem, just a blip—don't worry about it.*

They were like peacocks, bragging about their huge salaries, New Century's enormous share of the market, how so much money was being made every day, every week. They cheerfully confirmed they were all on double commission: *Takes a tough man to sell this stuff, and New Century is prepared to pay well for the best.*

I asked them if they gave much thought to the possibilities of defaults when the resets began. They dismissed this with even more panache. *Not our concern, pal. Our job is to sell the mortgage policy. Period. Right after that it's someone else's problem.*

I asked, did they think some of the less wealthy guys would still be able to afford the reset payments? *Hope so, otherwise it's back to the ghetto, right?*

Was proof of income or assets needed before the mortgage is granted? *Hell, no. They just need to state their income. No docs. That's why we work here.*

You guys ever worried some of these no-doc borrowers might just take the money and run, without making payments? *I just told you, it's not our problem. We're salesmen. New Century makes it easy for us.*

They all knew one of the big attractions of New Century stock was the 10 percent dividend it paid. The stock was held up by that. It was one of the highest dividends on the New York Stock Exchange, and it was quite obviously too good to be true. If the market went down and that dividend had to be cut back, the stock would have to crash. Anyone could see that, but it did not faze the bodybuilders. *Look, man, right here we got a great company and we're killing them out there in the market. Let's just fly with it. Three of our top guys have made $74 million over four years, with cash and stock. That's a goal for all of us. And New Century's gonna make that possible. Universal home ownership, right? That's our target. New Century for the new century. You gotta love it.*

They told us the corporation had taken their top salesmen to the Bahamas on a luxury liner booze cruise. Actually it had been a themed booze cruise, under the banner "The Best Damn Mortgage Company. Period." They'd even hired the railroad station in Barcelona, Spain, for another heavy-drinking junket for top employees. New Century chiefs made huge charitable contributions, and sent one high-flying exec to a Porsche-driving school.

"Guys," said our new buddy, "right here you're looking at a new shade of blue chip. That's one of our mottoes."

You couldn't dislike these New Century heroes. But their knowledge was awfully one-sided. For a start, they knew nothing of Pete

Hammack's evidence of heavy stock selling among the company's three founders. Neither did they volunteer anything about some shaky accounting practices, which had caused concern to a Maryland financial research outfit, currently flagging problems with New Century's third-quarter earnings release.

Neither were they aware of the anger of a California lawyer, Alan Ramos, who was plainly infuriated that his client, an elderly lady about to be evicted from her three-bedroom home northwest of Stockton, had been made an enormous "senior citizen" loan. On checking the documents, Mr. Ramos found that her income section had been left blank.

"Blank?" he exclaimed. "How does it even get past the first person who looks at it?"

Right there I guess we had the New Century way. Its loan originations had been $6.3 billion in the year 2000 and were expected to hit $60 billion this year. This was a corporation that unloaded thousands of mortgages, every month, onto Wall Street mortgage securitization guys who weren't anything like as smart as they should have been.

Dave Gross and I left that bar in mild amazement. That whole group of cocky, relatively dumb bodybuilders was so pleased with their lives, so unaware of what could happen, so far behind the advanced thinkers of Wall Street. You know what they say: when it's seven o'clock in New York, it's 1991 in California. Make that 1981.

"There's something really rotten about this place," I told Dave. "We're in the Wild West of mortgage lending."

He said he agreed, and was really shaken by the totally careless way the bodybuilders wrote mortgage agreements, how they could not give a damn whether the money was paid back or not. For one bright shining moment I decided I had seen the light. Because in that restaurant, crammed with self-satisfied know-nothings, we had gazed upon the amoral soul of this housing boom, the crux, the fulcrum, the place where so many dreams would begin, and where surely heartbreak and financial collapse must follow.

We were both struck by the curious remoteness of the guys with whom we had spoken. They acted as though the fortunes of neither the corporation nor the borrowers had anything to do with them. They were like hired guns, oblivious to the fate of their victims or the outfit that had hired them. Both in their own minds and in ours, they were men apart—for slightly different reasons, of course.

Both Grossy and I thought they were a breed, rather than a clan. They were professional salesmen who rode the waves, and when one wave petered out they would find the next one. I thought of that Philadelphia bucket shop, where high-pressure tactics were used to sell penny stocks; they would say anything, promise anything, just to get the sale done.

These guys we'd just left were the same, remote from the reality of what they were doing. They moved in a flock, migrating from one sales scam to another, probably about every five years. And they were good at it. I recognized that much, even though I'd personally have given the bastards a run on a vanload of pork chops. Never forget your roots, right?

At this point in August, the New Century stock was at over $40 and rising. It would be pointless trying to persuade the mortgage guys back at the office that this market was surely heading for a very hard brick wall; Dave Sherr and his boys would surely laugh at us, as they had done before. And we flew home that night wondering what the hell to do. The fact was, we couldn't find out the volume of subprime that had been sold to Lehman, but we had discovered much about a hardworking, hard-partying culture upon which our corporation's future might depend.

The following day, straight off the red-eye from Los Angeles, we were met at JFK and whisked into the office, where we immediately caucused with Larry and Pete Hammack, both of whom were waiting for us. We already suspected New Century had been taking wild chances with its lending, but now we needed to move fast.

Larry said the $20 puts were 50 cents each for six months, "let's buy 10,000"—which effectively meant we could make a $500,000 bet that New Century's stock would go below $20 between September and March. This was crazily cheap, we thought, but the market was calm, no volatility. We bought a pile of the puts; we bought the $20s, the $25s, and the $27.50s. Just the $20 puts we purchased made us short a million shares below $20 a share. That's not counting all the other puts we bought. If New Century went down, we'd make close to $30 million. I guess that's why Lehman stood us a couple of nights in the Beverly Wilshire.

But on the next day we wanted to up the ante on New Century—short them big-time. And with a position of this size it meant I needed the approval of Rich Gatward. By now I had a solid relationship with the old tiger of the equity trading floor, though we all had to be on our A-game in our dealings with him, and I understood he would not hesitate to bawl out anyone who wasn't. But he and I had developed excellent trust in each other, and he never once turned me down on a well-presented trade, especially against a subprime candidate. He was the toughest, but also the fairest, of the Lehman department heads that I knew. I presented him with our full plan, the complete picture of New Century, along with a sprawl of outstanding spreadsheets compiled by Pete Hammack, who came to the meeting with me. The sheets demonstrated what we could lose and what we might win depending on the price of New Century's stock, from $60 all the way down to $5. I admit I had some trepidation, because we'd been on a clandestine mission and wanted to keep it very quiet. I also had no idea whether Rich had close friends up in the mortgage department. But he never faltered, that fast analytical mind of his slicing up the information we presented.

Finally, after careful study, he said, "I think you've got something here. And this work is great. Put the trade on, and keep me posted." Rich was not as bearish about New Century, but he still trusted Larry and me, and he backed us every last inch of the way.

I contacted Susquehanna, an outside broker, the domain of Matt Durso, a good old buddy of Dave Gross. I told him I wanted a menu for 30,000 put contracts on New Century—that's known on Wall Street as a gorilla trade. Big.

"Jesus," he said, "what do you guys know?"

"Matt, we've done a ton of research on this," I told him. "We don't like the company. And we don't think the dividend's safe. Also, they're registered as a REIT [real estate investment trust], and we think the REITs are vulnerable in a falling housing market."

I told him we were looking to pay 55 cents per put on one of the options on his menu, and he came back wanting 65 cents. I checked with Larry, who snapped out one of his creeds: "You limit orders, you limit profits. I don't want to nickel-and-dime. I just want to get it done."

A limit order is just a way of lowballing, trying to undercut the trader's market, hoping to buy at a lower price. But when the market keeps moving away from your bid, you end up chasing it, like a

Bedouin riding his camel toward a mirage. We had no time for that on a trade this hot. So I did that part of the deal and put on a $650,000 initial trade. At the end of the day, in total, we spent $5 million and bought all 30,000 put contracts. God help Matt Durso, I thought. He and Susquehanna were taking all that risk. Little did I know that in October, New Century would grind ever higher.

We were now in mid-September, and there was developing a feeling of disquiet throughout Wall Street. Yet more evidence was emerging about the stresses on the housing market. And I have to say, our trip to the West Coast was becoming more public than we anticipated, and so were the huge short positions.

There was no word from the mortgage guys, at least no formal word, but there was a buzz about the Asset-Backed Securities Index, or ABX. That's the index that tracks the prices being asked and paid for the subprime mortgage bonds, the CDOs. The ABX was a system of quivering sensitivity, programmed to practically suffer a thrombosis if those bonds moved a couple of ticks downward.

And what made the situation that fall even more jumpy was that no one could remember the son of a bitch twitching a tendon, never mind moving a muscle. The ABX was static; the mortgage market had been dead calm for years, a graph line unlike any other. There were dead people whose heartbeats were more erratic. The index was as straight as a gun barrel, all through the entire upsurge on the U.S. housing market.

The ABX normally trades at par (100) because it's a measure of the strength and value of mortgage bonds. On Tuesday morning, September 19, the ABX slipped to 97–99: the trader, who sets the market, would buy at $97 and sell to you at $99. The ABX had fallen very, very slightly, only three ticks, but in certain places that caused big consternation.

Larry and I went for a drink at a nearby sports bar, Tonic, that evening, and ran into a colleague, Eric Felder, head of our high-grade credit business—that's the traders who deal with investment-grade corporate debt. He knew as much as anyone about Lehman's credit derivative business and was highly respected all over the Street.

Eric was a real up-and-comer, a bull by nature, but as soon as we saw him, he began to tell us he was very bothered by something he had noticed that day. His question was, "Did you see that move in the ABX today?" We could see the concern on his face. "It dipped. First sign of volatility I've ever seen on that index. This, guys, is serious. If it drops one more time this week, we better short it. I guess the mortgage guys are still long. And if this keeps up, that's not gonna be good."

I asked him how this might affect New Century, and he was not optimistic. Larry said immediately he was going to double, maybe triple, our short position against the California brokerage.

The next day the ABX dropped to 96–98. I increased the short on New Century yet again. Both Larry McCarthy and I understood why the CDOs were dropping. There were more sellers than buyers, more people watching that ABX, more people paying attention to slight upticks in the default charts, the repossessions, the failures on first-mortgage payments. Maybe there were even people quietly recollecting the words, months ago, of both Alex Kirk and Mike Gelband.

Larry and I did not have all the answers. But we had found out one thing: Lehman had underwritten $101 billion in mortgage-backed securities so far that year, and a whole lot of it was subprime and Alt-A. Holy shit!

By any standards 2006 had been a ride through choppy waters for Lehman, especially with the housing market now shipping water. Short of a miracle, neither of us could see how the mortgage department could come out whole, not with the raft of CDOs they had. For all we knew, the traffic light had already malfunctioned. Which may have been what was causing the ABX to develop a nervous twitch, with everyone lining up to make an exit.

Even the Delta bonds, which seemed like a steady and reasonable bet to increase in value, had suffered a couple of diabolical moments. One of them, back in April, was so dire at the time, I couldn't bring myself to mention it in this narrative, especially as I had made the original market for the bankrupt airline.

Back on April 17, the bonds had rallied to 26 or 27 cents on the dollar. But then things went south, especially Hezbollah's missiles, which started bombarding Israel, and the world oil market, as usual, instantly wet itself. Up went the price of jet fuel. Then the pilots threatened to go on strike. We still had a boatload of the bonds, bought cheaply, but still, $425 million in face-value worth? As the hours ticked away, the strike grew more and more likely. Everyone was saying it was going to happen, and that Delta's entire fleet would be grounded, resulting in zero cash flow and a highly negative balance sheet.

Everyone, that is, except for one person. Jane Castle said, "The pilots are bluffing. Trust me. And the bonds are still worth fifty-two cents."

We were close to table max, that is, the maximum amount of money we could put on the table. After that, we couldn't buy another bond, whatever the price. And the market wasn't listening to Jane. The bond price dropped to $23, then $22. And then something truly nerve-wracking broke out.

It was two-thirty on that Monday afternoon when my direct line to the sales desk in our San Francisco office suddenly lit up. John van Oast, our man in command, was on the line with the worst possible news. T. Rowe Price, a huge mutual fund with five thousand employees out of Baltimore, Maryland, wanted to sell their Delta bonds. I knew they might have been holding about $120 million face-value worth of convertibles, and they were one of our biggest customers, with about 20 percent of Delta's entire convertible bond issue. They were a real traditional company, founded in 1937, currently with almost $400 billion under management. T. Rowe Price had to be accommodated.

"Larry," yelled John from California, "I got 'em on the wire right now, and they need a bid on Delta convertibles."

I called back, "Twenty-one, twenty-two, ten million up!"

"Hold it," replied John. "Be right back."

Seconds later he was on the line again. "They appreciate the bid, but what they really want is a cleanup bid."

Jesus Christ. They want to sell them all. The blood drained from my face. I told Larry the state of the battle. I knew he'd go low since we were already near table max.

For a moment there was silence. Then Larry called it: "Eighteen bid for the lot!"

For the first time in my life I saw a bead of sweat on his brow, and maybe even a slight tremor on his hand as he scribbled down a note.

Van Oast yelled, "They got a hundred and twenty to go. All I need to hear are the two beautiful words."

The numbers flashed through my mind: $120 million face value on bonds times 18 cents, that's $21.6 million for cash. Larry nodded curtly. "You're done!" he replied. And the deal was complete.

Larry, for once, was a bit over his skis. We were about an inch and a half from table max, which meant five bucks was a lot of money to spend. Larry had just spent more than $21 million. Somebody's budget was about to get slammed. "I'd better go see Gat," said Larry. "Jesus Christ!"

Several weeks later I took a call from the head trader at T. Rowe Price, who reminded me, "I've been in this business a long time. With that airline going down, that was probably the gutsiest call I ever heard. McCarthy?"

"Who the hell else?" I replied.

A few days after we had bought all the bonds, the Delta pilots called off the strike, and the price went back up to 24–25 cents on the dollar. Gatward was thrilled because Larry, Jane, and I had persuaded him to share the risk, and he'd taken most of it at 18 cents. So far as Jane was concerned, there was no reason to sell any of them. So we all just hung in there with our gigantic load of Delta convertibles, all through the summer of 2006.

And now we must fast-forward to a cold November day on Seventh Avenue. I was walking to work, contemplating our vast short position on New Century and our even vaster long position on the Delta bonds. The first one was probably as much my fault as anyone's; the second resulted from advice from Jane, but I had made the market. And the entire department understood the dimension of our gamble. There were not yet jokes being made about it, but we'd been in there with Delta for almost twelve months, and our corporate year ended in November.

I reached our building and stopped downstairs for a cup of coffee. It was not yet six-thirty, but there were already a few people in there. First person I saw was an equity trader I knew well, Jim Everett, who turned to me with a grin and said, "Big day for you guys."

I hadn't the slightest idea what he was talking about, and I must have looked kind of blank.

"Haven't you heard?" he said.

"Heard what?"

"U.S. Air just made a hostile bid for Delta. At least fifty-five cents on the dollar for the bonds."

I think I nearly died of happiness. Chills ran up my spine, and my pulse was racing as I headed up to the trading floor. I can't remember the ride up in the elevator, can't even remember if there was anyone else sharing it. I was just running the numbers through my mind, and the key ones were that we now owned about $720 million worth, face value, of the bonds and we'd bought most them for well under 25 cents on the dollar.

I came out of that elevator like a greyhound out of a trap, running to my desk and hitting the button to switch on my screen. And there it was, the hostile bid from U.S. Air. *Fifty-five cents.* I called Larry on his cell phone. He hadn't heard either, and said he'd be there in just a few minutes.

I could tell he was beside himself, not just with excitement but with a sense of relief, because he'd been the motor behind our enormous position. He'd relied on Jane's assessment, but he'd personally sanctioned almost the whole of Lehman's expenditure. If this had ever gone badly wrong—say, if the bonds had slipped to being worthless—Larry McCarthy would have taken the lion's share of the blame.

It was not yet seven o'clock, but by now everyone in the entire bank knew about the drama, and a lot of them knew we were about to make a colossal fortune for the firm. The atmosphere was electric, nothing less, as our group moved into gear, because trading was expected to start early, maybe around seven-thirty.

The place was packed, and every single eye was on us, especially me, the market maker. But suddenly there was a shift of focus, and we turned to the entrance to the trading floor to see Jane Castle walking in. A huge burst of applause broke out, a spontaneous cry of joy, just for her. Through all the months, through all the doubts and all the fears, she'd never wavered in her valuation of Delta Air Lines, and everyone knew it.

The smile on her face would have lit up Yankee Stadium, and she walked straight up to me and gave me a sweeping high five that darn nearly broke my wrist. Moments later Larry came in, wearing a brand-new suit and looking like the king of the world, and another burst of applause ripped into the morning air. When it died down, he looked over to Joe Beggans, who was about to start trading the Delta bonds, and, with a huge grin on his face, held out his hand and shouted, "Gimme the keys, Joe. I'm driving!" The whole place erupted.

When trading began, a lot of guys imagined we'd be selling as fast as we knew how. But not McCarthy. He crashed into the market and started buying the Delta bonds at 53 cents all over the Street. He actually chased the price up to 60 cents. And Jane was his co-conspirator, standing next to him, telling him they'd go to 65 cents.

Brent crude was crashing on the London market from $77 to $60 a barrel, jet fuel was down from $2.30 a gallon to $1.80, the pilots were flying, the aircraft were taking off, God was in His heaven, and our very own angel, Jane Castle, was telling Larry the Delta bonds could go to 70 cents.

Jane knew they'd had a positive cash build during their bankruptcy and had almost $4 billion in the can. Their last quarter's $500 million EBITDAR (earnings before interest, taxes, depreciation, amortization, and rent) was well above Street expectations. Their international flights had doubled, and there was now less competition from the budget airlines. In addition, Delta was valued at a fabulous, only 5.6 times EBITDAR, whereas the low-cost JetBlue stock was trading at 15.5 times. In addition, Jane had always passionately believed there would be a massive consolidation phase coming to the U.S. airlines.

The rest remains a blur until the moment Larry McCarthy decided to get out. "Okay, guys. Let's go," he called, and, for the first time for almost a year, we began to divest ourselves of the Delta bonds. Larry launched them onto the market with consummate skill, knowing, of course, that U.S. Air was out there waiting, begging to buy. By the time he had finished, Lehman had made a $250 million profit, the largest one-day triumph in the history of Lehman Brothers bond trading.

Larry was so elated by the turn of events and by Jane's determination to maximize that he announced our whole group was invited to a dinner he would host that night at Il Mulino, one of New York's most esteemed classic Italian restaurants. Almost everyone attended, except Jane. And there, at a meal during which no expense was spared, he proposed a toast to her. "If she was here," he shouted, "I swear to God I'd drink champagne from her shoes!" I chuckled, remembering that just before we'd all left for the restaurant, he'd actually picked up the phone and apologized profusely to the risk management department for the Delta bonds having gone up forty points. Sarcasm is supposed to be the lowest form of wit, but not on this day. How sweet it was. *Why don't you shove it up your ass, VaR?*

And all this was happening in the shakiest quarter the mortgage business had ever had. With the mortgages crashing all over the place, we saved their asses. Their numbers were off, their profits were off, and the losses were starting to pile up. The ABX was headed for 85–86, and our $250 million victory, in a way, lit up Lehman's year-end balance sheet.

The real estate boom year 2006, which had started out rich with promise, had, for those with the wits to notice, been steadily turning sour. But now, at the start of the New York winter, the landscape had turned rancid. Anywhere there had been a sign of decay, poor management, or just plain old trouble, that's what ultimately developed. Most indicators measuring the performance of the mortgage industry glowed in the darkness of disaster. Every chart that could possibly record a trend was recording a god-awful one, and getting worse. Repossessions were up, prices were down, defaults were climbing, mortgages weren't getting paid, and accountancy among the big mortgage houses was developing into sleight-of-hand as financiers struggled to hide the truth from an increasingly skeptical world.

The vastly experienced property brokers at some of the biggest investment houses in the business, Merrill Lynch, Goldman Sachs, JPMorganChase, Citigroup, Bear Stearns, and Lehman, had run headlong into the oldest, most obvious, most dangerous trap in their business: they'd gone into massive trades, with massively leveraged positions, without first perfecting their exit strategy, how to get out if a fire started. Right now they needed to reach the theater door, but everyone else was stampeding down the aisles, jumping over the seats, swinging on the chandeliers, and diving through the men's room window trying to reach safety.

All the signs had been out there for weeks, especially among the mergers and acquisitions. One of Larry's more graphic mottoes is that a sure signal of big trouble is when two pigs marry each other. And the pigs had been charging for the altar all year.

San Diego's Accredited Home Loans announced the purchase of Aames Financial, a Los Angeles giant with $6.75 billion in home loans, representing thousands of subprimes. Accredited must have been real at home with this, since they had $16.5 billion of their own in originations and were in worse trouble with defaults than the guys they bought.

Accredited was the outfit I'd told our guys to short just before I hit that screamer of a three-wood onto the ninth green at Cog Hill. (On reflection, it might equally well have been just after I missed the putt.) Anyhow, we'd been shorting Accredited for months, and I thought they and Miss Piggy Aames would make a perfect couple.

Wachovia Bank and Trust, out of Charlotte, North Carolina, the nation's fourth-largest bank holding company, spent a whopping $25.5

billion to buy Golden West Financial, a mortgage giant chock-full of adjustable-rate mortgages and currently shuddering from the impact of reset-led defaults.

Then in November 2006 Merrill Lynch took over San Jose–based First Franklin, one of the nation's leading originators of non-prime residential mortgage loans. Merrill somehow managed to get mixed up with a sister corporation to Franklin that went by the name of NationPoint. Online mortgage sales were its specialty, and the previous year the pair of them had lent a staggering $29 billion. They represented Subprime City. And now Merrill paid $1.3 billion for them, which under the current circumstances was tantamount to buying a nuclear bomb, fully primed, armed, and timed, with no particular destination keyed in. I hate to use up yet more of my supply of hindsight, but I can say precisely one thing that could never be disputed—if Mike Gelband or Alex Kirk had been in charge at Merrill, that merger *never* would have taken place.

By Christmas 2006 we'd been hearing rumors for a while that MGIC, an investment corporation based in Milwaukee, would team with the Radian Group in Philadelphia to spend $259 million to buy Fieldstone Investment Corporation of Columbia, Maryland, a nationwide residential mortgage banking company with a hefty accent on nonconforming borrowers. Fieldstone wouldn't exactly enter the marriage with an appealing dowry: in the first nine months of 2006 they'd lost $28.3 million, which was not too bad for a piggy. By year's end Fieldstone was the twenty-third-largest lender in the country, specializing in home buyers with the poorest credit. So we started shorting all three companies. (The deal would be announced in February 2007.) Looking back, this was an increasingly desperate attempt on our part to level up the Lehman balance sheet while this horrendous mortgage picture continued to unravel. Everywhere you looked, there was trouble. Privately Mike Gelband, Larry, and the rest of us had an unnerving instinct that this whole thing could blunder forward into unimaginable chaos.

We'd already received a shock when yet another ominous signal came ripping through cyberspace concerning the biggest home builder in the country, the Dallas-based construction giant Centex. The previous spring Centex had missed its earnings target by a country mile, and there had been huge consternation. But then the industry somehow rallied in the summer, and it seemed the good times might be back for

Centex. But in the middle of October 2006, they'd announced yet another horrific miss on their earnings sheet, making 69 cents per share instead of the forecast $1.40. It was the buzz of the trading floor. And this was not make-believe money, like our romance with the credit default swaps, the bets, and the IOUs. When Centex threw up its hands, this was real down-and-dirty cash. Centex did not gamble and scheme. Centex built homes—bricks, concrete, and wood—all over the country, thousands of them. They were bigger than Beazer. And they were not joking. They'd announced a massive cut in their landowning options, which, to those in the trade, is a classic sign of big problems. When a builder doesn't need land, that builder senses trouble ahead. In the third quarter Centex had orders for 6,828 homes, down 28 percent on the previous year. These were record levels of contract cancellations, and the corporation was so concerned that they were prepared to abandon huge land options at a predicted walkaway cost of $90 million. I guess that must have been tough to swallow, but, hey, in this market, a builder's gotta do what a builder's gotta do.

All the ominous signs that this endless housing funfest was about to end were sending tremors through the market. But perhaps most of all, it was attracting cruising sharks, investors and analysts whose business was the blood of the mighty. In a way, our group represented Lehman's private shark tank, but we were just trying to clean up the firm's act, rebalance the books, and make up for the coming losses. The real sharks were out there on the Street, circling, scenting blood, trying to spot weakness in our ancient merchant bank, weakness that would allow them to thrust forward and feed, dumping huge short positions on our stock. In some ways, they were echoing us with the mortgage houses, but these sharks were outsiders, intent on our downfall, less sympathetic, and a whole lot more ravenous.

Wall Street sharks are apt to cruise in deep waters. One of the few times they surface is at those regular conference calls when analysts and stockholders are free to get on the line and ask searching questions of the bank's management. Lehman's last-quarter 2006 conference took place on Thursday afternoon, December 14. In the chair was our chief financial officer, Chris O'Meara. Christine Daley and I had the phones rammed into our ears. She was really on edge, deeply troubled by the slowdown, and the subsequent buildup in our mortgage portfolio. And we were now hearing more confirmation of this, humming down the wire. "Wow," said Christine, "we're supposed to be in the moving business, not the darned storage business. I don't like the smell of this. Not one little bit."

When the discussion turned to the mortgage market, Chris admitted that Lehman's creation of CDOs was slightly slower than it had been the previous year. It did, however, "remain solid," despite what Chris stated were "the challenges from the U.S. housing market." That was a pretty economical way to describe the coming Armageddon, when the mortgage resets would do what Mike Gelband had said they would do, and bring the whole trembling edifice crashing down around our ears.

The fact was, the market was beginning to see the enormous problems that were ahead of us. Our corporate mortgage policy was revolving around the word *containment*. That word popped up again and again as the Lehman financial guys tried to explain the need for globalization in the hope of obfuscating the bald truth, instead stressing the grand world expansion strategies that set us apart from the pack. That meant unloading the CDOs all over the planet, especially to Europe and Japan. And the sharks sensed the tactic.

One of the Goldman Sachs analysts wanted to know, "What percentage of your mortgage business is now derived from outside the U.S. versus in the U.S.?"

Chris was fighting off his back foot, but he had an answer. "It is becoming an increasing percentage. We do not disclose that. But without giving you specifics around what's outside the U.S., recognize that it's a growing proportion of what we do, and we intend to keep growing."

The fact was, the Goldman analyst had worked out that there were few U.S. hedge funds, pension funds, or banks that would dream of buying the CDOs, given the alarm bells now regularly sounding throughout the U.S. housing industry. And he wanted to know where these things were getting sold. Chris offered some very obscure mentions of Korea, Japan, and the United Kingdom but stayed away from naming specific buyers.

The situation in places like Stockton, California, was beginning to come to a head. California newspapers were beginning to run stories of families seeing their mortgage interest rates reset and suddenly being asked for payments that came in at more than their monthly paychecks.

I understand I have occasionally talked of these situations with the mild objectivity that can walk hand in hand with remoteness, when a situation seems too far from home to be real, like famine in North Africa. But these cases *were* real. Here was a hardworking American man whom the bodybuilders had talked into taking out a mortgage that would cover the full price of a new house and provide some cash as well. And now, after the interest rate had reset to a much higher level, he was being asked for an astronomical repayment amount. If he paid it, his family would starve. And he didn't know the name of the person who held this mortgage, who was probably a banker in some Tokyo side street, twelve thousand miles away. So the homeowner's only alternatives were crime or the highway.

Judging by the recent crime figures for Stockton, many had chosen the former route. But those figures would go down, since the population of the town was plummeting downward as people abandoned their homes in droves. In the case of this particular family, they packed up their car with their possessions, called on friends and family to help, and headed back to the poorer areas of Oakland, whence they'd come. Before finally leaving the family had ripped up the carpets, hauled out the appliances, and even cut out the copper pipes, then placed the keys in the mailbox and vanished. No one actually knew they had gone until two months had gone by without a mortgage payment being made. And then it became clear to someone: this was a subprime mortgage that was not about to get paid. In Stockton alone, there were dozens, and then hundreds.

And what about the bodybuilders? They didn't care. They were still out there, still selling, still raking in the old double commissions. Still leaving $100 tips to pretty waitresses. And still—*vroom vroom*—hammering those sleek, shiny 160-mph sports cars straight down the highway.

By mid-December, the defaults were on the rise and beginning to show up in the national charts. The market for CDOs and all mortgage securitizations was grinding to a halt, and one hell of a jam was developing at the theater door. It was becoming impossible for Lehman to sell these bonds in the United States. And the first people to panic, right in the middle of the Christmas holiday, were the ratings agencies, who were looking at a major credibility gap that was just beginning to spotlight them. And that was not to their liking, because these agencies, Moody's, Standard & Poor's, and Fitch, were supposed to be judging other people's credentials, not having anyone else judge their own.

But the stats were coming out and they were not looking good. In 2001, Moody's had revenues of $800.7 million; in 2005 they were up to $1.73 billion; and in 2006, $2.037 billion. The exploding profits were fees from packaging the CDOs and for granting top-class AAA ratings, which were supposed to mean that they were as safe as U.S. government securities. But in the past few weeks things had changed drastically. Back in 2003, Moody's, S&P, and Fitch had each downgraded 113 CDOs between them, a couple every three weeks, out of all the thousands of issues. In 2005 that figure had crawled up to 172, which meant that each of the three agencies downgraded one issue every week. In the dying remnants of the year 2006, they downgraded 1,305, many of them straight from AAA to junk—BB or lower. It's also known colloquially as closing the barn door after the horses have bolted into the fields.

How on earth could a bond issue be AAA one day and junk the next unless something spectacularly stupid has taken place? But maybe it wasn't just stupid. Maybe it was something spectacularly dishonest, like taking that colossal amount of fees in return for doing what Lehman and the rest wanted, giving those CDOs an utterly undeserved rating, tantamount to the standard of the Federal Reserve, when they must have known they were dealing with a bunch of out-of-work no-hopers.

Forgive me a harsh judgment, but I think those raters were a bunch of half-assed, dishonest villains who would do anything for a fast buck. I just don't believe they were that stupid. And anyway, I believe a plea of "stupid" is probably the saddest of all defenses.

In the days surrounding Christmas 2006, there was evidence that the rating agencies were approaching panic stations. They were letting it be known that their own assessments had been wrong. And it came out publicly on December 27, on Bloomberg, that certain Lehman bonds, four of them, representing mortgages and home equity loans to some of the riskiest U.S. consumers, were about to have their ratings cut. Moody's admitted the potential for losses to investors had "rapidly increased" because consumers were facing financial difficulties. Ratings for securitizations on three other Lehman bonds, subprime home loans made the year before, were also put on Moody's list of possible downgrades. A total of thirty bond issues, with $416 million in balances, were affected.

Everywhere you looked the ratings agencies were rushing for cover. They were announcing ratings cuts all over the place, citing banks and lenders and issuing warnings, especially about subprime mortgages that were less than a year old. The truth was, all three of the big agencies could see the unexpectedly high levels of late payments and foreclosures piling up. They weren't that stupid. They could read the charts as well as we could—not as fast, but just as carefully. And now they were responding, threatening to look more closely.

The best numbers available said that defaults on subprime ARMs were running at 27 percent, the highest level for new loans for five years. About 3.2 percent of them were either delinquent by ninety days or more, or already foreclosed or repossessed. The overall rate of late payments on all subprime loans in the previous quarter rose to 12.56 percent.

A study was also issued by the Swiss bank UBS that warned of Lehman's subprime loans. They also named an Anaheim, California–based lender, Fremont General, as the issuer of the fourth-worst-performing bonds in the nation. Some of the worst had been issued by Goldman Sachs, General Electric Company's WMC Mortgage, and Morgan Stanley.

Right about then, we thought this could get really ugly. The principal monitoring trade group, the Securities Industry and Financial Markets Association (SIFMA), calculated that the total value of all mortgage-backed securities issued between 2001 and 2006 had reached *$13.4 trillion.* CDOs now represented America's greatest export and, thanks to the bodybuilders, were still surging forward. They dwarfed the high-yield corporate bond market, which is a snazzy way of describing junk bonds, those high-risk investments that have such a checkered history but have made vast fortunes for the lucky ones.

I hate to use the word *fraud.* But the CDO case comes very close, because its bedrock was a gigantic group of people, thousands and thousands of homeowners, who must surely default on their repayments. Even the bodybuilders knew that, despite turning a collective blind eye. And if the friggin' lugheads knew, there must have been a lot of other people who knew. My own department at Lehman was the first to know. And Alex Kirk was the first to flag it, in May 2005—one year and seven months before it started to fall apart. Mike Gelband yelled it publicly, with facts and figures, for everyone to hear, from Fuld downward, at 7:06 A.M. on June 7, 2005—one year, six months, and three weeks before. I was right there. No excuses. Many at Lehman Brothers had heard the warnings, and all through those months heard the rumors.

And it wasn't just people inside Lehman. The highly respected Lawrence Lindsey, former director of President George W. Bush's National Economic Council, who as president of The Lindsey Group was a highfly paid consultant to Lehman, made substantial monthly presentations to both high-level managing directors and members of the Lehman executive committee that reported directly to Dick Fuld and Joe Gregory. Lindsey was just as, if not more, bearish as Gelband and Kirk about the pending problem with mortgage resets and the impact on the economy of the growing problem of negative home equity.

Kirk, Gelband, and Lindsey had sounded the warnings. I accept there were people who honestly did not believe it. And you can never fix stupid. But our department knew beyond a shadow of a doubt that this CDO bullshit was utterly, totally, mind-bogglingly loaded with peril. If we'd been an oceangoing liner, maritime law would have required us to fly a flag announcing: *Danger: High Explosive Aboard.*

That figure of $13.4 trillion, the number of mortgage-backed securities sold by Lehman, Merrill Lynch, Bear Stearns, Morgan Stanley, and the rest, bears examination. If $1 million in $100 bills is two feet high, it would take three Washington Monument–sized stacks of money to make $1 billion. To make $13.4 trillion, that would be about twenty thousand Washington Monuments—twenty thousand stacks of $100 bills, each almost six hundred feet high. Laid end-to-end like the centerline down the middle of a highway, the bills would measure 5,075 miles, the distance between the New Century parking lot and the General Motors Building on the banks of the Detroit River and back—traveling across the Nevada Desert, straight over the top of the Rockies, past Denver, and heading across Nebraska, Iowa, and the Indiana flatlands before reaching the eastern end of Lake Erie and swinging north to the Motor City. And just to move from the absurd directly to the completely ridiculous, if you converted them all to $1 bills, the stack would reach the moon, 230,000 miles away, with a couple of million left to blow on a summer home on the Sea of Tranquility.

Whichever way you examine it, $13.4 trillion is a very decent amount of cash, enough to carpet the earth. But the money was not real, nor would it materialize. Right now, even as we contemplated the reality during the Christmas holidays in 2006, there were families bailing out of houses that were about to be repossessed, running for their lives, without even the slightest intention or the wherewithal ever to repay their mortgages. If things continued to get worse, the amount of cash that the mortgage holders might actually collect out of that $13.4 trillion might not reach even the top of the Cape Canaveral launch pad, never mind anywhere near the moon.

And speaking of the moon, I should mention that at precisely this time, this Christmas, I reached out and touched its glowing outer edges with my own fingertips, like ET just before he went home. Seventeen years had passed since I graduated from UMass and set my sights on a seat at one of Wall Street's top tables. Seventeen years since my high school buddy Jack Corbett had informed me that my chances of achieving this hovered somewhere between slim and none. It had also been almost seventeen years since a succession of New England finance hotshots had evicted me from more offices than any other applicant since records began.

These had been years of barnstorming commotion, years of desperate aims and objectives and what I considered to be titanic effort. My own single-minded quest had, for me personally, demolished all before it, including a marriage that lasted only a year before being swept away in the fiery wake of my own ambitions.

Step by step, through the little bond company above the dry cleaner, I had reached for the moon. Up into the stratosphere to Morgan Stanley, and then the break for which I had prayed for so long: a coveted place on the trading desk at Lehman Brothers. This was a place where, for the first time in my life, I seemed to matter. It was a place where mighty weights of responsibility had been rested on my shoulders, where great men finally treated me as an equal. It was a place where, in my mind, I once had stood alone, making the market for the foundation of the biggest trading victory in the 156-year history of Lehman Brothers; a place where I had helped to forecast both the coming Armageddon and what to do to protect ourselves. It was a place where I had the effrontery to believe I belonged, and where I profoundly hoped I would always be received with respect.

And now I was being invited up to the suite of rooms on the twenty-seventh floor where the annual bonus hearings were held, where Rich Gatward and Larry McCarthy presided over meetings with all of their people, reminding them of their strengths and weaknesses, and handing them their annual bonus package. When it was my turn to go in, they both stood up and shook my hand. It was then, and still is, the proudest moment of my entire life. In the two years I had been there I had made the firm just shy of $50 million hard cash. In 2006 alone, with the Delta bonds and subprime shorts, I had been responsible for $35 million of trading profits.

They both treated me as if they were aware of every last dollar I'd made. Neither of them sought any credit for anything they had contributed. They never did, no matter what the circumstances. They made me feel as if I had done it all on my own. And when they gave me my piece of paper, my eyes raced down it to find the number that mattered. And there it was, a glistening seven-figure bonus.

"You're hitting two-ninety," said Larry. "Nice going, buddy."

In those fleeting seconds I considered I had achieved my life's ambitions. I was in the majors and suited up, my name was on the lineup card, and I was ready to swing the bat with the best of them. I'd come from so far back. I'd started so darned late. But somehow I'd made it. Even my dad might admit I'd proved some people wrong.

No day ever passes when I do not think with profound gratitude of those moments when I stood up there with Rich and Larry and received my million-dollar reward. No day. No night.

How d'you like them apples, Corbett?

It was no surprise that Larry and Rich had been wearing such broad smiles, because the year-end results for Lehman, despite the mounting problems in the real estate market, were extremely good. The firm had $46 billion in revenues, with profits of around $4 billion, or $6.73 per share. Generally speaking, that was good enough to keep us patronizing bars and restaurants like Il Mulino, Ben Benson's, Tonic, Nobu 57, Rue 57, Felix, Pink Elephant, Frederick's, and Ono at the Hotel Gansevoort.

Life was exquisite that winter. Quarter by quarter, Lehman had been coining money. In 2005, Q1 revenues were $7.39 billion, Q2 $7.33 billion, Q3 $8.6 billion, and Q4 $9.05 billion. In 2006, the revenue breakdown was Q1 $10.3 billion, Q2 $11.5 billion, Q3 $11.7 billion, and Q4 $13.1 billion. As gravy trains go, this was not half bad.

No one, however, was looking very hard at the dark side to this magnificent state of affairs. And that dark side was leverage, the amount Lehman Brothers had borrowed in order to lever up their balance sheet, taking bigger and bigger positions, which they could afford only if they used someone else's money. It made the profits look fabulous. But in order to appreciate the shining fabulousness of the profits, you had to ignore the fact that in order to attain them, Lehman had actually borrowed by now thirty-two times their own worth, or more simply, around $480 billion, mostly to cover purchases of mortgages from places like New Century. Some of us thought that was probably a bit steep, especially since the number in 2004, a mere twenty-four months earlier, had been only twenty times Lehman's own worth.

I always found the numbers to be mind-blowing and so did Larry, Alex, Rich, and Mike. But we were in a minuscule minority. Even the SEC, which is supposed to keep a sharp weather eye out for situations of obvious danger, paid not the slightest attention to the condition of Lehman, any more than they did to the other banks with highly leveraged positions, like Merrill Lynch and, more important, Bear Stearns, which were leveraged even higher than we were.

The House Financial Services Committee held fifty-six hearings in 2006, and they covered every possible unforeseen happening that could befall the western part of planet Earth. They discussed everything, from flood insurance to transparency in financial reporting. As a matter of fact, they spent hours and hours on those subjects, and even longer talking about the obfuscations that had brought down Enron so many years ago. That was the tactic of spreading out wider and wider until the truth is forever obscured. Not one of those fifty-six gatherings of the U.S. government's financial watchdogs touched directly upon the issues that were in danger of bringing the entire world economy to its knees—the off-balance-sheet securitizations, the RMBSs, CDOs and CLOs, the deadly leverage in the system.

Indeed, the Securities and Exchange Commission chairman, the fifty-four-year-old Harvard-educated Christopher Cox, was summoned before that committee in September, just as the credit bubble was reaching its peak. This was by any standards a momentous brain to face the congressmen. Chris Cox not only had earned his MBA at the Harvard Business School but also had earned a doctorate in law from Harvard, where he edited the law review. He served in the White House as a senior associate counsel to President Reagan starting in 1986, at the age of thirty-four.

If he couldn't get it, who could? Answer: no one. Because Cox, speaking at a session to celebrate the Sarbanes-Oxley Act, the signature legislation of the post-Enron era, felt compelled to observe: "We have come a long way since 2002. Investor confidence has recovered. There is greater corporate accountability. Financial reporting is more reliable and transparent." Sometimes, Mr. Cox. Not always. And there were at least ten people in my department at Lehman who on that very same September day could have put you straight.

Right now there seemed to be a local, statewide, and nationwide policy to ignore the encroaching truth. Uncle Sam had removed his top hat and put on his ostrich suit in order to bury his head in the sand, or perhaps somewhere with even less sun. However, there was one new set of numbers that came sidling out of the darkness, like Caliban slouching sideways: there was an increase of 35 percent in U.S. house foreclosures for December. More than a hundred thousand properties were taken away from owners who were unable to pay their mortgages. Merry Christmas, New Century.

Meantime, on the other side of the Atlantic, the oldest and third-largest banking corporation in the world was facing up to a burgeoning wave of shocking news that seemed to be growing worse by the day. The global mammoth HSBC was putting together a warning that its bad-debt charges would be 20 percent larger than forecast.

HSBC, a major player in the low-quality-mortgage game, made no attempt to disguise the ominous trend that was emerging throughout its North American mortgage operation. The 140-year-old London-based bank was by far the largest so far to specify this obvious forthcoming problem, and its directors were prepared to go on the record, saying that the current slump in U.S. real estate prices had made it more difficult for strapped homeowners to refinance in the traditional way. They had but one chance. And that was to run.

HSBC had a global payroll of almost sixty thousand and in 2003 laid out $15.5 billion to purchase Household International, the disgraced predatory lender from Chicago. This allowed HSBC to break swiftly out of the blocks and into the shaky mortgage business before most banks were organized. It now looked as if they might be first in, first out, because they were citing a $10.56 billion charge and squarely admitting that their predictions about defaults and repossessions were way off target.

The truth was, a vast operation like HSBC could ride out a storm like this. A lot of much smaller shadow banks really did not have a prayer without some serious federal help. And one of these was none other than New Century, whose black-glass house of cards was about to cave in.

In the days before HSBC made its formal warning, New Century admitted its third-quarter earnings would have to be revised. They accurately forecast a resounding fourth-quarter loss, as the early payment defaults hit home. They further said they would restate results for the previous three quarters in order to correct accounting errors. The glossy mortgage provider slashed its forecasts for loan production in 2007, and in one day its stock crashed 29 percent. When it hit $15 I went down to discuss the situation with Rich Gatward. He said: "Double our short position. You're right, these guys are crooked." We'd stuck to our guns for almost six months, holding on to the shorts—and now the cards had turned, and we were on our way to a $28 million profit.

In a sense, we were not yet tuned in to a dark subterranean move along the deep tectonic plates of Wall Street. That stern warning from HSBC had not gone unnoticed. The market did not react, but there must have been an underlying seam of fear, unspoken but present, because on February 27, 2007, there was a major hiccup on the Chinese stock market, and on the following afternoon, Wednesday, just before 3:00 P.M. the Dow Jones Industrial Average suddenly and for no apparent reason dropped 178 points in a single minute and then kept falling. Alex Kirk, heading into a meeting, exclaimed, "Holy shit!" as he walked past my desk. Ten minutes later, when he came out of the meeting, it was down 546, its biggest single-day rout in five years. "What the hell's going on?" he asked. But no one knew, and there was an aura of quiet unease right through the trading floor. I could see some of the younger traders, looking worried, some of them scared. Alex Kirk, frowning, said, "It doesn't add up. Markets don't drop like that in sixty seconds. There's something wrong here."

Larry didn't believe it either, and in the middle of the drama, in the middle of what was a stupendous freeze of pure terror throughout the floor, he was the only man who moved. With people all around him paralyzed with indecision, he waded into the churning market all on his own, to buy three million shares of SPYs (an exchange-traded fund that tracks the S&P 500) in the hole, that is, at the low point as the market plummeted. Alex, standing next to him, ordered a tight stop-loss on the trade (i.e., he limited the amount that could be lost). But he allowed Larry to put over $400 million on the line, waiting for the numbers to climb back up.

In the end they did recover, and Larry made $6 million in something like twenty minutes. Some people later put the plunge down to a mysterious high-tech computer glitch, and maybe it was. But the S&P hadn't suffered more than a 10 percent correction in four years. And glitch or no glitch, that sudden crash frightened the life out of many traders, a lot of whom suspected it could have been a tremor before the real earthquake.

Well, the home of all earthquakes is reputedly California, and just a few days later, right up the street from the San Andreas Fault, we had a real good one. New Century admitted it was going to be late filing its annual report with the SEC. The following day the company disclosed there were U.S. Attorney's Office and New York Stock Exchange investigations into trading on its stock. Immediately federal bank regulators announced a crackdown on loose lending standards on subprime mortgages.

Seven days later—six months since Dave Gross and I had shared a couple of beers with the bodybuilders—New Century stopped making new loans, and the stock price collapsed totally. They went straight to bankruptcy.

And what now for the lugheads? I supposed they would just move on to the next scam. They were a breed, and the collapse of New Century would not unduly concern them. Guys like that understand innately there are almost certainly hidden problems with all the products they carry into the market.

I wondered if those salesmen in the restaurant would ever remember Dave Gross and me, a couple of guys in from New York who asked a lot of questions, most of them negative, some of them almost accusatory. Would our presence out there, sitting in that bar, ever ring a bell with the hotshots who had told us how great it was to be a part of the New Century family? How fast the cars and the women were? How rich they would all become, how perfect life would be out there on the road, moving the poor from semi-ghettos onto the lush banks of the Delta and the sprawling new developments in Nevada?

To them, when it all went wrong, none of it would matter. Nothing would be laid at their door. But for us in the financial world it would surely come home to roost. If this went the way we thought it was going, lives would be ruined. Men who had worked brilliantly and faithfully for decades could get wiped out in a crashing stock market, with its attendant bankruptcies. People whose wealth is tied up in corporations so often leave their private stock options behind, unable to claim their rightful rewards after a lifetime of work.

And there were other aspects, stuff that only some of us could ever understand. Not just the sadness of ruin, the undeserved sword of Damocles slashing down on a family or a small business. Some people have no difficulty grasping the sorrow and heartbreak that may lie ahead. And I am one of those. I don't usually admit to such sad deliberations, but I am nonetheless aware that I harbor them. I suppose it's a weakness. But I am not ashamed of it. And it's why I despise the bodybuilders. Because the anguish of other people will always matter to me.

9

King Richard Thunders Forward

And they summoned Prince Mark and told him to saddle up his white battle charger and go to it—storm the boardrooms, lay siege to the world's most grandiose commercial real estate, and the hell with the expense. And the risk.

ASIDE FROM THE subprime mortgage market, where the lunatics were now in total command of the nuthouse, there was another kind of craziness lurching around on Wall Street in the winter of 2007. It wore a merry smile and there was bright optimism in its eyes. However, when it was exposed to a harsh light, it would become the face of bleak stupidity.

I refer to the Apparition of Plenty, a grinning wraith, wandering around a market awash with cash, with billions of dollars from China still flooding in for U.S. Treasuries, still making money a very cheap commodity. Generally speaking, it was impossible to go out of business in the United States in the first half of 2007. On the same subject, I should confirm it was still pretty tough to fail in the second half. Huge corporations could borrow limitless amounts anytime they wished. So could medium ones. The little ones? No problem. Bankers could borrow with impunity; investment bankers could have anything they needed. My great-aunt Matilda probably could have hit Bear Stearns for a couple of billion to open a Cuban cigar shop, despite the fact that (a) importing anything from Cuba was illegal and (b) she had passed away in 1954. Even General Motors, under a preposterous weight of debt and liability, could borrow. So help me, bankrupt Calpine could, and did, still borrow.

Logic had flown the coop. Rolling loans, short-term thinking, and easy-come money dominated the landscape. Secure a billion-dollar loan for thirty days, borrow again to pay it back, then again, then again. Just keep borrowing and paying back. It could go on forever. It was a physical impossibility to go bust. In the entire year, major bankruptcies in the United States were few and far between. Globally, the default rate was at an all-time low. In 2009 there will be probably five thousand in the United States alone.

Of course, most people never gave the matter much serious thought—probably they were too busy filling out loan applications. But there was one person in our organization who was giving the matter profound consideration. And that person happened to be the one analyst in all of Wall Street who had called the Calpine bankruptcy first, and also the insurmountable problems of General Motors: Christine Daley.

As one of Lehman's top two analysts of distressed debt, she was gazing at a market that was defying gravity. Calpine was on the floor with gigantic debt, and I had bought the bonds for as low as 10 cents on the dollar when they filed for Chapter 11 protection. Insanely, the bonds went above par to 120 cents on the dollar! General Motors, which, logically, should have tumbled into the Detroit River, had its stock selling at $32 when it should have been about 27 cents. The truth was, in this pumped-up credit bubble, Christine's market in distressed bonds had ceased to exist. There wasn't any distress, but Christine could see no real reason why there shouldn't be. Which was right and proper, since there wasn't a reason, or at least not a logical one. It was just the way things were. The very brilliant Christine Daley was in an intellectual dilemma, a situation to which she was unused.

Slowly, over the long dark weeks of midwinter, she ran into the same recurring problem: recommending short positions, spotting real live trouble, and then watching the bonds go up, rising on a flood tide, as people with money to spend continued their desperate search for some value, some return, on their cash. They were buying corporate bonds because of the insatiable thirst for yield above the low rates being paid for Treasuries.

In her view we were looking at weeds—priced not as flowers, as Warren Buffett had observed, but as emeralds. And over the weeks I watched Christine become ever more gloomy and frustrated. We talked often, and she would ask the unanswerable question, "What the hell am I supposed to do? I locate a corporation that cannot possibly survive, crippled by debt, floundering around, losing market share, with a future that adds up to zero, and the stock goes up. And then the bonds."

And every day the Dow Jones kept chugging along at around 12,700, not much volatility, and very few scares. Christine still looked as beautiful as ever and arrived every day immaculately turned out, but I often caught her looking somewhat reflective, and I could see she had much on her mind. She was the lonely vulture with nothing to buy.

I knew she believed the bonus pool in the distressed-debt department was going to hell, and one late afternoon she said, "We're never going to make a lot of money this year. So what's the point of working?" It was a pretty good question, but my trading world was wider than her researcher's domain, and her position was much worse than mine. I could still operate. She couldn't.

Together we sat and stared at new tables that had just been released showing the main players packaging lower-quality mortgage-backed securities. Right at the top of the 2006 table was Lehman Brothers, with over $50 billion worth of subprime on the market, up there ahead of the giant RBS Greenwich Capital, the U.S. fixed-income investment arm of the Royal Bank of Scotland (founded 1727). The Scots were $4 billion behind Lehman. And behind both of them came two more Wall Street behemoths, Morgan Stanley and then Merrill Lynch, which was over $16 billion behind. In fifth position was Countrywide Securities. Between them these five had over $200 billion out there swinging in the warm breezes of the Sunbelt, all five hoping fervently the poor were going to keep writing checks even though they could not prevent them from growing bigger and bigger with each passing month.

Both Christine and I had heard the rumors that the mortgage guys were having trouble moving the CDOs, those securitizations of mortgages. Actually, we'd probably heard more than that, but in the strictest confidence, since this wasn't the kind of stuff you want to make a great deal of noise about. As bad news goes, that hovers somewhere between chilling and terminal. Because if our guys couldn't move them, neither could anyone else, and that theater door was getting real jammed up.

Maintaining these rolling loans, which were acquired to buy the mortgages in the first place, was plainly becoming very difficult and very pressured. The idea was to repackage these mortgage-backed securities and get them turned around and sold in the fastest possible time, before the original loan money had to be paid back. But now it was just possible Lehman was getting stuck with them, these red-hot potatoes, which can so seriously damage your hands.

I remember mentioning to Christine that the engine of this business was the bodybuilders, who were still out there, working for whoever was still in the game—not New Century—and they were still selling mortgages. It was not like turning off a faucet. You couldn't shoot them. And Lehman had obligations to the brokerage houses. If they could no longer move the CDOs, this was a shocking problem.

Remember, when it came to assessing trouble, Christine Daley was widely considered not just the best on Wall Street but one of the best there had ever been. And she was worried. I could see that. With her own field of operations temporarily in shreds, I sensed she was losing heart, becoming engulfed by the blind illogic of the market and of some of the people with whom she shared this enormous building.

One of these was our corporate president, Joe Gregory, the right-hand man of the reclusive CEO, Dick Fuld. Now, Dick had somehow evolved into a very strange president and chief operating officer, remote from his key people, apparently allergic to the engine room of the business, and jealous of his hold on power. But Joe Gregory was a regular, run-of-the-mill, ho-hum financial follower, loyal to his master, Richard Fuld, but with few of the necessary tools and instincts to serve as president of Lehman Brothers. He suited the boss fine, however, since he posed not even the semblance of a threat and would do anything in the world for the chief.

Joe's fixation was a subject called diversity. He was consumed with it. His aim was the mission of inclusion. He had an entire department devoted to it, headed up by a managing director. Great rallies were staged in New York's auditoriums, with free cocktails and hors d'oeuvres served for up to six hundred people, all listening to Joe or one of his henchmen pontificating. "Inclusion! That must be our aim!" he would yell, as if we were running a friggin' prayer meeting.

In Joe's view, it was the culture of the corporation that mattered. Joe believed that inclusiveness would carry us to victory. If the culture was right, then all would be right. Which was all very well, but down in the trenches, where a trader might sweat blood to make a couple of million dollars, most of us were a bit tetchy about Joe Gregory going off and spending it on a cocktail party for six hundred people.

That might not have been fair to him, but that's the way it seemed to us. Especially when it emerged that the top dog in diversity was earning well over $2 million a year and that the diversity division had a bigger budget and more people than risk management! Which was unusual for a hard-driving merchant bank with billions on the line every day, and where control of financial risk was absolutely paramount. The whole scenario really bothered a lot of people, especially hard-nosed traders who, after hours of real stressful work out there fighting the world, were then being marched off to these meetings and rallies to support Joe's trumpet call for equality. People who spend all day long concentrating, making big decisions, dealing in millions, are sometimes a bit tired after a 6:00 A.M. start.

This included Christine, who, with a husband, two small children, and a gorgeous apartment to maintain down in the Tribeca area of the city, was really not ready for this sideshow at the conclusion of her working day. Joe's mission for diversity drove her mad. She had no time for any of it, but Joe Gregory had us all over a barrel: he had major control over our bonus compensation, and he made it clear there would be extra money for those who rallied to his cause. Most of us did not care about the cause, but the prospect of this thirty-first-floor loyalist lopping a couple of hundred thousand off our annual check because we weren't in there pitching for the cause of the day was seriously irritating. Harsher judges than I considered Joe hid behind his unusual fixation, appearing to fight the world's woes while staying well clear of the gundeck.

Christine's view of the market was it was behaving irrationally and almost certainly showing classic signs of a top, with dozens of corporations trading at values far, far beyond reality. She also believed that when the president of a trading investment bank was spending his time staging hugely expensive rallies for minority groups, that might have been the ultimate demonstration of a market peak. There was too much undeserved cash flying around, it was all too easy, and there was too much time to find oddball ways to spend it. The essential weirdness of the situation—a bankrupt Calpine still borrowing, GM stock priced way above where it should be, and then the rallies on top of it all—might have been the last straw for Christine. She just could not deal with it. Also, she was permanently concerned about the coming catastrophe in the mortgage game, and certain in her own mind that Lehman had to get out of CDOs, downsize their risks, and stay out. So one morning in February she came to me and said, "Larry, how are we going to make any money this year? There's zero value in this marketplace. But I've probably got enough to live out my life. And I'm quitting. Maybe I'll come back when these idiots start to blow up. But right now there's nothing here for me."

I ought not to have been surprised. And perhaps I wasn't. But the awful truth of her words drove right through me. Christine, my friend, my buddy, my ally, my kindred spirit, always there, always ready to help. You don't find many people like that, not in one lifetime. And now I was losing her. I do not recall ever feeling that sad at any other moment in my career. Not even when Steve Seefeld and I parted on the rainy sidewalk of Greenwich Avenue seven years earlier.

There was nothing I could say. And nothing more she wanted to hear. Her logic was impeccable. She needed to go. And she knew how I felt about her. Nothing more needed to be said. Except before she left my desk she said, "Just so you know, Larry: I didn't really believe you about the subprime crisis last year. But you called it."

I muttered something about blind luck, and gave her a hug. She was wrong, of course. Alex Kirk had called it in May 2005, when he made the steroid comment to Larry and me right outside that 7:00 A.M. meeting. All I can say is, I knew Alex had hit it right on the button, and I had acted ever since to try to contain the coming disaster. Christine had not been party to that somewhat historic moment, and neither Larry nor I had ever revealed the identity of the true prophet.

Meanwhile, Joe Gregory was out there on various stages, facing the television cameras, waving his arms in the air like some kind of a messiah, blathering on about the culture, basking in his gigantic earnings, getting to and from his $32 million beachfront home in the Hamptons via private helicopter, limousine, and God knows what else. When he did settle down to some real work, he was there only to do the bidding of his boss, Fuld: keep those derivatives going, those CDOs, the lethal swaps, and the highly leveraged commercial real estate deals. That way the stock stayed high, the balance sheet looked great, and the personal bonus checks for the two men at the top of the tower would keep them in a style to which they had undoubtedly become accustomed.

It was, however, blindingly obvious to the big brains in the organization that the two top guys were living in Delusion City. Both of them were devoted to the commercial mortgage-backed securities—CMBS—another gigantic securitized debt portfolio, this one based on huge buildings not yet paid for with real money. Again, Lehman was slicing them up and packaging them, getting them rated AAA, and selling the bonds to banks, hedge funds, and sovereign wealth funds all over the world.

Instead of the vast army of struggling homeowners, this derivative, the CMBS, offered the backing of major corporations in the form of cash flow paid by rents to those who owned the buildings. And so far as Dick and Joe were concerned, this was perfect: a hedge against the residential real estate, a safe diversification. Except that in the current global asset bubble, no one was diversified, nothing was safe. They simply did not understand that Lehman was concentrated, that commercial real estate was equally as vulnerable as residential property. Just another top-of-the market illusion of solidarity.

Christine Daley understood this, understood we were heading for trouble. And now she was leaving. The rest of us were caught in a trap, because Lehman had us in golden handcuffs. Our equity holdings in the firm were growing, but even if we left, it would be months, maybe years, before we could get our hands on the money. Each year we left behind enormous sums payable only in the firm's stock sometime in the future. This had unquestionably played on Christine's mind. She had been with the firm eight years, and by leaving when she did, she was able to sell some of her stock, which must have given her a substantial sum.

She had, however, decided not to remain in New York. It might be the city that never sleeps, but it is also the city that never stops swallowing people's money. And she set about finding a new, more economical place for her family to live, utilizing the same kind of research program she had applied in her quest to expose Calpine. Everything was considered—climate, schools, universities, housing costs, taxes, and the surrounding countryside.

Eventually she chose Nashville—Music City, the fast-growing capital of Tennessee, situated on the banks of the wide and winding Cumberland River, home to the Country Music Hall of Fame, and the stamping ground of Hank Williams, Loretta Lynn, Barbara Mandrell, and Emmylou Harris. Nashville is also a place of learning, with sixteen colleges and universities, including Vanderbilt, and six graduate business schools. Nonetheless, the image of this consummate, clued-up New Yorker, Wall Street's soignée diva of distress, strutting around that warm, slow, and easy southern city is one that escapes me still.

We gave her a farewell dinner within a few days of her departure, since Nashville was beckoning. Twenty of us gathered in the Blue Fin, a classy Times Square restaurant at Broadway and 46th—Larry McCarthy, Alex, Schell, Joe, Jane, and the rest—and there were no attempts to persuade her to change her mind. We all knew Calpine's CFO had tried that for months before he realized he was still dancing through raindrops.

But there was something else at that dinner. Amidst all the jokes and laughter, I think we all knew Christine was onto something. She was getting out with as much of her bonus money as possible, and Larry told me he was sure she was making the right decision. It was as if we all sensed there was a death wish about the Lehman top management, that something was so wrong we might not survive. I mean that. I was thinking the unthinkable: that our ship might go down unless we, the experts on distress, could get hold of the helm and correct our course.

Everyone knew that Christine's market had, temporarily at least, dried up. And we wished her well, trying to hide a nagging feeling that she was at least two steps ahead of the game. Alex, typically and generously, picked up the tab, and Larry and I escorted her down to find a cab. We stood on the sidewalk for a few minutes, finally kissed her good-bye, and then she was gone, heading south down Broadway, toward another, calmer world. I felt desolate as I watched the taillights of her cab speeding away down the Great White Way.

Back at the factory, I had a team of analysts burning the midnight oil, poring over charts and statistics, locating photographs and converting them into slides. Larry and I were preparing the mother of all presentations, to convince the top Lehman executives that this ship must swerve away from the course set by Dick Fuld and Joe Gregory, who had not personally been on the bridge for about five years. And, in the opinion of the growling McCarthy, their chosen lookouts were a sight worse than those two comedians who missed the giant iceberg from the crow's nest of the *Titanic*. Those guys didn't have binoculars. The Lehman lookouts couldn't see at all.

Around this time I could see Larry becoming extremely irritated with the situation. Every time I spoke to him, he snapped out some thought that had been preying on his mind: "Subprime is already spreading to Alt-A, and then it's going to spread to the banks. And then it will spread to our high-yield market. Dick and Joe think it's 'contained'—well, it's not, it's contagious."

Occasionally he walked around the mortgage floor, and he could smell they were losing money. He could sense they were saying as little as possible, like a bunch of nervous rabbits frozen in the headlights, their links to the trading floor long gone.

Our analysts Pete Hammack and Ashish Shah kept coming up with startling truths, especially the huge increase in homeownership since 2002. It had climbed to an all-time high of 66 percent as the shadow banks and mortgage companies shoehorned people into homes, persuading them to go into heavy debt. Now, suddenly, I unearthed a horrific fact: in February 2007 the total dollar value in real estate in the United States was worth approximately $20 trillion. Which seemed like a big number, except that in 2005 it had been about $23 trillion, before everyone started bailing out of subprime. In Larry's opinion, underwriting standards were being totally compromised. The bodybuilders had done their worst. And now we faced a gathering storm. Larry said as much to Dave Sherr, the global head of the mortgage securitization business, who rounded on him and retorted, "You don't know what you're talking about. You're an idiot."

Larry fired back with a favorite expression of his: "And you're a high kite," meaning someone who is essentially drifting around the stratosphere, spaced out, high on their own importance. I doubt Sherr understood precisely what McCarthy meant, but I am certain he got the drift. For drift, read rift. The two hardly ever spoke to each other again.

On Friday morning, February 9, 2007, in a third-floor conference room, the senior managing directors gathered to hear Larry's findings. He's worth listening to when he's studied something for about one-hundredth of a second, never mind a couple of months. And no one wanted to miss it, except for the two chowderheads up on the thirty-first floor, who once more demonstrated their limitations by ignoring the entire proceedings. But forty-five of the top Lehman operators crowded into that room to hear a thirty-page presentation.

Larry, characteristically, steamed straight in, citing the crashing figures for home equity values, pinpointing the uptick in residential mortgage defaults, and railing about the standards of underwriting and the massive exposure so many Wall Street firms now had to subprime mortgages. He declared the warning by HSBC to be more important than any other issue, and he lambasted our own management for believing the problem was somehow "contained."

He scorned the latest unemployment figures, which were indeed moving lower, because there was hard evidence the subprime problem was already spreading to Alt-A mortgages and to construction corporations, not to mention the biggest brokers. "There'll be a domino effect," he said. "And the very next domino to fall sideways will be the commercial banks, who will swiftly become scared and start deleveraging, causing consumer borrowing to contract, which will push out the credit spreads. The present situation, where no one thinks there is any risk whatsoever, in anything, cannot possibly last."

In that room, he did not need to elaborate. But I'll explain what he meant. The credit spread refers to the difference between Treasuries, which were paying around 4.5 percent, and the yields of corporate bonds and the mortgage-backed securities, which were probably around 7 to 8 percent. Larry felt that these yields may suddenly spike up to 9 or 10 percent, which is known in the trade as widening the spread. It happens when the market senses higher risk and it becomes necessary to lower the price and up the yield in order to move the bonds. Larry McCarthy could see this coming, clear as daylight.

"That contraction in consumer borrowing," he said, "will strip the steroids out of the market. And there will swiftly be a very big correction, which will lead to higher unemployment." He added that the Fed would surely move to cut interest rates, but there would still be a very hard landing. "Many people today believe that globalization has somehow killed off the natural business cycles of the past," he said. "They're wrong. Globalization has not changed anything, and the current risks in the Lehman balance sheet put us in a dangerous situation. Because they're too high, and we're too vulnerable. We don't have the firepower to withstand a serious turnaround."

At this point Dave Sherr offered a short speech for the defense. He said that the mortgage market and the corporate bond market were not correlated. He rebutted Larry in short, terse sentences, reiterating once more that, in his opinion, the ace distressed-bond trader did not know what he was talking about.

"Dave," snapped back Larry, "you mortgage guys have been giving us the mushroom treatment for months, keeping us in the pitch dark and feeding us shit." He added that we were not being told the whole truth, and that as a company, we were not moving nearly fast enough. "These derivatives and all the leverage in the system are giving everyone a false sense of security," he said.

He pointed out that our risks were enormous in so many fields, not just in the CDOs but also in commercial real estate, in leveraged buyouts, and especially in credit default swaps, the voodoo section where people could bet against a corporation or a bond without having a principal interest in the operation.

"I know a little about gambling," he confirmed, with awesome understatement, "and I know a lot about risk. We have too much. Far, far too much. And we need to cut it right back, and start a counteroffensive, with the heaviest short positions we've had for years, before this whole insane market goes straight down the tubes."

Aside from those who were already singing from the same hymnbook—including Alex Kirk, Mike Gelband, Rich Gatward, Joe Beggans, Pete Schellbach, and Jane Castle—there were many worried faces in that room when Larry concluded. A few of the younger guys may have been skeptical, but the majority took his conclusions seriously.

After the meeting Schell told Larry he was glad it had all finally been said. But he did wonder why it had to be right now. Larry turned somewhat theatrically to the window and pointed at some imaginary horizon. "You see that right out there?" he demanded hypothetically. "That's a fucking iceberg, and we're headed straight for it, flank speed. Even the goddamned *Titanic* tried to swerve."

Pete commented on how Dave Sherr had reacted with such anger, calling Larry to task. But the old stock market high roller just grinned slyly and commented, "As you go through life, old buddy, you'll probably find that empty cans usually make the most noise."

Right then Lehman Brothers needed noise—anything to drown out the forthcoming cacophony of the corporate conference call that would take place on March 14, because there were surely numbers and stats, obvious to McCarthy and his tribe but perhaps not quite so obvious to the analysts, who were currently circling the coral reefs of Wall Street and probably tearing at the shattered carcass of New Century.

On the appointed day we opened the lines with Chris O'Meara, our slick-talking chief financial officer, in the chair. It turned out to be one of the longest conference calls in the history of Lehman, as Chris parried the polite cut-and-thrust of the sharks with long-winded, convoluted, barely comprehensible explanations that might have baffled Einstein in his prime.

The first point that caused a ripple of consternation throughout the vast network of shareholders and researchers who were listening in was Chris's revelation that mortgage-based securitization volumes had decreased to $22 billion from $40 billion the year before. He stopped short of the shining truth that the U.S. market for questionable mortgages had collapsed. He also never mentioned that not only were the mortgage holders running for their lives but U.S. investors were finally saying no—and that finance houses appeared to have no alternative but to start moving those toxic loans abroad in ever-greater volume. That way they could cripple the entire globe, instead of just America. Chris attempted to belittle the importance of this development by mentioning, somewhat loftily, that subprime mortgage securitization accounted for less than 3 percent of Lehman's total revenues. What he did not say was there was a growing mountain of these things piling up, not sold, unloved, massive potential liabilities, yet deftly removed from the balance sheet by means of the qualified special-purpose entities. In other words, accounting sleight-of-hand, witchery, trickery, sorcery, or skulduggery. Now you see it, now you don't.

Just read this outrageous mangling of the language to conceal the truth at any price. O'Meara's antagonist was Michael Mayo, a hard-eyed analyst from the Prudential Equity Group.

MAYO: You said under 3 percent. But that's still a possible domino effect from subprime to other areas. What other exposure do you have to the subprime market?

O'MEARA (an air of pure incredulousness in his voice): To the subprime market?

MAYO: That's what I had in mind.

O'MEARA: Okay. So there's—the situation you're talking about, warehouse lending, or . . . ?

MAYO: More generally, what's your total balance sheet exposure to subprime mortgage, either direct or indirect?

O'MEARA: We have a fair amount of sort of exposure. We talked about the residual interests, which represent sort of a levered exposure. We also have whole loans, but all of it is subject to the same hedging principles we talked about earlier. And it's been working quite effectively.

MAYO: But when you said the hedging offset the losses, the hedging offset the losses in which areas?

O'MEARA: Essentially everything. Our objective is to offset the risks as we are moving these instruments, and holding the instruments, in what we'll call our client warehouse, as we're moving them from raw product into securitization.

Listening as a stockholder on the line, you could have wondered whether he worked for the New York Philharmonic or a meatpacking factory. And even Chris felt the need to have another stab at clarification.

"Mike," he said, "if we're making secondary markets and taking positions that we're distributing and sponsoring client activity while that's in the warehouse and on the balance sheet, we're trying to hedge the components of risk that exist: the interest rate risk, the prepayment risk, the various risks that exist. We're actively, dynamically trying to risk mitigate."

I'm not sure what a coast-to-coast "Huh?" sounds like. But I guess it would be very much like a dull thudding sound, like a lead balloon landing in a bottomless dollop of bullshit.

From where I sat, it seemed that the Lehman rear guard was growing weaker. All around me there were more critics of the direction the company was headed. And the mood among the analysts on that conference call was one of unmistakable skepticism, audible in the tone of the questions, the barely suppressed disbelief in the voices. What had been, a year previously, a small group of Lehman personnel crying out in the wilderness was now a growing army of mutineers, both inside and outside the firm.

The trouble was, the corporate direction was created at the very top, on the thirty-first floor, at the steel whim of the artless old commercial-paper trader Dick Fuld and the thirty-year Lehman veteran Joe Gregory. These two men controlled many things way beyond

Seventh Avenue: thousands of families, mortgages, college educations, second homes, alimonies, vacations. Indeed, they controlled lives. And to risk upsetting either of them was more than most people could afford.

In the teeth of what was now open criticism about the firm's policies, Dick and Joe began a long, out-of-step march to nowhere. Their determination to buy hedge funds was becoming voracious. By now, they also bought into Europe's largest hedge fund, GLG Partners (London), and another UK-based operation, Marble Bar Asset Management. Right after the conference call, they bought a 20 percent stake in D. E. Shaw, the global investment and technology development firm. Back in London, they purchased 20 percent of the $5 billion hedge fund Spinnaker Capital, specialists in emerging markets. Fuld, with the help of Dave Goldfarb, also took a stake in Blue Bay Asset Management, another huge European fund. And, being thoroughly global men, and indeed men to whom the world is an exceptionally small place, they pounced to acquire Grange Securities, one of the largest sellers of, of all things, CDOs in Australia.

Likewise Lehman had previously purchased a 20 percent share in a major U.S. commodity hedge fund, Ospraie, which managed about $2 billion of assets. Unlike the astute Warren Buffett, who despised investing in hedge funds, "Decouple Dave" Goldfarb and Dick Fuld couldn't get enough of them.

Lehman bought, needless to say, with borrowed money, at the top of the market. These were purchases thoroughly deplored by Larry McCarthy and totally disapproved of by both Mike Gelband and Alex Kirk. The foreign purchases were inspired by the avowed belief of Fuld, Gregory, and Goldfarb that globalization meant decoupling from the U.S. market because it was no longer all-powerful, that China and the emerging Asian economies had stripped the crown from America and rendered all men and markets equal. If the United States continued to falter, then there were smaller but stronger markets bursting out of the East that would make up the slack.

Decoupling. The wave of the future. The globalization of world commerce, the only answer for brilliant investment bankers, as the U.S. of A. finally took a backseat on the world trading stage. Sounded good. Sounded incontrovertibly modern and farseeing. In fact, it was absolute garbage, meaningless, untrue, unadulterated Crap. That's my capital C. Because without Uncle Sam, the rest is inclined to be second-rate. When the United States stops buying, the whole shebang bites the dust. But it would be many months before the rest of the world's market makers understood that and stampeded back into U.S. dollars.

Another tactic that met with almost universal disapproval was Fuld and Gregory's latest act of pure bravado in buying back Lehman's stock at $75 a share, to counteract rumors of growing problems on the balance sheet. It was a primitive form of reply, but Fuld was never a subtle man, and like his old mentor Glucksman he reacted to adversity with teeth-baring aggression, once threatening to ram his fist down a critic's throat and rip out his heart. Which stood up interestingly against Glucksman's fabled action of publicly ripping his own shirt off his back in uncontrollable fury.

Under fire, Fuld's instinct was to hit back instantly rather than bide his time. Stung by the rumors of trouble in his kingdom, he decided to charge into the market and start buying Lehman stock, which he must have suspected was already wildly overpriced. With our potential debt, how could it possibly be anything else? And so, with the ever-faithful Joe standing with him, shoulder-to-shoulder, Dick pounded the market and spent a staggering $1.6 billion of the firm's money on purchasing Lehman shares for the bonus pool as well as for investment purposes.

Mike Gelband actually considered that the boss had almost certainly lost it. For it was beyond the comprehension of that most brilliant risk-taker and trader that anyone could be that out of touch with reality. "Buying it?" yelled Mike at one point. "He should be fucking selling it, to raise capital."

But Fuld and Gregory were men of the twentieth century, not the twenty-first. They thought they were still in the 1980s and that they could play a high-stakes game of poker, never showing weakness, keeping their cards close to their chest, employing intimidating tactics, Texas Hold'em, with a mighty pile of chips. Used to work. Not anymore. Modern markets are much more sophisticated. There is an army of eagle-eyed hedge funds on the lookout for misplaced hubris and out-of-touch management, especially when there's crushing debt.

They thought they could bluff it out, and they flatly refused to slow down the mortgage origination platform, and to reduce our most vulnerable positions. In answer to the most recent troubles, we had a CEO and a president, both full of bravado, swearing that our latest setbacks were just blips on the horizon of the big picture. And the only way to silence our detractors was confidently to repurchase our own stock in massive quantities, never mind the price. That'll show 'em, right?

You did perhaps notice, four paragraphs back, I mentioned the word *kingdom*. I did not do so lightly, and I am mindful that this nation first fought a bloody war against its masters and was then refounded on the absolute principle that it must forever be rid of England, with its monarchs, hereditary princes, dukes, peers, and all the other paraphernalia of a kingdom. There are very few Americans who would today wish for a reversal of those principles and a return to the old ways of the United Kingdom, where inherent privilege still, to an extent, prevails. I do not think Richard S. Fuld Jr. or Crown Prince Joe would have been among that vast majority right here in the United States, because they turned Lehman Brothers into nothing short of a straight-down-the-line kingdom. King Richard ruled from a palatial paneled office with his own personal conference room and private bathroom.

Henry VIII, George III, William the Conqueror, Ethelred the Unready, and the rest would have been right at home up on our thirty-first floor. If someone could have constructed a decent moat and portcullis around 50th Street and Seventh Avenue, they'd probably have sent for their crowns and ermine and never gone home. Because Richard Fuld had taken several leaves out of the royal playbook, ruling the place with absolute authority, unchallenged, unencumbered by advice, and mostly unbowed. Whatever he wanted, decreed, or demanded was the way things worked. There was a tiny group of courtiers who were allowed to speak, but they understood it was best to go heavy on respect and decorum, or they could easily be on borrowed time at the Tower of Lehman.

In addition to Joe Gregory and the ex-CFO Dave Goldfarb, both yes-men, there was another character, obeying the whim of the king. He was Steven Berkenfeld, the forty-five-year-old chairman of the Investment Banking Commitments Committee, the eight-person panel whose responsibility was to approve or disapprove giant corporate loans. It did no such thing. It said yes when Dick Fuld wanted it to say yes, and no when he wanted it to say no. They were big on respect, short on incurring the displeasure of the king.

King Richard had even turned Lehman's board of directors into a kind of largely irrelevant lower chamber. This was yet another group which he wanted to rubber-stamp his decisions and collect generous fees. It was not recruited to supply leading edge and lucid wisdom in the current wild marketplace, but for agreeing with the monarch, accepting his all-knowing take on the bank's investments. Above all, the board was created not to rock the royal barge as it made its stately way downstream.

In the United States, the titles of king, prince, emperor, czar, duke, lord, and viscount have been banished for more than 230 years, since the Revolution. Thus the boss settled for "chairman" as his underlings' required form of address to him.

The Lehman Board contained no Prince Hal, the swashbuckling young future Henry V preparing to lead his troops to victory at Agincourt. Nor did it contain a wise and scheming old operator like Pete Peterson, who walked with kings from other realms and nurtured different skills. Dick Fuld's court contained not one director who could safely claim to be an old Lehman hand, wise in the ruthless ways of the market. In fact, only months before the Lehman directors had accepted the resignation of the veteran actress Dina Merrill, who at the age of eighty-three was an eighteen-year director not widely consulted about the modern, savage upward and downward swerves of the Stock Exchange. Merrill had, however, played a mean Sylvia Blair in the 1950s production of *Desk Set,* with Katharine Hepburn and Spencer Tracy.

Nine members of the ten-person board were retired. Four of them were seventy-five years of age or older. One was a theater producer, seventy-five-year-old Roger Berlind; one was a former CEO of the energy giant Halliburton, Thomas Cruikshank, seventy-seven; one was the chief economist at Salomon Brothers in the 1970s and '80s, eighty-one-year-old Henry Kaufman. The last of this septuagenarian-plus quartet was the former senior partner at McKinsey and Co., John Macomber, age eighty.

In addition, there was Marsha Johnson Evans, a former Navy admiral and head of the American Red Cross; Sir Christopher Gent, a former CEO of England's cell phone empire, Vodafone; Roland Hernandez, the former chairman and CEO of the Spanish-language television company Telemundo Group; Michael Ainslie, former president of the auction house Sotheby's; and John Akers, the retired chairman of the board and CEO of IBM.

Only two of them had direct experience in the financial services industry—and they were all from a different era. None of them was tuned in to the massive securitization of the modern economy, the minefield of credit default swaps, derivatives trading, and all the risks those products created. On that board, there was no stern voice of censure, of warning, of old-fashioned logic. There were only the deep melancholy tones of Henry Kaufman, known locally as "Dr. Doom," who believed the world was on the verge of global calamity and that the Fed was remiss in its idle oversight of commercial banking. Old Henry was on the right track, but the fire in his belly was dimmed, and the chairman had little trouble silencing him.

From this disparate group of old stagers, Lehman created a risk committee, chosen and controlled by Fuld himself. It met only a couple of times a year, which was an unusual way to monitor the company's ongoing risk, as it continued to accumulate a massive portfolio of real estate assets. And right here we stumble upon the one man in the organization who might well have acceded to the title of prince.

This was the somewhat aloof former lawyer Mark Walsh, the forty-six-year-old head of Lehman Brothers commercial real estate investments. He was a prince among the worker bees, the blue-eyed boy of the thirty-first floor, the favorite of Fuld, with an expandable departmental budget that would have made the eyes of the Sun King water. For not even Louis XIV, that most profligate of spendthrift French monarchs, builder of the Palace of Versailles, had access to cash on that scale.

Mark Walsh had been at Lehman for twenty years. After seventeen of them, he had taken complete charge of the firm's global real estate group. Right now he held the keys to the kingdom, with astounding personal authority to commit capital any way he saw fit. Mark was by nature a risk taker. Fuld liked that a lot, and he loved the way his young real estate Turk went for high-risk, high-return bridge debt and equity financing for large acquisitions. He also liked the fact that Mark was a proven moneymaker over the years at Lehman.

Before long every other branch of Lehman's commercial real estate business was answering to Mark Walsh. He shared responsibilities with no one, and was building a Lehman portfolio of billions and billions of dollars' worth of buildings, mostly huge. At this time estimates were that Lehman had $30 billion worth of commercial-mortgage-backed securities exposure, more than triple that of Morgan Stanley, which had a much bigger balance sheet. Go get 'em, Prince Mark.

I hope he'll forgive that final burst of informality, because, like

Fuld, this studious-looking character was utterly distant from the rest of us. Neither Christine Daley, Larry McCarthy, nor I had ever met him. He was just this shadowy junior god who spent money as if it was going out of fashion and could do no wrong in the eyes of the king. Some thought all it represented was too much power, too much autonomy, in too few hands.

But Mark Walsh's popularity with the great powers was boundless. Dick and Joe even presented him with his own domain, a kind of corporate fiefdom at 399 Park Avenue, one of the greatest high-rise buildings in Manhattan, occupying the entire block between Lexington and Park Avenues and East 53rd and East 54th Streets. The world HQ of Lehman Brothers Real Estate Partners was bang in the middle of the glass skyscraper that housed the main offices of Citigroup and a host of other blue-chip companies. Nothing was too good for Mark. Hell, the annual rent paid for the Property Prince's 436,000 square feet of office space was $43 million! That was more than it cost the Sun King to build Versailles.

And these were turbulent times. Despite the continuing deluge of available cash, another little zinger of a scare came winging in on Friday evening, March 2. The NYSE-quoted company Fremont General, a mortgage industry leader out of Santa Monica, California, suddenly announced it was getting out completely from subprime mortgage lending, citing mounting pressure from loan repurchases and likely regulatory action. That rather bland statement plainly obscured an absolute uproar out there in the golden West, because the FDIC was in there, in some kind of towering rage, slapping a cease-and-desist order on Fremont. They cited loans made to subprime borrowers who couldn't pay them back. And they demanded sweeping changes to Fremont's residential and commercial mortgage business, alleging the company had violated Section 23B of the Federal Reserve Act by engaging in shady transactions with its own affiliates.

When the cage of the FDIC gets that seriously rattled, it's usually accompanied by a SWAT team screaming into the offending corporation, brandishing chains, padlocks, bolts, and bars. Wall Street was buzzing with tales suggesting that this had indeed happened, and that half the executive committee had been on the golf course when the feds came marching in. In any event, workers were warned of layoffs, and Fremont set about trying to sell their entire mortgage operation, confirming simultaneously that it would delay its latest earnings report.

There had been a total of about two dozen mortgage lenders either closing or selling out their businesses in the past year, and Fremont's very obvious problems sent a lightning bolt through all the investment banks, especially Lehman, which was sailing very close to the same cold, gusting breezes that capsized the Santa Monica flagship. Fremont's demise was very good news for Rich Gatward and me, as we had a large short position on it. We pocketed over $5 million profit for the firm that next Monday as the news of Fremont's tough day on the course crushed its stock by 20 percent.

The latest casualty, in a sense, drove Dick and Joe ever closer to the Lehman commercial real estate business, which they both thought represented a vital hedge against the forthcoming collapse of the residential market. And there, at the head of this crusading cavalry of hope and glory, rode the white knight himself, Prince Mark, fresh from a sensational 2006, with his sword arm ready to cut a mighty swath through any challenge that presented itself.

But it was not just Fremont that was driving our thirty-first-floor monarch toward commercial real estate. It was also the trumpeted success of the Wall Street private equity firm the Blackstone Group, managers of the world's largest buyout fund. Blackstone in 2006 agreed to terms to purchase billionaire landlord Sam Zell's Equity Office Properties Trust for about $39 billion, the biggest takeover of a real estate company in the history of the world: office buildings in New York, Washington, and Los Angeles, 580 of them. It was their eleventh publicly traded real estate takeover in the past two years. And it made Blackstone owners of the premier office portfolio in the country, ahead of the crowd, especially Lehman.

Dick Fuld's dark eyes must have glowed with envy, not least because Blackstone was owned and run by two old Lehman men: Pete Peterson and Stephen Schwarzman. Peterson, his former boss and effortless superior, the co-CEO who had been so brutally fired by Dick's old mentor, Lew Glucksman, who had, in turn, groomed the young Richard Fuld to eventually replace him. Schwarzman, another elegant and richly talented banker, a man who had gazed with mere amusement at the pushing and elbowing of Glucksman and his ambitious disciple Fuld.

Blackstone's two vastly experienced sophisticates now operated a leveraged-buyout business that had opened up a brand-new era in American finance. These were two men who Richard S. Fuld Jr. would like to see fail. And now they were on the rise, making money and headlines faster than he was, and announcing the launch of an IPO. Jesus Christ! They were going public and probably going to collect a billion dollars each. Dick Fuld would have walked barefoot through broken glass to beat them to it.

But he and Joe could not prevent it. They could only try to match it. And they summoned Prince Mark and told him to saddle up his white battle charger and go to it—storm the boardrooms, lay siege to the world's most grandiose commercial real estate, and the hell with the expense. And the risk.

Mark gathered his troops and began a search for the finest real estate deals on earth. They would all cost a lot of money, but he had a lot of money—at least his master, Fuld, appeared to be able to lay hands on a lot of money, even if it was borrowed. There was nothing too big for Mark, because he had the unreserved backing of the king of Lehman and the support of Prince Joe.

And there was nothing too big for them. Mark had already been permitted to spend billions upon billions on European real estate, and even while he was assembling his forces, Lehman was right in the thick of two massive deals that involved almost $50 billion—both leveraged buyouts, together involving more than four times the entire net tangible equity value of the investment bank on Seventh Avenue.

The first was a major investment in the biggest buyout ever, the $45 billion takeover of the Texas energy colossus TXU Corporation. Our old friends Kohlberg Kravis Roberts, which for so long had held the world buyout record, $25 billion for the tobacco and snack company RJR Nabisco, now teamed with the Texas Pacific Group to make the purchase.

The smaller Lehman partnered with giants Goldman Sachs, Citigroup, and Morgan Stanley to partake in this massive undertaking to take TXU private, just as the energy company began a program to build no fewer than eleven coal-fired electric power plants in Texas, to the outright fury of the green lobby. It was never made public whether Fuld was swayed in his judgment by the fact that Henry R. Kravis was about to upstage his longtime rivals, Peterson and Schwarzman, as the new master of the takeover universe, a distinction he had lost when Blackstone grabbed what seemed like half the occupied office space in the free world.

The second deal that involved Lehman was the $3.1 billion takeover of Claire's Stores, a three-thousand-property necklaces, handbags, and headbands corporation out of Pembroke Pines, Florida, a few miles west of Fort Lauderdale. Apollo Management was the buyer, with Bear Stearns, Credit Suisse, and Lehman providing the finance. Between them they took a family corporation with no debt as of October 2006 and almost $250 million in the bank directly into a bankruptcy situation with debts of $2.5 billion, ten times its annual earnings.

I don't know what it was about the Lehman chiefs and debt, but they seemed to be drawn together in an unending dance of death, swept up in the euphoria of the times. And what times they were. In this twelve-month period, June 2006 to June 2007, nine of the ten largest LBO deals in history were launched. And Fuld and Gregory were fighting, scratching, and clawing their way into the contest, trying to eat with the big dogs, the men with the big commercial bank balance sheets, Citigroup, Bank of America, and JPMorganChase.

With hindsight, the investment banks Goldman Sachs, Bear Stearns, Lehman, Morgan Stanley, and Merrill Lynch ought not to have been competing. Indeed, before Bill Clinton signed the repeal of the Glass-Steagall Act in 1999, it would have been illegal to do so. But now it was all different. And the much smaller Lehman Brothers had a chairman and a president who were determined to join in the biggest financial operations on the planet. There was a ferocious leverage arms race among bankers, and Lehman was prepared to stretch themselves out in order to achieve their aims. And boy, were they ever stretched. At first, liabilities that totaled twenty-two times our worth seemed okay. Then it was twenty-six to one. Now, in the late winter of 2007, it was thirty-four to one and rising. By year's end it would be forty-four to one.

In the opinion of Dick and Joe, the boys at 399 Park Avenue were the light of the future. And in the middle of March, Mark Walsh struck—in probably the most expensive square mile of the most expensive real estate outside one of the world's most expensive cities, in the heart of one of the most expensive countries in Europe. With the blessing of the board, he actually went in on his white charger and purchased the largest office complex in France, in the heart of the Parisian business district: two enormous round thirty-nine-story glass towers, like a couple of upturned tubes of tennis balls standing on end, in the shadow of the legendary Grande Arche de la Défense. He paid $2.81 billion for Coeur Défense, the name given to this most prestigious construction, right in the center of La Défense, the space-age French skyscraper "city" of modern architecture and multinational corporations, which stands twenty-nine miles west of the Cathedral of Notre Dame.

At the time, Lehman was in the hole for about $465 billion. So why the hell not? In for a penny, in for a pound, right?

Coeur Défense was built in 2001 for $886 million. Three years later, when Goldman Sachs' Whitehall Fund bought 51 percent, the building was valued at $1.8 billion. Three years after that, Mark Walsh's real estate group bought it for $2.8 billion, which meant it had increased in value by $330 million a year. The deal was financed by commercial mortgage-backed securities.

In a sense, Coeur Défense was the crown jewel of Lehman's property empire in Europe. Flush in the center of the largest new office development in Europe, it did not come cheap. But that was no problem in these freewheeling days of ready cash, and the forthcoming CMBS sales would finance it with ease. Just so long as those bonds kept selling on the world market.

No one could accuse Mark Walsh of lacking guts. He'd already been involved in enormous deals in California and China, and he was working on a whole bunch of new ventures. I am obliged to say that Larry McCarthy really resented the way the Lehman balance sheet swayed in favor of the real estate guys. I guess he believed the commercial game was as lethal as the residential business. The entire diversification theory was a complete anathema to him. He believed it was a fraud, some kind of a bear trap. But Mark Walsh was not finished yet. Not by a long shot.

At the time I detected no appreciation by our highest management that we were right in the middle of a global asset bubble. Everything was awash with liquidity, at the top of its price range: steel, real estate, almost all commodities, corporate bonds, fine art, wine, LBO deals. Everything was expensive. So expensive that Wall Street's diva of distress had fled nearly a thousand miles and five states away, to the guitar-and-fiddle lands of the good ol' boys beyond the Appalachian Mountains.

And those massively overvalued prices had polarized the corporation. The group that surrounded Dick and Joe was blindly unaware, since they could always get hold of cheap money, while truly great financiers like Mike Gelband, Alex Kirk, and Larry McCarthy were spitting mad at what they saw as the potential destruction of the entire corporation.

Looking back, it's clear to me that it all affected Mike Gelband the most. By March, he was an out-and-out bear. As Lehman's global head of fixed income, he could not possibly approve of the program to buy back our own expensive stock on the open market just to show strength. And he found a way to tell Dick Fuld precisely how crazy he considered that to be. He was absolutely convinced the markets were at a top, and that Lehman was using leveraged money to buy leveraged hedge funds on margin. In his view this was the road to hell.

He scorned the whole concept of Lehman Brothers' diversifications, because the new "investments" were being conducted at the pinnacle of the market. He was certain of that. And he hated the current fad of buying commercial real estate in India, Asia, and Europe because they were all at the top of their markets—known in the trade as "top-tick prints."

Mike wanted subprime eliminated from Lehman's operations. He wanted to fire the bodybuilders and slash by half Lehman's program of originating mortgages. At the urging of Alex Kirk and Tom Humphrey, he had gone around Joe Gregory and begged Dick Fuld for a reduction in Lehman's mortgage origination at BNC and Aurora. This infuriated Gregory. And that was not the only battleground Mike was carving out for himself.

Mike never believed in decoupling, a strategy based on the idea that the United States was finished as the world's number one world financial power. He wanted to downsize, regroup, and stay healthy. And he repeated his concerns and fears both to the heads of departments and, over and over, to the men in the big chairs on the thirty-first floor. No one could have listened to him and still believed the chairman and his president any longer knew what they were doing.

This was the voice of a very senior Lehman managing director, and it was one of cold reasoned logic. We all knew that, but it was not anything Richard S. Fuld wanted to hear. He wanted risk, more risk, and if necessary bigger risks, because that was also the way to the big bucks, the multimillion-dollar bonuses for him and Joe Gregory. He was never going to listen, perhaps because he would be so rich by the time the end came that he would not care one way or another what happened to the firm. Maybe that's being uncharitable. But the fact remained that Mike Gelband was a vastly superior financier. He'd been with the firm twenty-six years, and just as only the very rich understand the difference between themselves and the poor, only the truly brilliant comprehend the difference between themselves and men of moderate intelligence.

Time after time, as a member of the Lehman executive committee, Mike voted against big spending projects, railing to Joe about blowing out all the fabulous profits accrued between 2004 and 2006. Mike stayed awake nights churning over in his mind the unchallengeable truth that Lehman had so many brilliant people, all being led by a couple of commercial paper traders out of touch and out of their depth. The World War I British Army was once described by a German general as "lions led by donkeys." Mike Gelband's opinion of the chain of command in Lehman's little army could scarcely have been more succinctly phrased.

Here he was, the head of fixed income, the only expert on the subject on the entire executive committee, and his recommendations to protect the firm were being resolutely ignored. Mike warned them of the coming credit crunch. He warned them of the lethal danger of that $15 trillion to $18 trillion of leverage out there, the credit derivatives issued between 2001 and 2007. It was a paper phantom that Lehman had done more than its fair share to create. At one meeting he pounded the table and shouted, "This is not going to be just a credit crunch. This is going to be the granddaddy of all credit crunches. And you're trying to buy into a giant global asset bubble." This took place in the middle of a Dick Fuld–inspired attempt to buy yet another inflated hedge fund. And again Mike voted no. He voted no—no—no, over and over. And not once during all these anguished months did one member of the Lehman board of directors call him to clarify his overriding concern about the future of the company he so loved. Not once. Although whether they even knew of his concerns he has no idea.

The trouble was, Dick Fuld could not understand the technicalities of market finance at the highest level. And when Mike tried to explain, the boss just glazed over and tuned out. One day Mike was attempting to point out the enormous dangers to the firm caused by SIVs—structured investment vehicles. These were like supersized CDOs that borrowed in the commercial paper market and bought mortgages and other debt involving colossal leverage, billions of dollars. And if the surging commercial paper market ever froze up, Mike thought, the global financial system might cave in.

The chairman didn't get it. But he realized he needed clarification. In front of Mike, he called Henry Paulson, the secretary of the United States Treasury and a former CEO of Goldman Sachs. Dick did not even try to get into the details of the problem, and quickly handed the phone to Mike, who pointed out with immense clarity the serious problems recently developing in the asset-backed commercial paper market and its deadly potential impact on the giant leveraged SIVs, to which Wall Street and the largest commercial banks were exposed. Mike thought this would lead to a serious credit freeze, one that he believed was shimmering on the horizon. To this day, Henry Paulson, with a supreme grasp of the subject, insists that the first person ever to warn him of the coming catastrophe was Mike Gelband, of Lehman Brothers, in that phone call from Dick's office.

Still, Fuld wanted Mike to accept his view. The chairman decided to bully him, to belittle him publicly, rather than relying on mere persuasion. "I don't want you to tell me why we can't," he said at one meeting. "I want you to be creative, and tell me how we can. You're much too cautious. What are you afraid of?" Then Joe Gregory began to harass the firm's one world-class expert on fixed income, telling Mike how Dick was not happy and that it was essential Mike begin to take much more risk, make bigger deals, relentlessly pursue growth. "You just have to make a change in direction," said Joe. They wanted him to buy hedge funds, take out leveraged loans, purchase real estate all over the globe, get into commodities—steel, gold, and oil. What mattered was to catch and then pass Goldman Sachs, Citigroup, and Blackstone, to show them who was boss.

Joe invited Mike to a private lunch meeting in the executive dining room on the thirty-second floor. But the two men had very little in common. Both of them observed company policy by wearing suits and ties up there in the holy of holies. But while Mike ate seared tuna, with no dessert, Joe hit a major plate of pasta. And Joe's views, so far as his guest was concerned, were absurd. Later that day, Mike confided to Larry and Alex, "Neither he nor our chairman understands the dangers of securitization, the leverage in the system.They cannot understand. And they will never understand. When I beg either of them to listen to what I am saying, their eyes glaze over."

On the evening of that luncheon, Mike Gelband, close to tears, had a long discussion with his wife, Deborah. He was an extremely rich but modest man, uneasy with glitzy people, and uninterested in private helicopters. He and Deborah understood that he needed to be true to himself and his conservative principles, that he needed to make a stand for what he believed was right. And in Mike's opinion, enough was enough.

The following day he took the elevator up to the thirty-first floor, walked into Joe Gregory's office, interrupting a meeting, and quit. "You said I was to make a change, Joe. And that's what I'm doing."

Dick Fuld's right-hand man was scared. No doubt about that. He tried to backtrack, called Dick, tried to reason with the departing head of fixed income. But Mike had made up his mind. And his departure made Wall Street headlines.

The news broke the following morning on the Bloomberg tape, and Larry McCarthy was not so much shocked as shattered. Mike Gelband was his lineman, our blocker, the big hitter who was a huge sponsor of all of our risk and short positions. He'd had the most phenomenal career, punctuated by success after success. In a democracy he'd have been swept to power, most certainly by Larry McCarthy, who regarded him as the most talented guy in the building. The chairman and his deputy had somehow found a way to lose him, and that had to rank as one of the most stupid acts he'd ever seen anyone do—anywhere.

On the day Mike left, May 2, 2007, everyone trooped down to the third floor around eleven to say good-bye. So many people wanted to shake his hand that a huge receiving line formed. Everyone owed him something. He was such a big part of our strength and standing in the corporation. His presence made us count. Some of the women were in tears as the great Lehman banker moved from friend to friend. How could anything ever be the same again?

Mike could have saved his job, could have gone on collecting $10 million to $20 million a year, every dollar of it earned. But he was not that kind of guy. Like Larry, Mike was certain we were steaming toward the iceberg, with a balance sheet he thought was catastrophically over-leveraged. He had to be true not only to the firm but to himself, and he could not countenance the wishes of the chairman. And so he walked away from one of the highest-paying jobs on Wall Street, walked away from those enormous earnings. It took a real man to do that.

He came over to say a last good-bye to Larry, Joe, and me. And there was a strange silence throughout the trading floor as he did so. When he finally turned away and walked toward the door, there was a sustained and heartfelt burst of applause—not the raucous outpouring that greets a touchdown or a home run, just a fierce clapping of hands, like the kind that greets a pitcher when he's finally relieved in the eighth with his team out in front after a long job, brilliantly done. For the record, he did turn around one last time and, typically, just smiled and nodded to his fans. If he'd been wearing a cap, he would have doffed it—for the good times.

I glanced over at Larry and could see how upset he was. For the first time, the old poker player was wearing his heart right where everyone could see it. And somehow I knew, with pure certainty, that Larry too was about to jump ship. We completed our afternoon's trading and left the building in a somber mood. Already things seemed different.

I arrived on the trading floor the following morning at around six, opened a couple of markets, and waited for Larry, who showed up at eight o'clock. I will not easily forget the sight of him as he marched along the corridor wearing a 1960s Lilly Pulitzer suit in lime green, sky blue, and white, with little plovers woven on it. He wore no socks, light brown loafers, and a preppy blue Vineyard Vines tie with a little Santa Claus motif.

"What's with the tie?" someone asked, presumably trying to take their eyes off the rest of him.

"It's kind of a battle honor," he joked instantly. "For all my years here, getting you guys paid." Last word, as always, to Santa McCarthy, who had, in fairness, always guarded the interests of his troops with enormous generosity.

And even now he was about to deliver his morning largesse. In his arms he carried two large brown bags that contained fifty sandwiches for the traders, salesmen, and assistants who surrounded him. He was always aware how hungry people can get who were up soon after 4:00 A.M. and had been hard at work for three or four hours before the rest of the nation got out of the sack. Today he had a gourmet selection of egg, cheese, sausage, and ham. He never wanted to eat alone.

"You're going, right?" I said, somewhat unnecessarily.

"I can't stay," he replied. "Not the way things are moving."

"It's Mike," I said.

"Not entirely. But he was my main man. And I hoped he and I, with Alex, could turn us away from the goddamned iceberg. But now we're probably gonna hit it. And I don't want to be here for that."

For the second time in less than twenty-four hours I was looking into the eyes of a top-class Lehman managing director who was leaving. I actually felt physically sick, and the whole floor somehow, by some strange act of telepathy, now knew that Larry McCarthy was following the revered Mike Gelband out the door. *Everyone* felt physically sick. This was not just bad. This was chilling. And the balance of power would now tip away from the distressed-debt department.

I never remember the trading room being so quiet. Every eye in the room watched as Larry went up to human resources to conduct the traditional Lehman Brothers exit interview. When he came back I asked him what he'd told them, and he laid it right out, both barrels.

"I told them I'd heard a lot about Dick Fuld over the years. He's a former commercial paper trader, but not once, not one time in all my years here, did I ever see him on the trading floor. Not even on the day me and the guys had the single most profitable day in the history of Lehman's fixed-income division—two hundred fifty million clams, and the guy's a no-show."

It's hard for Captain Cool to show outrage. But I could see it on his face at that moment, just at the memory of that shining day when we sold the Delta bonds and never even received a note or a handshake from the head of the corporation.

"I said I just thought it was very odd, that's all—a pretty unusual way to stay close to your troops."

For the rest of the morning Larry walked around saying his goodbyes and spending time with the support staff, Janice, Olivia, Maribel, Sylvia, and Jessica. He told me he was leaving the building right after lunch, but he didn't mention precisely what lunch would mean on this day. It turned out he'd ordered twenty carts of food from the outstanding steakhouse Ben Benson's. That's where he ate, and that was the food he wanted for his guys. When fifteen waiters started pushing them in I thought the A train had veered off its tracks. There were huge metal trays of prime rib, filets, porterhouses, creamed spinach, mountains of potatoes. There was enough shrimp and lobster to feed the population of Martha's Vineyard. Larry had decreed, "No plastic," so there was only the finest cutlery and linen napkins. The feast cost him around $14,000.

He and I talked quietly while we dined, and he came up with some true McCarthyisms—"Never tell anyone on Wall Street your problems, old buddy. Ninety percent of those you tell don't care, and the other 10 percent are glad you have them."

He told me to stay short in this market, no matter what. "Because something doesn't smell right. There's a lot of funny money flying around, crummy coupons on crummy credits, distressed debt trading at par. Crazy LBO deals one after another. This smells like the top to me—it's got all the makings."

Like Mike, Larry was really uneasy about the amount of debt Lehman was carrying. We could not know the precise details, but we knew it was thirty-four times our tangible equity value, which added up to a little over $500 billion. That's only half a trillion, and if you say it quickly enough, it doesn't sound that bad. But it did to Larry, and I know that was one of the reasons he was going. Same as Mike.

I remember he attempted to misquote the old Republican senator from Illinois, Everett Dirksen. "You know what he said, right? A billion here, a billion there: pretty soon you're talking real money."

But Larry was not really joking. He was upset, serious, and concerned. "You know," he said, "this is one of the most prestigious merchant banks there has ever been. Lehman. That's a name for the ages. But we don't have any bread. Not real bread."

"I understand," I replied. "How can anyone who owes half a trillion dollars have any bread? We're one of the great and feared Wall Street institutions. But we're fucking broke."

"Larry," he said, "the Texans have a pretty good phrase for that: big hat, no cattle."

I guess I was the last good-bye, after Gat and the guys from the second floor had sought him out for their final farewell.

"I gotta go," he said to me. "I love you, buddy, but I'm out of here while the going's good." He gave Gat, Terence, and me a big hug, picked up his briefcase, and headed for the exit in his Lilly Pulitzer suit, a defiant figure who had made over $400 million profit in a four-year Lehman career.

There were eighteen rows of people between Larry and the door, and one by one they stood up and applauded as he walked past, just as they had with Mike.

Larry never looked back. But just before he reached the glass doors, he raised a clenched right fist high in the air. And then he was gone. Something in the soul of Lehman Brothers was gone with him, and it never came back as we steamed ever onward toward Larry's iceberg.

10

A $100 Million Crash for Subprime's Biggest Beast

It was impossible to move the CDOs on. The goddamned cat was out of the bag, and we were staring at an ugly, sneering face engraved on a very hot potato.

LARRY McCARTHY HAD scarcely aimed his black Mercedes-Benz north up the FDR Drive when a detonation four thousand miles away on the banks of the Rhine River triggered an explosion on Sixth Avenue in New York, about a block from the Lehman tower. UBS, based in the city of Basel, suddenly decided to shut down one of the storied names of Wall Street, Dillon Read Capital Management, located on the Avenue of the Americas at West 50th Street. Time: immediately. Reason: first-quarter losses of $124 million. Cause: U.S. subprime mortgage defaults.

The news ripped through the financial world, sending a shiver through our trading floor, which had not yet recovered even a semblance of equilibrium after the departure of Gelband and McCarthy. The collapse of Dillon Read shocked everyone, but nowhere worse than at Lehman Brothers. We currently stood at the top of the table of subprime lenders, and this was bad enough without yet another hedge fund crashing. Dillon Read, with Wall Street roots going right back to the 1920s, had been acquired by the giant Swiss bank UBS and then relaunched in 2005 with an investment of almost $3.5 billion.

Its sudden failure, so heavily linked to subprime, came hard on the heels of the New Century bankruptcy and the subprime distress signal fired skyward by HSBC and Fremont General. And now we were hearing ferocious rumors that General Motors' first-quarter profits were off 90 percent because of mortgage losses at its 49-percent-owned GMAC finance company because of subprime defaults. And anyone still standing in the brokerage game was in the process of rushing for cover—but not in time to prevent the carnage.

The lawyers were on the march, with lawsuits flying around like artillery shells all over the country as people swore to God they had been sold mortgages they simply did not understand. They were confused by the interest rates and the closing costs. There were allegations of unfair and discriminatory loans, reckless and predatory lending. Words like *deception, high-pressure, irresponsible,* and *falsified* were sworn before judges. And then there were the accusations of companies deliberately altering the income and employment statements of applicants. In one courtroom, a plaintiff swore, by all that was holy, the mortgage broker had placed $5,000 in her bank account, photocopied the statement, and then removed the money, in order to qualify her for a loan.

There were continued allegations of overstatement of assets. There were legal actions, class actions, rearguard actions, and chain reactions. The national watchdog, the Center for Responsible Lending, estimated that loans for 2.2 million people would end in foreclosure—that's one-fifth of all subprime loans made over the previous two years. In California's still-frenzied real estate markets there were now accusations of credit card offers—"platinum equity cards"—with activating phone numbers attached. When the applicant hit the buttons, a mortgage broker was on the line, trying to sell a house. And still the bodybuilders were out there, signing people up, while their home offices just kept on loading up the mortgages and moving them in tranches to the Wall Street investment houses. By now on the trading floor we were hearing of U.S. banks flipping loans to banks in Europe and Asia—not just selling them CDOs and RMBSs but handing over the original loans.

Meanwhile, the theater door was slammed tight and locked. No one could get out. The market for CDOs was much weaker by now, and the lines had to be kept open to the foreign banks and hedge funds. But the shuddering noises from both the Alps and the Far East were growing louder. And from where I stood Larry's iceberg was getting ominously close. There were not yet lengthy stories in the national magazines, but there were some worrying reports starting to appear in the financial press, at this point mostly about court cases, with occasional charts and statistics designed to illustrate a worsening situation. An unmistakable fear began to manifest itself on trading floors throughout the city.

This did not concern us in the distressed-bond trading division because fear, uncertainty, and falling revenues were our stock-in-trade. Right now, the stock market was refusing to go down, but it must surely be a matter of time before this changed. And one of our top guys was heavily into a plan he thought was obvious but no one else had considered. Peter Schellbach believed that Countrywide, the nation's number one mortgage lender, was about to go bust. That was an outlandish thought in a bank like ours, but that was Schell's view, and he was rockin' and rollin' his way toward proving it. Night after night he would pore over charts and reports trying to get a handle on this $26 billion giant of the mortgage industry, which operates out of Calabasas, on the north side of the Santa Monica Mountains, west of Los Angeles. Countrywide was synonymous with its founder, chairman, and CEO, Angelo Mozilo, a clever self-made man, whose father had been a butcher in the Bronx.

Angelo had taken hundreds of millions out of his mortgage business, mostly selling stock options, but Schell had him pegged right now, discovered him selling a hundred thousand Countrywide shares a day in the middle of the subprime crisis, in which his firm was deeply implicated.

Indeed, Countrywide was one of the true pioneers of the programs to provide financing for low-income borrowers in the 1990s, in response to the urgings of the Clinton administration and its firebrand official Roberta Achtenberg. Angelo was regarded as king of the shadow bankers, appearing on Jim Cramer's show on CNBC, and having his name linked to people in high places, like Senator Chris Dodd, for whom he provided a mortgage that saved the Connecticut Democrat around $75,000 in interest payments.

Schellbach was sure of his ground. A former newspaper reporter, he had a fantastic knack for the deepest kind of research, and when you add that to his wonderfully eloquent command of the language and his gifts as a musician, he was probably some kind of modern-day Renaissance man. He earned $3 million to $4 million a year, maybe more, and lived in a big, roomy apartment on the Upper West Side of

Manhattan with his wife, Jackie, and two sons. Inside the firm he had a towering reputation for accuracy and judgment. Like Larry, and like me, he'd never met the chairman.

But now he was onto something. Countrywide's gigantic portfolio of subprime mortgages could not, in his opinion, permit the corporation to stay afloat, and he was recommending we take huge short positions on both the stock and the bonds. Just then Angelo Mozilo was in the process of a stock-selling program that would gross him $129 million before the summer was out. Schell could have lived with this. Just. But at the same time, Angelo was publicly touting the stock and using shareholder funds to buy it back and support the $45 share price. And that Schell could not live with. There was something very wrong with Countrywide, and the old rock guitarist did not require a consultation with S. Holmes in London's Baker Street to work out the answer.

The fact was, in the year 2000 Countrywide had had mortgage revenues of $2 billion, with net income of around $320 million. In 2006 that revenue figure was well over $10 billion, with income of $2.5 billion. Now it was plummeting, and Schell was detecting a $6.5 billion crash, which he thought would finish them. So far as Schell could predict, there was no way Countrywide, with enough subprime defaults to capsize the space shuttle, could avoid losing possibly up to $700 million in the current year.

We were so busy on that first afternoon without Larry and Mike it was hard to get our bearings. And it was not until the following morning that the appalling reality set in. They weren't coming back. Right next to me, Larry's chair was empty. We had lost our fighter ace, and there was no replacing Major McCarthy, the man with the fastest cannon on Wall Street, the dive-bomber of distress, everybody's hero. Well, nearly everybody's. I still talked to him just about every day, but even so, the sight of that empty chair haunted my dreams for many, many months. To a lot of people, he was lost forever, and they still miss him.

That first day, a young trader came up to me and said, "It's not the same, is it? I mean, without him." He never even said Larry's name. He didn't need to. If he'd said the same thing six months later to anyone on the floor, he still wouldn't have needed the name.

The absence of Mike Gelband also had a terrible effect. He and Larry had represented the glue of our team. They held us together, creating that magical shared loyalty. In the opening days of May 2007, we were a bit lost without those two powerful influences, especially Mike Gelband. And for months afterward, people still wondered in their thoughts and conversations how Dick and Joe could possibly have forced him out.

The old team was still full of buddies, since many of us had been handpicked by Larry McCarthy. But there was a sadness and a feeling of disquiet about the troubles that might be lurking in the immediate future. Larry had been through three bear markets in his career, and whenever there were bullets flying, it was really comforting to see him in there with us, working along the cutting edge of the risk.

Right now I had to dismantle Larry's ledger. I had to get in and find his trades, and he had told me I'd find that a lot of fun. He was right. First thing I located was a billion dollars' worth of subprime shorts on corporations like Countrywide, Radian, MGIC Insurance, Fannie Mae, ResCap, and Washington Mutual. They were huge amounts, both shorts and puts—Larry had hit Beazer Homes and Centex, not to mention the ratings agency Moody's. From what I could tell he was in for over $1 billion and was trying to jack it up to $3 billion at the time he resigned.

He'd done something extremely ambitious with Countrywide. From what I could tell, he'd bought a massive amount of protection—a billion dollars' worth of credit default swaps at 18 basis points. That's the equivalent to shorting the bonds at slightly above 99 cents on the dollar, just a tick under par. He believed the bonds could go to 50, then bankrupt the corporation.

Some of the young traders told me later that if everything had been left in place just the way Larry had planned, he personally would have made the firm $1 billion of profit in 2007. Secretly, I took that as one hell of a compliment, because there was no doubt in my mind that Larry had acted on everything I had told him. He'd taken my best ideas and, as it were, put his money where my mouth was. Schell and Hammack had helped me, but it was I who had briefed Larry on those big hitters who had somehow mislaid their bats.

Meanwhile, the Dow Jones average during May and June raged ever upward, above 13,500, battering to death those with short positions on the big subprime corporations. At the time it was hard for me to sleep. I used to walk disconsolately home from the office, worried out of my mind as those mortgage-related outfits we'd shorted powered upward. In one week I lost $8 million, and I had to report to

Schell and Gatward, who were sympathetic, because they too were watching various corporations defy gravity. Anyway, they knew I had been $38 million up on the year, and they both believed it was merely a matter of time before there was an almighty crash.

Some people appeared not to be worried about the present market situation. One of these was Mark Walsh, who continued to do the bidding of his masters, buying massive chunks of real estate all over the world. Right in that time frame, he pounced again, teaming with the owners of Rockefeller Center, Tishman Speyer, for a $22.2 billion leveraged buyout of the Archstone-Smith Trust, which owned 360 luxury apartment buildings from Houston to New York, Phoenix to Fairfax County. This was real estate at the highest level. Tishman Speyer was one of the top corporations in New York, with world headquarters above the ice rink at Rockefeller Plaza. This was not inappropriate, because they and Mark Walsh overpaid heavily for Archstone, probably by $3 billion, and Prince Mark was suddenly skating on very thin ice. The deal, of course, paralleled the 2006 Blackstone purchase of Equity Office Properties Trust, which was about twice the size, and which had placed the little green god of envy squarely on Dick Fuld's shoulders. When Mark Walsh sought backing from Lehman's corporate balance sheet for the Archstone deal, he received it quickly and in full. Fuld could at last see a chance to slice into the lead established by Peterson and Schwarzman in the high-prestige game of collecting enough apartment blocks to reach halfway to the stars.

But Archstone was not worth $22.2 billion. This was the top of the market, and there was a bidding war to acquire it. Goldman Sachs was in there, hot and heavy, and Fuld was determined to prove Lehman could play in this league, against the big guns of Wall Street. With the bidding already too high, Goldman pulled out, and with the greatest joy, Fuld told his blue-eyed boy to keep charging, sword drawn, and pay what he had to for a big share of Archstone's apartment empire.

There was no way Fuld was going to allow Mark Walsh to back off. Right from the start, right from the moment he had been given almost carte blanche, there could be no backing off.

"Thanks mostly to Blackstone, we've missed three big ones," Dick had told Mark. "Don't miss any more."

I'd never suggest that Fuld was blinded by envy or that he was a particularly vengeful man. But with Dick, it was not always about judgment. There was often something personal.

The Archstone deal was completed early in the coming October, and another honking multibillion-dollar loss was on its way to the Lehman balance sheet. But that much was not really clear in the spring of 2007, and with the stock and bond markets still blundering upward, despite incontrovertible evidence it should have been going the other way, we in the distressed division had almost nothing at which to smile. Except for an event on June 6, to which everyone was looking forward: Larry McCarthy's going-away party. It was scheduled to take place in the Red Lion, one of New York's landmark live music spots, situated south of Washington Square, a little bit west of Broadway. And there, in the richly paneled dark wood interior, with its red leather chairs and fifty-foot bar, we would all have drinks and dinner together for the last time.

Christine Daley was there, and Jane Castle, Mike Gelband, Alex Kirk, Rich Gatward, and his great friend Bart McDade. Larry's beautiful wife, Suzanne, flew up from their horse farm in Wellington, Florida. Everyone who had really mattered in Larry's life, 120 of us. It had to be everybody, because Larry was a man who always had time for the less important people, and he was generous to them with time and money, far beyond the call of duty. I guess we'll never know how many people he helped in times of trouble. But believe me, it was a whole lot. If anyone had been left out, Larry definitely would have noticed, and most definitely would have sent a chauffeur-driven limousine to pick the person up from wherever they lived. He might even have gone himself. But he would not have tolerated anyone not being invited. You have to know him as well as I do to understand that. The guy's got a heart the size of the Empire State Building.

We'd rented the whole place, and the music was great. Schell and his band superbly played Grateful Dead favorites right there in this cathedral of rock 'n' roll to this trading floor brotherhood, which had never been more closely knit. We were all together, standing among the pictures of musicians like Jimi Hendrix, Mick Jagger, Keith Richards, and Jerry Garcia. The speeches were hysterical, especially Larry's. He mentioned that the CDS (credit default swap) traders were currently working on bringing down the whole world. He observed that some of the women wore clothes to work his wife wouldn't wear in the bedroom. He picked out our most senior salesman and said he was the last one left who used to work for Drexel Lambert (deceased 1990). He said that Joe Beggans would take over his mantle as the world's greatest trader, and that the brand-new electric guitar Pete Schellbach had purchased this week, which had cost him thousands, was a stone-cold certainty to have marked the top of the market.

Despite the laughs, the evening turned out to be sadder than Larry's last day. His close friends gathered around him at the end of the evening, knowing this really was the last time, and that all the sorrow that now engulfed us could be laid at the door to the big office on the thirty-first floor. There weren't many dry eyes out there on the sidewalk as we waited for cabs on that warm June night.

But the epitaph of the evening was not written until the following day, when Bart McDade walked in at four minutes past six, instead of six o'clock sharp, as he had unfailingly done every day of his working life.

Someone called out, joking, "Hey, Bart, running a little late today?"

But our famously good-natured equity chief never smiled. And he never broke stride. He just said quietly, "We retired a legend last night."

And, in a way, that brought down the curtain on an era. The future was uncertain. The vexed question of Lehman's debt and exposure had been the subject of Mike Gelband's last stand, and he had been not just ignored but forced out of the firm, which meant, broadly, that nothing much was going to change on the thirty-first floor, where our two leaders were demanding more power from the turbines as we headed into the ice field.

Alex was now our great hope of sanity. He and Mike had implored Dick and Joe to slam on the brakes, to cut that $500 billion debt drastically. They had proposed that instead of being thirty-four times leveraged, we cut back to twenty-five times, which would bring the debt down to $380 billion. Instead of that, we were headed straight up to $660 billion, and it was driving Alex Kirk quietly nuts. Over and over he tried to issue warnings. But he was not winning. Mark Walsh was still spending money as if it had gone out of style, Lehman was still obligated to buy thunderous wads of shaky mortgages, all our short positions were going the wrong way, and the corporate bond prices were following the Dow upward. Amazingly, the Lehman Brothers high-yield bond index ground to its all-time tight credit spread of 231 basis points over U.S. Treasuries. That's under 7 percent for a high-yield bond!

Blackstone's initial public offering took place on June 22 and netted two enormous fortunes, one for Pete Peterson, and one for the CEO, Stephen Schwarzman. They received the bulk of the $4 billion raised in equity—Schwarzman sold shares worth $700 million, and the now eighty-one-year-old Peterson collected $1.8 billion in that single day. Altogether, the Blackstone IPO valued the corporation at close to $40 billion, and first-day trading saw the shares rise from $31 to between $35 and $38 on the Big Board. It was the largest IPO on Wall Street in five years, since the collapse of the dot-coms. The biggest buyer of the brand-new Blackstone public stock was a 5 percent stake in the corporation purchased for $3 billion by the enormous Jianyin Investments, owned by the Chinese government.

So while Fuld fretted and fumed at the injustice of a world that made towering heroes of such men as Peterson and Schwarzman, there were other, more advanced ways of looking at the situation. The fact was that even though Stephen Schwarzman was retaining, for the moment, 24 percent of the Blackstone stock, the two founders had essentially got out right at the top of the market. As the news broke on the trading floor, the bearish Pete Schellbach growled, "Look out. Schwarzman and Peterson are selling stock, and we're buying hedge funds." These Blackstone financial tartars had been early and right so often, we had almost lost count.

Since Dick's old mentor Lew Glucksman had hustled him unceremoniously out of Lehman's front door, Pete Peterson had never looked back. He and Stephen were the best, and they had both worked for Lehman. I am sure their loss was felt as keenly in another time as we felt that of Mike and Larry. And our chairman had been indirectly involved in the departure of all four of them.

By now we were approaching the halfway point in the year. And among the many hostile problems with heavy artillery ranged against us beyond our Seventh Avenue garrison, there was one that was becoming more urgent than all the rest. Because this one was already clambering halfway over the ramparts, its ass pointing up toward the sun. I refer, of course, to the CDOs, which had swiftly developed into a major disaster area.

On a bright June day, we all gathered for a crisis meeting in the trading floor conference room. In the chair was Jason Schechter, senior vice president and global head of cash CDO trading, who had supervised the construction of a hybrid collateralized debt obligation comprising credit default swaps on ninety high-yield rated companies. It was perhaps the most dangerous junk bond ever invented. In attendance were Pete Schellbach, Joe Beggans, Pete Hammack, Ashish Shah, Eric Felder, Jeremiah Stafford, who was a trader in high-yield indexes, and Jane Castle. I was sitting with my buddy John Gramins, a good-looking and fast-talking trader in leveraged loans, and a nine-year Lehman veteran. He was around thirty-three, and lived on the Upper West Side of Manhattan near Peter Schellbach. Like me, he had been handpicked for the firm by Larry McCarthy.

The overwhelming reason for the meeting was that the NINJA loans were blowing up all over the country. Poor homeowners were bailing out as the resets slammed them into a financial Guantánamo Bay, with no prospect of an early release and no escape from the crippling interest payments. Their only way out was to leave everything, write off the payments they'd already made, and get out under the cover of darkness, keys in the mailbox.

I realize I have mentioned this in a small way at various points, but this was different from what had happened in late 2006. This was nothing like a few guys in over their heads; now there was a whole scattered army on the march, getting out of their new homes and going back to the poorest areas of the cities, where they could afford to live. The shining era of the $400,000-a-year bus driver was drawing to a close. There would be no more ludicrous lying on loan applications. And the days of the slick-talking bodybuilders were already numbered. In places like Stockton, there were practically traffic jams at three o'clock in the morning as the residents piled into trucks and vans and hit the road, mostly to vanish without a trace.

And as thousands of mortgages ground to a shuddering halt, the little ripples that had been slightly irritating to the financial world were now not ripples at all. They were big white-foamed breakers crashing onto the beaches of Wall Street and threatening to drown anyone who was late taking cover.

The march of the NINJAs was public. There were no secrets left. There was nothing more to be hidden. The collapse of so many shadow banks had taken care of that. Any mortgage brokerages involved in subprime were in desperate trouble, and the crisis was creeping inward from its outer reaches in Iceland, Shanghai, the Swiss Alps, and London.

Everyone at the table knew that even Lehman, the biggest beast among the subprime lenders, was finding it impossible to move the CDOs. The cat was out of the bag, and we were staring at an ugly, sneering face engraved on a very hot potato—that's the big tranche of tens of thousands of mortgages for which Lehman's selling price would need to be drastically cut.

The first news to hit us was confirmation of a huge hung deal—a $2 billion CDO that we could not move at par. All over the world, big investors were starting to discover the true value of their supposed AAA mortgage-backed securities, the ones officially stamped, signed, and certified as riskless by Moody's, S&P, and Fitch. There was a kind of global cry of agony: *Holy shit! We've been conned by one of the great scams, investment-grade bonds backed by American trailer trash.* Lehman had been forced to drop the price, selling the CDO at a $100 million loss at 95 cents on the dollar. It was the first time we'd taken a hammering on a CDO—and the trouble was, it might not be the last. In the trade, a loss like that is known as "taking a hickey," and we'd sure taken one.

And that was only half the story. Jason Schechter explained that the SIVs, the same securitized products that had driven Mike Gelband to leave the firm, were starting to unwind in two of America's greatest banks, Citigroup and Bank of America. These two institutions were the biggest buyers of subprime securities on the planet, and they were some of Lehman's biggest clients. They had used the lethal concoction of depositors' money, their own awesome leverage, and borrowing in the short-term commercial paper market to stuff their coffers with billions of dollars of Alt-A and subprime toxic debt. They lumped the mortgages in with other debt to create a gigantic bond, the SIV, which they believed, grotesquely, would provide a positive income stream. Like CDOs, SIVs borrow in the commercial paper market at, say, LIBOR plus 20 basis points and lend by owning a portfolio of mortgages at LIBOR plus 200. In simple terms that is like borrowing at 4 percent and lending at 6. A perpetual free money machine, they thought!

But it was as if they innately knew the terrible risks, because they hid the SIVs away, kept them off the balance sheet, stored them in offshore havens, away from prying eyes. There was always something distinctly suspect about the SIVs of Citigroup and Bank of America. Neither of these mighty institutions, which surely were big enough to have known better, had considered, in the depths of their blackest dreams, that this housing market could come unraveled and slash the value of their colossal portfolio of SIVs, perhaps bringing both banks to the verge of bankruptcy.

But now the foundations of the housing market were beginning to tremble, and the size of the two commercial banks had made them prisoners. They could run, but they couldn't hide. They could sell some, but not all, because a massive sale of mortgage securitizations could bring down the whole edifice of Wall Street, flooding the market and sucking down the smaller investment banks in a terrible orgy of selling off cheaply.

Fear, that most terrible of Wall Street predators, was suddenly lurking in our conference room. That one big loss we'd taken could easily be repeated—and almost certainly would be repeated, now that a major AAA-rated security, issued by Lehman Brothers, had been sold cheaply, an almost unheard-of occurrence in the past five years. The moment investors find out there is greater risk involved in buying such securities, the yield rises as the bond price falls and they no longer trade at par. Once there's more risk, they want more reward.

These mortgage-backed securities had been paying only one or two hundred basis points over LIBOR, the interest rate banks charge each other for short-term loans, the lowest rate at which banks can borrow money. By June 2007, this was mostly around 5 percent, and the CDOs had hitherto been paying as little as 6 percent. But sooner or later the news would get out that Lehman had just lost $100 million, and investors would now want more for their money. They would look for six hundred basis points over LIBOR, perhaps more. The market for CDOs that contained a heavy dose of subprime mortgages would never be the same.

We were alerted that there was already a buyer's strike developing on a worldwide basis. Big investors suddenly did not feel the same about mortgage-backed securities. The CDOs, which for so long had provided a money machine for investors, now felt vulnerable. When Lehman dropped the price by $100 million, well, they'd just fired the "short" heard 'round the world. Right now it was a secret, or supposed to be, and the loss would not leak out for several weeks. But somehow there were already undercurrents. One of the important market clues delivered at that table came from Jeremiah Stafford, a thirty-two-year-old top trading operator. He was a senior vice president of credit derivative trading, but his most significant task was to trade Lehman's High Yield 9 Index (HY-9), which comprised one hundred equally weighted corporations and charted the ups and downs of their bonds. Jeremiah was, by now, very bearish. For the past three years he'd had hardly anything to do, since his markets were flat calm, with zero volatility. But now he was one of the busiest traders on the floor, because some of his biggest customers were stampeding to short the HY-9 index as a hedge against an impending credit crisis. "I'm seeing it," said Jeremiah. "Daily increasing numbers of sophisticated accounts selling the index short, as a hedge against credit spread contagion."

Everyone understood what was happening. And this was unnerving, because the near-moribund HY-9 market had been becalmed for a very long time, and the sudden explosion of activity could only have been caused by one factor: fear. Sudden dramatic protective changes, like the ones Jeremiah was reporting, manifest themselves for no other reason.

And it was not just the HY-9 they were shorting. They also wanted positions on the ABX, which tracks the value of mortgage-backed securities, and the LCDX (the leverage loan index), which tracks all the millions of dollars borrowed for hostile takeovers. (Remember the CLOs, the collateralized loan obligations, the steroids behind the buyouts?) Jeremiah was trading them all short, because that was all anyone wanted. Anyone with eyes to see could tell there was a coming sea change in the markets. This was not a shift or an adjustment; this was a deep, shuddering portent.

And then Pete Hammack made it worse by revealing there was a strong rumor that Bear Stearns was considering liquidating all of the assets held by one of its two hedge funds that were long in CDOs. He'd been told this by our mortgage guys, who had just seen a very hefty block of CDOs coming through the market with Bear Stearns' paw marks all over them.

Ashish Shah made it clear this was becoming a real marketwide problem, saying he knew that Merrill Lynch had nineteen hung CDOs that could not be moved at the right price. Those of us in this meeting were collectively beginning to recall the bitter words uttered by Mike Gelband, Larry McCarthy, and Alex Kirk in this very room three months ago: the dire quality of their warnings, the clarity of their thoughts. And those of us with longer memories could remember Mike's words of two years ago: *You cannot model human behavior with mathematics.*

We discussed the positive feedback loop—financiers' jargon for the world state of play. It means the global carousel that began on 9/11 when the Treasury dropped interest rates to 1 percent to stimulate the economy. The idea was to insert a large amount of almost free money into the economy, allowing people to borrow for cars, houses, credit cards, and store credit lines. In turn, the shadow banks were set up to lend money to prospective home buyers. With reasonable rates of repayment and a constantly rising housing market, people could use their homes like an ATM machine, taking out home equity loans and heading off on spending sprees at Sears, Home Depot, and other megastores. Awash with cash, the stores turned to China for zillions of inexpensive products, which came flooding into the United States and other Western markets. Everyone was getting rich, especially the Chinese, who proceeded to invest their profits in U.S. Treasury bonds, billions of dollars' worth. This ensured that interest rates were kept low, which triggered a thirst for higher yield among investors, and the cycle started all over again. What had begun as a friendly little zephyr of a breeze, circling cheerfully through the financial markets, was now gathering strength each time it came around, first into a good stiff blow, then into a gale, and now howling into a full-blooded hurricane, sucking up everything in its path.

It seemed that nothing could stop the loop. The population somehow could not function without cheap money. China could not function without massive orders from the United States for consumer goods. The big Wall Street commercial banks and investment banks had become dependent on the rising real estate market and the revenues from the sales of credit derivatives. And the Treasury was counting on the Chinese to hurl money at the United States, which held down interest rates. Everyone counted on everyone else to keep this financial tornado spinning.

But now a gigantic monkey wrench had been thrown into the works. House prices were collapsing, which meant that people who could not pay their mortgages were leaping from the carousel. That left the CDO market to go to hell as investors stopped buying. Without the easy money from the shadow banks, people were changing their spending habits, which completely screwed up the lives of Sears, Home Depot, and other retailers. They in turn stopped ordering from

China in those same vast quantities. And that put a brake on the amount of Treasuries China could buy from the U.S. government, which slowed down America's ability to borrow big sums of money from Chinese banks. Everyone was now screwing up everyone else. That's known in financial circles as the negative feedback loop, the precise opposite of the first one, the positive feedback loop. For the record, for anyone who might be very slightly confused: the first one, the positive loop, is great for all concerned, although not guaranteed to last. The second one, the negative loop, is a bitch.

I describe it so because once the loop reverses direction, it's extremely difficult to slow down. It all starts with those CDOs backing up at the traffic light. Remember what I said when Dave Gross and I were out at New Century? That it would start right there. And indeed, New Century was one of the first to crash in flames.

Now we were hearing that Lehman had taken a haircut to the tune of $100 million on the sale of a CDO. Which meant the game was over. As night follows day, events would unfold in a gruesomely predictable order. With the housing market slowing down, many people would run out of cash, and others would find their credit lines greatly diminished; this would prevent them from spending at the same rate, affecting especially retail stores like Sears and Home Depot. But it would also affect restaurants, main street stores, and car dealerships. When banks get scared, they pull back on lending. Similarly, when people get scared they just stop spending. Second homes, vacation homes, are put on the market, which drives prices down even further.

I have always been taught to be alert for the moment the pendulum stops swinging positive and turns negative. So far as I could tell, this was it. Lehman had caught a major cold with that goddamned bond. Jeremiah could see it all happening, right before his eyes. Ashish thought it was worse on the other side of the Street, at Merrill. Pete Hammack had heard of a potential collapse at Bear Stearns. Hell, this *was* it.

The only voice of reason still echoing in this particular room was that of Mike Gelband, and those two comedians on the thirty-first floor had made it impossible for him to work here anymore.

At our meeting, Jason Schechter had not revealed any kind of a master plan to steer us away from potential disaster. But it had been hugely educational, and no group of people anywhere in this vast office complex understood better than we the true nature of the ice floes that lay ahead when the subprime mortgage game finally detonated worldwide rather than just stumbling along causing trouble, as it was at present. The meeting broke up after a depressing hour. And no one was more depressed than Eric Felder. He was fiddling with his BlackBerry, and as we walked from the room, he said, "Guys, the lightbulb just went on for me . . . in the year 2006, possibly 50 percent of the growth in the United States GDP was bogus—CDOs, CMBSs, CLOs, and MBSs. Alex's steroids. Holy shit!"

No one had any miracle cure for the banking industry. No one really had any idea how to jump out of the way of that razor-sharp pendulum as it began its backward path, preparing to cleave its way through our industry, traveling in a different direction. The wrong way.

Twelve working days after that CDO meeting, on Wednesday, June 20, the Dow plummeted 150 points late in the afternoon because of the uncertainty concerning those two major Bear Stearns hedge funds. Both of them were packed with subprime mortgages, and rumors were rife that they would collapse. Indeed, Merrill Lynch, one of the funds' lenders, seized $850 million worth of assets that were backing the two hedge funds, and began to auction them off. A wave of selling hit the mortgage-backed securities market and drove down the price of the bonds. Behind the scenes there had been high drama at midnight, when a rescue plan blew up and the two hedge funds were very nearly shut down right there. By the closing bell Wednesday a lot of people probably wished they had been, because the funds were in crisis and they were dragging down the whole market.

The *Wall Street Journal* was spooked, and reminded readers that as of a few weeks earlier, the two hedge funds had held more than $20 billion of investments, mostly in complex securities, bonds backed by subprime mortgages—"made up of the relatively risky home loans to borrowers with troubled credit histories."

The newspaper mentioned, somewhat archly, that since 2000, Wall Street had created $1.8 trillion of securities backed by subprime mortgages. But now there was a housing slump, and the explanation for the mini-crash that day was clear: the slump was causing a spike in mortgage delinquencies, which hurt the value of the bonds. By the end of that Wednesday afternoon there were clear and obvious signs of investors becoming worried—it looked like thousands of them were trying to get out.

For the moment, the Bear Stearns funds were still breathing. Just. But we all stood back in anticipation of a wild rush to the desk of Jeremiah Stafford to pile fortunes into short positions on the HY-9, because if those Bear Stearns funds went down, they were big enough to cause nothing short of abject chaos in the markets.

Right now we were certainly not in chaos. The Bear Stearns situation was not, for the moment, life-threatening, and the market was still quite buoyant. But Wall Street's most sinister problems occasionally arrive without the thunder of the guns and the clash of mounted cavalry on the stock exchange floor. Some deadly problems come creeping in on cat's paws, unannounced, often unnoticed. They occur when the world's banks unobtrusively arrive at a single conclusion—individual decisions made quite separately but at around the same time. No one says anything about collective change. The consequences just come padding in, and suddenly there's a lightning bolt of fear crackling through the market. It was happening right now in those last days of June 2007. Maybe it was the Bear Stearns hedge funds, maybe the rumors about Merrill's unsold CDOs, maybe the avalanche of investors piling into Jeremiah's short index trades. But whatever it was, the commercial paper market, the lifeblood of us all, was suddenly contracting. There was a clear and definite reluctance on the part of banks and money market funds to lend to us speculators. Both Mike and Larry would have chuckled sarcastically, *No! How could anything like that possibly have happened?*

The signs were barely discernible, but on June 30 there was another minor hand grenade landing on the floor. Someone found out almost one in four of all Countrywide's subprime loans were delinquent—25 percent, up from 15 percent against the same period last year. In pure numbers that was hard to quantify, but Countrywide was still the biggest lender in the nation, with 62,000 employees in 900 offices financing around 200,000 loans a month, and right there we were talking thousands and thousands of homeowners not paying. And 10 percent of those were 90 days delinquent or more. It also emerged that many of these delinquencies were the direct result of savage resets, taking the homeowners' repayments from the low "teaser" levels, to double digits. Some carried prohibitive prepayment penalties, which made refinancing impossibly expensive. And it was right here that the commercial paper market finally faltered.

I'd like to explain commercial paper in a little more detail. For a start, commercial paper is short-term money, loaned out for thirty to forty days or less. This market is used by the biggest and best blue-chip companies. Commercial paper is the quickest, cheapest, and easiest way for them to raise a fast loan that is not regulated by the SEC. As an example, say Bear Stearns goes to JPMorganChase and requests a $500 million loan for fourteen days. Question: would you lend Bear Stearns half a billion dollars for just a couple of weeks when they were backing it with AAA-rated mortgage bonds and willing to pay 5 percent interest? Answer: probably yes, since that would mean a $959,000 profit.

Now, JPMorganChase isn't going to offer up that $500 million to any old applicant. But Bear Stearns is a highly respected bank, and they've done something similar many times before. The same would apply to Lehman, Morgan Stanley, Goldman Sachs, General Motors, or Countrywide. All of them have always paid back, with the interest, right on time. But in many cases they paid back with money from another short-term paper loan they'd borrowed from someone else. For banks with blue-chip lines of credit, it was possible to keep a huge loan rolling for months and months, paying back with borrowed money over and over. Simply put, they were taking short-term borrowed money and investing in longer-term mortgage-backed securities that paid a higher yield. In Wall Street jargon, this was known as the "carry trade" or the "positive carry trade."

The problem was, banks tend to keep an eagle eye on charts, trends, graphs, and indices. And right now there was one chart jumping off the screens of bank analysts all over the world. It was the big blue tracker of the amount of United States commercial paper outstanding weekly from 2001 to mid-2007. For the first four years, it was cruising at a rock-steady $1.25 trillion to $1.5 trillion. Then it began a steep upward climb, coinciding with the advent of the credit boom in housing. In 2005 it broke $1.5 trillion. In 2006 it was well on its way to $2 trillion and reached that level by Christmas. After the first half of 2007 it was $2.25 trillion and climbing, which represented a spike of $750,000 a week. Suddenly, without warning, the biggest banks started to haul on the reins. At first they weren't saying an outright no to their best customers. But they were hesitating, referring things to committees, making it more difficult to borrow, taking longer. That evening Alex Kirk took a group of us traders out to dinner and expressed his grave concern that the modern tenets of finance were causing the systems of financial plumbing to clog.

Then, right after the July 4 vacation, they started saying a categorical no to various clients. The situation at Countrywide was probably the catalyst, spurred by the vast number of mortgage delinquencies. When Countrywide's bankers said no, instantly Angelo Mozilo and his men slammed the lid on information leaking out about this crisis. But the giant mortgage shop could no longer roll its remarketable preferreds—those 4 percent loans that needed to be paid back in seven days. The commercial paper market had frozen on them.

Terence Tucker, our ace salesman, found out. A big hedge fund tipped him off, and the rest was like a wildfire. The three-month LIBOR ripped upward from 5.36 percent to 5.95 percent. It doesn't sound like much, but this was the biggest move in years. Gatward instinctively warned his traders, "Guys, this is the biggest move in three-month LIBOR since Long-Term Capital Management bit the dust back in 1998, take down risk now. I want to see all your long positions trimmed down before the close." You could feel the tension growing. I'll never forget how much louder it was becoming on the trading floor that summer. I hadn't heard anything quite like it in my entire time with the firm up to that point. It had a distinct higher pitch to it, like a nervous crowd in the fifteenth round of a close prizefight. This move in LIBOR could only mean one thing: banks no longer trusted each other in quite the same way. Remember, Countrywide was a shadow bank, with $300 billion worth of mortgages out there, a lot of it subprime. This was the first sign of big trouble. Countrywide was under a blanket of deep white frost, with no further access to cheap, fast money.

The situation immediately worsened rather than improved. Everyone was starting to find it difficult to borrow. The roof was falling in on the carry trade. It was no longer possible to borrow at those very low rates and lend at much higher ones, a tactic that had convinced many Wall Streeters that here at last was a method of trading made in heaven. And for a very few years after Greenspan slashed the rates in 2001, "borrow short, lend long" was a license to print money.

Then, in the middle of July, Bear Stearns' two hedge funds went bust. One was their Strategies Fund, and the other was the Strategies Enhanced Leverage Fund, both under the umbrella of Bear Stearns High-Grade Structured Credit. Through January 2007 they had forty months with no declines, but in the following four months the Enhanced Fund lost 23 percent.

And that's a lot worse than it sounds. They had $638 million in invested capital and had borrowed at least $6 billion, making $11.5 billion in bullish bets on the subprime mortgage market, plus $4.5 billion in bearish wagers to hedge their position. That's ten times leverage minimum. So when it crashed 23 percent, the margin clerks at Merrill had no choice but to seize their $850 million in collateral and dump it for 85 cents on the dollar.

All of this cast a dark cloud over Wall Street, setting off a chain reaction that would shake the CDO market globally. The SEC moved in to conduct a thorough examination of the Bear Stearns fund's balance sheets. The fund immediately suspended investor redemptions. Bear Stearns itself was doing an impressive impersonation of a nerve-wracked ostrich that had planted its head straight into the sand, without the slightest intention of coming back up.

The Strategies Fund was not in such dire straits as the Enhanced, being only six times leveraged. And Bear Stearns threw it a lifeline of $1.6 billion, because they thought it had a chance to survive. But they were wrong, and on July 17 they sent out a letter to investors telling them more or less what was going on, and that the funds were essentially worthless and would be disbanded.

"There is effectively no value left for the investors" was the eloquent phraseology of the letter, which failed to add an even more eloquent phrase about their own managers' inspired strategy in loading up the funds with CDOs strictly reliant on people who had no bread. Indeed, Bear Stearns was sanguine about this mildly embarrassing method of losing billions of dollars. "Our highest priority," they confirmed, "is to continue to earn your trust and confidence, each and every day, consistent with the Firm's proud history of achievement." Then they added, "Please contact us if we can be of service." This last bit was presumably aimed at specific investors who felt like dropping another $100 million in the world's worst mortgage-backed securities.

Another casualty of that black July was United Capital, a large hedge fund out of Key Biscayne, Florida, and a leading player in the asset-backed securities (ABS) market. By the eleventh of the month all four of their funds were closed down with combined losses of $630 million. This was doubtless a shuddering blow to their investors, but the toughest break was to its thirty-eight-year-old founder and CEO,

John Devaney, a man who had ridden the subprime wave and then crashed high and dry onto the sun-kissed but rock-hard Key Biscayne beach with a severely broken ego.

Along the way, during the rampaging boom years of the subprime bonanza, John had collected a Gulfstream jet, a Renoir painting, a $6.5 million vacation home in Aspen, Colorado, and an $11 million Sikorsky corporate helicopter big enough to transport a squad of leathernecks straight into Afghanistan. There was also the world-class 141-foot oceangoing tri-deck Trinity yacht that sported an eight-person Jacuzzi and five staterooms paneled in enough top-of-the-line cabinetmakers' cherrywood to redecorate Grand Central Station. It carried more than ten thousand gallons of fuel, was named *Positive Carry* as testimony to its owner's positive devotion to those glorious little commercial paper loans that had kept United Capital rolling along through the very best of times, and was registered—where else?—in the Cayman Islands. Housewise, John was in good shape. In Key Biscayne alone he owned seven of them, all mansions, total value of $78 million. His own residence was the $38.5 million West Matheson Drive waterfront palace that had featured prominently in the Al Pacino gangster classic *Scarface*. When the crunch came, and the banks suddenly slammed on the brakes that summer, it was all over for Big John. All of the above were sold, but he swore to God he would earn again the money his investors had lost. Financiers have calculated his was one of the largest hedge funds to go down in the viselike grip of the short-term credit squeeze, which forced so many to bail out and leave the market to sterner men.

Meanwhile, back on the Lehman trading floor, August brought no better news. The market was suddenly volatile, and after a strange July peak of around 14,000, it tumbled in mid-August to just above 12,800. Bank of America stepped in to save Countrywide and bought 16 percent of the ailing shadow bank for $2 billion after Countrywide's shares lost more than 66 percent of their value. In the end they went to $1. Lehman's rock 'n' roll guitarist, Pete Schellbach, had been right on the money. He shorted Countrywide when it was flying high and had pocketed over $10 million in profits for the firm.

It was clear, even to those accustomed to keeping their head well down at Lehman, that Dick Fuld had hit the spending gas pedal with a ferocity that would have made John Devaney's eyes water. Several days after the departure of Mike Gelband, Lehman began negotiations to buy the Houston-based energy services corporation Eagle Energy Partners for a total of $400 million. Lehman already owned one-third of it, which Mike had considered quite sufficient. And now they were going for the rest, as part of Dick Fuld's expansion plans.

Those plans were gaining ground with every passing week. By high summer Lehman was involved in multibillion-dollar commitments with TXU and Claire's Stores. Then there was the payment services giant, First Data from Denver, Colorado, in which the firm was involved with a consortium of banks in a $26 billion takeover deal. In addition to buying Eagle Energy, Lehman was also tied up with a group of banks trying to raise billions to refinance Home Depot.

And then Dave Sherr, of all people, and his team somehow got us into the old International House of Pancakes' $1.9 billion buyout of Applebee's, a chain of almost two thousand neighborhood restaurants out of Overland Park, right on the Kansas-Missouri border. My guys, almost to a man, hated it. Steve Berkenfeld, who obviously couldn't get enough of pancakes, rushed straight in and approved it. And again Lehman stepped up to the plate with financial support, this time for IHOP, boldly buying a corporation whose stock had been in steady decline. I think in the end we lost nearly half a billion dollars on this hung deal. Our salespeople couldn't move the debt at all. I'm not even sure Dick got out with a plate of secondhand pancakes. Old Dave thought securitization could save the world and even move an overpriced plate of pancake debt.

The magic of private equity was pervading the Lehman boardroom, and all of these big leveraged buyouts held immense appeal for Fuld and Joe Gregory. Both must have been aware of the firm's high-wire act with Lehman's debt. But both men were devotees, apparently, of the very suspect maxim that it's always possible to spend your way out of trouble.

In these barnstorming days, where the stock market was expressing a total disregard for reality, the private equity firms were happy to purchase a corporation at ten or eleven times its EBITDA. This is very, very high historically, especially compared to 2005 levels when the current LBO boom began, and likely to work only in a financial bubble. But Dick Fuld couldn't see this. Under him, Lehman's philosophy was akin to a golf cart, those little contraptions designed to allow golfers to zip around the course a bit more quickly than if they walked. Golf carts are all fitted with a governor, which is a device to keep the cart's top speed slow enough to be safe. Lehman's thirty-first floor was riding on a golf cart, but Dick Fuld had taken a sledgehammer to the governor and was currently making about 140 mph straight across the ninth green. Oil gushers, power stations, necklaces, handbags, home fittings, electrical goods, paintbrushes, pay slips, credit cards, wallpaper, and pancakes—Dick and Joe were in there. We were $82 billion out in leveraged mortgages, $30 billion in leveraged buyouts, $40 billion in CMBSs, $5 billion in the oil industry, $20 billion in hedge funds. God knows how many additional assets were kept off the balance sheet and currently hidden away in the middle of the Caribbean. Not to mention the fact that Lehman Brothers was well on the way to being leveraged to forty-four times our value—that's well north of $700 billion. We were somehow out there buying wildly overpriced skyscrapers with distant views to the friggin' Eiffel Tower, still buying hedge funds. And we were still up to our ears in apartments—we probably owned more than two hundred thousand of them worldwide. *Sunny, south-facing two-bedroom gem. Best deal on the market. Must see. Can't last.*

Those last two words made me shudder. I once sat down and calculated that if everything went well in terms of annual returns, Lehman could have paid back all that debt about five weeks before my 276th birthday.

Upstairs, the one deal in all the world that Dick Fuld wanted signed, sealed, and finalized was the $22 billion purchase of Archstone-Smith. Before the leaves in Central Park had turned to gold, Mark Walsh had it wrapped. Lehman's balance sheet went a slightly different color because of the massive overpayment. But Fuld and Gregory were very happy with the price and passed several times on the offer to exit the expensive transaction and pay the breakup fee, which would have possibly allowed Lehman to walk away from death's door. Even worse, several senior salespeople at Lehman I spoke with say they had large well-known clients that wanted to buy the Archstone debt that Lehman owned, but strangely Mark Walsh didn't seem to care about selling.

One man who did care, who cared with a ferocious inner rage, was Alex Kirk, the ranking member of the old crowd who still had the brains and the wherewithal to save us from the lunatic downhill ride we were all being forced to take.

Alex ranted about Lehman becoming a REIT with an investment bank on the side. He swore that in any other comparable organization, if indeed there was one, there would have been three men doing Walsh's job, not one. Someone should have insisted on oversight.

Using every ounce of his considerable power, he began a selling program in which he tried to unload Lehman's portfolio of leveraged loans. He put them on the market, hit bids, paid the penalty clauses, and slowly began to extricate us from both the debt and the consequences of a falling high-yield corporate bond market worldwide, not just in the United States. Alex's thinking was much like that of Mike and Larry.

But it was a tough and lonely battle for Alex to fight. In the end, I heard he took $1.5 billion worth of losses, while at the same time he was driving Joe Gregory mad, not to mention the dark, brooding figure of the increasingly remote Fuld. Again and again, Alex demanded to know if Gregory or his boss understood the risks, whether they understood what the hell was going on, and whether they in any way comprehended that someone, somehow, somewhere, had to find a way to hit the brakes. Months later I was told if Alex had not bothered with the aggressive selling campaign, Lehman, in the end, would have lost another $10 billion, a situation perhaps best illustrated when Coeur Défense was sold a year later for a billion-dollar loss.

By now, Alex, recently promoted to chief operating officer of fixed income, was very badly out of step with the two main powers. He was tougher and cleverer than either of them. And the prospect of his departure was too unsettling to be considered. So for the moment they just tolerated one another. But at least Alex understood precisely what he was doing.

Anyone with even low-voltage antennae could sense there was a huge sea change taking place in the corporation. Confidence was beginning to ebb away. And there were rumors of a new chief financial officer being appointed, our third in as many years—Christine Daley's classic sign of pending trouble in any corporation.

There was a chill in the autumn evening as I emerged late one night from a restaurant on 55th Street and Broadway. I was with my beautiful girlfriend, Anabela, a New York–based architect from Panama, and as we reached the south-running avenue that cuts diagonally across the west side of midtown Manhattan, I remember I paused for a moment and watched the limousines sliding through the traffic.

All around there were beautifully dressed ladies. Smartly dressed men in expensive overcoats were hailing cabs outside crowded restaurants. Doormen were blowing their piercing whistles to summon taxis.

There was the sound of laughter on the night air. Huge checks for costly dinners had been paid with ease. The staff had been extravagantly tipped. A feeling of unchecked prosperity pervaded everything.

And I was suddenly seized with a deep sense of foreboding. A feeling that had been shrouding me for weeks, ever since that CDO meeting, was inexplicably upon me. I thought of Mike and Larry, away from it all now. And I thought of lonely Alex, fighting his valiant rearguard action against the paper gladiators on the thirty-first floor.

I turned to Anabela and said, with chills running down my spine, "Take a long look at all this, honey. Because it's going to end. This time next year New York will not be anything like this."

She looked at me quizzically but said nothing. Which was just as well, because I could not really have answered. Not rationally. I simply knew, that's all.

11

Wall Street Stunned as Kirk Quits

We're heading into rough seas, and you don't have the talent in the right places. You have the wrong commanders, the wrong helmsmen. The wrong lookouts. You're doing every damn thing wrong.

THEY CARRIED OUR CFO, Chris O'Meara, out of the combat trenches with a few gunshot wounds and very muddy boots. After months of internecine warfare facing the light cavalry of Wall Street's analysts and researchers, Dick Fuld, his commanding officer, pulled him back from the front line to a more sheltered position. There are no medals awarded for ducking and diving in the face of the enemy, but Chris deserved one for gallantry under fire.

For hour after hour, this Georgetown-educated veteran chief financial officer had fended off a barrage of questions about the state of the battle at Lehman Brothers. On those wide-ranging conference calls he had faced interrogation about the firm's balance sheet, its exposure to the now-obvious mortgage calamity, its debt, its massive overseas expansion, its losses, its hopes, and its fears.

Regarding the last item, the answer was always that Lehman had none. Chris was not only in charge of the corporate cash but also often in command of corporate morale. Still, enough was enough, and the firm waited with eager anticipation for the commanding officer to announce his replacement, the new CFO who would face the anger of the guns.

Joe Gregory made the announcement. And it was not to a known Wall Street hard-ass that he turned. Instead he wheeled his great friend Erin Callan up to the front line. As shocks go, that one went.

Erin, a former tax attorney with a penchant for bright red leather jackets and a smile that would have melted the heart of a traffic cop, stepped up to one of the most demanding jobs on Wall Street.

Unlike Lehman's, her assets were solid. At forty-one, she was vivacious, intelligent, articulate, and fashionable. Educated at Harvard and New York University Law School, Erin Callan's career at Lehman had in recent years been in the investment banking division with a special focus on hedge funds. She had previously headed Lehman's global financial solutions group and the global finance analytics. She had been responsible for more than one hedge fund going public. And she was very confident in front of the television cameras.

However, Erin had one weakness: zero experience in the office of the comptroller in the corporate treasury department, which is an almost unheard-of omission on the resume of a chief financial officer.

I had nothing but admiration for Erin. Everybody liked her. But at this level, when we're talking about running the finances of a bank like Lehman, I would not have put her in quite that league. And that's the league you need to play in when the markets have crested and there is an iceberg the size of Mount Vesuvius lurking up ahead.

Erin enjoyed the attention more than most of us had anticipated. And she quickly became a business celebrity. Her good looks and fast mind enabled her to capture the television audience. In the opinion of Joe Gregory, we just had to get out there and tell our story, then all would be well. Confidence would improve, and by God, if there was anyone who could broadcast our side of the story, it was surely Erin Callan.

But even she had been slightly amazed at her promotion, which had come out of left field. And the fact that it had obviously been created by Joe Gregory cast a mild shadow over it, because everyone knew about his devotion to underdogs and minority groups. Maybe he thought a woman deserved a break to reach the highest rung on our corporate ladder. I imagine he knew he had just made Erin the most powerful woman on Wall Street, the only one with a genuine shot at taking over the helm of a major firm.

How this all came about was a great mystery, because it was difficult to find the catalyst. Was it a desire to move Chris O'Meara? Or promote and reward Erin Callan? That answer may never be revealed, but it emanated from the thirty-first floor and involved a truly bizarre set of circumstances that centered around Wall Street's queen of risk management, Madelyn Antoncic, holder of a Ph.D. in economics and finance from New York University's Stern School.

Antoncic, a Lehman managing director, had been chief risk officer, the one who determined the overall risk appetite of the firm by setting trading limits. Her experience was awe-inspiring: she'd worked at the Federal Reserve Bank of New York and then at Goldman Sachs, where she ran market risk management. For eight of her twelve years at Goldman she traded mortgage-backed structured products. She then moved to Barclays Bank, where she built a market-risk function, and then became treasurer of Barclays for North America. She was voted 2005 Risk Manager of the Year, an international award, and the following year she was named among the one hundred most influential people in U.S. finance. Her specialization was mortgage securities risk analysis.

She had greatly enjoyed her career at Lehman but found it difficult to accept that she might be asked to leave the room when there were tense issues involving risk being aired in front of the executive committee. After a presentation, the deal team was always asked to leave while the committee discussed the deal. But, defying all logic, Dick and Joe could request that their risk chief go outside with the wheeler-dealers. This was presumably because of her whip-smart, cautious mind, which dealt with the risk rather than with the maximum profits that might accrue, and the latter was basically all Dick and Joe wanted to hear about. They did not wish to know what she really thought. With a brand-new billion-dollar project on the table and an internationally recognized genius of a risk chief sitting right there, I would venture that asking her to leave the room was possibly the most outrageous move I've ever heard of, and certainly the dumbest. *Would the risk manager kindly leave the room?* I mean, that is preposterous.

But Madelyn was a bear by late 2006, advising caution, pullback, and extra study. Dick and Joe were just about as keen to listen to her as they had been to listen to Mike Gelband. So they just threw her out, on the grounds it saved a lot of trouble. I know that she believed that once Mike left, all semblance of sanity was lost, because it was obvious to anyone they would only discuss what they thought the firm could make. Not the possibility of loss.

I have been told by two close friends who were in attendance at one of those meetings that Dick Fuld, irritated beyond reasonable endurance by Madelyn's warnings, resolutely told her to "shut up." Which was a somewhat eccentric way to treat Wall Street's acknowledged authority on risk.

And so, on a sunlit September afternoon, Dick Fuld and Joe Gregory decided to make Madelyn's absence from those meetings even more permanent and got rid of her altogether, demoting her to a peripheral government relations job inside the organization. There is no record of precisely how much pain this caused Joe Gregory, who had spent half his life promoting women to positions of immense authority as a part of his multimillion-dollar program of inclusion.

Generally speaking, there was a group who by now believed quite sincerely, and without malice aforethought, that Richard S. Fuld and Joseph M. Gregory had essentially gone mad. In Madelyn's place they promoted the hitherto CFO Chris O'Meara, who was basically an accountant and had about as much experience in the supremely specialized business of risk management as Charlie McDonald. That's my uncle Rob's black Labrador. And into the white-hot seat of CFO they promoted Erin Callan, who had about as much experience of heavyweight corporate accounting as the aforementioned C. McDonald.

Now, it usually takes weeks if not months of assessments before appointing a CFO. But at the Tower of Lehman, deep into the reign of King Richard the Not-So-Great, it took about twelve minutes. Madelyn was given one day's notice, and the executive committee was never informed until it was a fait accompli.

Erin could scarcely have made her debut at a more difficult time. The obvious threat to the banking system brought on by less liquidity in the short-term commercial paper market was starting to come to fruition. Some rolling loans had stopped rolling altogether, as some banks, terrified of each other's losses and the risk of potential collapse, started to become leery of lending to each other. And they were not thrilled about lending to anyone else either.

Lehman was up to its eyebrows in debt, as well as bonds that had to be sold on. The deal-making party for so long enjoyed by private equity companies was grinding to a complete halt. And word was everywhere around Wall Street that Bear Stearns and Lehman were in the most trouble.

Lehman had managed to lay hands on sufficient capital to take part in its biggest LBO deals. But the issue with them was always to move fast enough to securitize them and sell the high-yield bonds and leveraged loans that made the LBO deals possible. The problem now, though, mostly due to the bank freeze, was a drastic lack of buyers. The big investment funds were not playing this game anymore, and the system was clogged with sellers. Which left billions of dollars of unsold securities on Lehman's books, as well as those of many other banks.

Bear Stearns was involved in financing a $28 billion leveraged buyout of Hilton Hotels, and another $7.4 billion LBO of Chrysler Corporation. Lehman was involved in three of the top five LBOs in the world: the $31.8 billion buyout of TXU, the $22.2 billion for Archstone-Smith, and the $26.4 billion for First Data Corporation. The securities right now could not be sold, which left a lot of very hard currency hanging out to dry in a firm like ours, which was not really big enough to partake of any of them in the first place, at least not in a major way. Estimates were that the big LBO lenders—the commercial and investment banks—were holding well over $200 billion of leveraged-buyout debt. Office rumors suggested we were on the hook for $15 billion, even after Alex's selling campaign. Not to mention the overpriced commercial real estate all over the friggin' world and our calamitous liabilities in the residential mortgages.

There were many jobs in the world of finance that any number of topflight traders and salesmen would have coveted. Chief financial officer of Lehman Brothers was not among them. Erin Callan had that. And hers was not the only appointment in Lehman that had raised eyebrows. Joe Gregory had brought in equities derivatives specialist Roger Nagioff to replace fixed-income savant Mike Gelband, but that was not a great success since Roger was stationed in our London office. That fell through in early February of 2008. Then Joe drafted the intellectual but inexperienced Andrew Morton from Treasuries, and that was not much of a triumph either. The whole process was reminiscent of the bizarre appointment of our former CFO Dave Goldfarb and making him global head of strategic partnerships and principal investing in 2006. The simple fact is that CFOs on Wall Street do not make that kind of a jump from accounting to risk-taking.

There was a theory that Dick and Joe liked to move people around because it weakened them, at least for the several months that it took them to learn their new business. But it stopped people from becoming dangerous—dangerous the way Mike and Alex were to Dick and Joe, who could not really understand the subject of high-tech modern finance and preferred to deal with people of comparable ability. It was an extraordinary mind-set, not wanting to be assisted and supported by the very best.

Alex was unafraid to speak his mind, and he banged the table during long, fractious conversations with Joe Gregory, and to an extent with Dick Fuld. He told them that key positions in the firm were being held by good people without sufficient experience. He cited Callan, Nagioff, and Morton. At one meeting he told Joe, "We're heading into rough seas, and you don't have the talent in the right places. You have the wrong commanders, the wrong helmsmen. The wrong lookouts. You're doing every damn thing wrong: buying hedge funds at the top of the market, buying back stock to impress the Street, holding on to astronomically priced real estate. You're buying when you should be selling. You're all over the damn place."

Now, there are some corporate presidents who would have given that very serious consideration, coming as it did from a man who had personally made the firm more than $250 million over the dot-com crash. Alex was a wartime general who thrived in times of market turbulence. But Joe Gregory was not such a character. He seethed about Alex, resented him, which was really odd, because any damn fool could see Alex had only the best interests of Lehman at heart.

With so many doubts being cast about her capacity to carry out her high-level duties, Erin might have been slightly fazed. But she was no such thing. Night after night she appeared on camera and stated our position. She was smiling, confident, and sure of her lines. She informed the world that all was well, our debt was manageable, and our worldwide profits were excellent. Lehman was the great globalizer. Lehman looked beyond local U.S. markets. The bank's horizons were wide. Its reach was far and thorough. Lehman was certain that its decoupling policy was correct. Yes, the chairman was buying back stock, but that was his privilege. A sign of bravado? Nonsense. A sign of inner strength.

The stock market, however, rallied in September, and in October reached an all-time peak, with the Dow over 14,000. Which was not good news for my group. All of us had taken massive short positions—

I refer, of course, to Eric Felder, Jeremiah Stafford, Peter Schellbach, Rich Gatward, and me. We seemed to have waited a lifetime for the market to turn down, and another lifetime while the stock market was surging upward.

I have no doubt that the executive suite on the thirty-first floor was knee deep in self-congratulation. And that Fuld and Gregory, were smiling away, certain in their own minds that for this great investment bank, it was right and proper that men like the know-it-all Mike Gelband and the brash, arrogant Larry McCarthy were out of here. Their pessimism was misplaced. They had plainly been wrong about everything, and stand by for a beautiful sleigh-ride, carefree, into the end of the year, where the big-bucks bonuses were awaiting. A new Manet for Dickie boy and another Sikorsky for Joey boy.

But on Thursday, November 1, shortly before lunch, the market finally shuddered. By the closing bell it had fallen 356 points. For a few brief sessions it held; then, on Wednesday, November 7, it tumbled again, another 361 points. On Monday the twelfth, it dipped through the 13,000 barrier, winding up at 12,988. On Monday the twenty-sixth, a further loss of 256 points from its high left the industrial index at 12,724, around 1,300 points below its peak. Bond prices were also crashing. It was the worst month in the history of the Lehman High-Yield Bond Index. (High-yield bonds back in June had been trading at an all-time low of only 231 basis points over Treasuries. They were now blowing out and yielding more than 500 over Treasuries. High-yield bonds were once again high-yield.)

There were two distinct schools of thought about this. Some people believed this was the start of something truly awful, since it had been the worst month in the history of the credit markets. Others, followers of the recent Dow form book, believed that nothing could shake the U.S. market. For them, the sensible idea was to hang right in there and wait for it to go right back up, then on to 15,000.

Confidence on the Lehman bridge was still high. And by the time Lehman held its fourth-quarter conference call, Chris O'Meara had been installed as global head of risk management. He introduced Erin Callan, taking her first quarterly conference call as CFO. This was essentially unnecessary, since Erin had made more television appearances than Lisa Kudrow in *Friends*. And, though lacking a leading Hollywood director, Erin was about as well prepared as any actress had ever been.

As the sharks circled, waiting to nail the Lehman rookie, a squad of assistants and writers formed a huddle around their quarterback. There were prepared scripts for every question, many of them masterminded by the old battle-zone warrior Chris O'Meara himself. And when the whistle sounded, the offensive coach sent her in, straight off the bench.

Our radiant head of finance stepped right up there. "Thank you, Chris. I want to take a step back for a moment and make some comments about full-year results. Despite all the pressures in the latter half of this year, our 2007 net revenues were a record $19.3 billion, representing a 10 percent increase over last year. That was the fifth consecutive year we've posted record revenues," she said. "Net income for 2007 was at an all-time high of $4.2 billion, $7.26 cents a share, up 7 percent on the prior year. This was achieved on a record first half and the successful navigation of the difficult market conditions we saw in the second half. All things considered, we are pleased with this performance. These results were a clear demonstration of the diversification we have achieved, and worked so hard for, over the past several years."

Erin stuck to her prepared scripts. Sometimes Chris stood up and helped, but in general terms it was like all the other conferences. The questions were often hostile but sufficiently convoluted to baffle anyone, even a person of extraordinary learning. And the answers would have brought a frown to the face of Confucius. One by one, the interrogators faltered, then died out of the conversation, making remarks like "Okay," or "I hear you," or "Thank you for addressing that question." Shoulder to shoulder on the ramparts, Chris and Erin had beaten back the enemy.

Meanwhile, by year's end, Alex's group, Schellbach, Felder, Hammack, Stafford, and me, had made an impressive contribution to the 2007 balance sheet by posting a $2 billion profit shorting all the usual suspects: the major mortgage corporations, real estate investment trusts, home builders, and restaurant chains—in other words, everyone who needs a thriving economy and access to credit to function.

My own contribution was a profit of more than $34 million. But Jeremiah, the most profitable trader on the floor, trading the high-yield indexes, had made $230 million. As the corporation lurched toward its inevitable high-spending destiny, we put in one hell of a performance. Everyone understood our contribution. And we waited for our just rewards when the bonus pool was announced.

It was, however, perfectly obvious that the two leaders had nothing but contempt for us. And when they sat down to work out the bonuses, they screwed us all. The traders' standard agreement on Wall Street had been a $20 million profit to earn a $1 million bonus. That went straight out of the window. My bonus, after my second straight $30 million year, was way down, nowhere near my expectations. It was the same all through the department. Dick and Joe just cut us all back—Beggans, Gramins, Schellbach, Stafford, Castle. And now we had no one to fight for us.

At first we wondered whether the guys on the thirty-first floor had finally accepted the true position of this outrageously leveraged corporation. But we quickly learned differently. Dick and Joe at the end of 2007 paid themselves stock bonuses valued at $35 million for Fuld and $29 million for Gregory, right up there with the largest bonus either of them ever received. And since they both knew that everyone would soon get to hear of this then you have to ask yourself what was going through their minds. This last, monumental feed at the trough of Lehman simply beggars belief.

I think when we found that out, we finally understood the character of these two men. And that discovery confirmed our worst dreads. They had set our course, flank speed, directly at the iceberg—vowing to spend our way out of trouble with money we didn't actually have. They had no intention of swerving either to port or starboard. They had essentially fired our best helmsman, and the most skillful navigator aboard, Kirk, was rapidly being sidelined. The bonus debacle put the lid on everything. In our opinion, Dick and Joe had decided to make themselves so rich that it wouldn't matter to them whether the ship survived or not.

Joe Beggans is a very cool customer, and I had rarely seen him so utterly exasperated as when the news broke that Fuld and Gregory paid themselves record bonuses for the year. "What the hell are they doing?" demanded Joe. There was, in his view, but one word to describe it: *unconscionable*. The *Oxford American Dictionary* is plainly in a blue funk about the word unconscionable and all its intonations. It offers a diatribe of definitions and similes—*unethical, amoral, immoral, unprincipled, indefensible, unforgivable, wrong, unscrupulous, underhanded, dishonorable, excessive, unreasonable, unwarranted, uncalled for, unfair, inordinate, immoderate, undue, inexcusable, unnecessary.*

Dick and Joe lived like a couple of potentates, and for them the occasional $40 million was very necessary. Fuld lived in an enormous Greenwich mansion, over 9,000 square feet, valued at $10 million. He had four other homes, including a mansion on Jupiter Island, one of Florida's garrisons of the big muckety-mucks in Hobe Sound, thirty miles north of Palm Beach. Dick picked it up five years previously for $13.75 million.

He also owned a vast $21 million Park Avenue apartment with three wood-burning fireplaces, and a spectacular ski chalet near Sun Valley, Idaho. His art collection was valued at $200 million, including a collection of postwar and contemporary drawings worth tens of millions, one of them by Jackson Pollock.

And so, with his stock and cash bonuses crammed in his rucksack, Richard S. Fuld took his Christmas break, smiling with his fellow potentate Joseph M. Gregory, who also headed home with a bank balance bulging with cash from his brutally indebted corporation.

As far as Dick was concerned, it was probably all more than fair. I mean, hell, that Peterson and Schwarzman had been paid a billion each, right? How could it possibly have been unreasonable for him and Joe to have helped themselves to a couple of modest little bonuses of $29 and $35 million? Compared to those Blackstone guys, they both felt like paupers.

The rest of us, devalued, demoralized, and generally pissed off at the bonus-cutting treatment they had leveled at us—we who had tried so hard—also made our separate ways home. We were apprehensive about what 2008 might have in store for us. In a sense, we were all slightly afraid to face the great unknown.

The stock market, utterly contrary to the end, and still in flagrant denial of the obvious, rallied over the Christmas period, the Dow climbing back to 13,550. But in the New Year reality came slamming home again, all the way from Wall Street to midtown Seventh Avenue. By January 8 the Dow had skidded around 1,000 points to 12,589. There was a brief rally, and then on Thursday, January 22, the Dow fell 458 points at one stage to a new low, but rallied to close at 11,971.

In the middle of this unpleasant trend, Ashish Shah, Lehman's own nuclear scientist of credit derivative research and analysis, had set his sights on another massive corporation he was quite certain would crash into oblivion before any of us were much older. And again it was a gigantic operation, sited in a seemingly impregnable sixty-six-story Wall Street edifice that dominated a large part of the financial district's landscape. I refer to American International Group (AIG), one of the world's major insurance corporations, the eighteenth-largest public company in the world, with offices in the City of London and in Lehman's very own Coeur Défense outside Paris. As big hitters go, AIG was out there swinging the bat as a component of the Dow Jones Industrial Average and the largest underwriter of commercial and industrial insurance in the United States. It was also up to its ears in insuring CDOs, one of its favorite heavy earners in the past three years.

Once more Ashish had spotted a corporation that was happy to race in front of an express train in order to grab a $50 bill. AIG had been collecting large premiums, accepting bets from nervous investors against the failure of these mortgage-backed bonds. In return they had agreed to pay out billions of dollars if the bonds dipped below, say, 60 or 70 cents on the dollar. AIG had, of course, written the insurance at par, on the basis that the securitization was rock solid, issued by banks like us, Merrill Lynch, Bear Stearns, and Citigroup and rated AAA by the agencies, same as Uncle Sam. No risk.

Ashish and Pete Hammack considered that AIG was getting into very deep water. Both of them knew those CDOs were currently becoming very dangerous, losing their par value. It was not quite time for those bets to be paid out, but the value of the bonds was sliding ever downward. Lehman had already taken a $100 million bath, and Ashish and Pete concluded, "We ain't seen nothin' yet."

AIG had really ridden the mortgage wave. After years of steadily writing highly profitable life insurance and insurance for floods, hurricanes, tornadoes, and sundry other acts of God, they had suddenly hit pay dirt. From 2002 to 2007 their revenues had almost doubled, exploding from $59 billion to $115 billion. That wasn't flood or tornadoes. That was the rampaging mortgage-backed CDOs, everybody's glorious profits.

And in the insurance world, it was not just AIG that might have hit the wall. It was also AMBAC Financial Group, one of the major bond insurers in the country. Their revenues had also more than doubled, from $725 million to $1.8 billion. Another huge bond insurance group, New York–based MBIA, was also headed for uncharted waters as the mortgage world spluttered and stalled.

The looming problem for all of them was they had been eager to accommodate Wall Street when investors began laying off colossal bets on the CDOs. There had as yet been no payouts, but Ashish was blowing a very loud whistle. In his opinion AIG was massively exposed, for billions and billions of dollars. They were the patsy at the poker table. Everyone had laid off their bets, but the board of AIG was not taking a hard look at their own position.

Remember one of Larry McCarthy's great slogans: *Always take a long look around any poker table for the sucker. If you can't find him, it's probably you.* AIG was, in the opinion of Ashish, that sucker, and they could go down for billions. Ashish was not just firing a soft warning. He and Pete Hammack were recommending we take one of our biggest short positions ever against AIG, MBIA, AMBAC, *and* Merrill Lynch. The latter, he believed, was in well over their skis, thanks to the lunatic calls allowed by their recently departed CEO Stan O'Neal. So far as Ashish and Pete could tell, Merrill was in for $100 billion, possibly as high as $140 billion, in long positions on CDOs, the worst on Wall Street. Whatever we considered to be a large short, Ashish said he would recommend multiplying it by three times.

At the last count in very early 2006, there was $26 trillion worth of CDS bets outstanding in the market. Now, in the beginning of 2008, it was $70 trillion, and throughout the world there were only seventeen banks carrying that risk. And, remember, there was another $15 to $18 trillion out there in credit derivatives, CDOs, RMBSs, CMBSs, CLOs, and ABSs, and the same seventeen banks had issued them between 2000 and 2007, including Credit Suisse, Goldman Sachs, JPMorganChase, Barclays, Bank of America, Citigroup, Royal Bank of Scotland, UBS, HSBC, and Lehman.

The numbers were just too big for anyone to make sense of. And somehow the $70 trillion was the less important number, because many of those were just bets between counterparties and investors. Some of them would win, some would lose. That other $15 trillion was real, and if that ever crashed, the consequences to the world banking system would be horrific, because there weren't sufficient reserves to pay out. Nevertheless, if the CDSs had been called insurance, the banks would have needed $5 trillion to $10 trillion in capital loss reserves. As it was, they needed nothing. And had nothing.

On the Lehman trading floor one of the few people expressing real concern over our corporate position was still Alex Kirk, who had for the past two months been telling Gregory that we simply did not have the balance sheet to hold on to our biggest deals. More than once he went into Joe's office and raged, "How many times do I have to tell you? We're forty-four times leveraged, and we cannot go on like this. We have to cut back in a big way, and all you do is keep saying we need to hit the gas pedal."

Joe's typical reply was that Alex was too conservative, that we needed to catch Morgan Stanley and Goldman Sachs, to play at the high-stakes table. "Growth, growth, growth, Alex. That's what we want and need, and we have to stay focused."

Vainly, Alex tried to reason with him, to explain that the securitization system had broken and was not coming back anytime soon. The repeal of Glass-Steagall had heralded a devastating new era, where the huge deposits in the commercial banks had enabled them to get into our game simply by buying and owning an investment bank. And now it was all coming home to roost. Our borrowing was stratospheric, just because Dick and Joe wanted to play in a game we could not afford.

"Where's the number?" roared Alex at yet another stormy meeting in Joe's office. "Where's the goddamned number? We tried twenty times leverage and that didn't work. So we tried thirty times leverage, and that didn't work either. Now we've tried forty times and that won't work. Well, what is the number? What will make you happy? One hundred times leverage? One thousand times? Where does it end?"

Alex was also furious over the farce being enacted about Lehman's supposed diversifications, because they were all in the same area. Lehman wasn't diversified at all. And as always, he railed against having the wrong people in the wrong jobs. Joe may have understood that Alex was correct, though I seriously doubt this. But Joe was more aligned with Dick than he was with anyone else. The two men had sat within a hundred feet of each other for thirty years. He may also have suspected that Alex believed Joe himself was in the wrong job. In the end he invited Alex up to his office on the thirty-first floor. And there, for the last time, he told Alex that the only aim of Lehman's senior management was growth, risk, and major deals. There was to be no pulling back, no more trying to trade out of our big positions in real estate. The only way was forward, and Alex needed to understand that.

Alex replied, "Joe, I'm not going to sit here and watch this happening."

"Then, Alex," replied Joe, "there's no place here for you. You can stay if you like. But it will have to be different."

Alex Kirk had run his course as one of the great Lehman financiers. He quit immediately, and while the resignation was no great surprise to his very closest friends, of which I was one, it had a shattering effect on the remainder of the trading floor. People were absolutely floored by it, and some of them walked around expressing disbelief that it had happened.

For most people it was the pure shock of the announcement; for others it was just the size of the gap he would leave. At the end of the afternoon, he and I said a private good-bye. We both spoke on the phone to Larry, and then he was gone. The team of Wall Street masters that I had joined almost four years previously had been well and truly decimated: Christine, Mike, Larry, and now Alex. To make matters even worse for me, my man Rich Gatward had also gone a few weeks earlier, transferred to Liberty View Capital Management, another of the many hedge funds Lehman owned.

For me at least, the place had the air of the Valley of Death, but I never stopped trying. I still gave it my all, still arrived earlier than almost everyone, still put in sixty-, seventy-, and eighty-hour weeks, but now I'd lost all my closest allies in deploying capital. I was suddenly all alone—and only a damn fool could have felt secure, or even wanted, in an environment where the two top executives in the firm had demonstrated not one shred of trust in the people I fervently believed were among the best there had ever been.

I looked around at the remnants of that supreme team, at Peter Schellbach, Joe Beggans, John Gramins, Jane Castle, and the rest. How long did any of us have in this poisonous atmosphere, where the big brains lived in fear of the small ones, high above us?

Right now there was no sign of turmoil, but there was a feeling of real unease. Not just at Lehman, where the departure of Alex had shaken every trading desk on the Street, but right through the financial industry. You could sense it: early 2007's feeling of robust confidence had just drained away. Rumors were everywhere, and they concerned especially Bear Stearns and us: losses and layoffs, mortgages and mayhem. It was darned unnerving, I'll say that. As we moved into March 2008, our two mortgage brokers, BNC and Aurora, were finally firing bodybuilders left, right, and center. The CDO market, now in its death throes, had screeched to a complete halt, leaving a swath of destruction right across the United States—especially in the ultrasecret warehouses of Lehman and Merrill, which both housed a mountain of this unsellable, multibillion-dollar junk.

I guess, secretly, I thought I was safe. With two $30 million years in succession, I was the most profitable trader on the convertible desk in 2006 and 2007. And I was number two behind Schell on the distressed desk in 2007. Yet the noose was tightening, because I was a member of the unwanted tribe, the group of cynics who believed that they alone were the people to save Lehman.

By Monday morning, March 10, it was clear something was going on. Little things that might not have been important at any other time suddenly assumed greater significance: people going missing for an hour, others not where they were supposed to be. The talk was that there would be some mass layoffs and that the balance sheet was heading south. I suddenly began to feel that if there were layoffs, I might be next, because of my close association with a different era and with people no longer at the firm. I had a bad feeling. I made it to my desk at the usual time, 6:00 A.M. But as the markets opened, I noticed Peter Schellbach was not there, and that was very odd. Three hours later, Joe Beggans picked up a house call and told me to go up to the twenty-fourth floor right away. I guess I knew right then it was over.

I walked to the elevator and reached the correct floor. But when I emerged there was a very depressing sight: there were signs all over the opposite wall giving directions. Plainly a lot of people were expected. I followed the instructions for the fixed-income division. When I reached the right door, I tapped and entered. Inside were Pete Ramsey, Rich Gatward's successor, and Pete Schellbach, and they both looked embarrassed. Schell told me that this had nothing to do with my performance or any other part of my work; they were just following orders. A lot of people were leaving over the next two weeks, and I was to be one of them. He told me that in his view, no one had worked harder than I had, and that a good severance package had been prepared, with shares of Lehman stock and full pay through September. It didn't make it any easier. I cannot describe how upset I was.

I went back down to my desk and told Terence and Joe I'd just caught a bullet. Then I went down to say good-bye to Jane, who was bewildered at the way things were going. "On one hand we're buying enormous buildings," she said, "increasing risk and leverage, and buying back stock. Next minute we're cutting back, reducing risk, and firing people." She told me she'd miss me, and that as far as she was concerned, I had the best market instincts she'd ever seen. Even that didn't make it easier, and I was struggling with tears as I went back downstairs to pack my boxes.

I hung around for a while, finding things to do, but the truth was I just didn't want to go. Then Schell came back and offered to help me carry my stuff down to the street. As we walked across the trading floor, I could see the kids watching me, and I could see the looks on their faces, all of them scared that it might be them next. It was the worst short journey I ever made, walking through there with my boxes.

Out on the sidewalk Schell shook my hand. Neither of us said anything, because anything that might have been said somehow could not be said. I climbed into a cab and we pulled out into the traffic. But, by God, I felt awful. I glanced back at the building and was seized by sadness. Lehman Brothers, where I had reached the holy grail, where I had fought it out on the trading floor with the best in the business. I was just so proud of it. I was proud of the people I had known. And I was proud of our many triumphs. I had loved every minute of my time there. I was proud of my achievements, and when I thought of them, somehow this bad day didn't matter. I'd been there. I'd made it to the top, and I had a pile of Lehman shares to prove it. I had no money worries, and I had a lot of friends.

Yet it was gone, and all my hopes and dreams with it. Gone forever, and there were tears streaming down my face as we pulled up outside my apartment building. Me and my two melancholy boxes.

Irrationally, I thought of three other Lehman faithful who had in the past been fired. There was Christopher Pettit, president and CEO, a charismatic, decorated West Pointer who had served in Vietnam, booted in 1996 in a poisonous web of intrigue in which he played no part. There was John Cecil, chief administrative officer and CFO, a brilliant financial thinker, edged out in 2000 by Joe Gregory for being too clever. And in May 2004, the likable Bradley Jack, president and co–chief operations officer, who stood too close in friendship to Dick, was exiled by Joe Gregory. Those were the landmarks that marked the stranglehold the strange axis of Fuld and Gregory held over the entire corporation. But, curiously, I still loved the memory of Lehman.

I'll never be able to explain how I felt about the firm. But perhaps someday someone will ask me how long I would have stayed if I could have remained a Lehman Brothers trader. And I can answer that: about a thousand years.

Meanwhile, as I slipped into temporary obscurity, Wall Street, with all its shocking underlying problems, was seething. And the place that was really roiling was a few blocks down the street, over on Madison Avenue, deep inside the world headquarters of Bear Stearns. Another glittering Manhattan fortress, impregnable in its day, was resting on foundations made of sloppy California Delta mud.

Bear Stearns was tottering. With crippling debt stifling its balance sheet and CDOs and other derivatives detonating from basement to rooftop, the venerable eighty-five-year-old investment bank, which had survived 1929, was gasping for air. The trouble with Wall Street air, as opposed to regular air, is that it consists of very large bundles of greenbacks, billions of them, and they are hard to acquire in stressful times. The overnight repo and commercial paper markets were, for the first time ever, just not available to Bear Stearns. These markets provide a nightly vote of confidence from investors globally on a financial firm's survivability.

In the week of my demise, there was effectively a run on Bear Stearns. Traders and investors who had never really forgiven the bank for the resounding collapse of those two hedge funds the previous summer were now refusing to deal, and Bear's lenders were literally closing it down, refusing credit. The stock, which had stood at $170 a share at the beginning of 2007, had become mired in the low $20s. The firm had huge trading obligations, chilling subprime exposure, and more than fifteen thousand employees worldwide. Identically to Lehman, Bear Stearns held mortgage bonds that could no longer be sold; they were trapped in the theater with the fire raging, trapped by their own greed, by their terrible borrowing, and finally by their inability to repay their loans.

Bear Stearns once had been among the most admired securities firms in the country. In 1929 they were the only Wall Street bank to lay off no one as the world collapsed all around them. That towering reputation for prudence followed them down the years and enabled them to open branches in just about every major American city and all over the world: Milan, London, Hong Kong, Tokyo, Mumbai, Dublin, Beijing, Singapore, and São Paulo.

But in that bleak week beginning March 10, Wall Street stood pop-eyed at a sight almost without precedent. There stood the gleaming limo, steam blowing out from under the hood, four flat tires, with the occasional deafening explosion from the exhaust pipe. It was pulled over onto the shoulder, and everyone was just hurtling past, staring straight ahead, all of them afraid to look.

Wall Street was terrified, because this was real. By Thursday, both the Treasury and the Fed had been called in. Immediately Henry Paulson and Ben Bernanke had funds transferred from the Treasury into JPMorganChase, which was instructed to finance Bear Stearns for twenty-four to thirty-six hours. Innovative windows providing liquidity such as the PDCF, primary dealer credit facility, had not yet been set. Uncle Sam had to use JPMorganChase to infuse emergency cash into Bear to get them into the weekend. Up until this point the government had never injected money into an investment bank. On Friday there was a near-desperate search going on to find someone to buy Bear before news of the looming bankruptcy at one of the most revered names in world finance caused outright global panic. The deadline would come around midnight on Sunday, when the Asian markets opened. And Sunday was pandemonium. With lines open twenty-four hours to Washington, meeting after meeting took place inside the Bear Stearns tower, trying to find someone to buy the bank at almost any price. The purchaser would need to assume support for around $30 billion of Bear's "less liquid assets"—that's the mortgage securities no one in their right mind would buy.

Right from the get-go, the hard-eyed CEO of JPMorganChase, Jamie Dimon, was out in front of the pack. He had 150 employees in there examining the firm's books and trading accounts. He looked interested, but no one could guarantee anything, and despite the somewhat comforting presence of the supportive Federal Reserve, Bear Stearns partners were preparing to file for bankruptcy first thing Monday morning. That's how serious it was. That's how desperate they were.

By late Sunday night, JPMorganChase had agreed to buy Bear Stearns for $2 a share, around one-tenth of the price at which the stock had closed on Friday. Both JPMorganChase and the Fed would guarantee the enormous trading obligations that had shoved Bear to the brink of total collapse. And the Federal Reserve agreed to finance the deal. After outcries from both investors and Bear employees, the price paid by JPMorgan was increased to $10 per share.

The fact was, despite the brilliant negotiating skill of Jamie Dimon and his foresight in comprehending the advantages of such a merger, Bear Stearns had been saved by the government of the United States. Jamie never would have done it without them. No one would have done it without them.

The news hit the wires late on Sunday night, and the world stood still. It was like a snowstorm in August: Bear Stearns snapped up for a bargain-basement price as it stood on the verge of extinction. My apartment was suddenly like my old desk, with the phones ringing, all the old familiar voices, Larry, Mike, Christine, Joe, and the rest.

The news hit the Far East Monday morning, March 17, right at the start of the trading day. In Tokyo, the Nikkei dropped 4 percent. But Wall Street opened to calm waters. The intervention and support of the Fed had not just saved Bear, it had saved everyone else. The Dow Jones Industrial Index held the line. A St. Patrick's Day massacre had been averted.

I could not work out whether I was still involved or not. But I had a considerable amount of Lehman stock that I could not sell for several years—half my bonus money for the past sixteen quarters. So it was deeply in my own interest for Lehman to prosper. Despite all of my forebodings, I wished them well in the serious task of protecting my Lehman shares. Beyond that I was in a bit of a void, not quite ready to make a move for a new job, nor just to sit here and feel sorry for myself.

As had occurred once or twice in the past, the sudden telephonic arrival of Larry McCarthy put things into perspective.

"Hey, buddy, what's up?" he said.

"Oh, hi, Larry."

"What are you doing?"

"Nothing."

"What do you mean, nothing?"

"Well, thinking."

"Bullshit. You gotta get your ass in gear."

"Who, me?"

"Sure. You and I got some serious trading to do. Come on. You just got fired, you got money all over the place."

"Well . . . I was just—"

"Jesus, Larry. Let's get steamed in. Bear nearly went, and we oughta start shorting these banks all the way down to zero. If we'd had a lick of sense last week, we would have done Bear Stearns."

"But we—"

"But bullshit. We don't need Lehman. We just get stuck right in there as if nothing had happened. Let's trade, buddy, trade. Short those stupid banks."

That Larry. He had a way about him. And although we would operate on a smaller scale than when we were risking Lehman's capital, we could still operate. I couldn't make $30 million, but I bet I could make $3 million. In fact, McCarthy and I would still be a pretty decent team. Lehman might have taken our platform, but they could never take our knowledge and our judgment.

And, speaking of knowledge and judgment, there was another billion-dollar event that very same week that shed a glaring light on some of our old adversaries during those turbulent early-warning days of the subprime. Dave Sherr, the forty-four-year-old Lehman mortgage chief who was so dismissive of the opinions of Larry McCarthy and Mike Gelband, suddenly left to start up his own hedge fund.

Now, Dave is not that bad a guy—misguided, but a decent enough character who was merely defending his own territory. To the death, that is. To the rip-roaring, spitting anthem of the guns, to the corporation-wide memorial service for the securitization process and CDOs. And I should mention he was being constantly leaned upon by Joe Gregory and his fellow bullies on the thirty-first floor. Dave may or may not have believed, but he sure as hell understood he needed to do as he was told.

And now, presumably with the blessing of the Lehman board, he had decided to go it alone. On March 20, 2008, Dave Sherr announced the launch of his hedge fund, named One William Street Capital Management. It was titled after the address of the fabled old Lehman Brothers headquarters, where Bobbie had sipped the finest red Bordeaux surrounded by his beloved Old Masters. Dave was starting with his back to the wall as well as a massive investment from Lehman, rumored to be in the region of half a billion dollars. A strange

Lehman investment in yet another hedge fund, given Bear Stearns being on death's door. Dave still believed that the mortgage market would rise again. He believed it was all at rock bottom, that the mortgage securitization market would make a storming comeback and CDOs would recover. All those times he had defended his little redoubt under withering attack, he had really thought it would all happen again and that he would once more make a fortune for his employers.

While Larry and I thought he might be wrong, and neither of us would have traded places with him, we both sincerely wished him well in his new venture; after all, we were indirectly investors in his fund through our Lehman shares. Dave had elaborate new offices on the thirty-ninth floor in the Time-Life Building on Sixth Avenue, opposite Rockefeller Center.

Like Julius Caesar, Lehman misjudged the Ides of March. On Sunday night, David Einhorn, the president of the hedge fund Greenlight Capital, was preparing a presentation that he would make to investors on Tuesday, April 8, 2008, at the Grant's Spring Investment Conference. And what a little ripper that was.

He started off with the minor criticism about the "cult following" historically enjoyed by Lehman management. He accused them of arrogance and took a dim view of their standards of disclosure, transparency, and cooperation with the investment community. He reminded anyone who was listening that mortgage originations and securitization had represented between 30 and 50 percent of Lehman's profits these last few years.

These observations were not being made by an average economist. Einhorn had a brain the size of the Coeur Défense. At Cornell University he graduated summa cum laude with distinction in all subjects.

He described Lehman's position as "dangerously exposed." But he regarded their global commercial real estate portfolio as a far bigger problem, and he pointed out that Lehman had more than 20 percent of its real cash tied up in the debt and equity of one single transaction, Archstone-Smith, with their 360 luxury apartment buildings and top-of-the-market price of $22.2 billion.

Anyone who had seen the presentation or read his monthly letter to investors so far understood that David Einhorn had not merely blown a whistle on the sleight-of-hand accounting Lehman was apt to pull. He'd borrowed a ship's Kklaxon, gone to the top of the five-hundred-foot-high Grand Central Tower above his East 45th Street office, and sounded the retreat for all to hear.

David's letters were eagerly awaited documents. He sometimes broadcast them, occasionally chatted about them to CNBC reporters, and quite often gave lectures based upon their content. The presentation he penned on that March evening might as well have been a hand grenade as far as Lehman was concerned. David Einhorn pulled no punches.

He said he had been shocked to see that in January Lehman had increased its dividend and spent $750 million to repurchase 19 percent of the outstanding public shares. He noted that in the quarter ending February 2008, Lehman managed to increase balance sheet assets (stocks, bonds, LBO corporate debt, CMBS, RMBS, et cetera) by another $90 billion.

"I estimate Lehman's ratio of assets to real tangible common equity to have reached 44 times," he wrote. That plainly calculated to a $748 billion asset risk over the real capital of $17 billion.

He complained that Lehman did not disclose the valuation it used on the Archstone investment. David stressed that commercial real estate prices had fallen 15 to 25 percent since the deal was announced. He found it "strange" that Lehman's realized and unrealized asset gains for the year were actually up by $400 million. Whoever else believed Callan's numbers, David Einhorn, one of the world's finest stud poker players, was not among them. Erin had not, after all, reported any kind of a loss yet.

In Einhorn's opinion, Lehman was "hiding" multibillion-dollar losses. And he stated that Lehman responded only "grudgingly" when asked for improved asset valuation transparency. And if they ever did provide that transparency, he wrote, "I suspect it would *not* inspire market confidence."

David's presentations should be read by every would-be Wall Street trader, analyst or investment banker. "The problem with 44 times leverage is that, if your assets fall in value by only 1 percent, that's half your real tangible equity. Remember Lehman only had $15 billion. Multiply that by 44 and you have $660 billion. Drop that by

1 percent and that's $6.6 billion. Right then that 44 times leverage becomes 80 percent. And all confidence is lost."

David already knew about Lehman's projected raising of $4 billion in capital in the next few weeks. In his opinion, investors were about to be duped, and the SEC, to avoid a crisis, was "turning a blind eye at Lehman's accounting." David's question on this issue was simple: "How can you raise capital without disclosing losses?"

He had noticed Lehman's reporting of losses was "consistently smaller than one might expect." There was always a modest profit that slightly exceeded the analysts' estimations. Not reporting any loss "smelled," in David's opinion.

This was a sensational enemy for Dick and Joe to have antagonized—an enemy who, in the not too distant future, would go on national television with CNBC's Maria Bartiromo and, quoting this very letter, spill the beans about Lehman's true situation. And remember, Lehman, like any major force decimated of its best commanders, was in a thirty-first-floor turmoil, with lesser men grabbing at the helm and a commanding officer who barely understood the complexities of derivatives.

Right now, the firm was down to the wire in its unspoken desperation to get some class men onto the bridge. There were just a few left, and their backs were to the wall, trying to cope with the beleaguered chairman and president.

There was Tom Humphrey, a man with twenty years' experience at the firm, now the global head of fixed-income sales, with hundreds of people reporting to him. Perhaps even more important, there was Bart McDade, the rising power on the executive committee, which had for so long been the private domain of Dick and Joe, easily malleable, without any backbone of its own.

There was a sea change going on at Lehman, and the rise of Bart McDade was at the heart of it. People liked him, and there were many who felt he should be swept to power in some kind of a palace coup. Perhaps his closest and most important confidante right now, in the absence of Mike and Alex, was Tom Humphrey, a genial, gregarious, hugely popular man whose sunny demeanor hid a street-smart brilliance and a calculating turn of mind. Dick Fuld and Joe Gregory knew that Tom Humphrey was a loyal, decent, and very smart man. What they never suspected was that Tom Humphrey was a card-carrying revolutionary who thought the pair of them might be out of their depth and no longer qualified to command the country's fourth-largest investment bank. Tom's close-knit group of friends were Mike Gelband, Alex Kirk, Bart McDade, and Larry McCarthy. He was one of us, and had been right at the heart of the mutineers' group that had for so long tried to curb the excesses of the Lehman leadership. Tom was less obvious than someone like Larry, but the flame of righteousness burned deep within him, and he was moving closer to the fulcrum of power with every passing week, his sword drawn.

Lehman's problems were mounting. But the biggest one was named Einhorn. Late in May he had given another speech of such paralyzing clarity that Lehman's stock went down 12 percent. David had decided he was not being told the truth. He did not believe Erin Callan's numbers and he wanted answers. But it was his obvious skepticism that did it. For the first time, publicly, the morals of the historic investment bank were being questioned. And everyone was talking about it.

On May 27 David was invited to an interview with Maria Bartiromo on CNBC during which he reiterated that Lehman had not provided specific disclosure and that it was up to them to provide much greater transparency.

"For the last six months," he said, "Wall Street has been playing a game of Who Has CDOs? And I think it's very peculiar that the first time a $6.5 billion pool of CDOs was disclosed by Lehman, it was very quietly on page fifty-six of their 10Q form filed months after this crisis had started." He told Maria he had grilled Callan and that "sometimes she refused to comment one way or another. But I do have a good responsibility to get my facts straight before I speak."

He added archly, "There is not enough disclosure here to know how bad the problems are. The numbers they reported didn't really reflect the full magnitude of the credit crisis. I think the risk-reward in the stock is poor from a long perspective. So we are short."

He wondered what incentive there was for companies to tell the truth. And he concluded with this damning statement: "And they seem to be upset that I've raised valid questions to which they do not have answers."

His previous week's comments had been bad, but this was a nightmare. There were many departmental heads who were now concerned. All of them had visions of their own stock diminishing by the week. David Einhorn, not only a hedge fund boss but also an author of considerable repute, plainly could not be stopped or silenced. Something had to be done.

By now, Bart McDade was being openly discussed as the near-certain successor to Joe Gregory as president. Constantly flanked by his great supporter, Tom Humphrey, the two of them were seen in conference often. And to no one's surprise, it was Tom who suddenly made the key move.

He invited twelve of his senior colleagues to a secret dinner at a private members' dining club on the Upper East Side on June 5. They were all from floors two through five, the floors that now formed the engine room of Lehman Brothers, so great was the financial world's mistrust of the thirty-first. The food was lavish, the claret would have met with the approval of Bobbie Lehman himself, and the bill was $7,000. There was one notable absentee among the assembled Lehman executives, though: Bart McDade, who, politically, could not make it.

Gerald Donini, who was the favorite to replace Bart as head of equities, was there, as were Eric Felder, global head of credit products; Skip McGee, head of investment banking; Jeff Weiss, a major investment banker with a place on the executive committee; and Richard McKinney, who had replaced Dave Sherr as head of global securitized products. Their stated objective was to figure out ways to help, to turn the ship around, to quell the headlong rush for growth as advocated by Joe Gregory, and, if possible, to allay the fears of David Einhorn. For that gimlet-eyed analyst had caused the Lehman management's credibility to plunge into free fall, with the concomitant danger that the firm would become a Wall Street pariah. The mood was, they told me, polite but fearful.

But the Bordeaux played its soothing role in freeing up inhibitions, and it swiftly became apparent that this select gathering had all the necessary qualities to provoke the most thoughtful and genteel of corporate riots. And as academic discussions became intermingled with profoundly held opinions, which were in stark contrast to those on the thirty-first floor, the mood changed. By the time Tom Humphrey began to pass around a decanter of rich vintage port, it had become blatantly obvious that drastic action was called for.

Either Dick Fuld or Joe Gregory had to go. Together they formed a duo that could no longer be trusted, principally because it seemed neither of them could stand to be among truly clever people. Dick retreated from them, while Joe, under threat or dissent, tended to evaporate his enemies. Generally speaking, that had proved over the years to be a lot of evaporation.

Fuld, blissfully unaware of the wrath to come, might have done better to have remembered his Shakespeare: *Uneasy lies the head that wears a crown*. Because at that dinner, in his absence, the divine right of kings was challenged and his iron grasp on power was irrevocably loosened. The men who should have formed his palace guard were, at long last, moving against him.

They did not intend to remove both him and Gregory, because of the crisis mode such action would provoke. But one of them was most certainly going, and so was Dick's longtime henchman David Goldfarb, the global head of principal investing, who had been right at the forefront of the massive property and hedge fund deals the firm had done in Europe and beyond. A former CFO, "Decouple Dave" was heavily under the influence of Fuld and Gregory, with all of their wild expansion plans. He had been shoulder to shoulder with Mark Walsh right at the sharp end when they bought billions of dollars' worth of assets in London, Paris, Australia, Asia, and even India. Hell, I reckoned he would have sanctioned the purchase of the Taj Mahal as a commercial property if it had come on the market.

And now they were going to clip his wings. The men with the wide horizons and limited understanding had only days to go before each was issued a short but compulsory leash. Dick Fuld and all of his cronies were facing the final roundup.

Four days later Lehman published its second-quarter earnings, and in response to the laser-powered searchlight of David Einhorn's probing, they admitted a $2.8 billion loss. In just a few months they had given back just about all of the 2007 gains, the first negative quarter in fourteen years. Down went the stock another 20 percent, making it 65 percent lower for the year.

There was now an urgency about sweeping the forty-eight-year-old Bart McDade to power. The tall, bespectacled head of equities was currently the most respected guy in the firm. He and Mike Gelband had been roommates at the Ross Business School at the University of Michigan. They had similar intellects, and both had stupendous track records. The way Bart had transformed the equities division from a ho-hum department into a Lehman Brothers powerhouse remains a legend.

As affable as Bart was, he was still full of unexpressed anger over the shameful treatment Mike had received. He believed that together he and Mike could have swerved the Lehman ship away from the iceberg. An immensely wealthy man, Bart lived on a spectacular waterfront cove in Rye, New York, right on Long Island Sound. He was a scratch golfer and board member at the prestigious Wingfoot golf club and had long threatened to retire and play the fifty greatest courses in the world. And right now he was hovering on the fringe of power at Lehman Brothers.

Two days after those earnings were announced, on Wednesday, June 11, he was in his office when Tom Humphrey arrived for an informal but historic chat. "We have enough support for this move, Bart," said Tom. "And I think you should make it."

Bart nodded curtly, shook Tom's hand, and walked straight to the elevator that would take him up to the thirty-first floor. He made the journey alone, and when he emerged from the elevator, he made straight for the great wooden doors that guarded the inner sanctum of Lehman Brothers, the sprawling private office of Dick Fuld, situated right in the northwest corner with views to the Hudson River. It was exquisitely furnished with antique chairs and tables, clocks, bronzes, and paintings, and it took up approximately one-quarter of the entire executive floor.

Bart strode right past the reception area, past the library, and into the office, where Fuld sat behind a huge mahogany desk. The longest-tenured CEO in the history of Wall Street looked up, slightly startled. Bart dispensed with formalities. He said straight out, "This firm has to make a change. The division heads are unhappy with the leadership right here on thirty-one. And the investment community has lost a degree of confidence in our stock."

Fuld, predictably, was furious. He summoned up a pugilistic expression, drawing on his bottomless wells of anger and resentment, that air of suppressed violence that had gained him so many boardroom victories and lost him so many friends.

"What the hell is all this about?" he snapped, barely controlling his temper.

And Bart, in that straightforward way of his, calmly explained that twelve of the most critically important departmental heads of the firm had met six nights before, and reached the only reasonable conclusion there was. If Lehman was to survive, a drastic change was required at the top. The present situation could not be permitted to continue.

"This was done behind my back!" yelled Dick, somewhat unnecessarily. He looked as if he might lose control. But Bart was not thrown off course. And now, for the first time, he was holding all the aces as he faced the Lehman boss.

"We have to do the right thing for the firm and the shareholders," he replied, and he issued the first ultimatum Fuld had heard in thirty years at the helm. Bart told him Joe Gregory was finished. He had to go. "Either that or . . ."

"All right," said Fuld through gritted teeth.

Dick Fuld met the fates with untypical acceptance. He knew that his devoted buddy Joe Gregory would face a corporate firing squad that afternoon. And Dick, a man who loved military similes and referred to Lehman's staff as his "troops," had no alternative but to accept the verdict of the court-martial that had taken place in a private dining club six days previously.

Fuld was squirming in his chair. He looked up at Bart and said, "You'll have to tell Joe. I won't do that." And perhaps for the only time in all those long years, the king of Lehman appeared deflated. The trademark pugnacious expression that had frightened the life out of generations of executives was suddenly gone. And, briefly, the fire died in those dark hard eyes. Dick was a trim, athletic man who stood only five foot eight, but to the few people who knew him, he often appeared to be ten feet tall. To Bart McDade just then, though, he looked about five foot two, slumped and diminished, his reign drawing to a close.

McDade left and walked along to the office of Joe Gregory, tapped on the door, and entered. Joe looked up, and again Bart made no attempt at small talk or pleasantries. He said, "Joe, you've done an admirable job behind diversity and philanthropy. But we're coming into a fierce storm here, and the department heads are not happy with your leadership. I've talked to Dick, and even he agrees we have to make a big change right here."

"What kind of a change?" demanded Joe, his hackles rising, his mouth turning down at the corners, the way it did when he entered defensive mode. "What are you talking about?"

"We think you should go."

"Go? What d'ya mean, go? I'm the president of the corporation. I've got millions of dollars of shares. What do you mean, go?"

"We have a new capital raise," countered Bart. "Four billion dollars, and the market is losing confidence in you and Dick. I mean, we just lost $2.8 billion. And your departure will help restore some faith."

Joe Gregory exploded. "What the fuck is this all about, Bart?" he yelled. "What's going on? Who the hell do you think you are?"

"Joe, believe me, I have the support of the departmental heads."

"Support? What are you talking about, support?" bellowed Joe. "This has to come before the executive committee."

"For the purpose of this discussion, Joe, I am the executive committee. Trust me, it's over."

"Well, when does the fucking committee meet?" roared Joe. "That's what I want to know. And I want answers."

"This afternoon. Three o'clock," replied Bart. "There will be a senior management meeting. It's just to complete the formalities. Don't doubt me. The divisional heads are united on this."

And so the final hours of the Fuld/Gregory duopoly rolled slowly on. At 3:00 P.M. the highest managers at the firm met in the large thirty-first-floor conference room. All the Lehman heads were there: many who had attended the court-martial dinner, plus Bart, Erin Callan, and the two main Lehman rulers, with Dick at the head of the table.

Bart stepped straight into the breach, outlining the gloomier aspects of the firm's position in the market. Skip McGee, head of investment banking, a powerful and popular leader, spoke in support of Bart, again making the irrefutable point that without a major change in the chain of command, Lehman might face an uncertain future.

Suddenly, from out of the clear blue yonder, Joe Gregory stood up and motioned to Erin, who, I am told, looked absolutely shocked. He said quietly, "For the good of the firm, Erin and I should step down," and gestured first to Erin and then toward the door. Some felt at that moment that Joe Gregory's peremptory announcement that Erin would step down with him was a complete shock to her and done without her knowledge. This would, conveniently for Gregory, allow the embarrassing spotlight to be shared, taking some of the glare off his failures. Erin was subsequently offered her previous position as head of hedge fund investment banking.

The remainder of the committee watched in silence as they

stood up and gathered their papers. According to my many close friends in that room, they did not precisely link arms, but together they walked off into a Wall Street sunset with their avowed and true ally, Richard Fuld, glowering at his assembled troops, knowing that he too might face the executioner's axe before he was very much older.

12

Fuld, Defiant to the End

"I've been in my seat a lot longer than you were ever in yours at Goldman," Fuld retorted. "Don't tell me how to run my company. I'll play ball, but at my speed." The Treasury chief glowered, and quite possibly at that moment, Lehman's fate was sealed.

DESPITE HIS OUTWARDLY calm demeanor in the conference room, Joe Gregory did not go quietly. Several observers said that there were "fingernail marks etched on the top of his desk." The fifty-seven-year-old deposed president closed the door behind him and his footsteps were not heard again. No one in the conference room spoke, and the men around the table waited for a few moments in silence. And then, with whatever dignity he could manage, Richard S. Fuld, a member of the Lehman board of directors for twenty-five years, stood up and without a word followed his oldest friend out into the limbo of the thirty-first-floor corridor.

Bart McDade, who was already standing, walked around the table and moved his papers to the place occupied for so long by the reclusive CEO. There was no acknowledgment of the dramatic usurping of power that had just been enacted. But when Bart finally took his place in the big chair, he became president of Lehman Brothers after an almost bloodless coup d'état.

Bart immediately called for a meeting of all key Lehman leaders, the more than 300 managing directors, the true brains and brawn from floors two, three, four, and five. They were the hub of the firm, the driving force that never once in all the recent strife had failed to make a profit. When they arrived, there was no celebratory mood among them, just expressions of the warmest possible wishes for the man they had unanimously selected to lead them: "Well done, Bart." "Everyone's with you." "We'll back you all the way, anything you need." Three of them just said, "Thank God."

Power had been transferred, and Bart's immediate objective was to place key people in their best possible positions. Erin, though, was a problem. Bart didn't immediately realize how embarrassed and distraught she was at that time and that she felt in her heart that it was time to leave Lehman, even though offered her previous position. Within days she left for her home in the Hamptons, where she spent the rest of the summer contemplating her fate. What she did realize was that she had been a mere pawn in the hands of Dick and Joe and had signed on April 8, 2008, the declaration prescribed by the Sarbanes-Oxley Act, the one in which both CEOs and CFOs had to swear they were telling the truth and hiding nothing when the corporate accounts were presented. Whether she even really knew the reality is another matter.

Meanwhile, one by one, Lehman's senior managing directors went back to their desks, leaving the president alone for a while with his thoughts. He believed Lehman's debt problems were massive, and he needed men who understood that with the same clarity he did. There were a lot of very good people at Lehman, but the two he wanted most were the two who had been too clever for Fuld and Gregory, two men whose brilliance had made them unacceptable—Mike Gelband and Alex Kirk. There were several others, of course, including Larry McCarthy, but in Bart's mind the two indispensable ones were Mike and Alex. Either one of them could have run the Federal Reserve if asked, and Bart knew he needed them back. Both of them. Right away.

He returned to his regular office on the second floor and immediately began to organize a meeting. In the end, the three of them fixed it for 2:00 P.M. the following Tuesday, June 17, at Alex's apartment on the Upper West Side. In the ensuing days, Bart's appointment as president was made official, and Fuld had been compelled to agree that the new boss should have free rein to run the corporation precisely as he wished. They always say a surrendering general never has any fight left in him. But this was a surrendering king, and he had even less.

Bart was in charge, and in his own mind he had one brief: to unload the insane long positions Lehman had in residential mortgages and commercial real estate. He thought that just might be possible if he could persuade Mike and Alex to rejoin the firm. But the unspoken dread that haunted his dreams was that Lehman might be so long on concrete it could never be sold. At least not in time. Not with real estate values plummeting all over the globe.

At precisely two o'clock on Tuesday, Bart and Mike arrived at Alex Kirk's apartment. The three old friends, whose words of wisdom had fallen for so long on deaf ears up on the thirty-first floor, were quickly united in a genuine, collective desire to save Lehman Brothers. They were also united in their belief that Lehman had never been rotten at the core, just at the head.

Bart had to take back that executive committee which was unused to challenging anything and had for years been totally under the high-paid spell of Dick Fuld and Joe Gregory, allowing itself to be led, blindfolded, into deep, turbulent, and possibly life-threatening waters.

Bart told Mike and Alex, "I believe with you two on board we could make it happen. We have sixty years of experience between us, but most of all we have trust. And we have the talent and skill to undo years of destruction." And Alex and Mike said almost in unison, "I just hope we're not too late."

Bart pulled no punches. He outlined the grotesque scale of the problem, highlighting the fact that the firm's balance sheet kept getting deeper and deeper into debt as the corporation tried to hold subprime and Alt-A mortgages that could not be securitized. Lehman had been taking on $5 billion a month in residential mortgage originations. So far as Bart could tell, with as yet only a cursory glance at the books, there was $80 billion worth of mortgages on the books that could not be shifted.

"Right now this firm needs some adult risk supervision," Bart said. "And you two are the best there is. We have to clean up twenty-four months of reckless growth with little regard for risk management."

Mike and Alex both knew the devils that had governed the decline of Dick and Joe: too many inexperienced risk takers at the helm, and too much personal competition directed toward Goldman Sachs and Blackstone, all of it at the top of the market. But that did not lessen the shock of facing Lehman's almost three-quarters of a trillion dollars of pure, unadulterated risk.

They were all worried about this enormous number. But Mike Gelband seemed for a few moments to be lost in thought. He sat back in a deep armchair, and the other two found themselves awaiting a reflection from their old and trusted friend. For a full minute he said nothing. Then he spoke in a quiet but firm tone of voice. "All three of us have been together before in a crisis. Like 1998, when Lehman was at death's door. The difference was, back then our balance sheet was $36 billion. It was manageable, possible. And we were conservative, playing from a small stack."

They knew Mike was going to a cold and dangerous place, from where there might be no return. But he spoke calmly. "It's different now," he went on. "The balance sheet is probably $150 billion bigger than when I left the firm. It's near $700 billion. That's too much money. Way too much. And Lehman may have borrowed itself out of the game. An investment bank can get just too big to succeed."

Alex Kirk nodded gravely and said, "It's become an endemic Wall Street problem. And no one can see where it ends." With that, despite the overwhelming nature of the task, Mike and Alex both stood up and said quietly they were honored to be asked and would return to work immediately.

Despite all that was facing him, there was a bounce in the step of Bart McDade as he headed back to the investment bank that had sufficient debt to buy Scandinavia.

Even with a new corporate president, there was an inevitable air of suppressed panic in the air at Lehman. It was so pronounced that even Fuld could sense he finally had to mingle with the troops, and he uttered no objection when Bart, a natural communicator, requested they make a grand tour of the offices together.

They visited floors two through seven, and Bart carried a small portable podium with him. At each destination he placed it in position and Dick stepped up onto it to introduce the new Lehman chief to the troops. Bart insisted that when Dick addressed them he be connected to the "hoot"—the floorwide communications system allowing everyone to hear his words. People were astounded. In the first hour and a half more people saw and heard Dick Fuld speak than had experienced that in the previous ten years. Dozens of them scarcely knew who he was.

Bart's own appearance on the little podium was less spectacular. Everyone knew Bart McDade, who was often walking around meeting people. And everyone really liked him. At least I think they did. I never met anyone who didn't.

For Dick Fuld, it was not so easy to climb down from the throne of Lehman. On the day after the meeting at Alex Kirk's apartment, a meeting of ten senior managing directors was called in the office of Andrew Morton, the second man to try to follow in the shoes of Mike Gelband as head of fixed income. Among them were Jerry Donini, Mark Walsh, Eric Felder, Rich McKinney, and Mo Grimeh, the Moroccan-born head of emerging market trading.

Dick Fuld had promised to attend, and for a while he sat quietly listening to the accounts of the potential losses that might occur in real estate and mortgages. He heard Eric Felder mention the profits being made by the hedging tactics, but finally he reverted to his old bullying ways, using them indiscriminately, ranting at guys who were not losing money, like Felder.

"I've had enough," he yelled. "Enough of the fucking losses. Enough!" He demanded answers, tried to bully them out of making further losses with an air of sheer belligerence, and raved on about hitting the ground running and fighting as a unit under the guns.

Now, a managing director at Lehman is an important executive. And these were not guys with whom to trifle. They formed a group of very clever people, ranging upward to very brilliant. And they stared at him in bewilderment. A major section of the group regarded Fuld as an out-of-touch old guy who was in office. After all, it was Dick Fuld who had somehow lost Gelband and Kirk, had somehow sanctioned the reckless nine-month buying spree initiated by Walsh, Goldfarb, Gregory, Berkenfeld, and Sherr.

Most people who attended that meeting regarded Fuld as a slightly pathetic, out-of-touch, confused old guy who was in office past his time, struggling with a 1970s playbook in a 2008 game. Lehman's balance sheet had grown to gargantuan levels, perhaps nearly impossible for one person to wrap his mind around. This was new stuff, losses, big losses, bigger than he had ever known or even dreamed about. He didn't fully understand the embedded leverage in modern advanced credit derivative products. The guy was confused, but he was also in shock, and he reacted the only way he knew how, the way that had always served him well. He started shouting, trying to intimidate people, as if to scare them into not making any further losses. On reflection, I guess it *was* pretty pathetic. But for me, it was sad rather than malicious.

Anyhow, Mike and Alex returned to the office on June 24, Mike as global head of capital markets, Alex, replacing Dave Goldfarb, as global head of principal investing. They both arrived around 6:00 A.M., and there was standing applause when they turned up on the third and fourth floors to make their rounds and shake hands with old friends.

By now Bart and many of his key people had moved up to the thirty-first floor, and the whole atmosphere changed immediately. What once had been a cold, almost eerie, library-quiet corporate seat of power, dominated by two men who led lives far removed from their staff, now became a thriving, cheerful place with the old teams led by Mike and Alex moving in, knuckling down to the urgent business of selling off Lehman's highly suspect assets.

Not everything changed, however. One of the new assistants told me that summer that Dick Fuld walked straight past her desk every single day and never once said hello, despite the fact she was the right hand of one of the great Lehman traders and risk takers. "Mr. Fuld," she told me, "walked right past me every day, as if I did not exist."

Meanwhile, the titanic task of going through the real estate books to try to unearth the truth was under way, essentially to assess the amount of concrete the firm had bought with borrowed money. What they found was nothing less than a horror story. Enclosed in a massive book the size of three Manhattan Yellow Pages, there were no fewer than twenty-four hundred line items contained in the records of Mark Walsh's transactions. Bart, Alex, and Mike were nothing less than appalled. The numbers alone were enough to cause a heart attack in any normal investment banker. But there was something so utterly out of control about what they had discovered that the issues instantly widened.

Plainly Walsh and his team, operating over on Park Avenue, had required no higher authorization. Anywhere else, they knew, purchasing on this scale would have damn near required an act of Congress. The questions began raining down on them: *Who knew about this? Was Fuld a party to the transactions? Or was it just Joe Gregory? If Joe knew, did he tell Fuld—or the executive committee, not to mention the board?*

Bart grilled Fuld, who seemed vague. Like Mike and Alex, Bart was frightened. This was beyond logic, this was beyond reason. The terrifying number of maybe $120 billion stood starkly before them. No one in all the world could unload that much commercial and residential real estate. The markets were in a downward spiral, and there were fewer buyers than there had been for years.

For a few moments they just stood there, literally overcome by the enormousness of the task before them. And then a thought flickered across their minds: *Lehman Brothers might be finished.* There was no satisfaction in having been proven right. Just a sense of profound sadness, and a fleeting moment of desolation at the magnitude of their problem—a problem so vast there might be no mathematical solution to what lay ahead.

Mike, the one who had been gone the longest, instantly tackled the valuations that had been entered onto the ledger. Unsurprisingly, they were all high, some assessed at their purchase price or sometimes higher. Like David Einhorn, Mike Gelband understood that the mortgage markets had dived and that if Lehman had to sell these positions at the current market value, down around 20 percent, billions of dollars' worth of assets would be stripped from the plus side of the balance sheet.

Everywhere any of them looked, there was nothing but trouble. Again Bart went back to Fuld, who was unable to shed much light on anything. And with every passing hour it seemed more and more probable that the tottering king of Lehman had cast a blind eye to many of the more unpalatable truths.

On one memorable occasion, Mike Gelband exploded: "I wish we could just locate someone with some real answers. I mean, hell, did anyone authorize any of this, or did it just happen?"

In the end, it did not much matter who knew or didn't know. The shudderingly huge commercial and residential portfolios remained, and with it unfathomable debt. And planted right in the middle of it, illuminated by the golden sun of the West, stood a name that in the end would live in infamy in the annals of Lehman Brothers—SunCal.

In some ways it was possible to trace Lehman's current problems directly to that corporation, to an enormous development site in the hot flatlands of central California, 120 miles northeast of Los Angeles. Located on the southwest side of Bakersfield, the site was a two-thousand-acre stretch of land upon which it was envisioned there would one day be six thousand homes, forming a recreational community built around a Greg Norman–designed golf course, boating and fishing waters, and a beach house. Lehman was originally in for $150 million in 2005. That made it both a lender and an equity holder. They called the site, with a Hollywood flourish, McAllister Ranch.

By June of 2008 McAllister Ranch was fenced off: three square miles of destitution, blowing sands like the Sahara, weeds like an abandoned tobacco farm, and a half-finished clubhouse. No houses. No grand lake for boating. Just a scene of dereliction, a place left to die quietly out in California's inland empire, the lands once designated to make untold fortunes in real estate development.

The bigger problem was that since Lehman had first climbed into this doomed enterprise, the original loan had increased to $350 million. And then, in addition, they had raised and loaned SunCal more and more, something close to $2 billion. It was nothing short of a black hole, and a bank the size of Lehman had no business being anywhere near it. SunCal would have made the accounts department gasp at a major multinational commercial bank, never mind a smallish Wall Street investment house with no depositor income.

With McAllister Ranch plainly on its way down the tubes, worth less than half of the purchase price in this market, and SunCal about to default, Lehman's accountants may have been somewhat opportunistic in scarcely recording any write-down on the investment on the balance sheet. It still showed almost the full value. I guess Gregory and Goldfarb thought Fuld might not want to hear much about write-downs.

Mike Gelband blinked in amazement. Every hour this grew worse. He and Alex grabbed the bullshitters by the horns and immediately transferred Mark Walsh's real estate operation back to the bullpen. Exit Park Avenue deluxe, back to the factory at 745 Seventh Avenue. They broke up Walsh's hundred-strong team and gave up trying to find out who was actually culpable for the gigantic losses. The fact remained that this crowd had meekly gone along with the out-of-control expansion plans, the massive overexposure to illiquid commercial real estate as laid down by Dick and Joe.

Mark Walsh himself was about to find life very different. The days of sitting there blinding Joe Gregory with the science of real estate ended for him like the slamming down of a drawbridge. Poor Mark, for so long the prince, now found himself under cross-examination that might have made a Gestapo officer blink. And he was ordered to report to the uncompromising Mike Gelband—hopefully to report sales, hundreds of them, to get Lehman out from under the debt created by Club 31, as that all-powerful stretch of skyscraper real estate was nicknamed by the rest of the staff.

Bart, Alex, and Joe also removed David Goldfarb from his position as head of principal investing and installed him in the brand-new, slightly ephemeral seat of chief strategy officer, no longer a big financial power with stop-go authority over major real estate investments. Remember, Decouple Dave had also been a final authority in the purchase of hedge funds, in which he was responsible for eight more of Lehman's major screwups that Alex was desperately trying to undo, write down, and sell.

Bart's great buddy, the brilliant Jerry Donini, a forty-four-year-old domestic equities whiz, was promoted to global chief—another neat move in line with their policy of trying to get the very best people into their right spots in the company, now, for a change, with access to "Club 31."

Erin's replacement as chief financial officer was the South African–born Ian T. Lowitt, Lehman's global treasurer, and a former Rhodes scholar at Oxford. His appointment was widely applauded, although Wall Street was still talking—reeling, actually—from a devastating lecture David Einhorn had delivered a month earlier at the prestigious Ira W. Sohn Conference in New York on May 21. He had made his speech at 4:00 P.M. right after the market closed, and before he spoke, the mere rumor that he might try to nail Lehman had already sent the stock down 2.44 percent that day, making it around 70 percent on the year.

Einhorn had disappointed none of the Lehman detractors, who were beginning to short the stock wholesale, much as Einhorn himself was. He argued that the firm did not recognize the declining value of some of its real estate holdings. He cast serious doubt on the value Lehman placed on around $6.5 billion of collateralized debt obligations backed by nonresidential mortgages. And he specifically mentioned a real estate venture called SunCal, in hard-hit central California. He said Lehman had not disclosed a material charge against that SunCal holding, and noted that Lehman had taken only a $200 million write-down of its entire nonresidential CDO position in the first quarter of 2008. That was about 3 percent. And like old Senator Everett Dirksen nearly said, "You start fooling around with a few billion here and a few billion there, pretty soon you're talking real money."

Einhorn scarcely had a good word to say about the way Erin Callan had presented the firm's financial report, with its suspect declaration of $489 million profit. And he reminded his big audience that she'd used the word *great* fourteen times, *challenging* six times, *strong* twenty-four times, *tough* once, and *incredibly* eight times.

"I would use the word *incredible* in a different way," Dave said.

It was not anything absolutely specific about that lecture. It was just the overall tone: David Einhorn thought there was something rotten going on in the Lehman accounting department. He never claimed inside knowledge, never even suggested he had a source inside the firm. He just recounted what the numbers were telling him. And the lack of transparency on those property write-downs had told him a great deal.

There it is again. That word *transparency.* Wherever there's trouble in big financial matters, that word pops up, over and over. I'd very nearly say capitalism cannot work without transparency. And whenever it tries, there's always a problem.

In the days that followed Einhorn's lecture, Lehman seemed to be under attack from a different source every day in some publication or other. Not just Lehman's stock but its reputation was being questioned. Both before and after the June 12 coup d'état, Dick Fuld was affected by this, but his rage diminished as more and more of his power was transferred to Bart McDade. The rage became a growl, and as the new men struggled with the ever-growing burden of the debt, Fuld finally grew more sanguine—not totally, but a little. In fact, those who remained in the wider information loop were often surprised by the calmness with which Dick Fuld increasingly began to accept bad news. It was as if he knew something that others didn't, as if he believed that in the end, all would be well: Lehman would take some hits, some of them savage, but nothing could genuinely knock the old firm from its pedestal.

It took a while to become clear why Fuld seemed so sanguine, but in the end it did. Eventually it became known that several months earlier, shortly after the Fed had moved forward to bankroll JPMorganChase's takeover of the stricken Bear Stearns on St. Patrick's Day, Dick had arranged a private dinner in New York with the seventy-fourth secretary of the Treasury. To most of the world, Henry Merritt

Paulson was possibly the most powerful of all the global investment bankers. To senior Wall Streeters, he was Hank Paulson, former chairman and chief executive officer of Goldman Sachs, far removed from the financial market trader, but nonetheless still widely regarded as a Wall Street insider, respected and esteemed, a lifetime free-marketeer, a Republican with rigid principles about capitalism and America's tried-and-true ways of doing business. But to a man like Dick Fuld—and there weren't many—Paulson was an equal, a fellow investment bank chief, no different from himself.

Fuld perhaps should have known better, because Hank Paulson's resume outlined a career of unusual toughness: one of Dartmouth College's best offensive linemen, All-Ivy, All-East, honorable mention All-American. The guy could hit. He'd worked as a staff assistant at the Pentagon. He'd been assistant to John Ehrlichman during the cauldron of Watergate. At Goldman he'd been one of the driving forces that made that bank the source of so much irrational envy in the mind of Dick Fuld. In his glittering career he had forged friendships and business associations with some of the biggest financiers in China. Also, he had more personal bread than Fuld. Real bread, that is. Not borrowed. In broad terms, Paulson was not a man to be taken for granted.

The dinner Paulson and Fuld had in the spring became known as the "huge brand dinner," a reference to the fact that Dick Fuld tried to convince himself and others that the meeting had gone his way, and ever afterward asserted that the Treasury chief had loved his idea of raising new capital and keeping the firm a single publicly traded entity. Elated at the success of the dinner, Dick had e-mailed his legal director, Tom Russo, and said categorically, "We have a huge brand with Treasury, and Hank loved our capital raise." In the months thereafter, several Wall Street journalists referred to the "cheerful" dinner and the amicable nature of the conversation. Articles appeared in *New York* magazine and *U.S. News & World Report* to that effect.

Wrong. It was in fact an antagonistic encounter, with Hank Paulson advising Fuld to sell both Lehman's assets and the firm, the former much more aggressively than had happened so far. While immediately after the Bear Stearns fiasco Paulson and Ben Bernanke had agreed that the Fed's PDCF, the Primary Dealer Credit Facility—known colloquially as the enhanced Fed window—should be opened to all investment banks for the first time, Hank took a poor view of the fact that Lehman planned to access this Fed window for cash, essentially taxpayer funds, while still taking on substantial risk. He actually gave Fuld orders, coming close to an outright demand, that Lehman get their act together. He wanted the place deleveraged in a big hurry, and he all but accused Fuld of dragging his feet. Hank was irritated that the massively leveraged Lehman, with Fuld's blessing, was investing in leveraged hedge funds. It was leverage on leverage, with taxpayer funds as the backup. Moral hazard, anyone?

He also advised they should consider seriously a secret but firm offer from the state-owned Korea Development Bank (KDB). It was believed to have been around $23 a share. Hank Paulson knew this offer had been on the table for several months and understood, doubtless from his Chinese friends, that it reflected a genuine desire on the part of KDB to own Lehman Brothers. He may not have been thrilled that Fuld had not accepted the offer, because an outright sale to one of the Pacific Tigers would have saved everyone a lot of trouble. He did, apparently, make his feelings on this point quite clear to Fuld.

"I've been in my seat a lot longer than you were ever in yours at Goldman," Fuld retorted. "Don't tell me how to run my company. I'll play ball, but at my speed."

The Treasury chief glowered, and quite possibly Lehman's fate was sealed at that moment. I am told Hank considered the Lehman chairman to have demonstrated something between arrogance and disrespect.

From all accounts, Hank Paulson was already worried about the calamitous effect a Lehman collapse might have on Wall Street, but he plainly did not consider Dick Fuld the right man to be at the helm. Doubtless Mike Gelband, during his time in the wilderness, had brought him up to date with other examples of Dick's less-than-inspired financial beliefs.

It was strange how Dick clung to two beliefs about that dinner right up until Bart, Mike, and Alex took over. Number one was that it had all gone well and that in the end, come what may, Hank would save both him and Lehman Brothers. Number two was a sense of security that the Fed PDCF window would never be closed to him. Both beliefs were misplaced.

And so the steady sound of the jackhammers crashing into Lehman's real estate, trying to knock down the terrible wall of debt, continued into July. Bart, Mike, and Alex worked tirelessly, late into the night, all the time further marginalizing Dick Fuld.

For several days, the markets held their own. Then, on Friday, July 11, there was another catastrophic bank failure, which instantly threatened to be the biggest ever. IndyMac Federal Bank, the Pasadena-based operation with assets of $32 billion and deposits of $19 billion, suddenly collapsed, closed down by the Office of Thrift Supervision and transferred to the FDIC. Right here we're talking bolts, bars, and padlocks, the biggest trouble there is in American banking, when the feds move in hard. Estimates were that the bank would go down for between $4 billion and $8 billion. IndyMac was the seventh-largest mortgage originator in the United States, and the largest savings and loan association in the Los Angeles area. It was the fifth American bank to fail in 2008 so far. Indeed, nothing on this scale had happened since the late 1980s and early 1990s. Between 2005 and 2007 only three other banks had failed in the entire country.

The cause was so predictable I have no doubt it made Hank Paulson cringe: low-doc mortgages, thousands of them. Not quite NINJAs or no-docs, but highly questionable loans to people who could not afford the repayments. It was not a major surprise on the Richter scale of probability, maybe a 3.4. IndyMac lost $614 million in 2007 and another $184 million in the first quarter of 2008 as the housing market cave-in moved sharply beyond the weakest borrowers and firmly into the Alt-As. With the complete collapse of the securitization market, outfits like IndyMac had no way to get new loans off their books, and the Pasadena bank was now steaming toward disastrous delinquencies.

Back in New York, investment houses with similar or related problems braced themselves for even bigger trouble. That Friday became a day of pure Wall Street theater: a towering city tragedy, like *Othello,* not a pastoral comedy, like *As You Like It*. This was not anything that anyone liked.

News of the bank collapse hit around midday. Then the oil market, which for several weeks had been doing a reasonable imitation of a rocket, shot up again to a new high of $147.27 a barrel on NYMEX, with every sign it might go higher. Forecasts of $200-a-barrel Brent crude flashed across the Atlantic. The whirling, bloodstained god of galloping inflation danced mockingly across the floor of the New York Stock Exchange.

The Dow, which had opened low for the month at 11,226, shuddered as traders slammed on the brakes. In midafternoon it briefly dipped below 11,000 for the first time since February 2006 but climbed back to 11,100 by the closing bell. All day Lehman shares had taken a pounding. After tumbling to an eight-year low the previous day, they fell $2.53 pre-market to $14.77, now making a 75 percent loss on the year.

Rarely had traders been more jumpy, and the sunlit second weekend in July was filled with apprehension for anyone who worked on, near, or around Wall Street, from bank presidents and bond traders all the way to the pretzel sellers outside the massive offices of Merrill Lynch. The city seemed subdued, the Hamptons depressed. Even Arturo Di Modica's three-and-a-half-ton charging bronze bull, Wall Street's symbol of America's strength and power, now gazed balefully up Broadway, and the light of battle in his eyes seemed unaccountably faded.

Monday was glum but uneventful. Then, on Tuesday, July 15, after the Dow reached 11,123, the market dived and the Dow actually closed below 11,000, at 10,963. It had not finished that low in two and a half years. Simultaneously, the price of oil took a steep decline, which, absurdly, seemed to cause more consternation than when it went high. The NYMEX price for a barrel of crude closed at $138.74, nearly $10 off its high the previous Friday. Gold hit a four-month high at $987. June automobile sales were reported to have declined more than 3.3 percent. But the worst possible news for any Wall Street investment bank was the near collapse of Fannie Mae, which suffered a 50 percent stock crash from $12.87 to, at one point, $6.82 in less than 24 hours. And that was off a high of $70 the year before.

Fannie Mae and the other government-backed mortgage giant, Freddie Mac, were two of the most gruesomely misleading corporations since Enron. Originally established to help make mortgage loans to lower-income families, they were, in the twenty-first century, way beyond that simple and quasi-philanthropic brief. They existed now only to buy gargantuan swaths of mortgages from the shadow banks. Data from *The Economist* shows that ownership of other firms' mortgage-related securities by Fannie Mae and Freddie Mac was up over 100 percent from 2002 to 2007. In effect, they were operating like Lehman or Merrill Lynch. They were thus effectively underwriting the mortgages on behalf of the government, but unlike Lehman and Merrill Lynch, they weren't trying to securitize them and unload them onto the world market as RMBSs and CDOs. They were keeping them on their books, billions of dollars' worth of mortgages they believed, wrongly, to be excellent investments. But now Fannie's earnings were out, and second-quarter losses had totaled $2.3 billion, the fourth straight quarter of red ink, for a grand total of $9.44 billion. Fannie Mae had pledged all those thousands of mortgages as collateral to raise more money, so that it could borrow more. It was a perfectly hideous loop, and between them, Fannie and Freddie owed $5.2 trillion, with leverage of sixty-five to one. Remember I explained that this kind of endlessly rolling loan system was known in the business as a carry trade. And now, at last, Wall Street was compelled to recognize that Fannie and Freddie constituted just a giant government-backed carry-trade hedge fund. As a government-sponsored entity Fannie and Freddie have access to sub-LIBOR financing. They could borrow at LIBOR minus 20 basis points and lend at LIBOR plus 180 by owning piles of mortgages. They were making a lot of cash on this carry trade but lost billions on the underlying real estate values behind all the mortgages they owned. I'm told you couldn't give away their shares on that Tuesday afternoon.

Back at Lehman Brothers, dark storm clouds were gathering, seen by some, ignored by others. The less perceptive carried on more or less as usual until the sudden arrival on the trading floor of Lehman's own private storm cloud: Mike Gelband emerging from the elevator like the Prince of Darkness from his thirty-first-floor grotto.

Mike had seen enough. Everywhere he looked, all around the sweep of Lehman's endless horizons, there were tempestuous winds building. Mike knew many things, and he had many ideas about how to stave off the oncoming doom. But what he knew better than anyone else was the urgency of selling our positions in almost every corner of the trading floors. *The debt. The debt.* No one was quite as scared as Mike about Lehman's borrowing.

All day he stalked around floors three and four, the trading ops rooms of high-yield and mortgages. He grabbed the list of positions and went from trader to trader, to Mark Walsh's guys and all the rest, naming positions and demanding, "Whose fucking position is this? I need to know now." Once he located the trader, he was yelling, "I want this sold *yesterday*! Am I clear?"

At last people began to tune in, to hear at last the gospel according to Saint Mike, once a mere cry in the wilderness but now echoing throughout the building. He was trying to get across one message: "We're in DEFCON 1!" That's the highest form of alert in the U.S. military: maximum readiness to repel a foreign attack on United States territory. For comparison's sake, the government sounded DEFCON 3 on September 11, 2001, and DEFCON 2 for JFK's Cuban missile crisis in 1962. That was the extent of Mike Gelband's concern.

All through the following weeks, amidst masses of ruffled feathers, the Lehman traders tried to obey orders, tried to sell whatever they could. But slowly it became apparent that the task was too great. In the end Bart, Alex, and Mike were beginning to accept that the only way out might be an outright sale of the entire firm to a bigger bank. But such a merger might prove beyond their hopes, because the chief executive officer was still Dick Fuld, and whatever else could be kept away from him, the sale of the corporation could not. That summer the Korean Development Bank had once more made an offer of around $18 a share, but Dick had turned it down. There had also been an approach from the huge Chinese finance house Citic Securities, suggesting a 50 percent interest in Lehman, but those talks had failed. Now the only serious interest came from KDB, which apparently was not concerned by the precipitous drop in Lehman's stock. They were still hopeful of buying the big American investment bank, and the U.S. markets evidently believed there might be a significant chance of that happening, because Lehman's stock rallied to $16.55 on Friday, August 22.

A Korean government minister actually made a statement confirming the interest, and a third offer of $6.40 a share came in, which would have valued the corporation at $4.4 billion. Fuld turned it down because he wanted $17.50 a share. The two sides were not even close, and from there everything went quiet and no more was heard. Lehman, given Hank Paulson's plain skepticism toward Dick Fuld, was on its own.

Worse yet, the dying of the Korean bank's interest caused Lehman's stock to continue its downward slide, to below $10. For the many thousands of us watching substantial stock positions still on hold from our bonus payments, we were seeing our life savings diminish by the day. Almost half of all I had earned at Lehman was payable in stock. If the stock price fell by half, so did our money. And the stock had done one hell of a lot worse than that in 2008.

At the end of that August, Anabela and I were on vacation on the Cape, and so was Larry. Both Larry and I had something to smile about. We had pulled off some great trades and made money pretty steadily since I left the firm. But I had given a big hunk of it back when I misjudged the oil market and took a major short position when crude went to $120. Of course, it continued rising to $148 before ultimately flopping back down into the $30s. Unlike a lot of people, I was right on the money with the coming oil crash. Pity I was three weeks too early! Luckily I bailed out long before the highs.

In those summer days on the Cape, every time Lehman stock even trembled or there was a glimmer of communication from Seoul, McCarthy and I were on the phone, encouraging, hoping for the oncoming rally. But it never came. And we just had to wait, gazing at Nantucket Sound from beaches where both of us had been brought up. We were two temporarily lost souls, still looking for the rainbow's end, while lesser men, or so we thought, struggled to help Bart, Mike, and Alex tackle the problems. If things did not look up pretty soon, we figured, we'd both end up driving the old pork chop truck down the very same highways I'd traveled twenty years before.

We were all back after Labor Day, and the following weekend, the two biggest mortgage lenders in the world, Fannie Mae and Freddie Mac, darned near went bust and took with them half the institutional investors in the country. Hank Paulson and Ben Bernanke went white with fear, and on Sunday, September 7, Paulson nationalized them both. The government fired the management and assumed 80 percent ownership of the mortgage giants, guaranteeing them each $100 billion if necessary. This sent a shock wave through the entire economy.

On September 8 there was another major surprise when Lehman brought its third-quarter conference call forward ten days, presumably to try to head off market fears that it might go under as soon as its results came out. But when the garrison is under sustained fire, there's usually first one hit and then another.

The next day, Tuesday, September 9, Lehman's bankers, JPMorganChase, called with some grim, maybe terminal news. Steven Black, their co–chief of investment banking, speaking directly to Dick Fuld and our CFO Ian Lowitt, announced that he wanted $5 billion in extra collateral, and he wanted it in cash. If not, that would be the end of Lehman's credit line. As of the next day, the tenth, there would be no more business. Lehman's accounts would be frozen. Which meant that the funds Lehman needed to operate from day to day, such as to pay salaries, bills, and expenses, would be unavailable. And, at this point, Lehman had no access to the commercial paper and overnight repo markets.

JPMorganChase's chief executive officer was Jamie Dimon, a fifty-two-year-old New York–born son of a Greek immigrant, Harvard-educated, and one of the greatest financiers on earth, creator of Citigroup and former CEO of BankOne. Wall Street legend has it that in October 2006, he called a top JPMorganChase executive in the middle of the Rwandan jungle, where he was checking out a coffee plantation, and told him to get the firm the hell out of subprime mortgages, "because this stuff could go up in smoke." You could have tied Jamie Dimon to the bow of a patrolling nuclear submarine, so sensitive was his sonar. Now he was worried about Lehman, had been for weeks, and that sonar was pinging like Lionel Hampton's vibraphone.

As far back as July, Dimon's risk department had been requesting collateral from Lehman because JPMorganChase's clients were becoming concerned at the bad news that kept emanating from 745 Seventh Avenue. The first request was for a straight $5 billion, which did not arrive until August. It came in structured securities that JPMorganChase found impossible to value but darned sure believed were worth a lot less than $5 billion. All the while Lehman was saying it would raise capital again, and Dimon may have believed this.

On September 4, with no further Lehman capital raised, JPMorganChase asked for another $5 billion in collateral, this time in cash, because they now knew that the first tranche of securities posted by Fuld had deteriorated to a value of only $1 billion. No further money arrived. Steve Black's September 9 demand for the $5 billion collateral was thus not entirely unexpected.

Fuld came up with $3 billion, which had the effect of making his bankers even more worried than they had been before. Then, along with the rest of us, Jamie Dimon learned Lehman was going to preannounce its losses the next day, and that Fuld himself would be on the line.

News of that preannouncement sped around Wall Street. There were those who believed this kind of preemptive strike, accompanied by a billion-dollar pep talk about the future, would take the sting out of Lehman's third-quarter losses. But JPMorganChase was horrified. In company with Citigroup, Jamie Dimon asked to see Mike Gelband, Lehman's head of capital markets. At the hastily arranged meeting, both these banking giants tried to persuade the corporation not to go ahead with the announcement, on the grounds it would spook the markets unless somehow capital could be raised.

The Lehman team claimed Fuld would reveal an upcoming sale of Neuberger Berman, its investment management division, for around $8 billion. Dimon's men thought it was worth no more than $3 billion, which was not much good since the firm required $4 billion minimum.

The following morning at seven o'clock in the fourth-floor auditorium, eighty of the Lehman faithful showed up for a meeting to discuss the fate of the firm. In a matter of hours, Richard S. Fuld would stand before the nation to plead Lehman's case. The auditorium was tense as Tom Humphrey and the newly appointed fixed-income chief, Eric Felder, briefed the troops on a survival plan, centering around the creation of an entity to house their shocking commercial real estate portfolio. It was to be called SpinCo, and Lehman would place all those huge cash-losing concrete liabilities in there, thus removing them at a stroke from the balance sheet, and sending the Lehman stock back to $20.

The auditorium went sepulchrally quiet. But suddenly, a voice of quivering rage and indignation was raised. Mo Grimeh, managing director and global head of emerging markets trading, a man to whom more than 150 people reported, was up and yelling. It was a never-to-be-forgotten outburst, referred to variously in the weeks to come as "the Mo-ment" or, alternatively, "Mo's last stand."

"That's it?" he roared. "That's fucking it? Well, what the hell have those fucking idiots up on thirty-one been working on for the past two months? This? You have to be kidding me. If this is all we have, we're toast."

At this point there was total chaos: shouting, arguing, raging, raised voices, furious faces. But no one was angrier than Mo, and he pressed on at the top of his lungs.

"All we've done is to take a dollar out of our right pocket and put it in our left," he yelled. "The heavy debt load would make it insolvent before it started. This is ridiculous. The market will see straight through it."

Everyone understood how hard the Lehman team had worked to put something together, and a lot of people believed it could temporarily work out. But the truth was SpinCo could not be activated until January, four months from the present time, and Lehman needed a buyer for the whole firm in the next three days. Mo had hit it: it wouldn't work, couldn't work. And by the time Tom Humphrey stepped forward to remind Mo that his time was up, the damage had already been done.

If Dick Fuld really intended to swing that plan in the conference call, he was, like Lehman, essentially on his own. And with most of the audience dumbfounded at the revelation that the bank had lost a shudder-inducing $3.9 billion in the third quarter, Dick Fuld stepped up to explain how all would be well.

On that Wednesday morning, he spoke with confidence, but the bombast was gone. He revealed his plans, but without the attitude that dared anyone to question him. The commitment was there, but this was not the pugnacious old warrior of the past. He spoke of "aggressively reducing our exposure to both commercial and residential real estate assets" (SpinCo). Of "substantially de-risking the balance sheet." And of "reinforcing the emphasis on our client-focused businesses." "This will allow the firm," he said, "to return to profitability and strengthen our ability to earn appropriate risk-adjusted equity returns." He blamed intense public scrutiny for causing significant distractions among Lehman's clients, counterparties, and employees.

In summation, he declared there was a concrete plan in place to exit "the vast majority of our commercial real estate." Lehman was reducing residential real estate and leveraged loan exposures "down to appropriate operating levels." The firm was in the final stages of raising capital, and the dividend was being cut to 5 cents a share.

The fact that Lehman Brothers was in debt to the tune of $660 billion was not given major prominence in the speech. The other lasting memory of that day was Fuld's assertion that Lehman's vast property portfolio had retained much of its value. There was a view inside the top tier of the firm that this could not be so, and Jamie Dimon could not accept this either. Lehman's principal banker was by now unconvinced that Dick Fuld's bank could ever get out from under that debt.

With awesome symbolism, Lehman's stock hit a ten-year low on the New York Stock Exchange in the middle of Fuld's speech, hitting $7, and thousands of employees saw their nest eggs, large and small, dwindle drastically. The speech did not help, and the revelation that the bank had lost a total of $6.7 billion in hard cash in six months was as bad today as it would have been next week. Only a very brave, and probably half-witted, soul could possibly have placed a bet on Lehman's survival.

The following day, Thursday, September 11, JPMorganChase found out their initial request for Lehman collateral of $5 billion had not been paid. Dimon, the same man who just six months before was used by the Fed to inject emergency funds into Bear Stearns, now ordered credit lines to Lehman halted. But somehow, pulling every string at his disposal, including raiding the London office for $2 billion, Fuld began finding the money, and by the close of business on Friday, he had delivered the $8 billion Dimon now demanded.

While Fuld labored to try to locate unencumbered funds, the three prospective Lehman saviors, Bart, Mike, and Alex, had been working for more than a week to pull together some kind of a merger with Bank of America. But that was never going to fly. What BofA really wanted was Merrill Lynch, and though the mighty Merrill's debts were worse than those at 745 Seventh, Merrill had sixteen thousand retail brokers with over three million brokerage accounts, mostly belonging to individuals. The retirees were especially lucrative—there was over $1 trillion in assets under management. In the ten days leading up to that Friday, the Lehman negotiators always thought there might be a deal, but by close of business, Bank of America, citing the fact that there would be no federal help, backing, or underwriting, was gone. Gone the way of the guys on the shores of the Yellow Sea. The fact that Hank Paulson had made no move to encourage or assist the Koreans was one thing, but when he refused to make any kind of move to help BofA save Lehman, that was a significant sign. And for negotiations supposed to be kept top secret, these were echoing around like calls to prayer in downtown Cairo.

It took about three and a half minutes for news of Bank of America's exit to reach Seventh Avenue, where the mood was already mutinous, with hundreds of people ready to sign a petition for the outright removal of Dick Fuld from the CEO's office. On the third floor of the building, my old domain, the hundred-foot-long south wall had become a giant billboard designed to insult and mock Fuld, Gregory, Goldfarb, Berkenfeld, Walsh, Callan, and the ancient board of directors, all accused of destroying this great institution. The Wall of Shame, they called it.

There was a giant photo of Dick and Joe arm in arm in tuxedoes with the catchphrase "Dumb and Dumber." There were pictures of Erin and Joe together arm in arm. Hank Paulson was portrayed sitting on Dick Fuld's head, with the line "We have a huge brand with Treasury." They had contrived photos of different board members in nursing homes, propped upright with walkers, with the caption "Voting in Braille only." There were dozens of quotes from Fuld and Gregory exhorting people to greater efforts, warning of the dangers of risk, urging traders "to execute like champions today." Where once those orders had rung around the Lehman floors like the commandments of the gods, now they were just hollow, the words of paper tigers. Silly, really. Big thoughts from little people.

Perhaps the most supercharged piece of bitter irony on that entire wall was a quote from Fuld himself uttered at a different time, when he still mattered. There was no illustration for this one. The staff had blown up and highlighted the stark words, stopping only just short of neon lights: "The key to risk management is never putting yourself in a position where you cannot live to fight another day."

Right now, what mattered was the only game left in town: the British-based bank Barclays. They had the mark of the cynical London street trader all over them, however, seeming to want the good assets but with no intention of taking the $50 billion worth of bad assets. The possibility did not look promising, but at least it was still alive.

By now news of Bank of America's withdrawal and the Treasury's disinterest had leaked widely, and the media, like sharks speeding toward a tropical shipwreck, were arriving in ghoulish anticipation. The big television trucks were parking outside. There were lights, cameras, microphones, reporters in search of interviews, photographers in search of pictures, desperate to find someone in tears, even someone too upset to talk.

The night wore on, and by 1:00 A.M. I had spoken to over a hundred people. My cell phone battery had run out as out-of-towners pursued us New Yorkers as if somehow we would know more. On Saturday morning, Bart and Alex, in company with Lehman's top legal advisor, Jim Seery, headed downtown to the Fed's Manhattan offices. While they sped south through the quiet Manhattan streets, I was awakened by the phone. And then again. And then again. By midmorning things were looking and feeling very bleak. And then, shortly before noon, someone called it, no ifs, ands, or buts. Guess who? Christine Daley, on the line from the far side of the Appalachians, way down there in Nashville, announced, "It's all over. They're filing."

I did not even bother to ask how she knew. Over the years Christine had been invited to every holiday party of every big law firm in the city that dealt in distressed or restructuring corporations. There was no senior lawyer in this field with whom she was not familiar. Someone had told her, no doubt of that. Christine's sources were always impeccable, and she always knew how the numbers stacked up.

In a sense we were both in shock. Because we were each about to lose a huge amount of money, as our bonus stock would shortly become worthless. Hell, I was still on the payroll, and Christine had years of work and reward tied up in those atomized Lehman shares, once worth $86 apiece and now on their way to zero.

"I guess we're finished," she said. "A triumph for a colossal failure of common sense."

At that moment the Lehman negotiators had their backs to the wall down at the concrete fortress of the Federal Reserve on Liberty Street, which, ironically, stands atop the biggest stockpile of gold bars on earth, surrounded by every kind of security, machine-gun-toting armed guards, and metal detectors. Bart, Alex, and Jim Seery fought for the life of the old investment bank they all loved. But they had to fight in the lair of Hank Paulson, and they suspected he had already decided to let Lehman go. He had creatively saved Bear Stearns but would not do anything for Bank of America in their attempt at a Lehman takeover, and he was not about to help Barclays. The Brits still seemed to want something of Lehman, though not everything, and early Saturday, having been there most of the night, they said a deal was possible, but they needed the approval of the Financial Services Authority (FSA), the British regulators in London.

Meanwhile, on another floor, Hank Paulson was in conference with Bank of America officials in their efforts to buy Merrill. To this day there are those who believe Hank was more interested in saving Merrill than he ever was in saving Lehman. Every few hours he fielded a call from Fuld, but the fact was, he disliked the man, and he believed that Lehman had arrogantly foisted most of their troubles upon themselves and should just go away.

Warnings that such a failure might lead to a world banking collapse concerned him but did not quite convince him he should step in and rescue them both. Hank took aside John Thain, his old friend and colleague from Goldman, now CEO of Merrill, and gave him a stern talking-to. Moments later Thain called Ken Lewis, CEO of Bank of America, at his home in Charlotte, North Carolina, and suggested a meeting. Perhaps unknowingly, perhaps unwittingly, and eerily similar to the BofA rescue of Countrywide months before, BofA and Merrill were being led to the altar in a marriage of convenience for someone. Some thought BofA was becoming the fifth branch of the U.S. government, JPMorganChase already being installed as the fourth.

But Lehman's position was not improving. They had teams of negotiators all over the building, in discussions with bankers and lawyers. Even Mark Walsh and his minions had arrived to help Barclays evaluate one of the most terrifying commercial real estate portfolios in the country. The Barclays guys were grilling Bart and Alex, trying to place a value on the corporation. One of their prime observations was "The Lehman valuations on these assets are insane—what the hell was Fuld doing? Him and this Gregory character."

By Saturday lunchtime, Barclays, unsurprisingly, had decided that whatever else they wanted, they did not want the Lehman commercial property empire. They were probably encouraged in this view by the findings of about three hundred other lawyers, accountants, and bankers who had also gazed in horror at the giant portfolio of concrete that Dick Fuld had so confidently praised on that Lehman conference call three days before. And everything was made more drastically difficult because Fuld, even when the writing was on the wall, had refrained from calling in the bankruptcy lawyers. Thus there had been no preliminary examination. The fact was, no one knew the answers to anything.

Right now all Fuld could do was drive the Lewis family nearly mad by calling the Bank of America boss every five minutes throughout that Saturday. If it wasn't the longest day in Lehman's history, it was surely the longest day in the lifetimes of Ken and Donna Lewis.

By Saturday night CNBC was talking openly about the demise of Lehman. They spoke as if the game was over, and anyone listening could have been in no doubt that Bank of America was out and the Barclays position was unpromising.

On Sunday morning, the streets around the Lehman headquarters were packed with reporters and television crews. A police line was established on the sidewalk as hundreds of Lehman employees began filing in, some carrying boxes, others with duffel bags. I took a walk along to my old office building just as the sorrowful procession of hardworking, talented staff members began to emerge one by one, holding their boxes.

I stood on the other side of the street and saw a few people I knew. Some of the women were in tears. Many of the guys were too upset even to look up. And the reporters crowded in on them shouting questions, demanding answers from people whose lives had just been shot to pieces, whose finances were decimated, lifestyles wrecked, in some cases, like mine, hearts broken.

I then saw Jeremiah Stafford cornered by the reporters. One of the toughest, fastest traders on Wall Street, whose expectations had been sky-high, he was just standing there with his box of possessions, wearing a Red Sox baseball cap. His life was in shreds, his dreams ruined, at least for the moment. I could see him fighting back the tears as he said how we had been expecting this for a while, but he and all of his closest colleagues would walk out with pride, knowing they had contributed. As he tore himself away from these intrusive strangers with their microphones and lenses and appalling sense of entitlement, he added, "It was a very great place to have worked." Right on, Jeremiah! He represents to me so much of what was right and so much of what was wrong with Lehman. There were so many talented traders like him, so many awesome hardworking investment bankers, salespeople, support people all over the globe. There were dozens and dozens of extremely profitable business engines and departments in the firm. It was like 24,992 people making dough and 8 losing it.

By now people were still arriving, driven by the fear that the Lehman bankruptcy might yet be so bad that the feds would move in and seize everything, bolting the doors, locking everyone out. But thus far Lehman had not filed, and while some may have thought there was still hope, most people knew it was over. Otherwise, why were there hundreds of media people camped outside the doors of 745 Seventh?

In fact, none of them knew about the single ray of hope that had glistened in one of the wood-paneled conference rooms of the Fed building shortly after nine-thirty that morning. Hank Paulson and the head of the New York Fed, Tim Geithner, had between them corralled a group of leading bank chiefs and convinced them to finance the SpinCo assets up to $40 billion. This was precisely what the guys from Barclays wanted to hear, and it effectively put a potential deal right back on track.

Bart McDade and Alex had, like everyone else, been at the Fed since 6:00 A.M. Mike Gelband was uptown at the law offices of Simpson, Thatcher, and Bartlett, Lehman's counsel, where they were tackling the massive problem of due diligence. Just before ten o'clock, Bart e-mailed Mike informing him there was a deal: Barclays was making an acceptable offer for the firm.

Mike, who perhaps more than anyone had strived to save the bank that had outright rejected him, was almost overcome with relief. But twenty minutes later, his hopes were shattered. A new e-mail came in from Bart, announcing there had been a problem. In truth, there were two major holdups. The first was the British regulators, the FSA, who would not clear the deal because they had no wish to involve the British financial system with American difficulties. Hank Paulson himself had stepped in and talked with the regulators in London, but to no avail. Some have said that the FSA was willing to share the risk with the U.S. Treasury, but Paulson yet again said no.

The more pressing issue was Barclays shareholder approval. There was no way Hank was going to place a United States Treasury guarantee behind a deal that might face some kind of mutiny from British stockholders. And this deal needed to be done that day. Lehman did not have enough money to open for business on Monday, not without borrowing, and Jamie Dimon was simply not up to extending any more credit to Lehman. And so the great bankers of the United States stared down the twin barrels of two insurmountable problems, regulators and shareholders, while Barclays backed away.

No one could say they didn't give it everything, but the enmity between Paulson and Fuld shimmered below the surface. In the end,

Fuld saw the Treasury boss as a Pete Peterson character, a smooth, highly educated Ivy League sports star, a dyed-in-the-wool investment banker who had risen effortlessly. Hank found Dick Fuld a somewhat graceless, arrogant character, devoid of humility even in this, Lehman's darkest hour.

And boy, was it ever dark. Huge arc lights split the night out on Seventh Avenue, generators roared, and reporters shouted as the evening wore on. Media from all over the world were there, performing their dance of impending death: CBS, NBC, the BBC, Sky News, ITV. *What's the mood like inside the building? How do you feel? How worried are you? What are the chances of a new job?* On this Sunday night their material was endless, because people were arriving all through the evening into the small hours, afraid of the lockout, afraid of losing years of mementos and personal possessions.

The old distressed-bond trading department was united as it had not been for more than a year, since Mike and Larry left. Everyone was on the phone to everyone else, in a mass commiseration for the old firm. Everyone, in their own way, was upset: Joe, Ashish, Pete, Grossy, Schell. But the two I recall being most hurt of all were a couple of the staunchest operators in the company: the hard-nosed ace salesman Terence Tucker, too distressed to talk, and Jane Castle, a hundred pounds of hell, too upset to come to the phone.

I had a long conversation with Pete Hammack, and as ever, he had assembled the facts and arrived at the firm conclusion that, no matter what, Hank Paulson had to save Lehman Brothers. There was no choice, he felt, because the calamity would be too great for the financial system if he let it go.

"The issue is the credit default swaps," said Pete. "There's $72 trillion of them out there held by seventeen banks, and Lehman must be sitting on $7 trillion of them. Likewise, since Lehman is a prime broker, what happens to all the other prime brokerages if Hank lets Lehman go? Right there you're talking Armageddon." Pete had thought it through. "If a hundred hedge funds have prime brokerage accounts with Lehman Brothers," he said, "each with $500 million at stake, that's $50 billion of stocks that will possibly be liquidated. And that amount of selling will cause a tsunami. Worse yet, all of these hedge funds are leveraged five times, maybe ten. That's $500 billion of selling, bonds, stocks, RMBSs, CMBSs, CDOs, et cetera. That's a mega-tsunami on steroids. That's what we have created, and Hank has no option except to stop it from happening." No modern market has ever seen that type of selling.

Larry McCarthy did not share Pete's opinion. "We're dead," he told me with rich and characteristic cynicism, "because Hank and his guys have seen the books." Like me, he thought all hope was gone, though our reasons were slightly at variance. Personally, I thought Hank Paulson was going to do something like Custer's last stand, riding bravely in defense of capitalism at the head of his troops, and let the market do its worst. Trouble with that was everyone might get killed. Worse yet, the son of a bitch was going to do it with my money.

All my life I've been a laissez-faire Ronald Reagan/Margaret Thatcher capitalist, swearing by the market, taking the risks, and the devil take the hindmost. But this one time I was looking for a government rescue, and I wasn't going to get it.

Around eight on that Sunday night the Lehman negotiators returned to the office from the Fed building and went straight to the thirty-first floor. Bart McDade walked into Dick Fuld's crowded office and told him there would be no rescue, that it was over, that Lehman Brothers had been mandated to file for bankruptcy.

The Lehman CEO was dumbfounded. Lehman might easily go down for $660 billion, the largest bankruptcy in the history of the world.

Despite a growing feeling that the feds did not care one way or another whether Lehman lived or died, they decided to give it one more try—to phone directly the Brooklyn-born Tim Geithner, head of the Fed in New York. One more plea. One more appeal.

Fuld's legal counsel, Tom Russo, made the call in front of perhaps fifteen silent onlookers, the entire Lehman executive committee. It was 8:20 P.M. They tried reaching Geithner but could only get through to his number two at the New York Fed. But with the most momentous failure in the history of U.S. finance about to happen, no one could track down Geithner. They buzzed, paged, and rerouted. But Tim had gone to ground. It might have been just happenstance, but there was a melancholy feeling that it might equally well have been deliberate. In those empty minutes, the fighting heart of Lehman Brothers began to fall apart.

But Mike Gelband and Bart were still in the game, and they decided there was one final card to play. It was a little embarrassing, but still a slender chance. One of Dick's executive committee members was George Walker IV, a top-flight Ivy League investment banker with a Wharton MBA. He was also a cousin of the president of the United States, George W. Bush. They shared a great-grandfather. Walker, thirty-nine, was the firm's head of investment management, and understood with everyone the gravity of the situation, the decimation of his personal capital, the loss of his career. Now Mike Gelband stood before him and begged him to call the president, to ask his cousin to intervene.

Walker was not at all happy at the thought of calling the White House. "I'm not sure I can do this," he said. But Gelband knew they were drowning men. If George would not make the call, it really was over. Mike took him aside and told him flatly that if this phone call failed, it would "unleash the forces of evil into the global markets." It was the same message that had been delivered shortly before to Geithner's number two. George went white, almost overwhelmed by the responsibility now being foisted upon him.

"I'm not ordering you," said Mike. "I can't do that. I'm on my knees, George. Please, please make the call. It's our last shot."

Eric Felder, the fixed-income chief, too implored him, saying quietly, "We are looking at an unmitigated disaster on a global scale, George. They don't understand what they are doing. Like Mike, I'm begging you."

Walker, distraught, pacing the room, looked over to Dick Fuld, who was on the line to the SEC. And then he went into the library and telephoned the president of the United States of America. Mike heard him request a connection to the private quarters of the president. It was obvious the operator was trying to put this family member through, but the delay seemed interminable, and finally the operator came back on the line and said, "I'm sorry, Mr. Walker. The president is not able to take your call at this time."

George Walker had failed, but he'd done his best. And now they all gathered around Dick Fuld's desk for the last time. Earlier in the day, the famous bankruptcy lawyer Harvey Miller and his team from Weil Gotshal had arrived and were now preparing for a bankruptcy filing that would be six times larger than any other Chapter 11 case in U.S. history.

Bankers were suggesting the $660 billion number was not far off the mark. They were talking $40 billion commercial real estate and mortgages, $65 billion in residential real estate and mortgages, and

$16 billion in high-yield leveraged-buyout debt—grand total $121 billion. In addition, there was another $300 billion worth of commercial paper, overnight repos, and Treasury debt. Lehman owed $100 billion more in stocks, corporate bonds, municipal bonds, and commodities, and another $100 billion in CDSs, CDOs, CLOs, options (puts/calls), and hedges on the ABX and the HY-9.

In the small hours of the morning, around two o'clock, Lehman Brothers filed for Chapter 11 bankruptcy. The 158-year-old investment bank was gone. It was Monday, September 15, in the year 2008. It was indeed the largest bankruptcy in history.

Hank Paulson had just made the decision that would obliterate the world's economy.

Epilogue

Written in Sorrow, Not Anger

Hours after Lehman's attorneys filed for Chapter 11 bankruptcy, Hank Paulson stood in the West Wing of the White House, and there, with the Stars and Stripes draped behind him, announced to the world that he had elected to allow Lehman Brothers to fail.

He uttered words of assurance to Americans everywhere that U.S. banks were safe and their deposits were insured by the FDIC. "I have played," he said, "the hand I was dealt." And he surely had, because in the hours that preceded that press conference he had made certain that the collapsing Merrill Lynch had been forced into the arms of Bank of America in one of the truly great marriages of convenience.

Immediately after the press conference ended, he was told the markets were tumbling. The Dow Jones Industrial Average went into a savage downward spiral, dropping 500 points on the day. Hank Paulson, the great Republican banker, had gone with his instincts, and now he wrestled with the momentous decision he had made. He was a man with a complete aversion to anything that smacked of nationalization, and he had made the call of a red-in-tooth-and-claw American capitalist. The fourth-largest investment bank on Wall Street had gone down. And the U.S. government had raised not one finger to save it. All around the world, the markets shuddered as Wall Street's tectonic plates began to rumble apart. Everyone was on edge, braced for a new shock, and there was not long to wait.

On Tuesday morning, September 16, right on the NYSE opening bell, shares in the world's biggest insurance corporation, AIG, slid 60 percent as a direct result of the Lehman bankruptcy. AIG had been an enormous player in the credit default swaps market and had taken billions of dollars' worth of bets against the failure of Lehman, simply because it seemed to them an absolute impossibility that it could ever collapse. They had promised all these people billions of dollars in payouts because it was unthinkable that Lehman could go down, but now it had. AIG did not have the cash to make the payouts they now owed. In addition, they had invested tens of billions insuring profits in the lethal CDO markets, which had collapsed with mass defaults by the mortgage holders. AIG was effectively insolvent.

On that Tuesday morning, the ratings agencies, suddenly quivering with self-righteousness, downgraded them, which required AIG to post collateral with its trading counterparties. Right there, AIG had a liquidity crisis. With the stock plummeting to a low of $1.25, 95 percent off its fifty-two-week high, the insurers were on the brink of bankruptcy.

Hank Paulson, who had just let the fourth-largest bank on Wall Street slip away, could not possibly allow the biggest insurance company in the world to go down the tubes with it. Against all of his capitalist instincts, he stepped in, and the Federal Reserve immediately announced the creation of a secured credit facility of up to $85 billion. In return, Ben Bernanke demanded and received an 80 percent stake in the corporation for the government. Bailout number four had just broken out, six months after Bear Stearns and nine days after Fannie and Freddie; the total of government guarantees was now at $314 billion. Strangely, Goldman Sachs CEO Lloyd C. Blankfein was the only major head of any Wall Street investment bank present in the AIG bailout discussions that day. Goldman was a large holder of AIG stock as well as an enormous counterparty to over $10 billion in AIG credit default swaps. A lot of Lehman employees still want to know why the Lehman rescue plan proposed over the weekend was so public, with more than eight investment and commercial banks looking under the Lehman kimono, while the expensive bailout of AIG just a few days later was so private.

But the biggest question on everyone's mind remains. How much did the Lehman failure cost the U.S. government in terms of massive additional bailout funds for AIG? With Lehman in bankruptcy and all the forced selling it created in the markets, some say Lehman's failure cost tens of billions. No one knows. If Lehman was saved, do you really think it would have cost an initial $80 billion and subsequently $180 billion in taxpayer funds for the AIG bailout?

With Lehman's bankruptcy filing less than forty-eight hours old, the full impact of the disaster hit the world's financial markets. The biggest banks on earth were, collectively, terrified to lend to each other, because none of them had any confidence they would ever get their money back. If it could happen to Lehman, it could happen to anyone. The heart of the global banking system, the credit markets, was frozen solid. There was no possibility of anyone securing a loan for anything, especially the investment banks. The short-term paper market ceased to exist. The safest, most solid banks in the world were unable to borrow money.

This was not just a difficult time, with banks stopping to catch their breath. This was a meltdown, and commerce in the United States was rapidly stalling. Hank Paulson was facing the beginning of the global credit crunch, the very same one Mike Gelband had warned him about on the telephone from Dick Fuld's office seventeen months before.

Just then Hank was gazing with horror at one of those mysterious Wall Street insider's charts known in the trade as the TED spread, a measure that perceived credit risk in the general economy. It's the difference between the interest rates for three-month U.S. Treasury contracts—risk-free T-bills paying roughly 1.5 percent—and the interest banks charge each other for short-term loans, LIBOR, around 2 percent. Historically the TED spread hovers between 10 and 50 basis points (that's 0.1 percent and 0.5 percent)—a tiny difference, and a very dull little chart, occasionally worth checking. The day after AIG crashed, however, the TED spread went into orbit, shooting up 300 basis points. It broke the record set after the Black Monday collapse of 1987. Visions of the Great Depression of the 1930s danced before Hank Paulson's eyes. According to this chart, the banks had slammed an enormous interest rate on every dollar they loaned. Reason: they did not want to lend, and this explosion on the TED spread signified they were not joking. They'd made it impossible for anyone to borrow money.

Even the dying breed of America's AAA-rated companies—and by now there were only six of them left—could not borrow money at that price. It's probably worth noting that in 1980 there were more than sixty nonfinancial companies that held the highest possible rating. Now there were only Automatic Data Processing (ADP), ExxonMobil, General Electric, Johnson & Johnson, Pfizer, and Microsoft, and even these uncontested champions of the credit food chain were left without nourishment.

And the floor of the New York Stock Exchange was vibrating, leaping up and crashing down, overreacting to every snippet of news. Nothing was merely okay or a bit suspect. It was either cataclysmic or

Christmas. News of the AIG government bailout sent the Dow up 154 points. But mass uncertainty, with no foreseeable solutions except government intervention, caused it to plummet 447 points the next day.

No one knew what to do. The only ray of clarity came from Ben Bernanke, who understood by now there was only one way forward—it might have been sideways, but at least it wasn't backward. The mild-mannered former Princeton professor understood that he and Hank now had to involve Congress and try to hold back the tide of financial disaster. There was no other way, and the creation of an emergency plan, drafted by the Treasury staff, was in Paulson's briefcase as he and Ben headed for Capitol Hill for the meeting that would suck the very oxygen out of the Senate conference room.

Because there, among the fourteen assembled senior U.S. senators, Hank Paulson uttered the home truth that more or less stopped the American government in its tracks. "Unless you act," he said, "the financial system of this country, and the world, will melt down in a matter of days."

No one spoke. And every last one of the assembled politicians remembers the moment when the conference room, behind the great ten-ton bronze doors of the Capitol, fell stone silent. This was no longer a discussion, a briefing, or a place for a financial decision. This was history. Whatever they elected to do would be remembered forever. Because Hank Paulson, in as many words, was plainly proposing the kind of action more readily associated with Soviet Russia or Red China—the potential nationalization of U.S. banks. Not one person sitting at that long table doubted that they were about to be asked to find billions of dollars to save the financial institutions. As with Fannie, Freddie, AIG—all in the last eleven days—that would mean dominant government equity in long-standing commercial corporations. Either that or America's most revered banks were about to go the way of Lehman. There could be no doubting the flat, calm severity of Hank Paulson's words. And the enormous intellect of Ben Bernanke plainly could find no alternative.

The senators remained hushed, all of them with conflicting thoughts rampaging through their minds. *Yes? No? What if I do? What if I don't?*

The Treasury secretary opened his file and presented his plan—a $700 billion request for taxpayers' money, to be used to buy the toxic CDOs from the banks.

A rising murmur of both approval and disapproval was heard all around the table.

"And we need it by Monday," added Hank.

The great capitalist had bowed to the inevitable. The plan was briefly elaborated, and the senators agreed to study it and then place it before the House.

The mere news of the plan's existence caused the Dow Jones Industrial Average to rocket upward and close 410 points higher. On the following day, Friday, September 19, it gained 361 points more. Hope was in the air, and the Dow was managing to cling to that 11,000 support point. It held on Monday the twenty-second, but narrowly breached it on Tuesday the twenty-third, closing at 10,854.

By this time Barclays Bank was back in the game. They paid $250 million for the Lehman businesses they wanted, and another $1.5 billion for the skyscraper at 745 Seventh Avenue. This saved upward of ten thousand jobs and Barclays lost no time in removing every last vestige of the Lehman name from the building. Barclays' blue insignia was everywhere.

The hearing at the U.S. Bankruptcy Court on Bowling Green, right opposite Wall Street's charging bronze bull, was packed with lawyers, the press, and Lehman witnesses. Lehman's case was presented with haste. In place of the one hundred to three hundred pages that normally accompany a massive Chapter 11 application for protection, Lehman's lawyers, Weil Gotshal & Manges, presented a fifteen-page document, alarming in its brevity, especially considering that this bankruptcy was bigger than WorldCom, Enron, Conseco, Texaco, Refco, Washington Mutual, United Airlines, Delta, Global Crossing, Adelphia, Mirant, and Delphi combined!

Weil Gotshal was called in far too late in the game, with little in the way of preparation by either the CEO or CFO of Lehman. Richard Fuld was playing his usual poker game until the bitter end; this time, the players included not just the Wall Street investment community but also Treasury Secretary Paulson.

Most likely, Henry Paulson knew that Lehman was not prepared for bankruptcy. But if Fuld tipped his hand and actually called Lehman's lawyers in for the normal three to four weeks of preparation for a bankruptcy of this size, then what little hope there was for a government bailout would have completely disappeared. Fuld was equally wary of tipping off the Street. He was afraid that if the shorts caught wind of Lehman's hiring counsel they would have then taken their short attack to a whole new level, blowing Lehman's credit spread on its debt deep into junk bond territory. But the lack of preparation for the bankruptcy meant that the haphazard selling of Lehman's global assets would be the fuel that fed the world's greatest financial crisis since the Great Depression of the 1930s.

No judge was ever more harassed than James Peck. Assailed on every side by vested interests, both political and financial, he had to approve the sale of the Lehman assets to Barclays. Otherwise, the deal could have fallen apart, and that most likely would have forced a Chapter 7 liquidation. Thousands of more jobs would then have been lost.

And so, holding the skimpy document, pressured by the White House, the Treasury, and New York mayor Michael Bloomberg, Judge Peck sustained the Chapter 11 and approved the hurried sale, aware as he did so that the very bedrock of U.S. justice had been threatened. No judge should ever be subjected to political pressure, as he most surely had been.

All of this, of course, affected many of the former Lehman employees who were out of a job and whose money had already vanished. Their thousands of stock options were now worthless, and family after family was wiped out. Tragically, months and up to years of severance pay owed to thousands of Lehman employees was wiped out and not paid by the court and Barclays. But the damage was even more severe to my Lehman friends in Europe. Many have questioned why someone in Lehman moved as much as $8 billion from our European headquarters in London to New York shortly before the filing. Lehman executives have said the firm typically collects money from its global units and then dispurses it every day, but serious questions will always remain. Employees in Europe were effectively locked out of their offices in what was essentially a liquidation of those business units. The pain to so many people I know in the United States and abroad was horrific. People I knew well were selling their houses, changing their children's schools, selling boats and SUVs. Even Joe Gregory had to sell his helicopter and his beachfront palace, and Dick Fuld's wife was selling art. Staff members who had bought real estate at the top of the market were in desperate trouble in the negative equity trap. And the reputations of Dick and Joe took a merciless hammering, because everyone now knew the CEO should have accepted the $23-a-share offer from the Koreans, the one Hank Paulson had recommended all those months ago. And if not that, surely Fuld should have grabbed the $18-a-share offer later in the year.

By now there were stories out in every financial publication that none of the Korean offers had even been taken before the board. Not for the first time, Dick Fuld had believed, with the implicit certainty of a medieval monarch, that he alone knew best, and so he'd rejected them out of hand—just another $19 billion blunder by the boss. And now there was nothing.

Meanwhile, the lawyers, trustees, and administrators were wrestling with the massively unprepared Lehman bankruptcy. Because the lawyers had not been called in much earlier, there was a level of confusion about the Lehman finances not seen in this world since Chiang Kai-shek made off with the entire history of China, the treasures of the Forbidden City, to the island of Formosa in 1949. The Chinese are still arguing about that. But there was no argument at Lehman. The bankruptcy officials were gearing up to start the sale of the remaining assets at fast, careless, sloppy prices. Already no one cared. It was as if they just wanted to bury our 158 years of history and leave no trace. And in a sense there would be no trace, just a lifetime of bitterness among excellent Lehman economists who knew, beyond doubt, that none of it ever should have happened. Mike Gelband had, after all, blown the whistle, formally and publicly, sixteen months before Jamie Dimon had hooked JPMorganChase out of the disaster zone in October 2006.

The stock market gains before that weekend of September 20–21 were instantly lost in the first two days of the following week, but the Dow hung on to the territory around the 11,000-point mark, sometimes a little up, sometimes a little down, while the politicians agonized over the possibility of bailing out the banks.

The bailout bill, with the backing of President Bush, was due before the House on Monday the twenty-ninth, and it did so in a tumult of polarization, as American politicians tried to decide who they were: U.S. capitalists, solid party-line congressmen, vote-with-your-heart liberals, or hard-nosed, pragmatic businessmen who had to make a tough but inevitable decision.

In the end, the American capitalists won. *We'll see the banks nationalized over my dead body . . . let 'em go, and let the markets do their worst.* The bill failed by a vote of 228–205. It was cross-party chaos. And simultaneously, every major economist in the United States, both on Wall Street and in Washington, went into cardiac arrest. Because this was no dress rehearsal. This was Armageddon. The credit markets were frozen shut, the world was about to close down for business. And these comedians in Congress had just rejected the only chance there was of averting world nuclear meltdown on the financial markets—the influx of heavy U.S. dollars as designated by Uncle Sam, straight from the Treasury to the places where they were needed. Like everywhere.

President Bush rallied his men. Hank Paulson went straight to the White House, but not in time to prevent the Dow crashing by almost 800 points to a new low, 10,365. It was the closest the U.S. financial world had been to pure shock since Black Monday, October 28, 1929.

The bill would come in revised form before the Senate on Wednesday morning, October 1. And when it did, the real heavyweights of U.S. politics bludgeoned it through by 74 votes to 25. When the bill came back before the House, in an acrimonious few hours, two days later, it was voted into law 263–171. This was just as well, because the markets were suffering a complete crisis of confidence. With the credit lines still frozen and no one sure what House Speaker Nancy Pelosi and her merry men were going to do next, the Dow had caved in another 500 points before that vote went through. Margin calls were raining in, hedge funds were going bust, and God knows what else.

The question was, would Hank Paulson's bailout bill save the world? Answer: not quite. On Monday, October 6, the first full trading day since the bill was passed, the Dow crashed down through 10,000, with an intraday low of 9,525. It closed at 9,955 in a day packed with fear-laden trading and volatility, a day in which the Volatility Index (VXO) broke 50 for the first time since 1987. This wasn't volatility. This was hysteria.

There were no brakes, and on Tuesday, October 7, there was another collapse of the Dow. It went down more than 500 points on the day, closing at 9,447. No one could remember traders being this scared. But they found out what fear really meant two days later, on Thursday, October 9, when the Dow continued its free fall, losing 682 points on the day. The VXO ripped straight up to an all-time high of 64, and the closing bell sounded out a chilling death knell of 8,579 on the Dow.

No one on Wall Street slept a wink that Thursday night. No one who had even the remotest concept of the untold damage being inflicted on the economy could possibly have found rest. There were people who stayed in their offices for the whole night, waiting for the dawn, waiting once more for the thunder of the heavy artillery blasting the U.S. economy apart.

October 10 came in with fire and fury. The Dow collapsed, with a difference between the intraday high and low of over 1,000 points. The VXO registered an all-time squeal of terror, closing at 76.94. No one had ever seen anything like it. At the closing bell the Dow stood at 8,451. But it was not the number, it was the nerve-shaking up-down frenzy that got it there. And the whole world was petrified.

Remember that 2007 Wall Street mantra of decoupling—the theory so beloved of Lehman's thirty-first floor, the Fuld, Gregory, and Goldfarb concert that allowed them to order the purchase of any damn overseas item they pleased? You probably recall the Coeur Défense and all those worldwide hedge funds? All of it was predicated on the unshakable modern belief that the new globalization of the world markets meant that America and its success or failure scarcely impacted the remainder of the planet. The rest of the global markets, both in Europe and the East, had caught up. They were so big and powerful, the United States had ceased to matter as the main man on the block.

Well, around 10:00 A.M. on Friday, shortly after the morning rituals of Danish pastries, French croissants, and Italian coffee, someone took that theory and kicked it straight in the ass, right into the middle of New York Harbor, directly into the sunlit gaze of the Statue of Liberty.

America was in trouble, and the world swooned. I hesitate to mention this, but several of them on the international stock markets were obliged to take time out to change their pants. Uncle Sam was in trouble, and no one could operate without him. The entire global economy collapsed in an undignified heap, whimpering and whining. The big fella was down. And what would now become of the rest?

Europe tanked first. Germany's DAX, the thirty blue chips, hit 4,308, down from a May high of 7,231. France's CAC-40, the forty top companies listed on the Paris Bourse, plummeted to 3,047 off a May high of 5,142. Spain's IBEX-35 index, the thirty-five most liquid stocks on the Madrid board, had fallen to 9,462 from 14,247. Ireland's ISEQ, the official list of equities on the Dublin exchange, dropped from a high of 6,460 to 2,751. Iceland was on its way to 677 from its May high of 4,942.

London's FTSE closed at 3,873; in May it had been 6,300. Russia's MICEX, their thirty largest companies, was closed on October 10, but the day before it had fallen to 637 from a May high of 1,966. China's CSI-300 had gone from 3,936 in May to 1,881. The Nikkei 225 closed at 8,115, having hit 14,343 on May 19. The Hang Seng Index in Hong Kong was at 14,398, from a May high of 25,822.

Nowhere was immune, no matter the distance from Wall Street. Australia's preeminent benchmark, the S&P/ASX-200 Index, had fallen just over 2,000 points from its May high and now closed at 3,960. Brazil had caved in from 73,440 to 33,230.

And this was only the beginning. The years of prosperity were over. The panic that marched on from the Lehman Brothers collapse became endemic. Iceland went bankrupt. The economy of Ireland crashed, making the short years of prosperity look like a mere blip in a poverty-studded history.

The economy in the United Kingdom very nearly collapsed. The Bank of England had to bail out the nation's lending banks. The Royal Bank of Scotland, which had so gamely chased Lehman up the table of subprime lenders, almost went bust for the exact amount it had loaned, and was saved by Great Britain's central bank.

Hank Paulson's $700 billion TARP (Troubled Assets Relief Program) proved a life support for the two biggest banks in the world, Citigroup and Bank of America. It provided cash for General Motors and the other U.S. car giants to stay afloat. Goldman Sachs and Morgan Stanley also received funds.

But meanwhile, Paulson and Bernanke were shocked by the sheer scale of the events of that Friday afternoon, only twenty-five days after Lehman closed down. The level of trouble that had caused them to go to Congress in the first place now seemed magnified several times over, despite the government rescue, as the world's stock exchanges imploded, and the Treasury chief was under no illusions about the potential of the catastrophe. He had to move again. He and Ben Bernanke had, somehow, to force the U.S. banks back into liquidity mode.

In Ben's opinion that could only mean compulsory capital injection from the U.S. government directly into the banks. Hank Paulson was immediately against it, because such a plan hammered against every capitalist principle he'd ever had. Visions of Tiananmen Square stood before his eyes, especially, on its west side, the all-controlling

Great Hall of the People, the largest central government building on earth. Hank loved China, but not that much.

By Sunday morning, Ben Bernanke had decided that if Hank had a better idea than capital injection, then let's hear it. But there was no better idea. There was no other idea. And on that afternoon, October 12, the Treasury secretary personally called every one of the chief executive officers of the nine biggest banks in the country and told them to report to his office in the Treasury Building, right next to the White House, the next day.

Right on time Monday morning, they all arrived—the CEOs of Citigroup, Merrill Lynch, Morgan Stanley, JPMorganChase, Goldman Sachs, Bank of America, Wells Fargo, Bank of New York Mellon, and State Street Corp. Inside the Treasury these icons of Wall Street were seated in alphabetical order on the other side of a huge table across from Hank Paulson and Ben Bernanke.

There was terrific tension in the air because these were Paulson's guys, men against whom he had competed when he headed up Goldman Sachs. Many of them were personal friends, and now he had to read them some kind of riot act. But he pulled no punches. He told them the U.S. banking system was in deep trouble, and he was not offering some kind of solution that warranted a general chat. His decision was not open to negotiation. The U.S. government was going to issue them a direct infusion of cash, tens of billions of dollars. And that would mean Uncle Sam was about to become a major shareholder in each one of the country's largest banks, right here, right now, in the Great Hall of Paulson.

Well, almost. But first there was a furious discussion, as was only to be expected. This conference table was capitalism incarnate. The idea of nationalization of the U.S. banking system was anathema to every one of the bankers sitting at it, though some recognized they were somewhat short of C-notes at that particular moment, especially Citigroup and Bank of America.

Anyway, it was all to no avail. The boss, working in harmony with the chairman of the Fed, had made up his mind. And now he produced from his file nine single sheets of paper, setting out the conditions for the transfer of cash in return for the major government stock holdings. Hank said he wanted every one of them back, personally signed by each CEO, before they left Washington, D.C., that night.

And all nine of them did so. The U.S. government had seized the reins of the financial world and taken a central role in the American banking system. Hank Paulson had taken a near-impossible journey, fighting his ideological hatred of government intervention in market problems. On that day, he effectively blew out $125 billion. And the following morning he stood before four giant American flags in the vast marble foyer of the Treasury and announced his decision to a waiting nation.

"Today, we are taking decisive actions to protect the U.S. economy," he said. "We regret having to take them."

At that moment Henry Merritt Paulson, who had spent his entire working life defending free markets, became the most interventionist Treasury secretary to hold the office since the Great Depression. And not even he could disguise his look of profound displeasure as he spoke.

Back in New York, there was a distinct slide away from the prosperity of the last decade. Restaurants and bars bore the full brunt of the layoffs on Wall Street—probably 150,000 by Christmas in financial services, owing to mass collapses of hedge funds and banks laying off thousands and thousands of workers.

The collapse of the derivatives had savaged financial institutions and brokerage houses alike. The crash of the stock market wiped billions of dollars off the value of U.S. corporations. Bankruptcies were announced almost hourly. Layoffs were nationwide.

Terence Tucker told me his commute from New Jersey in the good days used to take him an hour and a half. At the start of 2009, it took only forty minutes in light traffic to Wall Street.

Because of the location of my apartment, I occasionally walk past 745 Seventh. And I always stop and stare up at the floors where I'd found, I thought, the holy grail. Up there, behind the huge glass windows, we'd all fought it out, us against the world: Larry laughing, Grossy, Joe, Terence, Schell, Christine, Jane, Pete, Rich, Ashish, Mike, Alex, and Bart. Such days they were, with massive risks, tight camaraderie, and the endless joy of being right. And now we are all scattered, separate pieces, strangers, I suppose, in strange different places. It will always make me profoundly sad.

Even now I cannot quite understand what went wrong. How could it have gone wrong? As a team, we must have been judged world-beaters. I still stare up at those windows, and I am always left with the feeling that we all tried so hard, and yet some strange forces ruined everything.

It changed me. It stripped away all the careless glances at stock charts I have lived with all my life. The ramifications of those charts have a different meaning now. Where once I stared at the zigzagging lines, and just thought, *Up, down, win, lose, profit, crash, problem, solution, long, short, buy, sell,* now I see mostly people. Because every movement, up or down, has a meaning. I see it because I've been there. Every fraction of every inch of those financial graphs represents hope or fear, confidence or dread, triumph or ruin, celebration or sorrow. There's nothing quite like total calamity to focus the mind.

I find myself thinking of the families of the people I knew so well. The millions of dollars snatched from them undeservedly. I know what it meant to them, how lives were devastated, life savings obliterated.

Other people's anguish has always affected me. And I understand the psychological scars left on men and women whose careers were wrecked at Lehman. I have seen their tears, and I've heard their cries. God knows, there were people who committed suicide, threw themselves in front of trains, in this financial Armageddon.

Again I look up at those windows, and I know the ghosts of my old team will never leave there. Nothing could ever be that good again. Wall Street will never be the same. Lehman brought it down, as it brought down half the world. And, I say again, it never should have happened.

Acknowledgments

It was James Robinson who led me to this book. In the first place, he felt I had an untold story that I was bursting to unleash on the world. Second, his father is the renowned *New York Times* number one bestselling author Patrick Robinson, the man who wrote *Lone Survivor* for the heroic U.S. Navy SEAL Marcus Luttrell.

I never thought he would even consider it—not the vast jumble of thoughts cascading unchecked and undisciplined through my mind. But James talked him into it, and all through the winter of 2008–09 I commuted between New York and the Robinson family home in Ireland.

James held the project together, handling the mountainous volumes of research, preparing material for his father, who was obliged to spend all day on the writing, every day. Including Christmas.

I thank James for his unflagging support, both as my co-researcher and "interpreter" for his father. But above all I thank him as my friend.

Patrick Robinson has written many bestselling techno-thriller novels and, including this, has five times ghosted for other people. All of the other four made it to number one on a bestseller list. Believe me, I now understand why. I could never have done it without him, and he has my sincere thanks for everything.

I thank also Patrick's droll and urbane London literary agent, Andrew Nurnberg, who seized upon this book within five minutes of hearing we planned to write it. He never doubted its merit, never once saw it as anything but a potentially huge success. He instantly appointed a New York agent to share the responsibility, Larry Kirshbaum, who took us to one of the greatest publishing houses in the world. And I thank them both.

And equally I thank our editor, John Mahaney of Crown Publishers, who read it once and made up his mind immediately to acquire the work, no matter the opposition. His wise and thoughtful preparation of the manuscript evokes my complete admiration. And my thanks to Rik Sen, a doctoral student at New York University's Stern School of Business for his hard work and dedication in reviewing and checking financial data.

Most important, I would like to thank my beloved Anabela, who was there for me every step of the way. Her friendship, patience, dedication, and positive reinforcement were crucial in my completing this book. Anabela, I'll always remember—and be forever grateful for—the way you helped me through this unique experience.

As with any book as complex and detailed as this, there are more people to thank than I could possibly record, particularly as most of them would wish to remain anonymous, well clear of the firing line. But they know who they are, my colleagues from all over Lehman's countless corporate departments. Patrick and I thank them for the endless time they spent, filling me in on those events I did not see firsthand, making certain that this story, whatever else, is as accurate as any Wall Street thriller could ever be.

L. McD.

Index